Chinoiserie

HUGH HONOUR

CHINOISERIE

The Vision of Cathay

JOHN MURRAY

Printed in the United States of America

0 7195 2927 1

TO MY MOTHER

Contents

Contents

Chinoiserie

Preface

Several weighty tomes have been written—and more will no doubt appear—on various aspects of the artistic, economic, and philosophical relations between Europe and China. This is not one of them. My book is intended for those who, like myself, have a nodding acquaintance with Chinese art and have wondered how and why a European style called 'chinoiserie' should ever have come about. I have, perforce, approached the subject from a strictly European standpoint, attempting to discover how western artists and craftsmen, from the Middle Ages to the nineteenth century, regarded the Orient and expressed their vision of it. For chinoiserie is a European style and not, as is sometimes supposed by sinologues, an incompetent attempt to imitate the arts of China. It is the manifestation of an attitude of mind similar to that which brought about the eighteenth-century Gothic revival. Just as the architects of Strawberry Hill and Fonthill Abbey created fantasies based on a highly coloured picture of the Middle Ages, so the designers of such chinoiserie masterpieces as the *Grande Singerie* at Chantilly and the porcelain room at Aranjuez perpetuated their vision of a similarly fanciful and poetical world, distant in space rather than time.

To explain how this idealized vision of the Chinese Empire developed in Europe has been my first aim. I have then attempted to show how it was expressed in the arts and how chinoiserie gradually developed into an autonomous style which, in its turn, modified the European picture of the Orient. This curious process of cultural inbreeding, itself so similar in its intricacy to the involutions of a Chinese puzzle, may best be illustrated by a personal experience.

As a child I had a very clear idea of what China was like. The willow-pattern plates off which we ate each day afforded a vivid glimpse of the Chinese landscape, and I soon learned the story of the two lovers who, pursued across the hump-backed bridge by an angry father, were transformed into birds hovering amid clouds at the top of the plate. Chinese costumes were like-wise familiar to me for I, like other children, occasionally went to fancy-dress parties dressed as a mandarin—complete with embroidered silk suit, straw slippers, a pigtail dangling from the back of my head and drooping moustaches gummed to my upper lip. Certain blue and white ginger jars, brightly coloured enamel trays and lacquer panels in our own and other houses were pointed out to me as products of this distant land, and visits to Kew Gardens acquainted me with its architecture. All these objects induced in my childish mind a very distinct picture of China—a topsy-turvy land of brilliant flowers, weird monsters, and fragile buildings where most European values were reversed. And even when, years later, I discovered that they had all been made in Europe, the original impression remained at the back of my mind.

Paintings, pottery, and furniture made in China for the Chinese, and not for export, were rarely to be seen in Europe until comparatively recent times. Nor were accurate accounts of China available for the European reader until the early nineteenth century. Thus it came about in the seventeenth and eighteenth centuries that European writers built up the image of an eastern philosopher's empire based on their own interpretations of travellers' tales, some true, some partly true and others frankly imaginary, while artists produced chinoiseries which derived at second, third or fourth hand from anything that ever came out of the Orient. Many of these chinoiserie wares would baffle a Chinaman, as Oliver Goldsmith seems to have appreciated when he described the visit of Lien Chi Altangi, his Citizen of the World, to a lady of taste. Asked to examine the beauties of a Chinese temple in her garden, the bewildered oriental replied, with less than Chinese politeness: 'I see nothing, madam . . . that may not as well be called an Egyptian pyramid as a Chinese temple; for that little building is as like one as t'other.'

In attempting to relate the long and complex history of chinoiserie in a single volume I have been obliged to limit the scope of the work rather rigorously. Space, and my estimate of the reader's patience, has allowed me to describe and illustrate relatively few of the numerous delightful chinoiserie objects produced in the late seventeenth and eighteenth centuries. I have kept, as far as possible, to those which seemed both attractive and interesting his-torically. I have not dealt, save in passing, with Chinese export wares which play a rather ambiguous role in the development of chinoiserie. Nor have I been able to dwell at any length on the direct imitations, not to say fakes, of Chinese wares made in several parts of Europe, and especially Holland, during the seventeenth century and later. Such objects can have affected the vision of Cathay no more than the imports on which they were modelled.

The notes printed at the end of the text cite the principal sources of my information—where these are not quoted in the text—and also contain references to certain interesting manifestations of chinoiserie which I was unable to mention elsewhere. Further information about the buildings and objects illustrated will be found in the catalogue of illustrations. The notes have been arranged to correspond with the sections into which the chapters are divided, and as the individual sections are fairly brief I have dispensed with numerical references. I hope that these notes and catalogue entries will prove of use to any who wish to investigate particular aspects of chinoiserie. As the index refers to the authors of the works cited in the text, notes and catalogue, I have not felt it necessary to print a separate bibliography. I trust that I have acknowledged all the books and articles which have provided me with ideas or information.

To mention the names of all those who, in correspondence or conversation, have helped with advice or information would take several pages. Not only have they patiently answered my questions and supplied me with photographs but several have directed my steps in unfamiliar fields and drawn my attention to objects and printed sources which I might otherwise have overlooked. Among them I should particularly like to thank: Mr A. F. Bagshaw, Mr John Beckwith, Mr Gudmund Boesen, Mr David Carritt, Senhor Ayres de Carvalho, Mr Anthony M. Clark, Mr Edward Croft-Murray, Dr Peter Davis, Miss Yvonne Hackenbroch, Mr Miles Hadfield, Mr John Harris, Mr Calvin S. Hathaway, Mr John Hayward, Mr Terence Hodgkinson, Mr Geoffrey Houghton-Brown, the Hon. Mrs Ionides, Professor Klaus Lankheit, Mr James Lees-Milne, The Countess of Lichfield, Monsieur Robert de Micheaux, Mr Henry P. McIlhenny, Professor Ulrich Middeldorf, Mr Clifford Musgrave, Vicomte de Noailles, Mr L. G. G. Ramsey, Mr D. Snelgrove, Dr E. Steingräber, and Professor Vittorio Viale. I should also like to thank Mr Harold Acton for his advice and encouragement. And I am very deeply indebted to those who have read portions of the typescript and saved me from several errors and omissions: Mr Douglas Cooper, Mr Christopher Hussey, Mr Nicholas Powell and Mr F. J. B. Watson. Finally I wish to thank Mr John Fleming who has encouraged and helped me at every stage of the work.

Preface

For permission to reproduce the photographs in this book I am indebted to: Her Majesty the Queen, Christabel, Lady Aberconway, H.H. The Margrave of Baden, Mr A. F. Bagshaw, Mr Norman Colville, Mr C. L. David, Monsieur A. Fauchier-Magnan, Mr Hugh Farmar, Mr B. E. Hokin, Sir James Horlick, the Hon. Mrs. Ionides, the Earl of Lichfield, Major Nigel Martin, the Earl of Rosebery, Mr C. D. Rotch, Lord Sandys, Viscount Scarsdale, the trustees of the various public collections and the commercial organizations whose names are given in the catalogue of plates. The passage from *The Letters of John Chinaman* is quoted by kind permission of the publishers: George Allen and Unwin, Ltd.

ASOLO, *March*, 1961

CHAPTER I

The Vision of Cathay

I THE IMAGINARY CONTINENT

When the intrepid Jesuit missionary Matteo Ricci arrived at Peking in 1601, he surveyed the wonders of the city and then inquired the whereabouts of Cathay. Nineteen years spent at Macao and Nanking had familiarized him with China: now he wished to discover the fabulous land of which he remembered hearing such extraordinary and intriguing stories at home in Italy. It was some time before he could be convinced that he was already there.

Many later visitors to China have been similarly disillusioned. Like Ricci, they have found it difficult, if not impossible, to reconcile their preconceived notions of the country with its actual appearance. The Rev. Richard Walter, who went to Canton with Captain Anson in 1742, was distressed to find how unlike the Celestial Empire was to that 'well-governed affectionate family', of which he had read, 'where the only contests were who should exert the most humanity and beneficence'. A century later, Robert Fortune, the plant hunter, gazing from the sea at the barren hills of the southern Chinese coast, querulously demanded whether this could be '"the flowery land", the land of azaleas, camellias and roses, of which I had heard so much in England'. Even in the 1930s Sir Osbert Sitwell remarked that only when visiting the private apartments of the Imperial Family at Peking did he begin 'to grasp for the first time since arriving in China, how the idea of chinoiserie first seized upon our ancestors'. However charming the landscape, however picturesque the buildings and people of China might be, European visitors have frequently suffered a shock of disappointment on finding the reality so very different from the land of their dreams. Like Ricci, they discover that even in Peking, Cathay is still far to seek.

Cathay is, or rather was, a continent of immeasurable extent lying just beyond the eastern confines of the known world. Of this mysterious and charming land, poets are the only historians and porcelain painters the most reliable topographers. They alone can give an adequate impression of the beauty of the landscape with its craggy snow-capped mountain ranges and its verdant plains sprinkled with cities of dreaming pagodas and intersected by meandering rivers whose limpid waters bear whole fleets of delicately wrought junks, all a-flutter with bedragonned pennants and laden with precious cargoes of jade, porcelain, samite, silk, green ginger, and delicately scented teas. Beside their banks the palm and the weeping willow flourish amidst phoenix-tail bamboos and a proliferation of exotic flora. Giant flowers abound here: chrysanthemums which tower above the men who tend them, paeonies which dwarf the birds nesting in their branches, and convolvulus whose blossoms serve as hats, as parasols, and even, on occasion, as the roofs of huts. Indeed, the natural landscape is so beautiful that when laying out their gardens the Cathaians could desire no more than to reproduce it on a miniature scale, with paths serpentining round hillocks of artificial rock-work, sinuous rills, and forests of tiny gnarled trees. The fauna is no less extraordinary. Huge and fiery dragons lurk in every mountain cave; gaudy birds with rainbow-hued plumage swoop over the plains; butterflies the size of puffins hover round the pendant blooms of *Wisteria sinensis*; and diaphanous-tailed goldfish play amidst the water-lilies and chrysolite rocks of stream and pond.

The inhabitants of Cathay are small and neat. Hats, shoes, and cheekbones are worn high, while moustaches, pigtails, and finger-nails are encouraged to grow to inordinate length. Their similarity of appearance—like so much else about them—is proverbial, but they try to disguise it by the prodigiously rich variety of their clothes. Flowing robes of silk, elaborately embroidered with gold, are much in favour since they hide their diminutive stature while emphasizing the nobility of their bearing and the studied grace of their movements. A peace-loving and, perhaps, an effete race, they avoid martial combat save when ancestral voices are heard prophesying war and Tartar warriors clad in clinking armour swoop down on them from beyond the mountains. Their true talent is for a serene contemplative life. *Belles-lettres* are honoured in Cathay as nowhere else; the emperor himself is a philosopher and poet while the officials of his far-reaching benevolent despotism are chosen and promoted according to the excellence of their verses.

Save for the rustics who joyfully tend their flocks or drowse on the backs of water-buffaloes, and for the maidens who so elegantly carry their *famille rose* pitchers to the fountains, work seems ever at a standstill in this lotus land of everlasting afternoon, where the employment of leisure is commonly regarded as the serious business of life. Occasionally the courtiers may go a-hunting after strange beasts, mounted on fleet and magnificently accoutred ponies. But most of the inhabitants of Cathay pass their time less strenuously, gently wafting themselves to and fro in swings, or reclining in willow cabins to watch their cormorants retrieving goldfish from a near-by stream. For hours they will sit in their gardens, drinking tea out of tiny cups, rising only to dance a stately rigadoon to the faint twanging and high-pitched tinkling of their unearthly orchestras, while their children play complicated games, juggling dextrously with filigree balls of porcelain or ivory and flying fantastic kites.

This luxurious people has created a style of architecture to suit its leisured life. In a country of perpetual spring, where the prunus is always in blossom, no very substantial buildings are needed, and the climate permits a long duration to the flimsiest construction. The fancy of their architects has therefore been unbridled in the creation of delicate, brightly painted latticed garden houses, jade pavilions, pleasure domes open to the sky, little huts in trees which might be mistaken for the nests of exotic birds, tall pagoda towers built of porcelain, and spindly bridges spanning rivers which never have the discourtesy to run in flood. On the eaves of every building—absurdly wide and turned up at the corners—hang carillons of tiny bells, set a-jingling by the reverberations of great gongs booming from near-by temples.

Such is the vision of Cathay which shone in many a westerner's eye. That it bears no relation to the China of K'ang Hsi or Ch'ien Lung, and still less to that of Sun Yat-Sen, or Chiang Kai-Shek and Mao Tse-Tung, the Chinese themselves have for long been at pains to demonstrate. But even though the temple gongs and bells of Cathay are silent now, the gossamer pavilions decayed, the gardens over-grown and the quaint little people who tended them are dust, some memory lingers on of this bizarre land to the east of the world where most European values were turned topsy-turvy and where flourished a civilization more elegant and humane, more sophisticated and highly wrought than any the West has ever seen. Small wonder that European travellers to China have often been disappointed. For China is as far from Cathay as a Shang-Yin bronze cauldron from a Meissen *garniture de cheminée* in the Chinese taste.

This book is not concerned, save in passing, with China or with Chinese objects. The subject is *chinoiserie* which may be defined as the expression of the

European vision of Cathay. Before proceeding to it, however, something must first be said of the travellers' tales—some true, some half true and many wholly fictitious—on which the legend of Cathay was nourished. A full account of these, from Marco Polo in the thirteenth to the plant hunters in the nineteenth century, would fill a book far longer than the present. Here we shall merely glance at a few of the haunting stories which early travellers brought back from the East and which excited their wide-eyed and wondering listeners to evoke the vision of Cathay.

2   THE EMPIRE OF THE GREAT KHAN

Cathay was first revealed in all its splendour by Marco Polo, a Venetian who travelled extensively in Asia between 1271 and 1295, serving the great Mongol emperor, Kublai Khan, for about seventeen years. Some vague notion of this fabulous land had, of course, been current in Europe for many centuries. Greeks and Romans knew it as the source of precious silks, but during the Dark Ages the image of the country had so faded from the European mind that William de Rubruck, who took letters from St Louis to the Great Khan in 1252, was much surprised to find that the Chinese prisoners at the Mongol court were both ingenious and civilized. On returning to Rome, he sang their praises, declaring their skill as craftsmen to be excelled nowhere in the world, that they produced silk of the highest quality, made good wine from rice and wrote with a paint brush, combining all the letters of a word into a single character. But since he was unable to travel beyond Mongolia, his was no more than a Pisgah sight of the mysterious land. It was left to the adventurous and practical Marco Polo to spy out the country and record the fullest account of it that Europe was to read for many centuries.

Although master of at least four spoken Asiatic languages, Marco Polo was practically illiterate in his native tongue and might never have committed his extraordinary tale to paper had he not, shortly after his return home, been thrown into a Genoese prison. There he found a companion in one Rustichello of Pisa to whom he dictated an account of his travels in the frenchified-Italian (or italianized-French) which was the accepted literary language of both Genoa and Venice. This scribe was a practised writer of romances—he had already composed a somewhat inadequate version of the Arthurian legend—and he, we may surmise, was responsible for some of the more imaginative touches in the book they produced together. Surely it is to Rustichello that we owe the grandiose opening invocation which so magnificently serves as a cartouche to this first chart of Cathay:

> Great Princes, Emperors, and Kings, Dukes and Marquises, Counts, Knights, and Burgesses! and People of all degrees who desire to get knowledge of the various races of mankind and of the diversities of the sundry regions of the World, take this Book and cause it to be read to you. For ye shall find therein all kinds of wonderful things . . . according to the description of Messer Marco Polo, a wise and noble citizen of Venice, as he saw them with his own eyes. Some things indeed there be therein which he beheld not; but these he heard from men of credit and veracity. And we shall set down things seen as seen, and things heard as heard only, so that no jot of falsehood may mar the truth of our Book, and that all who shall read it or hear it read may put faith in the truth of all its contents.

That it was in many respects a truthful book, some six hundred years of subsequent exploration have proved—and many of the places Marco Polo described were not again visited by a European until the nineteenth century—but in the early fourteenth century Marco Polo seems to have been read mainly as fiction, and none of his discoveries was incorporated into the official map of Asia until fifty years after his death. How could a Venetian credit the existence of Kanbalu, a city which was declared to be larger, richer, and more beautiful than Venice, beyond the limits of the known world? How, indeed, could any European believe that a Tartar chieftain ruled an empire infinitely vaster, wealthier and better governed than Rome had ever seen? No more than the Emperor Ch'ien Lung, in the eighteenth century, was to believe in the existence of a prosperous and civilized Europe beyond his dominions. Marco Polo was therefore put down as an inveterate romancer and his book nicknamed *il milione* from the million marvels—or lies—it contained. On his death-bed, the legend runs, his pious relations besought him to save his soul by confessing how often he had departed from the truth in his book, 'to which his reply was that he had not told one half of what he had really seen'.

If Marco Polo was a faithful reporter of the things he saw, he was, none the less, a very gullible retailer of 'things heard' from others, and he was not always as careful as his prologue suggests to distinguish between his sources. Unconcerned with the ordinary life and habits of the people amongst whom he had lived in the East (apart from their religious practices which interested him deeply), he chose to record the marvels he had seen or heard about, and his recital of wonders contains the essence of the European vision of the fabulous East. His book is, therefore, the primary source for information about Cathay, and those who wish to travel thither must follow Marco Polo's route—through Persia and Timochain, where stands the solitary tree of the sun beneath which Darius and Alexander fought; passing near the luxuriant valley ruled by the Old Man of the Mountain; past Samarcan—that 'noble city adorned with beautiful gardens, and surrounded by a plain, in which are produced all the fruits that man can desire'—through Charcan, where chalcedonies and jaspers abound in the rivers; and finally across the desert of Lop which is haunted with evil spirits: 'Even in the day-time one hears those spirits talking. And sometimes you shall hear the sound of a variety of musical instruments, and still more commonly the sound of drums. Hence in making this journey 'tis customary for travellers to keep close together.'

The way now lies through the province of Tanguth, Kamul, where men formerly placed their wives at the disposition of travellers, the district of Succuir whence 'rhubarb is carried to all parts of the world', and onward yet for many a weary day's march until Chandu is reached at last.

> There is at this place a very fine marble Palace, the rooms of which are gilt and painted with figures of men and beasts and birds, and with a variety of trees and flowers, all executed with such exquisite art that you regard them with delight and astonishment. Round this Palace a wall is built inclosing a compass of sixteen miles, and beautiful meadows, with all kinds of wild animals (excluding those such as are of ferocious nature). . . . Moreover at a spot in the Park where there is a charming wood he has another Palace built of cane, of which I must give you a description. It is gilt all over, and most elaborately finished inside. It is stayed on gilt and lackered columns, on each of which is a dragon all gilt, the tail of which is attached to the column whilst the head supports the architrave, and the claws likewise are stretched out right and left to support the architrave. The roof, like the rest is formed of canes, covered with a varnish so strong and excellent that no amount of rain will rot them. . . . The construction of the Palace is so devised that it can be taken down and put up again with great celerity; and it can all be taken to pieces and removed whithersoever the Emperor may command. When erected, it is braced against mishaps from the wind by more than two hundred cords of silk.

Here we are but a step from Xanadu, the very heart of Cathay, for Marco Polo's description, though apparently so artless in its circumstantial detail, is suffused with such a glow of child-like wonder and delight that it inspired Coleridge to create the greatest literary evocation of the imaginary continent:

The Vision of Cathay

In Xanadu did Kubla Khan
A stately pleasure-dome decree:
Where Alph, the sacred river, ran
Through caverns measureless to man
  Down to a sunless sea.
So twice five miles of fertile ground
With walls and towers were girdled round:
And there were gardens bright with sinuous rills,
Where blossomed many an incense-bearing tree;
And here were forests ancient as the hills,
Enfolding sunny spots of greenery.

It may be doubted how much a traveller from a relatively backward country is impressed by a superior civilization: Marco Polo's book suggests that the finer points of Chinese culture escaped an Italian of the thirteenth century. It is, for instance, clear that Marco was less appreciative of the remarkable degree of religious toleration which Kublai Khan observed throughout his wide dominions than of what he supposed to be the Tartar's leanings towards the Christian faith. Nor did he perceive the value of China's most remarkable discovery—the art of printing. He could not, however, fail to be impressed by the Khan's efficient system of government, and he was much struck by the well maintained roads which facilitated communications throughout his empire. He also noted, with evident approval, the decorous way in which the Chinese behaved in Kublai's presence. 'In the first place, within a half a mile of the place where he is', Marco recorded

> out of reverence for his exalted majesty, everybody preserves a mien of the greatest meekness and quiet, so that no noise of shrill voices or loud talk shall be heard. And every one of the chiefs and nobles carries always with him a handsome little vessel to spit in whilst he remain in the hall of Audience—for no one dares to spit on the floor of the hall—and when he hath spitten he covers it up and puts it aside.

Such nice manners may well have surprised a Venetian who was accustomed to no such displays of *bienséance* in the Doge's palace. But even if Marco Polo failed to appreciate the high degree of civilization attained by the Chinese at a time when Europe was composed of a large number of warring states and European manners were, to say the least, rough, he firmly established the tradition of China as a land of wise government and elaborate courtesy which was to be developed many centuries later when Europe had learned to appreciate such qualities.

To Marco Polo, no less than to his stay-at-home contemporaries, the wealth of the East made the strongest appeal. Of the Tartar conquerors he remarks that 'the rich among these people dress in cloth of gold and silks with skins of sable, the ermine and other animals. All their accoutrements are of an expensive kind.' And throughout his book he stresses the prodigious riches of the Orient in gold, silver, and precious stones. He was also intrigued by the exotic natural phenomena, 'pears of an extraordinary size, weighing ten pounds each, that are white in the inside, like paste, and have a very fragrant smell', 'peaches of such a size that one of them will weigh two pounds troy weight', and bamboo canes 'four spans in girth and fifteen paces long'. Among the strange fauna he noticed were the great horned sheep now named *Ovis Poli* after him, 'bats as large as vultures and vultures as black as crows', bears the size of buffaloes, camelopards which, he says, are gentle in their manners, pheasants with tail feathers ten palms long, and a crane with wing feathers 'full of eyes, round like those of the peacock, but of a gold colour and very bright; the head is red and black and well formed'—a gorgeous creature of macaw-like brilliance which might be mistaken for the ho-ho bird. But the monsters, which were soon to play an important part in the vision of Cathay, rarely figure in the pages of this hard-headed civil servant, no doubt to the sorrow of his readers. Only once did he fulfil their expectations, when he mentioned:

> huge serpents, ten paces in length, and ten spans in the girth of the body. At the fore-part, near the head, they have two short legs, having three claws like those of the tiger, with eyes larger than a fourpenny loaf and very glaring. The jaws are wide enough to swallow a man, the teeth are very large and sharp, and their whole appearance is so formidable, that neither man, nor any kind of animal, can approach them without terror.

Some indication of the effect Marco Polo's book had on the popular imagination is given by the medieval illuminators' interpretation of this passage. They painted alongside it a miniature of a fiery dragon, a much more familiar inhabitant of their imagination than the crocodile which Marco Polo had painstakingly described.

Shortly before Marco Polo's death in 1324, a Franciscan missionary, the Blessed Odoric of Pordenone, set off for Kanbalu where he stayed for some three years. The account of his travels, written soon after his return to Italy, confirmed and even amplified the extraordinary story Marco had told. But the good Friar, realising how little credence was given to his predecessor's tale, evidently thought it useless to describe all the marvels he had seen, for he remarked at the outset, 'Of all I purpose not to speak, though I shall tell of many which shall seem to a number of people past belief. Nor, indeed, could I myself have believed these things, had I not heard them with my own ears or seen the like myself.' More observant of small matters than Marco Polo, he recorded many of those details of everyday life in China which have ever since fascinated the West, remarking on how the women's feet were bound, how the mandarins encouraged their finger-nails to grow to extravagant length and how the cormorant had been tamed and was used for fishing. But if Marco was inclined to exaggerate the riches of China, Odoric gave the same impression by his reluctance to provide facts and figures, declaring simply that 'any account of the magnificence of that lord (Kublai's successor), and of the things that are done in his court must seem incredible to those who have not witnessed it'. Such tantalizing remarks could hardly fail to open the door to a lively imagination.

To judge from the number of surviving manuscripts, the books of both Marco Polo and Friar Odoric enjoyed widespread fame. But neither approached the popularity of *The Travels of Sir John Mandeville* which may well be called a medieval best-seller, for more manuscripts of it survive than of any other book of its period—save prayer-books. The ingenious author of this work—probably Jean d'Outremeuse—has a claim to fame as the perpetrator of the most successful fraud in the whole history of literature, since his book had been translated into ten languages and was well known for five hundred years before it was proved that Sir John Mandeville had never existed, his travels had never taken place and his 'personal experiences' were mere plagiarisms and inventions. Hence its capital importance to students of the fabulous land of Cathay. Since 'Sir John Mandeville' had never ventured beyond the shores of the Mediterranean, he was able to give an unclouded impression of the European vision of the Orient. The author had, furthermore, a genuine literary talent—greater than that of Marco Polo or of Friar Odoric whom he plundered for details—and this enabled, or rather compelled, him to convert the Pilgrims' Guide to the Holy Land, which he set out to write, into a fascinating Gothic tapestry of myths, legends, surmises, and occasional facts which affords a fascinating glimpse into the medieval mind, however little it may tell us of the East.

According to 'Mandeville', the Orient was surrounded by an archipelago of islands which his lively imagination (aided by Pliny's *Natural History*) peopled with tribes of strange monsters, some with eyes in their foreheads, some without heads but with eyes in their shoulders, some with horses' feet, some with ears reaching down to their knees and, most strange of all, some with such great upper lips 'that when they sleep in the sun they cover the face with that lip'. 'In another isle', he calmly remarks, 'there are hermaphrodites.' Only once in the whole course of his travels did he admit defeat, conceding with becoming modesty: 'Of Paradise I cannot speak properly for I was not there, It is far beyond; and I repent not going there, but I was not worthy.'

In the centre of this phantasmagoric world stood Cathay, ruled by the Great Chan, or Cham, who styled himself, 'Chan, son of the high God, emperor of all who inhabit the earth, and lord of all lords'. Cathay is a great country, Mandeville declared, 'fair, noble, rich and full of merchants. Thither merchants go to seek spices and all manner of merchandises, more commonly than in any other part. And you shall understand that merchants who come from Genoa, or from Venice, or from Romania, or other parts of Lombardy, go by sea or by land eleven or twelve months, or more sometimes, before they reach the island of Cathay which is the principal region of all parts beyond.' Unlike Marco Polo and Friar Odoric, he showed no reluctance to particularize the Great Chan's riches, enlarging on the magnificence of his palace in terms which every European could comprehend. In the great hall there stood twenty-four pillars of fine gold and the walls were hung with sweet smelling skins of red panthers which 'they value more than plates of gold'. The 'montour of the Great Chan' stood in the centre of the palace, 'all wrought of gold and precious stones and great pearls; and at the four corners are four serpents of gold; and all about there are made large nets of silk and gold, and great pearls hanging all about it.' Naturally, the thrones of the great Chan, his empresses and children are made entirely from precious stones, as are the tables from which they eat. Even the ceiling of the dining-room is covered with a golden vine bearing many clusters of grapes, 'all of precious stones, the white are of crystal, beryl and iris; the yellow of topazes; the red of rubies, grenaz and alabraundines; the green of emeralds, of perydoz, and of chrysolites; and the black of onyx and garnets. And they are all so properly made, that it appears a real vine bearing natural grapes.' All the drinking vessels in this Aladdin's cave are of similar rarity: 'the cups are of emeralds, and sapphires, or topazes, of perydoz, and of many other precious stones. Vessel of silver is there none, for they set no value on it to make vessels of; but they make therewith steps, and pillars, and pavements, for halls and chambers.' Nor was this opulent display sufficient, for the Chan was said to keep in his own room a carbuncle, 'of half a foot long, which in the night gives so great a light and shining, that it is as light as day'. Thus did the author of Mandeville's travels enlarge on Friar Odoric's tantalising remark about 'the magnificence of that lord'.

'Sir John Mandeville' enjoyed the good luck which so often attends the barefaced mountebank. No sooner had he imposed his fiction on the public than the doors of the Far East began to close against the European who was soon excluded altogether from China. Extraordinary as it may now seem, his farrago of highly coloured nonsense was not only believed but accepted as the prime authority on the Orient for some two hundred years.

As late as 1340 Francesco Balducci Pegolotti stated in his merchants' handbook that the trade route from Tana on the Black Sea to Peking was perfectly safe—*sichurissimo*—whether by night or by day. But the Mongol Empire which had for a century maintained a *pax tartarica* throughout Asia, was already faltering and soon fell prey to the forces of Islam which set up an impenetrable land barrier between West and East. Finally, between 1368 and 1370, the Yüan dynasty founded by Kublai Khan fell, the nationalist Ming dynasty was installed on the Dragon Throne and China embraced a rigidly xenophobic policy. The curtain, which had been raised at the end of the thirteenth century to disclose a brilliant and intriguing picture of China, descended once more. The vision conjured up by Marco Polo, confirmed by Odoric and elaborated by 'Mandeville' was therefore to persist unaltered until the beginning of the sixteenth century when travellers could once again go to China and see for themselves.

3 THE TRIBUTE EMBASSIES

The distance which divides Holland from China is so great that regular intercourse between the two countries is hardly practicable. Indeed, there is no record of any previous Dutch embassy. Aware of the long and arduous journey of the present Ambassadors, WE were happy to give them audience and receive their tribute-presents. In earnest of our goodwill WE returned them gifts of suitable value. But when WE think of the danger of storm and shipwreck that besets the passage hither, WE are too solicitous of the welfare of the Dutch people to do more than permit them to send ships to China once in eight years, what time they may sell four cargoes and bring presents to OUR Court.

Mandate of the Emperor Shun Chih, 1656

A new chapter in the history of the imaginary continent opens in 1498 when Vasco da Gama's voyage to Calicut re-established a line of direct communication between Europe and the Far East. In less than a score of years the Portuguese reached the Chinese coast and began minor trading activities, but their piratical behaviour distressed the Chinese, who prevented them from making any deeper incursions into the interior. Had free commercial relations between Europe and China been permitted, then or later, the romantic haze which surrounded the Flowery Land would have been dispersed and the legend of Cathay would consequently have faded away. If, on the other hand, the Chinese had taken a still firmer stand and refused to concede any contact whatever with the outside world, the legend created in the fourteenth century would probably have survived unaltered until it died for lack of nourishment. As it was, China sanctioned a limited trade, for which her craftsmen ingeniously catered, and restricted foreign travellers to a few missionaries or the members of a 'tribute embassy' who were allowed to pass from Canton to Peking where they were accorded the privilege of making a *kow-tow* to the Son of Heaven. The Jesuits and ambassadors thus honoured, hastened to disseminate accounts of their experiences as soon as they returned home, and Europeans were thus given an occasional tantalizing glimpse of the fascinating country behind the Chinese barricade—a glimpse so brilliant and yet so fleeting that it merely whetted the appetite. Had the Chinese sought to cultivate the legend of Cathay, they could not have hit on a method more certain of success.

To the armchair, or rather joint-stool, traveller of the later Middle Ages, Cathay had appealed primarily as a fabulous land of barbaric splendour, but to the Renaissance humanist it appeared in greater conformity with the aspirations of his own time. A new note is therefore struck by Lorenzo Corsalis who, writing from Malacca in 1515, told Lorenzo de' Medici that the Chinese produce 'silk and wrought stuff of all kinds, such as damasks, satins and brocades of extraordinary richness. For they are people of great skill, and of our quality, though of uglier aspect with little bits of eyes.' Henceforth Cathay was to be populated by a race of strange little men, who were singularly skilful and industrious craftsmen, possessing a civilization different from but not inferior to that of Europe. The superimposition of this idea—which had been hinted by Marco Polo—on to that of a fabulous and prodigiously rich country increased the fascination of China and, moreover, made it worthy of consideration by the most classically minded European.

Europeans who succeeded in penetrating to Peking towards the end of the sixteenth century returned with a story scarcely less strange than that which Marco Polo had told, though it was significantly different. The gaudy splendours of Kublai's court had vanished to be replaced by more elegant displays of wealth. Juan Gonzalez de Mendoza, an Augustinian friar who took part in an abortive Spanish embassy to Peking in 1584, was particularly impressed by the architecture even of the houses of provincial governors, 'all of which are superbious and admirable', he thought,

> and wrought by marvellous art, and are as big as a great village by reason that they have within them great gardens, water ponds and woods compassed about. . . . All these houses are within as white as milk, in such sort as it seems to be burnished paper. The floors are paved with square stones, very broad and smooth; their ceilings are of an excellent kind of timber, very well wrought and painted, that it seemeth like damask and of the colour of gold, that showeth very well; every one of them hath three courts and gardens full of flowers and herbs for their recreation. And there is none of them but hath his fish pool furnished, although it be but small.

What a spacious vision of cultivated ease and sunny quietude this brief description must have conjured up for the denizens of dingy houses in the closely packed streets of Madrid, or Paris, or London. And how they must have stared to read of the clean paved streets within the towns and the no less wonderful roads which, league upon league, traversed the country.

But to the sixteenth-century imagination the practical ingenuity of the mysterious Chinese appealed less strongly than their weird yet strangely enlightened customs. Even those who had the misfortune to be imprisoned in China accounted it a valuable experience. For, as one remarked, 'the sentences which the officers pronounce are conformable to the laws of the kingdom; they judge according to the truth of the matter, which they inquire into themselves, without taking account of what the parties say; and so they are very correct in affairs of justice, for fear of the Visitation (from Peking) which they say is made every six months.' Naturally, the inhabitants of the England of Elizabeth I and the Spain of Philip II were impressed. That they found the religious toleration of China and the gentle Confucian creed less impressive, only suggests that they were as yet insufficiently advanced to comprehend such ideas.

By one of the stranger ironies of history, Europe first learned of Confucius from Jesuits who had been sent out to convert the heathen Chinese. The first and most endearing of these priests was Matteo Ricci who lived for nearly thirty years in China, the last nine in Peking, where he died in 1610. Realizing that the inspired 'popular' style of evangelism which St Francis Xavier had successfully employed in India would not appeal to the more sophisticated Chinese, Ricci resolved on a subtler approach, aimed at the mandarin rather than the coolie, and he set out to absorb the spirit of Chinese culture. He acquired sufficient command of the language to compose books which won the admiration of many *literati*, he assimilated the niceties of Chinese etiquette so completely that he gained the respect even of the unbending mandarins of the Board of Rites, and he studied Confucius so closely that he could bandy quotations from the *Analects* with the philosophers. The Precepts of Confucius he found astonishingly close to those of Christ, and he tried to persuade his listeners to accept the mystical element in Christianity. But here, of course, was the insuperable stumbling block, for the mandarins who had shown keen interest in Ricci's lucid exposition of his faith were clearly shocked by his belief in 'superstititions' which they thought little better than those of the Taoists and Buddhists. Although he had won an honoured place at Peking, both for himself and for his successors at the mission, neither he nor they accomplished the conversion of China. The mission had, however, a considerable influence on Europe, for not only did its members write accounts of their experiences in China, but the Society of Jesus published translations of the works of Confucius which were enthusiastically taken up by European savants towards the end of the seventeenth century. And thus the vision of Cathay was suffused with an ethereal light which, as we shall see, exerted an almost fatal attraction on the Deist philosophers of France, Germany, and England.

Meanwhile, the final touches were being added to other parts of the picture of Cathay. After the flight of the last Ming emperor in 1644 and the establishment of the Manchu dynasty, the Dutch government decided that the time was ripe to open normal trade relations with China, and dispatched an embassy to Peking. Shun Chih, the new occupant of the Dragon Throne, had, however, decided to maintain his predecessors' xenophobic policy. The ambassadors were treated politely as members of a tribute embassy from a dependent barbarian state, ceremoniously conducted to Peking, given handsome presents in exchange for the clocks, toys, astronomical instruments and firearms they had brought with them, were graciously allowed to make a *kow-tow* in the innermost court of the Great Within, and were then taken no less ceremoniously back to the coast with their purpose unachieved. But if the embassy failed in its politico-economic aim—as did those sent by other states in the subsequent two centuries —it was not without importance since the steward to the ambassadors, John Nieuhoff, wrote a full account of the expedition which was promptly translated into French and English and fixed the vision of Cathay on the European imagination.

John Nieuhoff was an observant traveller, and the picture he gives of China —glimpsed mainly from a junk on the Yangtze River, the Yellow River, and the Grand Canal to Peking—is essentially accurate. Yet one may doubt his knowledge of zoology as evinced by his description of 'Cats with long hair Milk-white having large ears like a Spaniel: the gentlewomen keep them for their pleasure; for they will not hunt after or catch mice, it may be for being too high fed'. The Pekinese, that most important denizen of Cathay, might have been allowed to make a more dignified first appearance on the European scene! With the flora he was more successful, and his account of the 'herbe cha' and the delicious beverage made from its leaves no doubt helped to popularize tea drinking in Europe.

In many respects, Nieuhoff's report did no more than confirm the tales of sixteenth-century travellers. He too was impressed by the Chinese system of government, and this citizen of the Dutch Republic commented:

> It is almost incredible for anybody to believe (unless they had seen it) in what State and Pomp these Idolaters and Heathen Princes live, and with what good order their People are Governed; for as well high as low Officers, in the Courts of the Vice-Roys (which are betwixt two and three thousand) manage their Affairs with so much quietness and expedition that all things were dispatched, and with like dexterity as in a private family.

And the fellow-countryman of Spinoza was surprised to note, 'that the whole kingdom is swayed by Philosophers, to whom not only the people but the Grandees of the Court yield an awful Reverence'. The novelty of his book lay in the visual picture it gave of China both by plates—taken from drawings made on the journey but touched up by the engravers—and by descriptions. He was much struck by Chinese buildings, noting that 'neither Wit nor Ingenuity were wanting in their contrivance', though he eschewed all Arabian Nights' apparitions of halls with silver flag-stones, pillars of massy gold and ceilings dripping with jewels. Instead he told of the porcelain tower at Nanking which may well

have appeared little less fantastic to his contemporaries than Mandeville's
'*montour*'. 'This tower', writes Nieuhoff,

> has nine rounds, and one hundred and eighty-four steps to the top; each round
> is adorned with a Gallery full of Images and Pictures, with very handsome lights.
> . . . The outside is all glazed over and painted with several Colours, as Green,
> Red and Yellow. The whole fabric consists of several Pieces, which are so
> Artificially Cemented, as if the work were all of one piece. Round about all
> the corners of the Galleries, hang little Bells, which make a very pretty noise
> when the wind jangles them.

In the Imperial gardens at Peking he observed that:

> All the Edifices, which are so many, are most richly adorned with guilt Galleries,
> Balconies, and carved Imagery, to the admiration of all that ever saw them;
> each dwelling having a large Pent-house so that you may walk dry in all
> weather: Most of the Timber which appears on the out-side of the House, is
> either gilt or covered over with a certain Gum, called by the Chinese *Cie*, much
> in use amongst them, and wherewith they colour or paint their Household-
> stuff, Ships, and Houses, that they make them shine and glister like Looking-
> glasses. All the Roofs of the Buildings are covered with yellow glazed Pantiles
> which shine, when the sun reflects, brighter than Gold; which has made some be-
> lieve and report, that the Roof of this Royal Palace was covered with Pure Gold.

Tartar gold had been replaced by Chinese lacquer, which was nearly as precious
in Europe, and Nieuhoff, with a house-proud Dutch burgher's eye for utility,
marked the good qualities of this substance, 'which is so beautiful and lasting,
that they use no Table-cloths at their Meals; for if they spill any grease or
other liquor upon the Table, it is easily rubbed off with a little fair water,
without loss or damage of colour.' He had, moreover, an eye for a garden.
And if he sometimes yearned for the trim parterres and regimented tulips of
his native land he was none the less susceptible to the sweet disorder and
engaging wantonness of the Chinese pleasance. 'There is not anything wherein
the Chinese shew their Ingenuity more than in these rocks or Artificial Hills',
he wrote,

> which are so curiously wrought that Art seems to exceed Nature: These Cliffs
> are made of a sort of stone, and sometimes of Marble, and so rarely adorned
> with Trees and Flowers, that all that see them are surprised with admiration.
> Rich and wealthy people, especially the great Lords and *Mandorines*, have for
> the most part such Rocks in their Courts and Palaces, upon which they squander
> good parts of their Estates. . . . If I should relate of all the other Artificial
> Ornaments, as of Gardens, Wildernesses, Pools, and other particulars which

adorn this [Imperial] Court, I should far exceed the bounds of what I intend, and perhaps to some of belief. . . .

In this passage lies one of the seeds which was to germinate in Europe and eventually blossom into that most attractive hybrid, the *jardin anglo-chinois*.

Seven years before Nieuhoff's *Embassy* first appeared in England, John Evelyn wrote to another Dutchman, Mr Vander Douse, who had also compiled an account of China:

> I have to the best of my skill translated yr. Relation of China . . . in ye mean time, it would be consider'd whether this whole piece will be to the purpose, there having been of late so many accurate descriptions of those countries in particular, as what Father Alvarez Semedo has publish'd in the Italian, Vincent Le Blanc in French; and Mandelso in high Dutch; not omitting the Adventures and Travels of Pinto in Spanish; all of them now speaking the English language.

The market was indeed glutted, but Nieuhoff's book made a notable impression none the less, adding many of the finishing touches to the picture of Cathay which was all but complete by the end of the seventeenth century. It is significant that Fischer von Erlach who gave in his *Entwurf einer historischen Architektur* (1721) the first appreciative account of Chinese architecture to be published in Europe, relied for his illustrations principally on the plates in Nieuhoff's book. Of the many books on China which appeared during the next hundred years the most important by far was Du Halde's encyclopaedic compilation—*Description géographique, historique, etc., de l'empire de la Chine* . . . (Paris, 1735)—but even this could do little more than sharpen a few details. Meanwhile, the Chinese Empire was drifting towards its conflict with the West, blissfully unaware of the vision of Cathay which shone so brightly in the eyes of European artists, poets, architects, and philosophers.

4   THE PHILOSOPHER'S EMPIRE

> Enough of Greece and Rome. The exhausted store
> Of either nation now can charm no more;
> Ev'n adventitious helps in vain we try,
> Our triumphs languish in the public eye. . . .
> On eagle wings the poet of tonight
> Soars for fresh virtues to the source of light,
> To China's eastern realms: and boldly bears
> Confucius' morals to Britannia's ears.

> WILLIAM WHITEHEAD, 1759

If no important additions were made to the picture of Cathay in the eighteenth century, it was viewed in an altogether different light, being moved from the traveller's fireside to the fashionable *salons* and even the studies of the *philosophes*. Cathay itself remained as vague as all such subjective visions—including those of Hellas and the Middle Ages—are bound to be, and hence, of course, its enduring charm. For all could plunge their hands into the lacquer bran-tub of Chinese travel literature and draw out a morsel to support their private visions of Utopia. As the French man of letters, Grimm, remarked in 1776:

> The Chinese Empire has become in our time the object of special attention and of special study. The missionaries first fascinated public opinion by rose coloured reports from that distant land, too distant to be able to contradict their falsehoods. Then the philosophers took it up, and drew from them whatever could be of use in denouncing and removing the evils they observed in their own country. Thus this country became in a short time the home of wisdom, virtue and good faith, its government the best possible and the longest established, its morality the loftiest and most beautiful in the known world; its laws, its policy, its art, its industry were likewise such as to serve as a model for all nations of the earth.

And of course, this lofty ideal was only made the more desirable by being set against a background as fantastically exquisite and as elegantly bizarre as Watteau or Boucher could conjure up. In the vision of a country where be-whiskered, pigtailed mandarins in dragon-encrusted robes were philosophers and where the *Analects* of Confucius were discussed beneath the bell-fringed roofs of jade pavilions, eighteenth-century Europe could recognize an enchantingly distorted picture of its own culture.

Cathay was, above all, the land of paradox. An exotic air of fantasy pervaded the scene—and yet, were not its curious little inhabitants more rational in their behaviour and beliefs than most Europeans? Esoteric religions flourished there, yet the kindly and enlightened Confucian philosophy, which embraced all the moral and none of the supernatural elements of Christianity, was the established religion. The empire was ruled by an absolute monarch who styled himself the Son of Heaven and made the despotism of Louis XIV look no more than a schoolboy's petty tyranny, but was governed with greater justice and liberality than any European state. How delightfully different and excitingly fresh it must have seemed to an age which was beginning to weary of the copy-book picture of Ancient Rome ruled solely by *gravitas* and *decorum*.

The Vision of Cathay

It should not be supposed that the philosophers who found in Cathay a reflection of their own beliefs and broadcast their interpretation of Confucianism throughout Europe, did so in any light-hearted or flippant manner. Very much the reverse. They promulgated their new doctrines as solemnly as they would have expounded the message of Aristotle's *Politics* or Cicero's *De Officiis*. Only the more superficial moralists like Addison and Lord Chesterfield, or the authors of 'Chinese Letters', like the Marquis d'Argens, Horace Walpole, and Oliver Goldsmith, used the Celestial Empire as a butt against which to play off the absurdities of Europe. Yet one may occasionally detect an undercurrent of fantasy rippling beneath the solemn disquisitions of even the most serious and convinced Non-Confucians. They pause sometimes in their higher flights to observe the grotesques on a Chinese screen and resume the debate by remarking sententiously: 'See how rightly and properly these absurd people behave while we, who are naturally so reasonable, often act in an irrational fashion'.

The first European philosopher to succumb to the charms of Cathay was Leibnitz, who declared in 1687 that he was immersed in 'the work of Confucius, the king of Chinese philosophers, which has been published this year in Paris'. Two years later he had made the acquaintance of and begun a long correspondence with Father Grimani, a Jesuit missionary in Peking, and in 1697 he published his *Novissima Sinica* in which he advocated an interchange of civilizations between China and Europe. The West, he conceded, had made great discoveries in mathematics, logic, astronomy, and metaphysics but seemed, in comparison with China, to be woefully backward in practical philosophy and political morality. Indeed, he continues: 'The state of affairs among ourselves seems to me to be such that, in view of the inordinate lengths to which corruption of morals has advanced, I almost think it necessary that Chinese missionaries should be sent to us to teach us the aim and practice of natural theology as we send missionaries to them to instruct them in revealed theology'. To promoting closer co-operation between Europe and China, Leibnitz devoted the rest of his life. He established societies in Berlin and Moscow, he plagued the Czar for assistance, and he evolved a theory of numbers to interest the Emperor of China who was reputed to be 'much addicted to the art of computation'. His labours were attended with little success, however, and the most that his society of Sciences at Berlin achieved was a licence to grow mulberries for silkworm culture.

In the theoretical field, Leibnitz's teachings had greater effect, for he attracted the discipleship of two notable men, A. H. Francke, who tried to establish Chinese as an academic subject in Germany, and Christian Wolff who embraced the doctrines of Confucius with such fervour that he was expelled from his chair at Halle University. With less dire results, Wolff's pupil Bülffinger also turned his attention to the moral and political philosophy of China, publishing in 1727 his vast compendium: *Specimen Doctrinae Veterum Sinarum Moralis et Politicae* in which he saluted China as the happy land where kings were true philosophers.

In France these matters were taken hardly less seriously, for at Paris resided the Jesuit mission which had introduced Confucius to Europe and had even published popular abridgements of his work, in which Chinese morality was pronounced to derive 'from the purest sources of natural reason'. And it was, of course, from the Jesuits that the young Voltaire first learned of China, hearing the good Fathers praise the rational religion of the mandarins while lamenting the foolish superstitions of the bonzes. Small wonder that he embraced the creed of the enlightened Confucius, declaring, 'I have read his books with attention, I have made extracts from them; I found that they spoke only the purest morality. . . . He appeals only to virtue, he preaches no miracles, there is nothing in them of religious allegory.' In Voltaire's hands Confucius was converted into an eighteenth-century rationalist and the cumbrous and decadent Chinese empire transformed into a Gallic Utopia. 'One need not be obsessed with the merits of the Chinese', he wrote, 'to recognize at least that the organization of their empire is in truth the best the world has ever seen, and moreover the only one founded on parental authority.' What, he asked, should European princes do when they hear of such examples? 'Admire and blush, but above all imitate.'

Meanwhile, the ingenious F. Quesnay, whom his pupils dubbed the 'Confucius of Europe', was concocting a system of political economy which would, he hoped, enable a European monarch to reorganize his kingdom after the Chinese pattern. His ideas, as might be expected, were reactionary. According to the physiocratic doctrine which he evolved, society was to be governed according to natural laws and the soil, as the only source of wealth, was to be the only object of taxation. It was, therefore, to China that he turned for an exemplar, stating in his great manifesto of Physiocracy, *Le Despotisme de la Chine* (1767), that there alone could one find a 'state founded on science and the natural law, whose concrete development it represents'. His proposals for a Confucian economy fell on deaf ears in Paris, but he attained a modest victory for Cathay by prevailing on Louis XV to follow the Chinese emperor's example of guiding the plough at the opening of the 1756 spring tilling—though it should be mentioned that this symbolical act was suggested to the monarch through the good graces of Madame de Pompadour who doubtless saw herself in the role of Ch'ien Lung's Fragrant Concubine.

But, despite the Neo-Confucians and the Physiocrats, many philosophers remained obstinately unconvinced of the moral superiority of the East. Early in the eighteenth century, Fénelon had contrived an imaginary conversation in which Confucius was routed by Socrates who belittled even the most remarkable achievements of Chinese civilization and roundly declared that the invention of printing was nothing to be proud of, still less that of gunpowder; that Chinese mathematics were lacking in method; that their architecture had no proportion, their painting no composition; and that they owed their undeniably exquisite porcelain and lacquer to a mere accident of geography. And lest there should be any mistake about its import, Fénelon entitled his dialogue *Sur la prééminence tant vantée des Chinois*. A little later, Montesquieu ventured to question the benevolence of the Chinese emperor's despotism for which he found no room in his theory of the state. Rousseau, moreover, cited China as a terrible example of how science and arts corrupt manners. 'There is in Asia a vast country in which the sciences are a passport to the highest positions in the State', he wrote.

> If the sciences really purified morals, if they really taught men to shed their blood for their fatherland, if they inspired courage, then the people of China would surely be wise, free and invincible. But as a matter of fact, there is no sin to which they are not prone, no crime which is not common amongst them. If neither the ability of its ministers nor the alleged wisdom of its laws, nor even the numberless multitude of its inhabitants, has been able to protect the realm against subjection by ignorant and rude barbarians, of what service have been all its wise men?

So much, thought Rousseau, for the rule of Natural Law in China.

The debate raged on throughout the greater part of the eighteenth century, with both sides drawing their ammunition from the same arsenal of travel literature. Only very occasionally did the cold light of common sense illuminate the discussion, save in England where Dr Johnson tried to shatter the legend of Cathay with the butt end of his pistol:

Boswell: What do you say to the written characters of their language?

Johnson: Sir, they have not an alphabet. They have not been able to form what all other nations have formed.

Boswell: There is more learning in their language than in any other, from the immense number of their characters.

Johnson: It is only more difficult from its rudeness; as there is more labour in hewing down a tree with a stone than with an axe.

And when Boswell remarked that the Chinese were surely no barbarians, Johnson curtly replied, 'They have pottery.' The last word must, however, go to Frederick the Great, a ruler less powerful but a poet and philosopher little inferior to Ch'ien Lung, who quietly remarked to Voltaire that the emperor of China hoped that Europe would one day make up its mind about his nation, and that those who had never set foot in Peking would desist meantime from praising it. But it was, none the less, with a glance towards the Dragon Throne that the philosopher king of *Sans-Souci* erected chinoiserie buildings in his park at Potsdam.

5 THE FALL OF CATHAY

The individual features which together made up the eighteenth-century vision of Cathay could all, or nearly all, be found elsewhere. America boasted a territory no less vast, replete with flora and fauna no less exotic. India was equally mysterious and the source of fabulous riches. Islam presented an art as engagingly bizarre—to say nothing of the lubricious charms of harem life. And, after the turn of the century, philosophers discovered that paragon, the Noble Savage, passing his blameless life and indulging his melancholy sensibility amidst the jungles of Africa or on the sun-drenched strands of Patagonia. But none of these lands alone could rival the infinite variety of China. And, moreover, as the eighteenth century proceeded, each of these distant countries seemed to draw nearer to Europe and consequently lost much of its enchantment. The America of George Washington and 'Gentleman Johnny Burgoyne' ceased to be an El Dorado of rainbow-painted macaws and picturesque feather-crowned aborigines. It was difficult for an Englishman to retain a sense of India's mystery when some recently returned nabob was lavishing his fortune on a sumptuous Palladian house in the neighbouring park. Nor was it easy for him to indulge in very exciting day-dreams of the sultan of Turkey's seraglio after Lady Mary Wortley Montagu had been received at Constantinople. China alone remained sufficiently distant and aloof to support a legend as romantic as that of Cathay.

But, alas, she was not to remain inviolate for ever, and once the isolation of China was broken, the vision of Cathay began to dissolve. The first cracks in her defences appeared as early as 1748 when Richard Walter published his account of *A Voyage Round the World* and described in singularly uncomplimentary terms the treatment Commodore Anson had received from the provincial officials of Canton. Anson, the first educated man apart from the Jesuits to visit China since the mid-seventeenth century, had towed a captured Spanish galleon into the mouth of the river at Canton where he attempted to restock and refit his ship. Every obstacle was put in his way by the local officials, and he gained a vivid impression of the corruption and inefficiency of the Chinese Government. Winding up his story, Walter remarked that Jesuit missionaries had led Europeans to believe 'that the whole Empire was a well-governed affectionate family, where the only contests were who should exert the most humanity and beneficence. But', he goes on, 'our preceding relation of the behaviour of the Magistrates, Merchants and Tradesmen at Canton sufficiently refutes these jesuitical fictions. . . . For we have seen that their Magistrates are corrupt, their people thievish, and their tribunals crafty and venal.' Anson had also discovered that one British man-of-war was a match for the entire southern Chinese fleet. Well might Grimm declare that 'the famous Captain Anson has, I think, been the first to correct our notion of this Mandarin government'. The report did not immediately cause the pagodas of Europe to rock, however, for it was accepted only by those who wished to believe in it, and Voltaire, for one, had little difficulty in brushing aside the unhappy incident. Canton, he explained, was a distant provincial town where it was only to be expected that the officials were corrupt and pettifogging; had Captain Anson gone to Peking he would have met with a very different reception. But once the seed of doubt had been sown, sceptics were not slow to encourage its growth and before long the vision of Cathay as a philosopher's paradise was undermined.

By the early nineteenth century the Chinese effusions of Leibnitz, Voltaire, and Quesnay were no longer credited, and Cathay dwindled once again into a land of fantasy, more appropriate to fairy plays like Gozzi's and Schiller's *Turandot* than to political and philosophical disquisitions. Meantime the first revelations of Anson had been confirmed by the reports of several other disillusioned and sometimes infuriated travellers to China, notably Lord Macartney in 1793 and Lord Amherst whose mission to Peking in 1816 foundered in an absurd pantomime of court etiquette. Those disclosures were soon followed by a spate of travel books which presented a more mundane and equally unromantic picture of Chinese life. Finally the advent of British troops in 1857 as a reprisal for the burning of a factory at Canton turned the exquisite vision of Cathay into the problem of modern China. And the wheel came full cycle when an eminent sinologue, G. Pauthier remarked that the Chinese 'whom we daily treat as barbarians, and who, nevertheless, had attained to a very high state of culture several centuries before our ancestors inhabited the forests of Gaul and Germany, now inspire in us only a deep contempt'.

Even so, a vision of the Utopian land still lingered at the back of the western mind. As late as 1901 the Cambridge philosopher G. Lowes Dickinson, in his *Letters from John Chinaman*, gave proof of its persistence. Employing a time-honoured formula, Dickinson, who had not yet been to China, attacked western civilization from an oriental viewpoint—and with such success that an American politician published an indignant reply in which he averred that John Chinaman 'had never seen the inside of a Christian home.' Dickinson's letter writer could not make any great claims for the wisdom and morality of the Chinese Government, so he confined his attack to the irrationality of the Christian faith in comparison with Confucianism (which may almost be equated in this instance with nineteenth-century liberal agnosticism), and the inexcusably brutal behaviour of western troops who had recently marched on Peking to rescue the staffs of the legations from imminent massacre by the Boxers. Dickinson's praise is reserved for the feudal agrarian system (much like that in William Morris's dream of the Middle Ages) and, more justly, the Chinese reverence for beauty. He also sketches one of the most beautiful literary evocations of the idealized land of Cathay:

> In China letters are respected not merely to a degree but in a sense which must seem, I think, to you unintelligible and overstrained. But there is a reason for it. Our poets and literary men have taught their successors, for long generations, to look for good not in wealth, not in power, not in miscellaneous activity, but in a trained, a choice, an exquisite appreciation of the most simple and universal relations of life. To feel, and in order to express, or at least to understand the expression of all that is lovely in nature, of all that is poignant and sensitive to man, is to us in itself a sufficient end. A rose in a moonlit garden, the shadow of trees on the turf, almond blossom, scent of pine, the wine-cup and the guitar; these and the pathos of life and death, the long embrace, the hand

stretched out in vain, the moment that glides for ever away, with its freight of music and light, into the shadow and hush of the haunted past, all that we have, all that eludes us, a bird on the wing, a perfume escaped on the gale— to all these things we are trained to respond, and the response is what we call literature.

CHAPTER II

The Beginnings of Chinoiserie

I SERICA: THE LAND OF SILK

A thorough investigation of the trade relations between Europe and the Far East would take us back to a very uncertain period of economic history. As early as the fourth century B.C. an active commerce connected Persia with India and perhaps with China: by this means Chinese wares may easily have been brought to Europe and European objects reached China. Not until the beginning of the first century B.C., however, did China participate directly in world trade, sending bundles of silks—so much finer than any materials woven in Europe—and perhaps some pieces of porcelain along the perilous caravan route which wound its way across Asia from the Yangtze River to the shores of the Mediterranean. At about the same time pottery vases of Hellenistic design began to reach China by way of the nomadic tribes of central Asia, for there was no organized trade in these wares. It is significant that the Romans called silks *serica*, deriving the term from the Greek word for China, just as eighteenth-century Englishmen were to call porcelain and lacquer: china and japan.

By the middle of the first century of our era the Asian silk road was well established (in the year A.D. 97 General Pan Ch'ao dispatched an official ambassador from the frontier in Turkestan to the distant land of *Ta Ch'in*, probably Syria) and some adventurous mariner had discovered the sea route across the Gulf of Aden which enabled merchants to travel from Rome to Muziris (modern Cranganore), the greatest of all Indian markets, in little more than sixteen weeks. Both routes were mentioned by an anonymous Roman writer of the first century whose description of China provides the earliest surviving account of the country in European literature. Beyond Chryse (modern Burma and Malaya), he writes, 'the sea comes to an end somewhere in Thin [otherwise rendered as Sin, Chin, or China]; and in the interior of that country, somewhat to the north, there is a great city called Thinae, from which raw silk, and silk thread and silk stuffs are brought overland through Bactria and Barygaza, as they are on the other hand by the Ganges river to Limyrice. It is not easy, however, to get to this Thin, and few and far between are those who come from it.' Roman merchants were quick to exploit the possibilities of the new route and silks were soon being imported into the Empire in large quantities.

This increase in the eastern trade was, however, regarded as a mixed blessing. The elder Pliny, for one, viewed it with a jaundiced eye, remarking that 'India is brought near by lust for gain'. The Seres, or Chinese, he said, carried their bales of silk to a river where they met the Roman merchants, and having obtained sufficient valuables in exchange for their wares hurried off, acting in contempt of the luxury to which they administered and, he adds with an admonitory wag of the finger, 'just as if they saw in their mind's eye the object and destination and result of this traffic'. As for the silken cloths which were becoming so fashionable, Seneca was disgusted by their gauze-like transparency: 'I see silken clothes, if you can call them clothes at all, that in no degree afford protection either to the body or to the modesty of the wearer, and clad in which no woman could honestly swear she is not naked'. But the warnings of the moralists were without avail, and three centuries later Ammianus Marcellinus complacently remarked that 'the use of silk which was once confined to the nobility is now spread to all classes without distinction, even to the lowest'. Pliny's gloomy forebodings might seem to have been fulfilled before the end of the third century when great material prosperity and, he would have said, an effeminate addiction to silk, began to exert an enervating effect on the empire. Barbarians from the north intercepted the trade route across Asia, others hindered Roman ships on their way through the Red Sea. Although Rome held Egypt and the Isthmus of Suez until the Arab conquest of 641, no direct trade between Europe and the Indies was possible from late in the third century until Vasco da Gama's voyage to Calicut in 1498.

Much of the silk imported from China was raw and woven in Syria into transparent gauzes, of the type which shocked Seneca. But patterned silk cloths were also popular and in the third century Dionysius Periegetes remarked that the Chinese 'make precious figured garments, resembling in colour the flowers of the field, and rivalling in fineness the work of spiders'. At this time, indeed, Syrian weavers occasionally copied the patterns on Chinese silks. A fragment of a third-century fabric found at Dura-Europos, for example, is decorated with a Han style design so closely imitated that one expert was deceived into believing it to be of Chinese origin though the technique (a weft rep) proves it to be Syrian. This fragment is the earliest recorded imitation of Chinese art in the West. Later, in the fourth century, after Constantine had adopted Constantinople as the capital of the Empire, an increasing quantity of silks was woven in Byzantium and a proportion of them is said to have borne patterns derived from the Far East.

During the fourth and fifth centuries silk was still brought to Europe by Asian intermediaries, but while the demand grew ever greater, transport across the continent became steadily more difficult and dangerous. Consequently the price rose, to the embarrassment of elegant and effete Romans who were accustomed to wear silk underclothes beneath their togas. A crisis came in the sixth century when the Emperor Justinian realized, apparently for the first time, that this lust for silk was enriching the Persians at the expense of the empire with which they were at war. He consequently fixed in 540 a maximum price to be paid for imported silk, but the wily Persians who had braved the perils of the caravan route, fully realized the value of their merchandise. Refusing to sell on any but their own terms, they bundled up their bales and trudged back towards the East, expecting, no doubt, to be recalled and offered a better price. For once, Justinian was inflexible and his courtiers were faced with the uncomfortable prospect of clothing themselves in linen or wool.

The ugly problem was soon solved by 'certain monks from the land of the Indians' or some blackleg Persian (according to another report) who offered, for a suitable reward, to smuggle the eggs of silkworms out of China. Loaded with gifts and encouraged with promises by the harassed Justinian, who must have realized that the silk in his own wardrobe would not last for ever, the smugglers departed and in due course returned with the precious eggs of the *bombyx mori* concealed in hollow bamboo canes. Success attended this desperate venture and as Gibbon recounts: 'the eggs were hatched at the proper season by the artificial heat of dung; the worms were fed with mulberry leaves; they lived and laboured in a foreign climate; a sufficient number of butterflies was saved to propagate the race; and trees were planted to supply the need of rising generations'. But it was with a heavy sigh that he added his inevitable comment. 'I am not insensible to the benefits of elegant luxury; yet I reflect with some pain that, if the importers of silk had introduced the art of printing, already practised by the Chinese, the comedies of Menander and the entire decades of Livy would have been perpetuated in the editions of the sixth century.'

2 CHINA: THE LAND OF PORCELAIN

During the six hundred years which separate the reign of Justinian from the Papacy of St Gregory X, Europe and China existed apart, as if on different planets. Occasionally some bedraggled and travel-stained barbarian merchant from the West may have reached the court of the Son of Heaven to be received as a tribute ambassador from a distant and sadly uncivilized province; but if so he never returned to tell the tale and no whisper of the momentous events which were taking place in China reached European ears. For whilst Europe was embroiled in a series of local wars and European arts were struggling for survival, China passed through the golden age of the T'ang dynasty, the tumultuous half-century of the Five Dynasties period and entered the serene era of Sung refinement. Before the Romanesque style had been brought to perfection in Europe, the arts of China had risen to their apogee and began to decline; before the birth of Dante nearly all the greatest masterpieces of Chinese literature had been written and, by means of printing, diffused throughout a continent. Convulsed by its own troubles, early medieval Europe had neither the time nor the inclination to look beyond the Levant, where the Crusades were being fought, to the distant Orient.

Nevertheless, oriental objects, mostly from Persia but very probably including Chinese silks, continued to reach Byzantium, and they account for certain strange motifs—phoenixes, peacocks, and dragons—which make so surprising an appearance among the sombre hieratic saints and emperors of Byzantine art. A phoenix of undoubted Chinese extraction figures in some tenth-century manuscript illustrations and, more notably, on the two ends of an eleventh-century ivory casket in the Cathedral Treasury at Troyes (Pl. 1). The birds on this casket may well be considered as the first specimens of European chinoiserie. Unlike the Syrian textiles of the third century, these panels are no mere copies, or fakes, of Chinese objects; they have been derived from a flat pattern on silk and worked out in relief in a different medium. And unlike the birds who strut and preen themselves on tenth-century manuscripts, their purpose is not illustrative but decorative. The casket is, however, a very lonely example of Byzantine chinoiserie, and it need not be assumed that the Far Eastern origin of the two birds was appreciated by their carver or that they were intended to satisfy anything more than a very generalized taste for oriental exoticism. They are, in fact, manifestations of a vogue for the exotic which attacked the Byzantine court under Macedonian rule and which was otherwise expressed in the Islamic motifs used to decorate enamels and textiles.

Some two hundred years after the Troyes casket was carved the land route between Europe and China was reopened, and Chinese wares were once again imported in quantity. In 1209 the Mongol chief, Genghiz Khan, made his first attack on China and six years later took Peking, whither his successor Otogai moved his capital from the Mongolian wastes, some time in the 1230s. Kublai Khan succeeded to the Mongol leadership in 1258, established himself on the Dragon Throne as the first Yüan emperor and by 1280, five years after Marco Polo entered his service, was the ruler of the whole of China as well as the greater part of central Asia. The conquest of China had been effected and now the ancient Chinese civilization began to subdue its victors. Kublai was the first to profit from this sweetening influence to which we may, perhaps, attribute his remarkable intellectual curiosity, tolerance and wisdom. Welcoming foreigners to his magnificent court, he opened the way from the West to the Far East, and those merchants who took advantage of it returned home with objects to illustrate their stories of the incredible riches of that prince and the exquisite craftsmanship of the Chinese. Among the treasures Marco Polo brought back were a Tartar belt of silver (probably his insignia of rank), a feminine head-dress enriched with gold, pearls and various stones, the gold tablet given him by the Great Khan on his departure, a Buddhist rosary and numerous stuffs of silk and gold thread, not to mention the various curiosities which, on account of their slight commercial value, were unspecified in the inventories of his effects.

It would be very interesting to know whether there were any paintings among the souvenirs brought back from China by Marco Polo, or by his contemporaries and immediate successors. For the recorded presence of Sung or Yüan dynasty scrolls in Italy would finally solve the vexed question of oriental influence in *trecento* paintings. Chinese dragons with bats' wings, metamorphosed into devils, began to make their appearance in illuminated manuscripts and sculpture before the end of the thirteenth century; but these are mere symbols of the kingdom of darkness (then popularly associated with Tartary) and are treated in a purely European manner. The earliest picture to reveal an apparently artistic (as opposed to iconographic) oriental influence is the *St Louis of Toulouse Crowning King Robert of Anjou* (Museo di Capodimonte, Naples) painted by the Sienese Simone Martini in 1317. Here the faces of both figures have a strangely oriental cast while the saint wears a mitre decorated with dragons which suggests that the painter may have seen some specimen of Chinese art at the court of King Robert. The influence is more fully developed in the same artist's *Guidoriccio Fogliano* (Palazzo Pubblico, Siena) of 1328 where the composition has an airy spaciousness strangely reminiscent of Chinese paintings and unlike anything in earlier Italian art. This fresco has, indeed, been compared with a twelfth-century scroll by Chao Po-chü (Museum of Fine Arts, Boston) in which the presence of an army is indicated, with characteristic oriental economy, by a group of pennants fluttering over the brow of a hill, as in Simone Martini's painting. Nor is it wholly without significance that the *Guidoriccio Fogliano* 'reads' from right to left, like a Chinese scroll. Ambrogio Lorenzetti may, perhaps, have drawn inspiration from a similar source when he painted the landscapes and townscapes in the Palazzo Pubblico at Siena a decade later. But, unfortunately, no Chinese painting is known to have been in Europe at this time and the possibility of an oriental influence on Italian *trecento* paintings must therefore remain hypothetical. (The influence of Indo-Persian miniatures on such early fifteenth-century artists as Stefano da Verona and Benozzo Gozzoli is generally recognized.)

No such doubts and difficulties afflict the study of the Chinese influence on fourteenth-century textiles, for many of the Yüan period silks imported from China still survive in cathedral treasuries. Richly coloured and decorated with bold stripes or seething with weird oriental beasts, many of these fabrics were made into dalmatics, chasubles, and copes while others were probably used for household decoration and personal adornment. Some specimens are woven with Islamic or, more rarely, orientalized European motifs which suggest that even at this early date the Chinese were catering for an export market. While the *pax tartarica* established by Kublai Khan reigned over Asia, bales of these materials were carried from China to the Middle East and to Europe along the caravan route which Balducci Pegolotti declared to be perfectly safe whether by night or day. That this great influx of brocades and embroideries, so much finer in quality and richer in colour and design than any Europe could produce, should have aroused admiration and stimulated emulation is hardly surprising.

By the middle of the fourteenth century the weavers of Lucca—then the most important centre of the silk industry in Europe—were busy imitating oriental designs. At first they copied precisely the fire-breathing dragons, playful lions and phoenixes which had rampaged on Chinese stuffs since the Han dynasty and which had first caught the fancy of Europeans several centuries earlier. Presumably they appealed on account of their exoticism, representing the fabulous East about which so many stories were now circulating. But in copying the oriental motifs the weavers altered them slightly, modified the relationship between them and finally absorbed them, together with patterns and inscriptions from the Middle East, into the great repertory of Gothic ornament (Pl. 2).

Oriental textiles also affected the related art of embroidery and a cope of mid-fourteenth-century German origin (Musée Historique des Tissus, Lyons) is worked in brick-stitch with a Chinese fret pattern of squared scrolls—an unusual example of the adaptation of an abstract Chinese design at this date. Most of these fourteenth-century fabrics have faded and all but disintegrated (more so than the Yüan silks on which a higher value was probably placed) and one may now catch a glimpse of their original brilliance only in such a painting as the *St Ursula* by the Cologne Master (Rudolphinum, Prague) where the saint is clad in a dress resplendent with chinoiserie phoenixes.

Small quantities of Chinese porcelain also reached Europe in the Middle Ages, though there does not seem to have been any organized trade in this commodity. Marco Polo, however, apparently felt no need to describe the material which he mentioned only once, to remark on its small cost at 'Tin-gui' and to give a garbled description of how it was manufactured. His account suggests that specimens of porcelain might have been seen by his readers, who would have been principally impressed to learn that no fewer than eight cups of this precious substance could be purchased for a Venetian groat. For, in comparison with the rough vessels which were the best that European potters could make, even the simplest piece of Chinese porcelain—such as the jar in the Museo di S. Marco at Venice which Marco Polo is reputed to have brought back with him—must have appeared exquisite indeed. The earliest recorded example of porcelain to reach medieval Europe is somewhat later, however: a greyish-white bottle converted into a ewer by a silver mount embellished with the arms of Louis the Great of Hungary who died in 1382. In the fifteenth century Chinese porcelain was included in the gifts given by the sultans of Egypt to various doges of Venice, the first of which was presented to Doge Foscari in 1442. It was probably from the collection of one of these doges that Giovanni Bellini derived the Ming porcelain bowls which he painted in his *Feast of the*

Gods (Pl. 3) thinking, no doubt, that porcelain was the only fit material to hold nectar and ambrosia.

After Vasco da Gama's voyage of 1498 had reopened the sea route to the East, porcelain was brought to Europe in ever-increasing quantities and soon all but the poorest monarchs could boast a few choice specimens in their treasuries. In addition to numerous porcelain vessels, the Emperor Charles V owned a set of plates (now at Dresden) decorated in China with his cipher and badge, and an inventory shows that Philip II of Spain had a collection of no fewer than three thousand pieces. Even Henry VIII, in remote and uncultivated England, owned one piece—a 'Cup of Purselaine glasse fation with two handles garnisshid with siluer and guilt the Couer garnished with iij Camewe heddes and thre garnettes'—and three more were added to the Jewel House as handsels to Queen Elizabeth in 1587 and 1588 (Pl. 4). So great indeed was the demand for Chinese porcelain in Europe, that even before the end of the sixteenth century Chinese potters had begun to produce blue-and-white wares expressly for the European market.

Towards the end of the sixteenth century, Loys Guyon declared that he wished to treat of porcelain because many great lords and connoisseurs of curious things were unaware of what it was made or (which is strange) whence it came, despite the estimation in which it was held by Christian no less than pagan princes. They use it, he says, to serve 'salades de grand prix, fruicts et confitures' at the tables of Popes, Kings, Emperors, Dukes, Marquesses of Italy, but above all, he adds with an unreliable instinct for protocol, at the tables of Emperors and Dukes. Despite the quantities that had been imported into Europe, an aura of mystery still hung about these vessels of gem-like quality, elegant form and quaint decoration. Magical properties were, of course, attributed to them no less than to other rare substances such as rock crystal and ostrich eggs, then believed to belong to the griffin, which were mounted to serve as cups in the later Middle Ages and the sixteenth century. In his account of *Vulgar Errors*, first published in 1646, Sir Thomas Browne set himself to examine these magical properties: 'that they admit no poison, that they strike no fire, that they will grow hot no higher than the liquor in them ariseth'. But, with his characteristic mixture of scepticism and credulity he was bound to confess that 'such as pass amongst us, and under the name of the finest, will only strike fire, but not discover Aconite, Mercury or Arsenic; but may be useful in dysentries and fluxes beyond the other.'

How far the owners of porcelain vessels believed in their magical attributes one cannot judge, but they do not seem to have doubted the wild stories of how this fine and precious material was made. For these, as for so much else in early chinoiserie, Marco Polo must be held primarily responsible. 'The process was explained to me as follows', he roundly declared,

> They collect a certain kind of earth, as it were from a mine, and laying it in a great heap, suffer it to be exposed to the wind, the rain and the sun, for thirty or forty years, during which time it is never disturbed. By this it becomes refined and fit for being wrought into the vessels above mentioned. Such colours as may be thought proper are then laid on, and the ware is afterwards baked in ovens or furnaces. Those persons, therefore, who cause the earth to be dug, collect it for their children and grandchildren.

But this tale was insufficiently romantic to be left unembroidered; some travellers declaring that the clay, and others that the vessels themselves had to remain buried for a century or more to acquire the right degree of hardness. One writer, indeed, would have nothing of so prosaic an explanation and asserted that porcelain was made from the shells of eggs and lobsters—not without some regard for etymology, perhaps, since the word porcelain is probably derived from the Portuguese word for a shell. These legends persisted, sometimes as convenient literary devices (they appear in the burlesque poem *Embarras de la foire de Beaucaire* as late as 1716), long after they had been denied by later travellers, who offered more plausible though still inaccurate explanations as to the origin of this mysterious substance—for they did not realise that the secret of true porcelain lies in the felspar mixed with the clay and the high temperature at which it is baked. Sir Thomas Browne remarked, 'Gonzalez de Mendoza, a man imployed in China from Philip the second King of Spain, upon enquiry and ocular experience, delivered a way different from all these', and then proceeded to describe a method disappointingly similar to that commonly used for making coarse tiger-ware and slip-ware pots. In fact, the attractive legends had been dispelled but not the mystery of fine porcelain; and the problem of how to make it in Europe remained to trouble the minds of the ingenious for many a long year. Kings besought their scientifically inclined subjects to consider the matter—Philip II may well have instructed Mendoza to study the Chinese potter's method—and alchemists abandoned their search for the philosopher's stone in the hope of discovering the constituents of porcelain. Indeed, the receipt for the first true porcelain made in Europe was discovered by an alchemist, Johann Friedrich Böttger.

The Beginnings of Chinoiserie

The first recorded attempt to produce porcelain in Europe was made in the factory of the Medici Grand Duke Francesco I at Florence in about 1575. Here imitation porcelain was made from many ingredients which included sand, glass, powdered rock-crystal, the white earth of Faenza and the clay of Vicenza. But although much finer than majolica, the soft-paste wares produced at this factory could never be mistaken for oriental porcelain, and most of them seem to have gone awry in the firing. The surviving examples—of which some forty are recorded—have a somewhat hazy glaze containing minute bubbles and are nearly all decorated in blue on a white ground with designs which derive from Chinese vessels made in the reigns of Chia Ch'ing (1522–66) and Wan Li (1573–1619). A bottle in the Louvre has a design of pine trees beneath which browses an unmistakably Chinese deer, another shows long-tailed birds roosting amidst exotic flowers and foliage (Pl. 8), while a large dish in the Metropolitan Museum, New York, is adorned with a group of European figures parading stiffly in a wide Chinese landscape—probably the earliest specimen of the delightful Sino-European mixture which was to become so popular in the eighteenth century. Other vessels are decorated with Islamic motifs, which may have appeared sufficiently eastern to be thought Chinese by the Medici potters, and a few have classical masks.

At about the same time Venetian potters are said to have made occasional use of Chinese features in their grotesque decorations, but there was no widespread vogue for chinoiserie as such in a country where high renaissance theories of art reigned supreme. It almost seems as if the Medici potters employed oriental designs from a belief in sympathetic magic, decorating their vessels with the blue-and-white patterns that could be imitated so much more easily than the substance of Chinese porcelain. But although they had anticipated the free use of Chinese motifs by some forty years and the production of soft-paste porcelain by more than a century, the Medici potters failed to produce true porcelain of a brilliance and hardness to rival the Chinese. The valiant experiment seems to have been written off as a failure and on the death of Francesco I in 1587 the production of the factory was abruptly halted.

From the little that is known about this factory it appears that Medici 'porcelain' was primarily, if not exclusively, intended for the Grand Duke's personal use or as presents for other rulers. Its wares, being known to few, exerted no scientific or decorative influence and the brief life of the factory can be regarded as no more than an isolated though remarkable incident in the history of both ceramics and taste. But even if the wares had been intended for the open market, they would hardly have met with much success. In the late sixteenth century large collections of Chinese objects were still rare and in the hands of too exclusive a minority to have created a popular vogue; and as they were probably valued more as expensive curiosities than as examples of exquisite design, imitations were not in demand. The vastly increased influx of oriental merchandise in the seventeenth century was necessary to create a popular fashion for the arts of the East and a consequent demand for imitations.

3   THE EAST INDIA COMPANIES

> Menez-moi chez les Portugais
> Nous y verrons, à peu de frais,
> Des marchandises de la Chine.
> Nous y verrons de l'ambre gris,
> De beaux ouvrages de vernis,
> Et de la porcelaine fine
> De cette contrée divine
> Ou plustôt de ce paradis.
>
> PAUL SCARRON, 1640

The Portuguese, to whom Pope Alexander VI had ceded the eastern half of the undiscovered world, established themselves in 1511 at Malacca, then the gateway to the Pacific, the principal market for cloves and nutmegs, and the most westerly port used by Chinese merchantmen. Within a few years their ships had reached the Chinese coast and Thomas Pires had been dispatched as the first Portuguese ambassador to the Son of Heaven. In 1517 Pires arrived at Canton where he was forced to cool his heels for two years while the offended potentate of a province near Malacca whispered damaging stories in the emperor's ear—stories that were amply confirmed by reports of a Portuguese adventurer, Simon d'Andrade, who was engaged in piratical activities off the Chinese coast. Eventually Pires was summoned to Peking, accused of being a spy and sent back to Canton where he was promptly imprisoned. All hope of a commercial treaty had, therefore, to be abandoned; but Chinese merchants were anxious for trade and provincial governors were prepared to condone the not unremunerative presence of the Portuguese on their territory. And so for a brief period Portuguese factors were allowed to live and establish warehouses at Ch'uan-chow and Ningpo, whence they were later expelled, as a reprisal for further damage caused by their less scrupulous and law-abiding compatriots. But, at last, in 1557, they received official permission to rent land and carry on trade at Macao—a desolate promontory in the Canton estuary—which was for nearly three centuries the most important link between China and the outside world, and has, to this day, remained in Portuguese hands.

Meanwhile, the Portuguese had reached Japan in 1542 and soon set up a flourishing trade, which was considerably helped by a Sino-Japanese war during which they profited from both sides. In 1571 the Spaniards, coming from the East as Pope Urban's bull had directed, established a trading base in the Philippine Islands, and ten years later the fierce rivalry which might so easily have developed between the two powers was happily averted by the union of the Spanish and Portuguese crowns.

The next arrivals on the scene were the Dutch, whose fleet first reached Canton in 1600 and whose East India Company was founded two years later. Although the combined forces of Spain and Portugal foiled their attempts to open up a regular trade route, the Dutch were able to establish a base, first in the Pescadores and then on Formosa, whence they could deal with both Chinese and Japanese merchants. They later contrived to obtain a monopoly of the Japanese trade and were responsible for all the Japanese porcelain and lacquer which reached Europe in the later seventeenth and the eighteenth centuries, besides much Chinese merchandise as well.

English means of commerce with China were less direct; in 1579 leave had been obtained to trade in the Ottoman Empire and install a consulate at Constantinople, the terminus of the caravan route across Asia. In 1600 the English East India Company was incorporated. But a licence which James I granted to Sir Edward Michelborne and others in 1609, permitting them to trade 'to Cathay, China, Japan, Corea, Cambaya' was of little avail in the presence of the well-established Portuguese. In 1612, however, they set up a base in Siam whence they secured direct contact with Chinese merchants if not with China itself. France was the last great power to reach the Far East. The Spanish and Portuguese kept her ships out of Chinese waters for many years and, until 1678, the Dutch prevented them from trading freely even in the Indies.

Throughout the sixteenth and well into the seventeenth century, therefore, the Portuguese and the Spaniards held the key to the China trade, and Chinese objects reached other European countries by way of, or in spite of, their ships. They sold their wares throughout Europe and it was to their stalls at the *Foire de Saint-Germain* that Scarron directed the connoisseur's attention in the mid-seventeenth century. Less regular methods had, however, been employed to bring oriental goods to England in the late sixteenth century when many a stately Spanish carrack, weighed down with eastern merchandise, was diverted to our shores by the official pirates of Queen Elizabeth's fleet. One of the most notable was the *Madre de Dios*, taken off the Azores in 1592 and brought safely to harbour at Dartmouth where its glittering and redolent cargo was trundled out onto the quay. 'Upon good view', wrote Richard Hakluyt:

> it was found that the principal wares after the jewels (which were no doubt of great value though they never came to light) consisted of spices, drugges, silks, calicos, quilts, carpets, and colours &c. The spices were pepper, cloves, maces, nutmegs, cinamon, greene ginger; the drugs were benjamin, frankincence, galingale, mirabolans, aloes, zocotrina, camphire; the silks damasks, taffetas, sarcenets, altobassos, that is, counterfeit cloth of gold, unwrought China silke, sleaved silke, white twisted silke, curled cypresse. The calicos were book-calicos, calico launes, broad white calicos, fine starched calicos, course white calicos, browne broad calicos, browne course calicos. There were also canopies and course diaper towels, quilts of course sarcenet and of calico, carpets like those from Turkey; whereunto are to be added the pearle, muske, civet and ambergriece. The rest of the wares were many in number but less in value; as elephants' teeth, porcellan vessels of China, coco-nuts, hides, ebenwood as black as jet, bedsteads of the same, cloth of the rinds of trees very strange for the matter, and artificiall in workmanship. All which piles of commodities being by men of approved judgement rated but in reasonable sort amounted to no less than 150000 li. sterling which being divided among the adventurers (whereof her Majesty was the chiefe) was sufficient to yield contentment to all parties.

Such were the loads of riches brought each year from the Orient to Europe; the sonorous catalogue is alone sufficient to express the sixteenth-century vision of the prodigious East.

By the end of the sixteenth century Chinese porcelain and a few pieces of lacquer had found their way into the houses of rich merchants. In 1599 Thomas Platter noted that Mr Cope of London had a cabinet of curiosities which contained 'earthen pitchers from China and porcelain from China'. But as Hakluyt's description suggests, such objects were then regarded as mere curios on a level with elephants' teeth and coconuts, the quantities imported being as yet insufficient to create a fashion for Chinese art. Porcelain vases, lacquer cabinets and even silks were brought home in the spice ships as 'perquisites' which might be appreciated by the company's directors or court favourites whose protection was desirable. The directors of the English East India Company certainly guarded their privilege jealously, hastening to the docks as soon as the ships arrived and grabbing everything they could lay hands on, with the result that, on one occasion at least, nothing was left for other purposes. Such avaricious behaviour caused a public scandal in 1613 when the governor of the company was forced to command 'that measures be taken to stop the clamour; whereupon some of the committees promised to return to the warehouse what they had. Twenty pieces of calico were placed at the disposal of the Governor for presentation to the Lord Admiral and other applicants.' Notice was, however, taken of the increased demand for oriental textiles and a few weeks later a sub-committee was appointed to discover 'how Callicoes and Pintathoes (painted cloths) will sell here, that so it may be to give unto the factors for buying and sending hither'.

Next year, greater care was taken with the cargo of the *Clove*, the first (indeed the only) English ship to return from Japan, which carried a rich load including 'Japanese wares, scritoires, Trunkes, Beoubes [screens], Cupps, and dishes of all sorts, and of a most excellent varnish'. To prevent the market from being flooded, the lacquer wares were sold slowly, with such good effect that 'small trunks or chests of Japan stuff guilded and inlaid with mother of pearle having sundry drawers and boxes' which fetched only £4. 5s. and £5 respectively in 1614 brought as much as £17 apiece four years later.

One result of the considerable increase in oriental imports was that objects which had previously been accepted as interesting curiosities were now eyed with greater discrimination. And in 1610 the connoisseur of orientalia makes his first appearance on the scene in the person of one Jacques l'Hermite who spurned a consignment of lacquer sent to Holland from Bantam, judging it far inferior to that which came from Japan. A few years later, Sir Thomas Roe, who was James I's ambassador to the Moghul court from 1615 to 1618, wrote from Agra: 'I thought all India a China shop, and that I should furnish all my friends with rarities; but this is not that part. Here are almost no civil arts, but such as the straggling Christians have lately taught.' Uninterested in mere Indian curiosities or Indo-Portuguese wares, he wanted to buy genuine Chinese objects which, to his regret, he found 'as dear as in England'.

The growing vogue for orientalia is also indicated by the steady increase in the prices charged for Chinese or Japanese objects. To quote an exceptional example, a 'cabinet of China worke' given as a wedding present in 1613 to Princess Elizabeth of England (the daughter of James I, known to historical novelists as the Queen of Hearts) was valued at £10,000. High prices reserved the most delicate Chinese porcelain, the finest Japanese lacquer and the most elaborate Indian textiles for the very rich, but as the fashion gradually extended down the social scale a lively demand was created for cheaper objects. A vogue for Chinese arts had come into being and European craftsmen were obliged to imitate oriental wares to satisfy less affluent collectors with pretensions to fashion and also to swell the collections of great noblemen for whom the spice ships brought back a still insufficient quantity of eastern objects.

4 FROM 'CHINA WORKE' TO CHINOISERIE

In the anonymous play, *L'Ile des Hermaphrodites*, published in Paris about 1600, there is a tantalizing reference to cabinets 'ornez à la fascon de la Chine où il y a toutes sortes d'oyseaulx et d'animaux représentez' which, it is very tempting to suppose, were the earliest European imitations of oriental lacquer. Only a little later Marie de Médicis was employing a skilful cabinet-maker named Étienne Sager to 'make with lacquer gum and gold decoration in the manner of the same country (China), cabinets, chests, boxes, panelling, ornaments for churches, chaplets, and other small articles of Chinese goods.' Moreover, she placed a seller of Chinese wares in the gallery of the Louvre where she also set up the notable *ébéniste* Laurent Septabre. At about the same time the imitation of lacquer was practised in Italy, and when William Smith wrote to Lord Arundel from Rome in 1616 he was able to list among his many accomplishments that he had 'been emploied for the Cardinalles and other Princes of these parts, in workes after the China fashion wch. is much affected heere'. Unfortunately, no fragment of such work is known to survive and we must turn to more northern countries for the earliest extant imitations of lacquer made in Europe.[1]

Such imitations were produced in England in the first two decades of the seventeenth century, and an inventory of the 'goodes and household stuffe' in the possession of Henry Howard, first Earl of Northampton, on his death in 1614, shows that he owned both oriental and pseudo-oriental furniture. His 'China guilt cabinette upon a frame' and his 'China cushen embrodred with birds' may well have been of eastern origin, but his 'large square China worke

---

[1] The imitation lacquer produced in Europe is of an entirely different substance from true oriental lacquer and is frequently called 'japan' to distinguish it.

table and frame of black varnish and gold'; his 'paire of crimson velvett chairs richlie imbosted with copper and blewe and white flowers china worke'; his 'small table of China worke in gold and colours with flies and wormes upon a table suteable', and, most notably, his 'field bedstead of China worke blacke and silver branches with silver with the Armes of the Earl of Northampton upon the headpiece' must have been of European manufacture. Alas, none of these preposterous objects has survived, but a small group of similar wares dating from the same period gives some indication of what they must have been like. These consist of a ballot-box (in the possession of the Saddlers' Company) which is certainly English and dated 1619, a cabinet in the Victoria and Albert Museum (Pl. 7), and a box containing twelve roundels in the same collection. All are of oak painted in gold and silver on a thickly varnished black ground, and they all seem to have been decorated by the same hand. The Saddlers' ballot-box has no specifically eastern features, but the cabinet and the box of roundels are both embellished with the same curious figure of a man wearing a long robe and mitre-shaped hat, standing amidst exotic trees of a markedly oriental aspect; though in the background of the cabinet scene a very English-looking windmill is to be descried on a distant hill.

The fashion for imitation lacquer also appeared in Denmark in the early seventeenth century and a room in the Rosenborg Slot, Copenhagen, was decorated with 'lacquer' panels in about 1616. Here the panels are of dark green varnish with designs finely picked out in gold and they are set in frames of imitation tortoiseshell. Most of them represent delicate little junks, one of which is dressed for a regatta, all a-flutter with pennants and guided by a youthful figure with six-foot plumes nodding from his turban, who stands behind the dragon-headed prow (Pl. 5). Another panel depicts the interior of some magnificent temple or hall of audience—perhaps the Great Within—where numerous figures kneel around the illustrious priest or potentate squatting on a carpet in the centre, while elephants and monsters look down from between the Ionic pilasters on the upper walls—an extraordinary jumble or chop-suey of oriental and European motifs.

Strangely enough, the only European countries which seem to have remained more or less immune to the influence of orientalia in the first half of the seventeenth century were those most intimately connected with the China trade—Spain and Portugal. So far as is known, Spain produced no imitations of Chinese art. Perhaps she imported sufficient quantities to supply every demand. Portugal had indeed been susceptible to the influence of Indian architecture early in the sixteenth century but absorbed its motifs into her national style. Far from imitating eastern goods at the beginning of the seventeenth century, the Portuguese were busy encouraging Indian workmen to carry out European patterns in native materials, such as mother-of-pearl and ebony—with alarming results. Only a few potters in Portugal seem to have employed oriental motifs in the decorations of their wares.

Elsewhere in Europe the fashion for oriental decorations was becoming a rage and craftsmen in all countries were busy imitating, somewhat falteringly, the quaint scenes found on cabinets, porcelain vessels and embroideries imported from the East. To supplement these sources, at least two engravers now produced sets of oriental-style designs. The earliest recorded was published by Mathias Beitler, a Dutchman, in 1616 and consists of a group of minute engravings of trees, bridges, little Chinamen, cats and some purely fanciful creatures. Seven years later Valentin Sezenius, a Dane, began to produce another series which contains an extraordinary mixture of classical and oriental features including long-tailed birds, wispy trees, and rickety buildings on stilts (Fig. 1)

Fig. 1   Etching by Valentin Sezenius, 1626

which seem to anticipate Pillement, and amongst which Chinese boatmen, Pan, Orpheus or amorous Dutch couples in Rubens costume are equally at home. Such designs were intended primarily for small enamel jewels though they may possibly have been applied to silver work. There was also a demand for oriental textile patterns, and as early as 1608 Thomas Trevelyon included drawings of strange flowers, of a type later to be called *fleurs des Indes*, among the 'Designs for use in the Decorative Arts' in his unpublished *Epitome of Ancient and Modern*

History. So great, indeed, was this vogue for exoticism in Jacobean England that John Taylor, who printed an ordinary set of patterns called *The Needle's Excellency*, felt bound to claim in limping verses that they had been:

> Collected with much praise and industry
> From scorching Spaine and freezing Muscovie,
> From fertile France and pleasant Italie,
> From Poland, Sweden, Denmarke, Germanie,
> And some of these rare patterns have been set
> Beyond the bounds of faithlesse Mahomet,
> From spacious China and those kingdoms East
> As from great Mexico, the Indies West.

Soon this taste was to be exploited in England by a company founded in 1625 to weave hangings with Indian figures, histories, and landscapes, but, alas, none of its works is known to survive.

No attempt seems to have been made to imitate oriental porcelain for some decades after the failure of the Medici experiment. In 1628, however, a Dutch potter named Christian Wilhelm began to produce at Southwark, vessels decorated in blue and white with motifs adapted somewhat crudely from Ming ceramics. And in 1637 a pottery in Hamburg was making similar blue-and-white earthenware dishes. Little is known about either of these factories, both of which seem to have gone out of business before 1660 when two more notable potteries were already producing blue-and-white wares of much higher quality—the group of factories at Delft in Holland which in popular parlance has given its name to all such European vessels, and the factory at Nevers in France.

The origin of the Delft potteries is still uncertain and the few known facts may be briefly stated. In 1614 one Claes Janszoon Wijtmans obtained leave from the States General to erect a faience factory (*pourcelainbackerij*) for the production of wares like those of the 'Indies'. Excavations on the site have turned up only potsherds of majolica type, decorated with purely European designs of pomegranates, oranges, birds, beasts, and flowers, and it was not until the middle of the seventeenth century that the great age of Delft pottery began with its famous blue-and-white wares. At first the majority of these were closely imitated from the Chinese and Japanese porcelain vessels which the Dutch were at this time importing into Europe. And throughout the subsequent hundred and fifty years the Delft factory was to turn out a stream of imitation, not to say fake, Chinese vessels, some of which are so close to their prototypes that their European origin may at first sight be mistaken.

Some of the Delft pottery painters did, however, break away from the practice of imitating Ming decorations, in the 1650s, to paint tiles, jugs, and plates with engaging little figures dressed in fantastic clothes and posed in absurd attitudes, which represented their vision of Chinamen (Pl. 9). Later in the century painters with greater daring gave free rein to their sense of fantasy, combining elements from Chinese and Japanese porcelain and freeing them from all strict oriental conventions. They produced objects, sometimes of such fantastic shapes as the tall pagoda-like tulip vases (Pl. 14), on which all the decorative motifs in the oriental potter's repertoire have been exaggerated; the Japanese ladies are more attenuated and the pot-bellied gods stouter, the dragons, monsters and weird birds more fantastic, the buildings more exquisitely flimsy and gimcrack, and the gargantuan flowers and trees more luxuriant. It was for long believed that the artist responsible for this development was Aelbrecht Cornelis de Keizer, who began his career in 1642, but the mark formerly attributed to him has now been assigned to a younger potter and it seems improbable that many wares in an unrestrained chinoiserie style were produced at Delft before the 1670s.

The Nevers pottery, although it produced few wares either as fine or as fantastic as those made at Delft towards the end of the seventeenth century, has a better claim to have originated the chinoiserie style in European ceramics. As early as 1644 this factory was imitating the shapes of Chinese vessels, though the example of this date (Fitzwilliam Museum, Cambridge) is decorated with a biblical scene and not with chinoiseries. But by the 1650s vessels of both Chinese and baroque patterns were being decorated with either European or oriental designs—mandarins and dragons figuring on exuberant baroque ewers while grandiose mythological scenes derived from contemporary painters appear on chaste Chinese vases. Possibly because France imported no porcelain direct from the East at this date and the potters therefore had few prototypes to imitate, or because the public demanded something more than mere copies, the earlier oriental Nevers decorations are freer in style than those produced at Delft in the 1650s. The figures and even the birds and flowers, though similar to those on late Ming porcelain, have been transmuted by a characteristically French elegance (Pl. 10). Nevers also produced pottery with drawings in white on a *bleu persan* ground, thus reversing the traditional blue-and-white colour scheme to create a startlingly new decorative effect which almost seems to emulate lacquer. But only very rarely, even in the later years of the century, did the Nevers potters produce those delightful *mélanges* of oriental—Chinese, Japanese, and Indian—motifs so gaily devised by their contemporaries at Delft.

Eastern fabrics grew increasingly popular as the seventeenth century proceeded and were imitated in both France and England. Even Cardinal Mazarin, an enthusiastic and percipient collector of orientalia, owned, so his inventory of 1653 reveals, 'Dix pièces de serge de soye à plusieurs couleurs façon de la Chine faites à Paris'. The factories where such textiles were woven were no doubt intended primarily to satisfy the ever-growing demand for materials 'façon de la Chine'; but they may also have been established to help the French textile industry to compete with the fashionable imports from China and India from which it was soon to need more effective protection. At about the same time, however, the English East India Company began to organize its textile trade on remarkable new lines, without heeding the plight of native industries, and a very extraordinary episode in the history of taste ensued.

In 1643 the London directors of the East India Company began to complain that the Indian fabrics sent home were not properly adapted for the English market. Their factors at Surat were sharply informed that:

> The Pintadoe [painted cloth] Quilts came safe to our hands and we have disposed of some part of them in sales at 50sh/- each piece. They serve more to content and pleasure our friends than from any profit that ariseth in sales, your first cost, freight and custom being put together. Of these 60 or 100 quilts will be as many as one year will vent. Those which hereafter you shall send we desire may be with more white ground, and the flowers and branch to be in colours in the middle of the quilt as the painter pleases, whereas now most parts of your quilts come with sad red grounds which are not so well accepted here, and therefore let them be equally sorted to please all buyers.

Since the Indian craftsmen applied their colours with the aid of resists and mordants, reserving the pattern against the coloured ground, some pressure had to be exerted before they would condescend to change to the more difficult reverse technique of reserving their patterns in silhouette against a white ground. The London directors then realized that the only way to secure the production of goods wholly acceptable to the English market was to send patterns out to India. Accordingly, in 1662 they wrote to their factors at Surat: 'We now send you herewith enclosed several patterns of Chints for your directions and desire you to cause a considerable quantity to be made of these workes.' This experiment was obviously a success and in 1669 the directors decided to improve on it, telling their factors: 'Now of late, they are here in England come to a great practice of printing large branches for hangings of Rooms, and we believe that some of our Callicoes painted after that manner might vent well, and therefore have sent you some patterns, of which sort we would have you send us 2,000 pieces.' It might be assumed that the patterns thus dispatched for copying in India were of purely English origin, adorned with Tudor roses, red brick houses and heraldic animals, but as Mr John Irwin —who first unfolded this strange story—has pointed out, they were, in fact, English designs in the Chinese taste. His point is proved by the existence of an English crewel work embroidery (Pl. 11) of about 1680 and two Gujarat hangings of approximately the same date, all three of which are clearly based on a common English original in the 'China fashion'.

The significance of this startling discovery, in the wider context of the history of chinoiserie, is that the English conception of what eastern fabrics should, ideally, look like was sufficiently distinct by the 1640s to necessitate the instruction of eastern craftsmen in making textiles in the English 'China fashion'. This extraordinary episode was not to end here, however, for the Indian weavers, being by nature unable to copy exactly the English designs unwittingly created a new, doubly, if not trebly, cross-bred style. And finally yet another twist was to be given to the story when, to quote Mr Irwin, 'chinoiserie of this even more hybrid kind had become so far removed from genuine Chinese tradition that it was exported from India to China as a novelty to the Chinese themselves'. In the eighteenth century, therefore, Chinese weavers were producing fabrics adorned with the now famous 'tree of life' design, based on Indian patterns, derived from English originals which were an expression of the European vision of the Orient. There can have been few more bizarre incidents in the whole of taste.

5 ENGLAND: THE LAND OF TEA

By the second half of the seventeenth century a vogue for orientalia was well established in nearly every part of Europe. It would hardly be an exaggeration to say that no princely palace or Grand Ducal mansion was considered complete without its porcelain cabinet glittering with blue-and-white plates, bottles, and jugs. Best beds were everywhere being hung with chintz and covered with pintado quilts; ladies of fashion could not hold up their heads without a calico gown or, at least, an Indian shawl to wrap about their shoulders; and every gentleman's library boasted a prominent shelf groaning beneath the weight of lavish folios of oriental travels. There was certainly no lack of such books in 1662 when, as we have already seen, John Evelyn was constrained to declare that another volume on China would not be 'to the purpose'. But so completely was Europe captivated by Cathay, that these works enjoyed an ever-increasing popularity, sharpening rather than cloying the appetite they fed. Their authors disseminated an account of the Orient which was no less intriguing for being occasionally accurate; and their illustrators provided European craftsmen with a new source of oriental designs.

To these enthralling travel books, Europeans were also indebted for yet another benefit—the mysterious drink made from the 'herbe cha' which travellers had tasted in China and described in glowing terms. Indeed, it seems more than likely that without their enticing accounts of this strange and sooth-ing beverage, the Dutch East India Company might not have ventured to import tea into Europe. Samples had been brought to Holland in the early seventeenth century, it is true, but not until about 1650 was the tea trade developed commercially. Within a comparatively short time tea had become, for most European countries, a major import from the East: for England it was almost a necessity of life.

Tea seems to have first reached England in the 1650s, by way of Holland, and in 1658 Thomas Rugge noted in his *Mercurius Politicus* that the 'excellent and by all Physicians, approved, China drink, called by the Chineans Tcha, by other nations Tay alias Tee, is sold at the Sultaness Head Coffee-House, in Sweetings Rents, by the Royal Exchange London.' Next year, the same writer states that 'Coffee, chocolate, and a kind of drink called *tee* [were] sold in almost every street' in London. But it must still have been something of a novelty, for on September 25, 1660, Samuel Pepys recorded 'I did send for a cup of tee (a China drink) of which I had never drunk before.' The beverage proved popular and the English East India Company began, very cautiously, to enter the tea trade importing 23 lb. in 1666 and 143½ lb. in 1668. These modest cargoes were soon found to be inadequate and before the end of the century no less than 20,000 lb. of tea was being shipped annually to England. Thereafter the figure soared steadily higher, and although tea was imported into all European countries, England continued to take the lion's share, making it her national drink. Sovereigns and their courtiers elegantly partook of it—when not taking council—poets celebrated its glories, and even that great philosopher and severe China-phobe, Dr Johnson, professed an inordinate partiality for the oriental beverage. Only so bold a buccaneer as Captain Stratton could remark that 'some are fond of tay and stuff fit only for a wench'.

Tea brought China into the very heart of the European, and more particularly, the English home, and naturally the impedimenta connected with tea drinking—kettles, pots, cups, and caddies—were strongly influenced by Chinese patterns. Genuine Chinese porcelain vessels were, of course, preferred, but before the end of the seventeenth century cups and teapots of an oriental flavour were being made in Staffordshire. Specially designed kettles and caddies do not, however, seem to have made their appearance in Europe until the eighteenth century, and they must therefore be considered later. In a far wider sense, the tea trade was to have a decisive influence on the subsequent history of chinoiserie, for it encouraged merchants to travel to China itself whence they were to return, in the nineteenth century, with exotic plants which are now familiar in every European garden and also, alas, those detailed and circumstantial accounts of the country which brought about the decline and eventual extinction of the legend of Cathay. Robert Fortune dispelled the mystery which hung about the drink itself by investigating the process of tea cultivation (about which the Chinese had prudently been secretive) and by collecting the seeds with which the first Indian tea farms were planted.

The importation of tea was the last major innovation to be made in the China trade. By the middle of the seventeenth century the picture of Cathay had been firmly stamped on the European imagination. Oriental wares, particularly textiles and porcelain, but also considerable quantities of lacquer, were flooding the markets of Paris, London, and Amsterdam. European craftsmen had, moreover, begun to imitate the arts of China, Japan, and India—between which no very nice distinctions were yet drawn—and from these a few of the more audacious began to develop a new decorative style. The court of Shun Ch'ih was providing a source of gossip and speculation no less titillating than that of Louis XIV or Charles II. In fact, the West was displaying unmistakable symptoms of a serious bout of China-mania.

CHAPTER III

Baroque Chinoiserie

I CHINOISERIE AT THE COURT OF LOUIS XIV

When Louis XIV decided to erect a pavilion for his favourite concubine, Mme de Montespan, he hit upon the novel idea of following a Chinese plan. This little pleasure house, called the *Trianon de porcelaine*, was designed by the court architect Louis Le Vau and built in the park at Versailles during the winter of 1670 to 1671. So quickly was it raised that it seemed almost to have sprung out of the earth with the spring flowers among which it must have appeared an enchantment. The first of many exquisite but ephemeral buildings which were to adorn the parks of Europe, the Trianon fathered a numerous progeny of Chinese pagodas, latticed tea-houses, kiosks and 'Confucian' temples, in every corner of Europe from Drottningholm to Palermo and Sintra to Tsarskoe-Selo.

A curious allegorical romance published in 1698, *Contes moins contes que les autres: Sans Paragon et la reine des fées*, presents a whimsical account of the Trianon's conception and sheds some light on the way in which China in general and this building in particular were regarded at the French court. The story concerns Sans Paragon (Louis XIV) and Belle Gloire (Mme de Montespan), a princess of China who was 'sans contredit la plus belle et en même temps la plus fière princesse de la terre'. Whilst accompanying Belle Gloire for a sail on the canal in his park, Sans Paragon asked her opinion on his stately demesne. Coldly, the princess replied that riches were so common in the Chinese Empire that her father, the emperor, had always preferred simple, clean houses to superb palaces. Having reached the end of the canal, Sans Paragon, ever anxious to please the princess, jumped ashore and struck the earth three times with his wand. There immediately appeared a porcelain castle surrounded by a parterre fragrant with jasmines and sparkling with little fountains. 'Le tout ensemble', declared the anonymous author, 'faisoit le plus agréable effet qu'il fût possible de voir.'

Although said to have been inspired by the tall porcelain pagoda at Nanking, the *Trianon de porcelaine* was but one storey high and coated with faience, not porcelain, tiles made at the potteries of Delft, Nevers, Rouen, and Lisieux. This porous material was unable to withstand the winter frosts and the cost of repairs proved prohibitive. Partly for this reason and partly, one may guess, because Mme de Montespan, for whom the building was erected, had been succeeded in the king's favours by Mme de Maintenon, the Trianon was demolished in 1687, only seventeen years after it had been conjured up. We may, however, obtain some impression of its appearance from contemporary descriptions and engravings.

According to Félibien's description of Versailles, the Trianon was 'un petit palais d'une construction extraordinaire'. It consisted of one large and four smaller single-storey buildings ranged round a court and all decorated with faience which caught the eye of every visitor. 'Considérons un peu ce château de plaisance', wrote the poet Denis,

> Voyez-vous comme il est tout couvert de faïence
> D'urnes de porcelaine et de vases divers
> Qui le font éclater aux yeux de l'univers.

Plaques of porcelain tiles decorated the cornice and the corners of the main building. On the entablature there were balustrades, loaded with vases, and the roof was decorated with painted tiles representing scenes of putti chasing animals, vases of flowers and various birds—all 'représentés au naturel'. Indoors, all was blue and white, a colour scheme then thought deliciously Chinese. Most of the walls were coated in highly polished white plaster on which ornaments were picked out in blue, and in the central salon the cornices and ceiling were similarly treated, 'le tout travaillé à la manière des ouvrages qui viennent de la Chine', to quote from Félibien again. The *chambre des amours* was wholly furnished *à la chinoise*, the chairs being covered with blue-and-white or gold-and-silver cloths. In the bedroom, incongruously called *la chambre de Diane*, the bed itself was adorned with putti in the European style, but the hangings were of white taffeta striped with blue, gridelin, gold, and silver, while tables and *guéridons* were painted blue and white 'façon de porcelaine'. Inventories reveal that a final touch of exoticism was given by Chinese flowered embroideries which presumably added gaiety and warmth to the otherwise somewhat chilly *décor*.

Contemporary descriptions of the *Trianon de porcelaine* might easily lead the modern reader to suppose that it was a bizarre trifle, a rococo building born before its time and anticipating such glittering extravaganzas as the porcelain rooms at Capodimonte and Aranjuez. Engravings reveal that it was nothing of the kind. They record a group of five single-storey buildings in an uncompromisingly late seventeenth-century classical style, with pilasters between their windows and high mansard roofs. Even the bright colours of the roof, the effect of which is lost in the engravings, must have been more strongly reminiscent of Portuguese *azulejos* than of any oriental building. Indeed, few would suppose that the Trianon was intended to have a chinoiserie appearance. Yet Félibien remarks that the building was suggested by 'l'engouement pour la Chine' which raged at the French court at this period. And it has even been suggested that the pavilions were disposed in imitation of the central courtyard of the Imperial Palace at Peking.

The *Trianon de porcelaine* illustrates the attitude to Chinese art which prevailed at the French court in the later years of the seventeenth century. Père Louis Le Comte doubtless spoke for many of his contemporaries when he wrote from Peking in the 1690s that 'the imperfect notion the Chinese have of all kinds of arts, is betrayed by the unpardonable faults they are guilty of'. Although he found Chinese buildings gaudily decorated with lacquer, marble, porcelain, and gold, he declared that the 'apartments are ill contrived, the ornaments irregular, there wants that uniformity in which consists the beauty and convenience of our palaces. In a word, there is, as it were, deformity in the whole, which renders [Chinese architecture] very unpleasing to foreigners, and must needs offend anyone that has the least notion of true architecture'. No such deformity was allowed to afflict the *Trianon de porcelaine* which was as magnificent and exotic as faience tiles, a blue-and-white colour scheme and embroidered hangings could make it.

Seventeenth-century inventories and descriptions of the French royal palaces abound in references to furniture and textiles *à la chinoise* and *façon de la Chine*. Cabinets, tables, screens, chairs, *guéridons*, hangings, and upholstery are thus described in the many volumes of the *Inventaire Général*. Unfortunately, not a single example of these chinoiseries is known to survive. To account for their disappearance is a little difficult, for it can hardly be supposed that all the *façon de la Chine* furniture and textiles in all the royal palaces was destroyed by accident, burnt during the Revolution, or sacrificed to subsequent changes in taste. An explanation is suggested by the *Trianon de porcelaine*, for if, as seems probable, these objects were decorated in the very restrained style of that build-ing they would now pass unrecognized as chinoiseries. The cabinets *façon de la Chine*, for example, which abounded at Versailles, may well have been of plain black varnish emulating the lustre of oriental lacquer but not its bizarre decora-tion. Similarly, the damasks *à la chinoise* may well have been embellished with flowers only slightly more exotic than those to be found in Europe.

There can be no doubt, however, that the king and his courtiers were impassioned collectors of Chinese and other eastern objects—embroidered silk hangings, lacquer cabinets, gold filigree (particularly loved by the king and his mother) and blue-and-white porcelain vases. Indeed, the inventories and litera-ture of the period reveal that in the early 1670s the court was in the grip of a severe fit of China-mania. To account for this vogue several reasons may be advanced. First of all there was the perennial desire for magnificence and exoticism which oriental objects satisfied. For even though the porcelain vases at Versailles were set in heavy silver or ormolu mounts and the lacquer cabinets on gilt classical stands which emphasized their opulence (one was even adorned with silver reliefs of the Labours of Hercules), they still appeared extremely bizarre. They also provided a little light relief to the otherwise too solemn *décor* and introduced a whiff of pleasant fantasy into rooms heavy with the incense burnt to the god-king Apollo-Louis. And, in addition, they had an associative value readily appreciated by a court which revelled in allegory and thrived on symbolism. For however strange and unclassical, Chinese art was recognized as being the product of a mighty empire. And at Versailles where every painting and nearly every decorative device celebrated some aspect of Louis XIV's *gloire*, the oriental objects included in this gigantic and carefully contrived stage set may well have been intended to hint at the monarch's universal sway. When he lay upon his bed beneath an Indian quilt, or sipped his *bouillon* from an exquisitely mounted celadon bowl, picked nectarines from a Chinese porcelain plate, or took physic from the blue-and-white jars in the royal pharmacy, or when he donned an oriental costume for an evening's masquerade, *le Roi Soleil* may well have considered the Son of Heaven as an alternative role to that of Apollo or Alexander.

Yet oriental objects did not appeal to the French court solely on account of their associations. There was also an economic reason for their popularity with Louis XIV and his ministers. For though exorbitantly expensive to the private collector, the choicest examples of Eastern lacquer could be obtained relatively cheaply by the king through the *Compagnie des Indes*. It is probably no coincidence that as the massy silver furniture at Versailles went into the melting pot to pay for the wars of the League of Augsburg, the supply of lacquer furniture was increased. The crown could, moreover, command the most brilliant craftsmen in all Europe—those of the Gobelins factory—to create furniture which had the same glossy richness, the same opulence and, to contemporaries, the same associative value as that imported from the East. Hence the vast quantities of oriental and *façon de la Chine* furnishings and other objects which were to be found at Versailles and other French palaces by the end of the seventeenth century.

From the court, the vogue for chinoiserie spread to the city and the provinces. As early as 1673, only two years after the *Trianon de porcelaine* was finished, the *Mercure galant* reported that the king's example had been followed by his courtiers and even the bourgeoisie were everywhere converting garden shacks into pleasure houses. Within a few decades the fashion had spread to Germany and other parts of Europe. But, alas, none of these seventeenth-century trianons has survived, nor have any prints, drawings or detailed descriptions of them. Their role in the history of chinoiserie therefore remains obscure.

The Trianon seems also to have encouraged the popularity of blue-and-white Nevers and Rouen faience, while the *façon de la Chine* furniture displayed in royal palaces inspired commoners to indulge a similar taste. Oriental furniture and porcelain, brought to France in ever-increasing quantities, became annually more popular and the influx of Indian textiles caused a revolution in dress design, driving out the heavy gold brocaded stuffs in favour of light printed fabrics from the East. It was partly to combat this oriental competition and to protect their own trades that French craftsmen began to produce more objects in the chinoiserie style. By 1683, indeed, *toiles des Indes* had been imported in such vast quantities that Louvois deemed the French textile industry to be in need of tariff protection. In the following year, however, the oriental cult was given further stimulus by the arrival in Paris of ambassadors from Siam.

This embassy was not, as contemporaries probably believed, a spontaneous gesture on the part of the King of Siam. It was organized by a Greek named Constant Phaulkon who had seized political control in Bangkok and hoped to shore up his unstable position with the help of the French. The ambassadors reached Paris in 1684 bringing with them an attractive supply of gifts; they were presented to the king, entertained by the royal family and taken to see the opening of the *Parlement*. When they returned home a French envoy and his train, bearing a pompous letter from his Most Christian Majesty to the King of Siam, went with them. In 1686 a second Siamese embassy arrived in Paris; a far grander affair which met with an even more magnificent reception. The ambassadors drove triumphantly through the city seated in royal coaches and were formally received at Versailles where they made their kow-tow in the newly decorated *Galerie des Glaces*. They had brought with them an opulent array of presents carefully selected to demonstrate the advantages of trade with Siam: exquisite cups and ewers of Japanese gold and lacquer, an abundance of glittering K'ang Hsi porcelain, and bales of richly coloured Chinese embroideries, which attracted the envy and admiration of every oriental fancier. This embassy so caught the popular imagination that almanacs for the following year were decorated with a print of the ambassadors' reception at Versailles, and highly imaginative engravings of the King and Queen of Siam—seated on elephants with a distant prospect of Chinese pagodas—were widely circulated. Even in the provinces, the embassy was celebrated with fêtes and masquerades. At Autun, for instance, a mimic King of Siam presided over the festival of the Arquebussiers, selected candidates for his seraglio—with what Gallic winks and nods one may only too well imagine—sampled the new burgundy at every *loge* and tipsily drove round the town as cries of 'Vive le roi de Siam!' rang out from the windows of the Jesuit college.

For various reasons the Siamese embassies brought disaster to Phaulkon and led to a massacre of Europeans at Bangkok. But the news of this unhappy outcome did nothing to quench the enthusiasm for the East which the Siamese had stimulated in France. The Jesuits, those jealous guardians of the chinoiserie cult, lost no time in pointing out that Siam was a very insignificant kingdom, far from China, and that the beautiful objects which the ambassadors had brought were not of Siamese but of Chinese origin. As a counter-attraction to the Siamese embassy, Père Couplet produced the choicest rarity in his collection of orientalia, a very docile Chinese boy named Mikelh Xin from Nanking. He was said to speak passable Latin, though no French, and was, of course, a convert to Christianity. Picturesquely dressed in a green silk tunic and dragon encrusted robe, the slit-eyed lad was presented to the king who examined him with interest, heard him say his prayers in Chinese and watched him eat with chopsticks. Little is otherwise known of Mikelh Xin save that he made a brief visit to England where he was painted, crucifix in hand, by Kneller (Kensington Palace). He was one of the first of many young Chinamen brought back to Europe by missionaries, and like his successors he was probably much petted by those savants who were undergoing instruction in Confucian philosophy from the Jesuits.

The sharp growth of imports from the East; the taste of the court; the Siamese embassies; the encouragement of the Jesuits; all these factors contributed to the growth of chinoiserie in France during the 1680s. What of its artistic manifestations? Although so surprisingly few examples can now be traced, these enable us to obtain a glimmering of the principles which underlay the style. Most numerous among the survivors are the blue-and-white pottery vessels made at Rouen, Nevers, and Marseilles. The ewers and vases produced at these factories were frequently decorated with motifs taken from Chinese porcelain but modified by a French accent. A fine example is a large Rouen plate decorated in the centre with an attractive Chinese garden scene, in light blue, dark blue and brownish-red, surrounded by a formal floral frame (Pl. 13). A similar scene, surrounded by classical grotesque masks, decorates a wall cistern of full-bodied baroque shape (Musée Céramique, Rouen). On these faience wares the Chinese figures have been given greater solidity than on any oriental prototype and are surrounded by *lambrequins* or borders of flowers tidied into such symmetrical orderliness that they have lost all trace of eastern exoticism.

Of the *façon de la Chine* textiles which were used for upholstery we know little though we may hazard a guess that they bore the same relationship to eastern fabrics as French faience bore to Nanking porcelain. A taste for exoticism was also answered by a series of tapestries—*Les Tentures des Indes*—woven at the Gobelins in about 1690 from designs by Jan Jans the younger. These hangings, however, are exotic only in subject-matter for they perfectly conform to European laws of perspective and composition. One depicts the Indian king enthroned beneath a parasol of Chinese make, surrounded by half-naked attendants and a profuse assembly of strange fauna; another shows Indians in scanty feather loin-cloths pursuing various objects of oriental venery (zebras and the like). Somewhat later the Beauvais factory produced a tapestry of a specifically Chinese subject—a luxuriant landscape with a dumpy pagoda in the distance and an exotic bird flying overhead. This panel, which seems to have been very popular, for it was often repeated, has none of the freedom of rococo chinoiserie tapestries; nor, of course, has it any connexion whatever with fabrics imported from the East. A strain of more elegant and whimsical fantasy is revealed by a large embroidered panel, in the Musée des Arts Décoratifs, Paris, which is usually assigned to the late seventeenth century. Somewhat in the manner of the Soho tapestries, which will be described later, it presents a number of independent scenes with little Chinese figures dancing, boating, shuffling across spindly bridges, squatting round tea tables or driving out in fantastic chariots. Similar figures and weird predatory birds appear on a needlepoint panel in the collection of Judge Untermeyer (Pl. 15). Here are the *dramatis personae* of the rococo chinoiserie scene but they still move with the grave solemnity of Louis XIV's courtiers treading a stately *chaconne* by Lully.

Lacquer enjoyed great popularity in late seventeenth-century France both for furniture and the panelling of rooms, though little has been preserved. One of the few survivors is the desk from which Mme de Sévigné wrote so many letters to her daughter, decorated with her coat-of-arms and festoons of flowers (Pl. 16). Although it was probably made in China this desk is painted in an unusual style clearly intended to satisfy the French taste for restrained exoticism. Much of the lacquer furniture produced in the 1670s and 1680s may have been still simpler, but towards the end of the century several Parisian *ébénistes* were making furniture which was decorated with chinoiseries. According to the *Livre commode* for 1692, 'Les sieurs Langlois imitaient fort bien les meubles de la Chine . . . Le sieur des Essarts . . . imitait le Lachinage en creux et en relief. Le sieur Langlois le jeune excellait pour les figures et ornements de la Chine.' The furniture produced by these craftsmen was probably similar to that made by their contemporaries in other parts of Europe. Perhaps some survivors may be lurking in English, German or Italian collections where their French origin is unrecognized. Small objects were occasionally inlaid with chinoiserie decorations and of these a few happily survive, notably a casket in the Wallace Collection, adorned with somewhat staid Chinese hunting and pastoral scenes worked out in laminae of tortoise-shell, mother-of-pearl, and stained horn.

The style of the chinoiserie decorations popular at the close of the seventeenth century is best seen in the engraved work of Jean Bérain I who occasionally made use of oriental motifs in his arabesques. Bérain's designs are in the lighter style which came into vogue shortly before 1700 and is sometimes regarded as the first phase of the rococo. It is significant that they remained popular throughout the first quarter of the new century and continued to be

used for the decoration of faience at Moustiers
and other provincial factories as late as the
1740s. But Bérain's sense of fantasy was always
rather restrained, and although the monkeys
who perch on his baroque scrolls, aiming at
each other with pea-shooters, might seem to
anticipate the singeries of Watteau and Huet,
their gravity brands them unmistakably as
denizens of the *Grand Siècle*. Indeed, his
monkeys, mandarins, pagods and Chinese
parasols are so discreet that they may easily be
mistaken for the fauns, senators, statues, and
fans which appear in classical and renaissance
grotesque decorations (Fig. 2). Bérain's contribution to chinoiserie was not, however,
confined to the realm of engraved decoration.
As an artist in the *Menus Plaisirs*, the adminis-
trative department concerned with the king's
personal expenses, he designed oriental masquerade costumes (Pl. 18) and organized some
of the chinoiserie *collations* and balls which
were among the most colourful entertainments
given at court.

Descriptions of these court masquerades
and other entertainments help to shed a little
additional light on the attitude to chinoiserie
which prevailed in late seventeenth-century
France. Chinese dominoes were first noticed
at the Mardi Gras ball of 1655 when Loret
remarked in his *Muse historique* on the diversity
of masks 'qui ridicules, qui fantastiques. . . .
Les uns ressemblaient à des chinois'. But soon
the Chinaman with his pendulous moustaches
and his pointed hat became as essential a part
of the masquerade as Pierrot or Harlequin.
Nevertheless, a slight stir was caused when the

Fig. 2 Engraving after Jean Bérain,
c. 1695

king himself appeared at a ball dressed in what the *Mercure galant* correspondent described as 'un habit, moitié à la persienne, moitié à la chinoise'. And his brother, who was never one for half-measures, astonished the whole assembly by the variety of costumes he wore at the carnival ball in 1685. First, he appeared masked as a bat, then fluttered away to return dressed as a Flemish woman; having cast aside his wide-brimmed hat and voluminous skirt he made his last entry somewhat surprisingly clad as a workman—but this costume was the most ingenious of all for by pulling a string he shed his rustic clothes to emerge 'vêtu en Grand Seigneur chinois'; and in this guise he danced and postured for the rest of the night. One wonders if he retained his ample periwig throughout this charming succession of metamorphoses.

Despite the court vogue for Chinese masques, chinoiserie does not seem to have made its *début* in the Parisian theatre until 1692 when the Italian come-dians performed Regnard and Dufresny's *Les Chinois*. The title is rather mis-leading, however, for no Chinamen appear until the second act when Arlequin steps out of a Chinese cabinet 'habillé en docteur chinois'. Later the cabinet itself opens to reveal as strange a combination of European and Chinese figures as were to be found on any faience dish; a pagod surrounded by allegories of rhetoric, logic, music, and astronomy, and a group of oriental violinists. The pagod commands the actors' attention.[1] 'Mais que signifie cette figure là-bas?' asks Roquillard.

> *Arlequin:* C'est une Pagode.
> *Roquillard:* Une Pagode? Qu'est-ce que c'est qu'une Pagode?
> *Arlequin:* Une Pagode, est . . . une Pagode. Que diable voulez-vous que je dise?

But the *Pagode* is, of course, Mezzetin who bursts into song beginning:

> Je viens exprès du Congo, ho, ho, ho.

To the general public, China was still a very vague, very remote and very fantastic country.

Some chinoiserie entertainments arranged to beguile the court for an evening were more sophisticated, the most notable being a ball given by the king on January 7th, 1700, at Marly and followed a week later by Monsieur's *collation*

[1] In French the word *pagode* may refer to a pagoda tower or to an oriental idol, called in English a pagod. Sometimes the distinction is far from clear, but a figure dressed *en pagode* is more likely to have looked like a squatting, pot-bellied oriental god than a tall tower hung round with bells.

à la chinoise at Versailles. The ball opened with a divertisement, *Le Roi de la Chine*, in which thirty musicians, all dressed in Chinese costumes, carried in the king of China on a palanquin. The dancer, Des Moulins, dressed as a pagod then executed a *pas seul* which was said to be most droll. Monsieur's *collation*, organized by Jean Bérain, was a very elaborate affair. The room in which it was given appeared to be filled with pagods; three statues stood on the buffet, three musicians and two singers *en pagode* played and sang, while no less than a dozen of the Prince's officers were similarly attired and stood by each table. At the entry of the young Duchesse de Bourgogne, in whose honour the party was given, all twenty pagods, animate and inanimate, nodded their heads in unison to greet her. The napkins and the table-cloths were of oriental stuffs, the plates were of porcelain; indeed this collation seems to have been the chinoiserie banquet *par excellence*. Some idea of how these entertainments appeared may be obtained from a satirical print of a Chinese feast given by the Margravine Sibylla Augusta of Baden-Baden in 1729 (see page 115). And it is to Germany, ironically enough, that we must turn for a reflection of other vanished splendours of Louis XIV chinoiserie.

2   THE EXAMPLE OF VERSAILLES

. . . Germany not only imitates France but always does double what is
done here.   DUCHESSE D'ORLÉANS, from Paris, 1721

In Germany the period between 1648 and 1700 was one of painfully slow recuperation from the ravages of the Thirty Years' War. Only in the last years of the century did the arts show signs of a revival. Numerous petty princes then began to turn their thoughts once more to the improvement and aggrandisement of their ancestral seats, and for inspiration they naturally looked to Versailles, that seventeenth-century cynosure of the polite arts and courtly manners. Dazzled by the brilliance of the Sun King's court, they promptly assumed the airs of a *grand monarque* and set about the equipment of their *Schloss* with all the essential ingredients—a monumental staircase, a *galerie des glaces* and an impressive series of state apartments some of which were modishly panelled in lacquer whilst others were decked out with lacquer furniture and oriental porcelain. Their gardens might not be as extensive as those designed by Le Nôtre, but they too had their canals, labyrinths, parterres, fountains, statues, and *trianons*. Thus chinoiserie came to Germany as part of the Louis XIV style and nearly all its manifestations dating from the first quarter of the eighteenth century bear a French impress.

Though the lacquered splendours of Versailles perished long ago, many a German *Schloss* or *Residenz* still preserves its eighteenth-century *chinesisches Zimmer*. One of the earliest is the Chinese room created for the Elector Franz von Schönborn in the Neue Residenz at Bamberg in 1705; here the Chinese taste is limited to a series of lacquer panels framed by carved swags of fruit beneath a louring baroque ceiling, heavily painted and stuccoed. A more debonair and accomplished specimen of this type of decoration is the *Lack-kabinett* fitted up between 1714 and 1722 in Schloss Ludwigsburg for Duke Eberhard of Württemberg's notorious mistress, the Grävenitz. Amid a profusion of late baroque, almost rococo, gilt scrolls forming brackets to hold porcelain trifles, are a series of large lacquer panels painted by Johann Jakob Saenger and depicting lanky, long-tailed birds, dragon-flies, and dragons sporting in an exotic garden where classical urns stand beneath gnarled trees (Pl. 22). These charming and exquisitely painted panels are of a type one can easily imagine to have lined the *petits appartements* at Versailles in the opening years of the eighteenth century.

Another German ruler who succumbed to the French cult for chinoiserie was the Elector Max Emanuel of Bavaria who had whiled away some tedious years of exile at Versailles. Shortly after his return to Munich he commissioned his court architect, Joseph Effner, to raise a little *Pagodenburg* in the grounds of his summer palace at Nymphenburg. As its name suggests, this strange little building was intended to resemble a Chinese pagoda, but it is no more bizarre than the *Trianon de porcelaine* had been. The exterior is almost ostentatiously classical, adorned with a giant order of Corinthian pilasters, and inside the hall and staircase are decorated with blue-and-white Delft tiles and paintings of European subjects. On the upper floor, however, there are two chinoiserie rooms, a little cabinet hung with Chinese wallpaper and an octagonal drawing-room lined with red-and-black japanned panels. The japanning, which is of high quality, is probably the work of a local Bavarian craftsman but harmonizes excellently with some handsome stools and tables made for the Elector in Paris.

In the first decade of the eighteenth century, the vogue for lacquer rooms also appeared at the other end of Europe, in Portugal; though whether this was the result of French influence is a little doubtful. In Portugal, as in Germany and France, lacquer seems to have been considered an expression of princely magnificence scarcely less essential than gilding and rare marbles. Portuguese painters developed a fine technique for lacquer which they applied not only to furniture and the panelling of rooms but to such unlikely objects as shrines and organ cases. Outstanding among them was Manuel de Silva who painted the library of the University of Coimbra in 1723. This library is, indeed, one of the most spectacular examples of lacquer decoration in all Europe—a series of three baroque rooms richly adorned with painted and carved trophies, garlands of flowers, armorial devices, putti, and spirited trumpeting angels which surround the vast green-and-red bookcases and balustraded galleries on which chinoiserie designs are delicately picked out in gold. Here motifs drawn from East and West have been happily combined to give an air of sumptuous richness which has seldom been equalled, though it must be admitted that the chinoiseries are so discreet as to escape the eye at first sight.

The taste for lacquer furniture was widespread in late seventeenth- and early eighteenth-century Europe. Unlike the French-inspired decorations, however, the furniture was usually of Dutch extraction. Throughout the latter part of the seventeenth century, Holland was vigorously exploiting the Far Eastern trade and had contrived to obtain a virtual monopoly of the lacquer imported into Europe direct from Japan—lacquer of far higher quality, incidentally, than that which came from China. Nevertheless, imports were insufficient to meet the demand and Dutch japanners—*japanisch Verlaker*—found a ready market for imitations, which they had begun to produce early in the century (Pl. 6). The Dutch japan made in the late seventeenth and early part of the eighteenth century was much closer to the original substance, both in texture and design, than that produced in any other European country and orientalists have sometimes been hard put to distinguish it from Japanese 'export' lacquer. It has even been suggested that Japanese lacquer workers may have been imported into Holland to school the native craftsmen. Dutch work of this period is of a refulgent glossiness richly decorated with chinoiserie scenes, trees, vases of flowers and birds, against a black ground. Cabinets appear to have been the most popular pieces of furniture to be decorated with this imitation lacquer; they were usually made both taller and shallower than those imported from the East. The delicacy with which the decorations were painted may be judged from a miniature example—an exquisite little cupboard for a doll's house, in the Rijksmuseum (Pl. 19).

One of the principal centres for the production of lacquer in the Low

Countries was the watering-place named Spa, near Aix-la-Chapelle, for centuries the Mecca of European hypochondriacs. A lacquer industry grew up here in the late seventeenth century and flourished throughout the eighteenth. All manner of objects from tiny snuff-boxes to vast armoires were produced for those who came to drink the famous medicinal waters and frequent the scarcely less celebrated gaming rooms. By means of this international clientele the lacquer produced at Spa—known as *bois de Spa*—was diffused throughout the length and breadth of Europe.

In the history of European lacquer, Spa has an additional importance as the birthplace of one of the most notable artists who worked in this medium— Gerard Dagly. Born some time before 1665, Dagly was trained from his youth as a japanner. At a fairly early age he went to seek his fortune in Germany where he attracted the attention of the Kurfürst of Brandenburg who appointed him official *Kammerkünstler* in 1687. His appointment was confirmed by Friedrich (the first king of Prussia) who succeeded in the following year. For this patron Dagly was principally employed in producing lacquer decorated with oriental motifs and he also appears to have painted stands for genuine eastern cabinets. In 1696, for example, he japanned four large black-and-gold coin cases—square Chinese-style cabinets mounted on stands with twist-turned legs. At about the same time he provided a suitable dado for a room in the Royal Palace which was panelled with large Coromandel screens (destroyed in the Second World War). For his designs he derived inspiration from the examples of Japanese lacquer in the royal collection. But he seems never to have been content to copy these originals, giving to the buildings an air of flimsier fantasy, endowing the figures, birds, and beasts with a quainter grotesqueness and partially 'correcting' the oriental perspective. Sometimes he further departed from eastern precedent by painting his designs in bright colours on a white ground (Pl. 21). His works enjoyed great popularity at the court of Friedrich and won him such renown that when the Kurfürstin of Hanover sent an English clock case to her Prussian son-in-law she felt bound to remark that 'Dagly makes much better ones.' The recipient of this gift was Friedrich-Wilhelm I who was evidently less impressed by Dagly's talents, for he included the *Kammerkünstler* in the clean sweep of unnecessary court officials which followed his succession to the throne in 1713.

Whilst in Berlin, Dagly attracted a number of pupils and imitators, the most notable of whom was Martin Schnell. A Saxon by birth, Schnell worked under

Dagly from 1703 to 1709 and then returned to his native city of Dresden where he produced lacquer furniture and bibelots of outstandingly high quality during the next three decades. He is best known for his japanned trays—probably the finest of their kind made in Europe—which are decorated with graceful clumps of flowers and engaging Chinese *genre* scenes (Pl. 20). Among his works on a grander scale one of the most notable is a handsome red fall-front bureau crowned by a stand for a porcelain vase, designed for the Japanese Palace at Dresden between 1720 and 1730. Schnell's chinoiserie decorations are more elegantly fantastic than those of his master Dagly and although they occasionally include individual motifs—a flowering tree, for example, or a hen and her chicks—copied directly from Japanese lacquer, they are in spirit still further removed from oriental originals. Indeed, his early works, produced in the 1720s, already tremble on the verge of the rococo chinoiserie style which he was to embrace whole-heartedly before the end of his career (Pl. 69). It is hardly surprising to find that he provided designs for the Meissen porcelain factory.

In the latter years of the seventeenth century the German potteries such as those at Hanau and Frankfurt-am-Main, were still under the influence of Delft. As we have pointed out, the Delft potteries had, in the early 1660s begun to evolve a true chinoiserie style. During the subsequent four decades they consolidated this new ground, giving to their blue and manganese ornaments an ever-increasing air of exotic fantasy. One of the most delightful and absurd products of this period is a bulbous wig-stand in the Victoria and Albert Museum, made at Samuel van Eenhorn's factory in about 1675 (Pl. I). The spherical head of this strange object is painted with a group of Chinamen picnicking beside a rock—or is it some weird Cathaian cactus?—which bursts into thorny blossom. One may well imagine how bizarre these oriental figures must have looked peeping through the face of a mynheer's elaborately curled perruque. The Delft potteries also began the production of *theepots* in the 1670s; fairly close imitations of Yi Hsing red stoneware teapots decorated with dragons or sprigs of prunus in relief.

The taste for porcelain gave rise to the creation of special rooms in which serried ranks of oriental vases and plates, reinforced by European pottery vessels, might be marshalled. A few such rooms survive in Germany (or survived until the Second World War), one of the earliest and most notable being that in the Charlottenburg Palace outside Berlin. Designed by Eosander von Göthe in about 1710, this *Porzellankammer* was arranged to show off a large collection, posed on a multitude of little brackets covering the entire wall space from floor to ceiling. The oriental effect suggested by the chinoiserie motifs painted on the dado, and just visible between the tall vases, was somewhat dimmed by the Roman gods and goddesses sporting on the stuccoed and painted ceiling. Such porcelain rooms probably had their origin in France, but they were also popular in Holland and England where a pattern was set for them by that prolific Huguenot artist, Daniel Marot.

A figure of European renown, Daniel Marot occupies an important position in the history of interior decoration. He was born and trained in France but in 1684 fled to Holland to seek refuge from the gathering storm of anti-protestant feeling. Almost immediately he was taken into the service of the Prince of Orange for whom he designed palaces and gardens and later worked in England, notably at Hampton Court. A designer of extraordinary versatility, he could apply his talents to any part of a princely residence, from the building itself and the trim parterres surrounding it, to the furniture, pottery ornaments, clocks, and even the key-hole guards. And he was equally prepared to work in the baroque or chinoiserie styles. Marot was not, however, an artist of very great originality and, like many later interior decorators, he formulated rather than invented a style. The lessons he had learned from Pierre Lepautre, André Charles Boulle, and Jean Bérain in the 1680s stood him in good stead for the rest of his career and he seems never to have made any stylistic advance. Indeed, the volume of engravings which he published in 1712, and on which his reputation principally rests, must have looked very *vieux jeu* in the Paris of the nascent rococo, even though it exerted a wide influence in Holland, England, and Germany. His classical decorations certainly derive from late seventeenth-century France and it seems possible that his essays in chinoiserie have a similar origin. In his great folio there is a design for a 'Chinese room', to be panelled in lacquer and fitted with little shelves for the display of porcelain, which would not have looked out of place in the Versailles of Louis XIV (Pl. 23).

3 RESTORATION CHINOISERIE

Whereas in France and Germany late seventeenth-century chinoiserie was an aspect of court art, in England, as in Holland, it enjoyed a far wider appeal

PLATE I Wig stand, made at Samuel van Eenhorn's factory, Delft c. 1675

and developed on different lines. Indeed, English chinoiserie seems to have been entirely uninfluenced by the court until the advent of William and Mary in 1688, by which time the style was already established as a popular phenomenon. James II, it is true, had shown a certain interest in the Jesuit translations of Confucius, but otherwise neither he nor his elder brother are known to have concerned themselves with the Orient. Mary, on the other hand, was an ardent devotee of the oriental cult, though her influence on its growth has perhaps been exaggerated. In a celebrated passage, Macaulay taxed the otherwise too blameless heroine of his *History* with the introduction of the Chinese fashion into her kingdom, declaring that she had 'acquired at the Hague a taste for the porcelain of China, and amused herself by forming at Hampton Court a vast collection of hideous images, and of vases on which houses, trees, bridges, and mandarins, were depicted in outrageous defiance of all the laws of perspective.' No doubt the estimable queen's passion for porcelain and Delft had some influence on the collecting activities of her courtiers, but she gave no more than a fillip to a vogue which had become general soon after the Restoration.

Some of the earliest indications of the Restoration taste for chinoiserie are to be found in the decoration of silver. The choice of this medium is, in itself, curious and calls for comment. Chinoiserie japan, pottery, and textiles produced in the first half of the century were all inspired by, if not directly imitative of, objects of similar materials imported from the Orient. But so far as is known, no silver or gold, apart from filigree, was brought to Europe from the East at this period. The notion of applying eastern-style decorations to silver tankards and bowls was therefore as novel as it was strange. Perhaps the patrons who demanded this type of work were influenced by the time-honoured practice of mounting porcelain vases in silver (Pl. 4).

The first known example of chinoiserie silver is a sconce made in London in 1665; a handsome piece of plate engraved on the support with figures of two orientals one of whom holds an inordinately long parasol over the other's head (Pl. 24). A tankard of 1670, in the Victoria and Albert Museum, by a different maker, is embellished with engraved decorations in a similar style. Although no other examples dating from the 1660s and few from the 1670s are known, there is no reason to suppose that these two objects, which have by chance survived, were either unique in their time or the earliest of their type. Nevertheless, the vogue for silver decorated in this manner seems to have become widespread only in about 1680, and the majority of surviving examples date from the subsequent decade. Among them are two complete toilet sets of 1683 (one consisting of six-teen pieces all of which are engraved with chinoiserie motifs) besides a large number of punch-bowls, montieths, porringers and caskets (Pl. 26). The peak of the fashion seems to have been reached in about 1688 when the Duke of Rutland ordered a pair of great bottle-shaped silver vases imitating Chinese porcelain in shape and decoration. Another pair of similar silver vases was made for him in 1696, but relatively few specimens of chinoiserie silver date from as late as the 1690s.

Save for the Rutland vases, all these objects conform in shape to the normal patterns of the period: the porringers are no more elaborate and the tankards no less robustly squat than their classically or armorially decorated contem-poraries. But the decorations, which are in much the same style on all known examples, are wholly frivolous. The first essentials seem to have been tall, wayward flowering trees and strange long-shanked birds. Oriental figures, sometimes more Indian than Chinese but usually of a Mongolian countenance, are often introduced—promenading, conversing with friends, battling on horseback, dancing to the music of weird instruments or standing wrapt in solitary contemplation. It is not known where these designs originated; the earliest silver pattern book to include the like was that published by de Moedler in London in 1694. The engravers, or those who provided the designs for them, may have looked at a few pieces of Nanking porcelain and Chinese lacquer cabinets, and they may also have glanced at the illustrations in Nieuhoff's *Embassy* and other travel books. They did not, in any event, copy eastern originals faithfully. Instead, they created an exotic decorative style which is wholly European in concept. An oriental might well wonder why these wispy figures are thought to possess any eastern qualities. In a markedly different style is a small snuff-box, given by Charles II to Nell Gwynne. This has chinoiserie decorations in relief, apparently in imitation of carved lacquer, but it seems to be unique (Pl. 25).

As we have already seen, the vogue for oriental and European lacquer was established in England during the early seventeenth century. Whether lacquer maintained its popularity under the Commonwealth is unknown, though improbable; but it was certainly in high favour soon after the Restoration. From the style of their heavy baroque bases, several English cabinets may be assigned to the 1660s and 1670s, but the earliest known dated piece of Restora-tion japan was made in 1679. This is a fairly simple table at Ham House, apparently made to stand beneath a mirror framed with strips of Chinese lacquer. Panels of lacquer (whether they are of European or oriental origin can seldom be ascertained from descriptions) were also used for interior decoration. In July 1682 John Evelyn recorded a visit to his 'good neighbour Mr Bohun, whose whole house is a cabinet of all elegancies, especially Indian; in the hall are contrivances of Japan screens instead of wainscot. . . . The landskips of these skreens represent the manner of living, and Country of the Chinese.' Evelyn, who shared his contemporaries' difficulty in distinguishing between the products of India, China, and Japan (and the three countries themselves, for that matter), clearly regarded this style of panelling as novel, but it was soon to become widespread. Before the end of the seventeenth century many an English house including Burghley, Chatsworth, and Hampton Court, boasted a lacquer panelled room.

Although it is difficult to believe that any 'English varnished cabinets might vie with the oriental', as William Whitewood claimed in 1683, there can be no doubt that English japanners had made great strides since their first tentative efforts at the beginning of the century. Oriental furniture was, of course, being imported in considerable quantity but it was not found to be wholly satisfactory. 'The joyners in this Country may not compare their Work with that which the Europeans make', remarked Captain William Dampier of the Japanese craftsmen whom he had seen in 1688; and, he continued, 'in laying on the Lack upon good or fine joyned work, they frequently spoil the joynts, edges or corners of Drawers of Cabinets: Besides, our fashions of Utensils differ mightily from theirs, and for this reason Captain Pool, in his second voyage to the Country, brought an ingenious Joyner with him to make fashionable Commodities to be lackered here, as also Deal boards.'

English japanners wanted the essential materials—the resin of the *rhus vernica*—with which to reproduce the consistency of oriental lacquer, but in time they succeeded in producing a glossy varnish, made from gum-lac, seed-lac or shell-lac, which is scarcely less lustrous and attractive. Their methods are minutely described in the *Treatise of Japanning and Varnishing* by John Stalker and George Parker, published in London in 1688. 'What can be more surprising than to have our chambers overlaid with varnish more glossy and reflecting than polisht marble?' these devotees of lacquer disarmingly inquire. 'No amorous nymph need entertain a dialogue with her Glass, nor Narcissus retire to a fountain to survey his charming countenance when the whole house is one entire speculum.' So carried away were they by the beauty and utility of lacquer that at the end of their preface they declared:

> Let not the Europeans any longer flatter themselves with the empty notions of having surpassed all the world besides in stately palaces, costly Temples, and sumptuous Fabricks; Ancient and modern Rome must now give place: the glory of one Country, Japan alone, has exceeded in beauty and magnificence all the pride of the Vatican at this time and the Pantheon heretofore. . . . Japan can please you with a more noble prospect, not only whole towns but Cities too are there adorned with as rich a covering; so bright and radiant are their Buildings that when the sun darts forth his lustre upon their golden roofs, they enjoy a double day by the reflection of his beams.

Their enthusiasm was, however, reserved for glossy painted lacquer with raised gilt decorations. For incised Coromandel lacquer they had nothing but contempt, possibly because they could not supply a recipe for imitating it satisfactorily. Coromandel, or Bantam ware as it was called (since it was imported from Bantam or the Coromandel coast), was 'almost obsolete and out of fashion', they sneered. 'No person is fond of it, or gives it house room except some who have new cabinets made out of old Skreens. And from that large old piece, by the help of a Joyner, made little ones . . . torn and hacked to joint a new fancie . . . the finest hodgpodg of Men and Trees turned topsie turvie.' Here, of course, they were mistaken, for although mirror-frames made of strips of Coromandel fitted inconsequentially together look displeasing and enjoyed but a brief vogue, Coromandel screens and cabinets held their popularity until well into the eighteenth century; and not without good reason, for they are among the most splendid pieces of furniture ever imported into Europe from the Orient. The Duke of Marlborough is said to have been so attached to a great Coromandel screen given him by the Holy Roman Emperor that he carried it with him to the wars. One may well imagine him gazing on its many little figures as his valet combed the bullets out of his wig after a heavy day at Malplaquet or Oudenard.

Apart from the provocative preface, Stalker and Parker's *Treatise* is concerned with practical matters and contains many engravings of designs suitable for application to japanned work. Some of these represent coveys of exotic birds, others are of landscapes (Pl. 12), and there are a few figured scenes, one of which shows a man pouring a jug of water on the head of another and is labelled 'A Pagod Worshipp in ye Indies' (Fig. 3). Like the engravings on contemporary silver, these designs cater for the vaguest of exotic tastes.

The authors claimed to have based them on imported specimens of lacquer but confessed that 'perhaps we have helped them a little in their proportions

Fig. 3   A design for japanned work; engraving from John Stalker and George Parker: *Treatise of Japanning and Varnishing*, 1688

where they were lame or defective, and made them more pleasant, yet altogether as Antick. Had we industriously contrived perspective, or shadowed them otherwise than they are; we should have wandered from our Design, which is only to imitate the true genuine *Indian* work.'

The art of japanning was by no means the prerogative of professional craftsmen, and there can be little doubt that Stalker and Parker's manual, though it provided designs for at least one notable decorator (Pl. 30), was intended primarily as a guide for amateurs. Indeed, japanning was numbered among the elegant accomplishments thought suitable for young ladies, and in 1689 Edmund Verney permitted his daughter to take this 'extra' at school, writing, 'I find you have a desire to learn Jappan, as you call it, and I approve it; and so I shall of any thing that is good and virtuous, therefore learn in God's name all Good Things, and I will willingly be at the charge so farr as I am able—though they come from Japan and from never so farr and looke of an Indian Hue and colour, for I admire all accomplishments that will render you considerable and Lovely in the sight of God and man. . . .' That the art of Japanning, like that of water-colour painting in a later age, rendered girls lovely in the sight of man is, perhaps, confirmed by Dryden's lines to Clarinda, written in 1687:

> Sometimes you curious *Landskipps* represent,
> And arch 'em o'er with gilded *Firmament*:
> Then in *Japan* some *rural Cottage* paint.

Nothing was sacred to these eager young japanners who seized on any object that could be embellished with Chinese figures. They may occasionally have worked on specially prepared furniture, small boxes, trays, and the like, but they seem often to have applied their varnishes to ordinary walnut pieces. The vogue for this pastime continued throughout the eighteenth and into the nineteenth century.

The professional japanned work produced in the fifty years between 1670 and 1720 was sometimes of very high quality. Every type of furniture was decorated in this way, and in 1697 the company of 'Patentees for Lacquering after the manner of Japan' (founded three years earlier) was able to offer 'cabinets, secretaires, tables, stands, looking-glasses, tea-tables, and chimney-pieces'. Other japanned articles made at the same time included chests of drawers, corner cupboards, day-beds, chairs, clock cases, barometer stands, and small objects for the dressing- or writing-table. Usually they were made of deal, oak, or pear-tree wood on patterns which were identical with contemporary walnut furniture. Large screens, similar to those imported from the East, do not seem to have enjoyed much popularity though they gave the japanners greater scope than smaller pieces of furniture. Cabinets were highly popular and have survived in considerable quantities. At first, they were closely modelled on Chinese examples and set on gilded or silvered carved wood stands heavy with putti, swags of fruit, or flowers and baroque scrolls. But in the course of time the design of both cabinet and stand underwent a profound and significant change. Towards the end of the century a lighter style of furnishing came into fashion and the heavy Restoration cabinet-stand gave way to a more elegant contrivance sometimes designed for the display of porcelain vases on the stretcher, while carved crests were occasionally added to the tops of the cabinets. Then, early in the eighteenth century, cabinet and stand were united to form a homogeneous piece of furniture which was japanned all over; cabriole legs replaced the sturdy angular supports and the rectangle of the cabinet was relieved by a gently domed top. By this time the oriental cabinet had been completely naturalized and converted into a piece of English furniture (Pl. 31).

From London the vogue for lacquer furniture spread to other parts of the country, and in 1705 one Sarah Dalrymple applied for a patent to carry on a japanning manufactory in Scotland. It seems probable, however, that japanned furniture reached Scotland before this date for an inventory of 1708 reveals that the laird of Thunderton had acquired several pieces with which to furnish his grim northern fastness. The brief list of objects in his 'strypt room' presents a strange picture of chinoiserie in the North. There were

> camlet hangings and curtains, feather bed and bolster, two pillows, five pair blankets and an English blanket, a green and white cover, a blew and white chamber pot, a blue and white bason, a black jopand table, and two looking glasses, a jopand tee table with a tee-pot and plate and nine cups and nine dyshes with a tee silver spoon, two glass sconces, two little bowls with a leam stoop and a pewter head, eight black ken chairs with eight silk cushens conform, an easy chair with a big cushen, a jopand cabinet on a walnut tree stand, a grate, suffle, tonges and brush.

One has only to people this bald description with the laird, his guns and dogs, his wife, his brats and perhaps an attendant gillie to conjure up a vision of a society which had fallen under the spell of chinoiserie and yet was as far removed from Hampton Court and Versailles as from Peking itself. The vogue for lacquer also attacked North America at the beginning of the eighteenth century and introduced a whiff of frivolous exoticism into the puritanically sober parlours of Boston. In about 1700 New England cabinet-makers were applying a somewhat coarse japan, vigorously decorated with chinoiserie motifs, to various articles of household furniture. A notable example is a chest of drawers on baluster legs probably made in Boston and now in the Metropolitan Museum, New York. Later in the century the fashion grew and many a highboy and low-boy was adorned with exotic flora and fauna of the type popular in England (Pl. 32).

The japan applied to English furniture at this period was in a wide variety of colours—black, tortoise-shell, vermilion, dark green (particularly popular for clock cases), yellow, and blue. English red japan was very popular abroad, in Spain and Portugal, as well as at home. In 1720 the Venetian Filippo Bonanni declared it to be of a hue more beautiful than coral—'si bello che vince il colore di corallo'. Against these lustrous or brilliant backgrounds designs were picked out in gold relief: wispy flowering trees, camels, giraffes and other strange beasts, dumpy buildings enclosed by fenced gardens, and distant views of craggy, cloud-capped mountain peaks. These little pictures were no doubt influenced by the paintings on oriental lacquer, but the designs were transposed into a European key. Who were the artists responsible for these glimpses of the flowery land? Though some were as talented as the average landscape and face painters of the day, their names have been forgotten and it is only by chance that we know of one, a Mr Lumley whom the Leeds virtuoso Ralph Thoresby visited in 1703 and deemed to be 'an excellent artist in many respects, paints excellently, japans incomparably'.

English chinoiserie pottery developed later than japan. The blue-and-white colour scheme, so intimately connected with China, had been employed at Southwark before it appeared at Delft, but not until the 1680s did unrestrained chinoiserie decorations begin to figure on jugs and plates made at Lambeth and Bristol. In 1671 John Dwight optimistically took out a patent (renewed in 1684) to make 'transparent earthenware commonly known by the name of porcelain or China' and, more realistically, 'stoneware vulgarly called Cologne ware'. Although he brought a series of legal actions in defence of these patents he never succeeded in producing porcelain. He was, however, able to decorate his pottery in emulation of oriental wares and he also made teapots which, like those produced at Delft, might easily be mistaken in a bad light for Yi Hsing pots. But the most attractive English pottery in the Chinese taste was made at Bristol during the 1670s and 1680s. A Bristol plate dated 1679 (Fitzwilliam Museum) is decorated in blue and white with a figure of a Chinaman squatting in a rockery. The oriental intention of this piece is clear though, as an historian of ceramics has pointed out, 'it could not remotely be mistaken for a Chinese original'. But some of the painters of the Bristol pottery became so orientalized that they gave an eastern cast even to European scenes. On a vase of 1685, for instance, the story of Lot is rendered in such a way that it might at first sight be mistaken for a mandarin's picnic.

Further indications of the late seventeenth-century vision of the Orient are provided by Chinese entertainments which were as popular in England as in

France; though it is significant that in England they took the form of stage plays rather than court masques. The Chinese first entered the English theatre in a ranting tragedy by Elkanah Settle, *The Conquest of China*, produced in London in 1675. Settle claimed that his 'Muse had History and Truth for her excuse' and the play recounts, or rather garbles, the story of the Ming dynasty's downfall. Certain elements derived from the accounts of the Manchu conquest, given by such writers as Martinius, Juan de Mendoza, and John Nieuhoff, were neatly tailored to fit an heroic tragedy. The names of the characters are exotic enough—Theinmingus, Zungteus, Quitazo, Amavanga—but they behave throughout with strict classical propriety; the Empire of China is frequently mentioned and there is a reference to the 'Pagode-Grove upon the Sacred Mount', but the scenes might otherwise be set in Rome as easily as Peking. In fact, there is very little that is Chinese about this gory and tedious drama. Settle was more successful when he approached China in a light-hearted spirit, in *The Fairy Queen* which was first produced in 1692.

The Fairy Queen is an operatic version of *A Midsummer-Night's Dream* with libretto by Shakespeare and Settle and music by Purcell. The original play was remorselessly cut and embroidered to bring it up to date, the most notable addition being a Chinese *divertissement*. 'While the stage is darkened a single Entry is danced', the book directs. 'Then a symphony is play'd; after the scene is suddenly illuminated, and discovers a transparent prospect of a Chinese Garden, the Architecture, the Trees, the Plants, the Fruit, the Birds, the Beasts, quite different from what we have in this part of the World. It is terminated by an Arch, through which is seen other Arches with close Arbors, and a row of trees to the end of the view. Over it is a hanging garden, which rises by several ascents to the top of the House; it is bounded on either side with pleasant Bowers, various Trees, and numbers of strange Birds flying in the air, on the top of the Platform is a Fountain, throwing up Water, which falls into a large basin.' In this enchanted setting, Chinese lovers sing duets to the stately harmonies of Purcell:

> Yes, Xanxi, in your looks I find,
> The charms by which my heart's betray'd. . . .

Six monkeys emerge from the wood to execute a dance and when they have finished 'Six pedestals of China-work rise from under the Stage; they support six large vases of Porcelain, in which are six China Orange Trees . . . the pedestals move towards the front of the stage, and the grand dance begins of twenty-four persons.' Hymen then appears on the scene to reconcile Oberon with Titania and then unite the Chinese lovers, a final quintet is sung and the opera brought to its close.

The *décor* must have contributed much to the charm of this elaborate spectacle, and one would like to know who designed it. The most likely candidate is Robert Robinson who seems to have specialized in exotic scenes, luxuriant with plants, birds, and beasts 'quite different from what we have in this part of the World', and who is known to have worked for the theatre. His only documented work is a series of exotic landscapes with figures, partly Chinese, partly Peruvian, which he painted in 1696 for a house in Botolph Lane.

A similar series, now in the Victoria and Albert Museum, has been attributed to him on stylistic grounds (Pl. 27). They are painted in green monochrome with gaily coloured figures: two panels depict feathered savages supporting heraldic achievements, but the other nine are of chinoiserie subjects with idols and potentates carried in palanquins or seated in chariots drawn by wild boars. An emphasis on the exotic splendour of the Orient marks these paintings as products of the baroque era but in other respects they anticipate the chinoiseries of the eighteenth century. They are the earliest known chinoiserie wall paintings, as distinct from lacquer panels. And although they cannot be regarded as masterpieces, even of chinoiserie, they must be accorded a position of some importance in the history of taste.

If, as has been suggested, Robinson was also responsible for the cartoons of the Chinese tapestries woven at the Soho factory in about 1700, he was an artist of greater ability than his surviving paintings suggest. One set, presumably the first, was woven for Elihu Yale the rich nabob and East India Company official who had been governor of the settlement at Fort St George (Madras) and returned to England in 1699. Yale is known to have brought back a collection of Mogul miniatures, and it seems highly probable that these provided the preliminary ideas for some of the figures on the tapestries. Each hanging has a dark-blue background on which there are a number of brightly coloured scenes of orientals riding, entertaining each other, enjoying picnics or making music amongst the giant trees of eastern gardens (Pl. 28). Yale's own set of tapestries, now in the possession of the university to which he gave his name, are bordered with swags of European flowers, but others have chinoiserie frames littered with teapots, cups, and vases (Pl. 29). To judge from the number of surviving examples, these Soho chinoiserie tapestries enjoyed some popularity, though they must always have been expensive. Other chinoiserie textiles and paper hangings were, however, available for less affluent devotees of the oriental cult.

In 1697 it was said that 'from the greatest gallants to the meanest cook maids, nothing was thought so fit to adorn their persons as the fabrick from India! Nor for the ornament of their Chambers like India Skreens, Cabinets, Beds, or Hangings, nor for Closets like China and lacquered ware.' Even allowing for the satirist's privilege of exaggeration, this statement is substantially accurate. Vendors of oriental merchandise and European furnishings in the Chinese taste abounded, and when, in the same year (1697), James Brydges (later first Duke of Chandos) was setting up house in London he was able to choose his eastern textiles from three shops. By this time the vogue for orientalia had spread throughout the educated classes. Many a citizen possessed a collection of Nanking and Delft; many a neat, square red-brick house included a room fashionably hung with exotic textiles or wallpaper. As early as 1663 Samuel Pepys had bought his wife a 'chint, that is, a painted East India callico for to line her new study', and a number of other rooms must have been similarly lined though none has survived the ravages of time. Some thirteen years later one Will Sherwin took out a patent to print broad cloth in 'the only true way of the East India printing and stayning such goods'. A cheaper substitute for embroidered or painted cloth hangings was provided by wallpaper, either imported from China or of English manufacture like the 'strong paper hangings, with fine Indian figures in pieces of about 12 yds. long and about half an ell broad at 2s. and 2s. 6d. a Piece', which were advertised in the *London Gazette* of 1694.

Oriental and oriental-style fabrics were also fashionable for clothes. It may be difficult to picture the severe John Evelyn in a waistcoat embroidered with chrysanthemums and dragons, yet his diary reveals that he had an eye for such articles of finery. In 1664 he noted some handsome embroideries that had been brought from China to London by way of Paris—'glorious vests wrought and embroidered on cloth of gold, but with such lively colours that for splendour and vividness we have nothing in Europe that approaches it . . . flowers, trees, beasts, birds, wrought in a kind of sleeve silk, very natural'. Within a short time, Europe was producing many garments as vivid and, to use a seventeenth-century word, as splendidious. Laying aside their stump-work, the needle-women of England quickly began to imitate the elegant freedom of Chinese designs. Similarly brilliant patterns were woven on English looms and soon after the end of the century weavers in all parts of Europe were turning out silks of an exotic and distinctly original appearance.

The evolution of the taste for these so-called 'bizarre silks', which were woven in France, Italy, Spain, Holland, and England, can be studied in some detail with the help of a number of dated designs which have recently been published. The patterns woven at Spitalfields appear to have been copied from French originals, for Paris was already the recognized centre of *haute couture*. Between 1707 and 1710, vaguely architectural designs with flowering trees, archways, and diagonal walls or screens on a diaper background were popular. Then a desire for more abstract—though no less bizarre—patterns made itself felt and in about 1715 luxuriant foliated designs began to win favour. It is hardly surprising to discover that although they were influenced by various parts of the East, from Persia to Japan, none of these patterns reproduces an oriental prototype. But despite the fashion for these European-made 'bizarre silks' imported fabrics from the East maintained their popularity—to such an extent, indeed, that the English textile industry was jeopardized and the weavers forced to complain that

> Ev'ry jilt of the town
> Gets a callico gown;
> Our own manufacks out of fashion.
> No country of wool
> Was ever so dull.
> 'Tis a test of the brains of the nation
> To neglect their own works,
> Employ pagans and Turks,
> And let foreign trump'ry o'er spread 'em.

This appearance of the satirist upon the scene in the early years of the eighteenth century marks a new period in the history of English chinoiserie and provides yet another indication of the widespread popularity of the cult. Fashionable collectors of orientalia first made their bow on the London stage in Charles Burnaby's *Ladies Visiting Day*, produced in 1701, avowing that they 'wou'd not give a farthing for a Monkey that wou'd not break three or four pounds worth of China'. Four years later the versatile Nicholas Rowe—author of numerous tearful tragedies, creator of 'haughty, gallant, gay Lothario', translator of Lucan and first editor of Shakespeare—devoted his only comedy, *The Biter*, to poking fun at English orientalists. The central character in this play is Sir Timothy Tallapoy, nabob of Kingquanoungzi (played by Betterton), who has returned from the East vastly enriched. He has also succumbed to the customs of the Orient and in one of his more revealing outbursts of peppery irritation declares:

> I will send forthwith to my correspondent in Canton for a new Pagode. I will marry my daughter to the young man I have provided for her . . . and after that I will incontinently espouse the most aimiable Mariana, and engender a Male Off Spring who shall drink nothing but the Divine Liquor Tea, and eat nothing but Oriental rise and be brought up after the institutions of the most excellent Confucius.

Needless to say, he is foiled in all these ambitions and returns angrily to the Indies. But the nabob had come to stay in English literature, and Sir Timothy Tallapoy is the ancestor of a long line of orientalized Englishmen who have returned from the Far East to put in a comic appearance in novels and plays. (The most attractive is Sir Oliver Surface in *School for Scandal* and the last of note Joseph Sedley in *Vanity Fair*.)

Many another satirist tilted at the oriental fanciers. Pope remarked how, at Hampton Court,

> One speaks the Glory of the English Queen,
> And one describes a charming Indian screen.

Later he observed of Chloë (Lady Mary Wortley Montagu):

> She while her lover pants upon her breast
> Can mark the figures on an Indian chest.

But the chinoiserie cult was faced with more solemn opponents, like Lord Shaftesbury who sarcastically declared: 'Effeminacy pleases me, the Indian figures, the Japan work, the enamel strikes my eye. The luscious colours and glossy paint gain upon my fancy'—and then asked how a man whose taste had been formed on such baubles could possibly appreciate the 'beauties of an Italian master'. Here speaks the voice of the new, the severe Palladian age. While Shaftesbury was politely scoffing at the vogue for eastern objects a more urgent protest became audible, that of English and French textile weavers vociferously complaining about the mass importation of oriental fabrics.

4 THE WEAVERS' COMPLAINT

'Odious! in woollen! 'twould a Saint provoke,'
(Were the last words that poor Narcissa spoke).
'No, let some charming chintz and Brussels lace
Wrap my cold limbs and shade my lifeless face.'
ALEXANDER POPE: *Moral Essays*, Ep. I, 1733

The great quantities of eastern fabrics imported into Europe in the late seventeenth century and so highly prized by the *haut monde* were viewed with a distinctly jaundiced eye by the textile weavers of France and England, for the new fashion had spread with alarming rapidity and now threatened their very livelihood. As early as the 1650s Cardinal Mazarin seems to have foreseen the danger and encouraged the production of 'serge façon de la Chine' to help the French industry compete with its eastern rivals. By 1683 the situation had become so serious that Louvois began to take more effective measures to protect the French weavers—measures made all the more necessary, as we have seen, by the arrival of the Siamese ambassadors bringing bales of precious Chinese stuffs as presents to the royal family. For although the *tessutiers* derived some benefit from the invention of a new cloth made in imitation of the ambassadors' robes and called *siamoisé*, this was offset by the fresh stimulus the embassy gave to the importation of oriental fabrics. A heavy tax was therefore imposed on all textiles imported from Holland and England (whether made there or in the East) and a ban was placed on the introduction of painted cloth (calico). Muslins and *toiles blanches*, which were not woven in France, were excepted from the restrictions, and the Compagnie des Indes was allowed concessions.

A minor war now began to develop between the Ministry of Finance and the Compagnie. In 1700, whilst the court was enjoying the *Roi de la Chine* masquerade, the Compagnie's trading ship, *Amphitrite*, was sailing back from the East with a rich load of exotic merchandise—the first to be imported into France direct from China. One hundred and sixty-seven cases of porcelain, innumerable bales of silks, gauzes, satins and unknown quantities of lacquer filled the holds of this merchantman whose arrival delighted the court. Not so the French craftsmen whose spokesman addressed a sharp letter to the director of the Compagnie des Indes. The cabinet-makers, potters, and textile workers were, he wrote, dismayed at the great quantity of merchandise the Compagnie was beginning to import. Although he recognized their right to bring the finest oriental wares to France, for the benefit of collectors, he criticized the importation of lower quality goods which might be sold in competition with French manufactures. As a result of this and similar incidents, the importation of silk and painted cloth was forbidden in 1714 except, in special circumstances, by the Compagnie des Indes. These restrictions helped to drive oriental fabrics out of fashion in favour of home-produced silks. And the wheel seems to have come full circle by 1735 when the Duc de Richelieu commended some samples of Indian brocade by remarking that they were the first he has seen which perfectly imitated those of French make—'Les connoisseurs mêmes s'y trompent', he added.

In England the troubles occasioned by the imports of eastern fabrics were more serious. An ever-increasing number of English merchantmen returned from the East each year laden with goods which flooded the markets and before the end of the seventeenth century the textile industry had begun to suffer. Between 1690 and 1700 the number of silk looms in operation at Canterbury decreased sharply while many Spitalfields weavers were thrown out of employment and forced to take unskilled work. In 1700 Parliament initiated a number of restrictions by banning not only the importation but also the wearing of Indian calicoes and chintz. This move was received with horror by the fashionable world and Samuel Pepys expressed doubt as to whether Lady Salisbury would ever think it worth returning from Rome to London 'under the infelicity oure inglish ladys are at this day very happrehensive of, from our parliament's avowed resolution to forbid the wareing of any more Indian silkes and calicoes'.

The first result of this law was to make smuggling a highly profitable, if perilous, business. As they sang in *The Weavers' Complaint*:

> The merchants all smuggle,
> And the trade's all a juggle,
> Carry'd on by leger-demain sir.

In 1708 Daniel Defoe—a violent and unreasonable China-phobe—was still protesting about the scant protection given to the wool and silk trades in spite of parliamentary restrictions. But the mania for calico and chintz continued unabated, much to the detriment of the long-established English textile industry, until finally, in 1719, the weavers of Spitalfields rioted and ran berserk through the city splashing *aqua fortis* on the dresses of any ladies they could find. Many rioters were caught and put in the pillory. And some imprudent women who went, dressed in all the finery of calico, to scoff, had their gowns torn from their backs by such weavers as had escaped punishment. There were similar outbreaks of violence in the provinces. Parliament was therefore forced to act again and in 1721 extended the ban on eastern fabrics to all cotton goods. The ladies were allowed two years' grace, but after Christmas day 1722 they were forbidden to use cotton for clothes or even for household decoration. How strictly this law was enforced it is difficult to tell, but it seems to have helped the wool and silk industries. In 1736 the law was relaxed a little, but even after this date Indian chintzes and Chinese embroideries could be introduced into England only by the smuggler.

5 BAROQUE CHINOISERIE

To dignify the bizarre, and often naïve, objects described in this chapter with the august title baroque, is to invite the scorn of every *Kunsthistoriker*. Nevertheless, the lacquer, pottery, textiles, and silver made between 1660 and about 1715 and decorated with chinoiserie motifs may conveniently be regarded as manifestations of the baroque spirit. For, different though their mediums and purposes may have been, these objects have certain stylistic features in common which differentiate them as clearly from genuine products of the Far East (or direct imitations of eastern originals) as they do from later chinoiseries. And it would be no exaggeration to say that these objects are closer in feeling to the classical baroque furnishings produced at the same time than to the rococo chinoiseries of the 1730s and 1740s.

But the use of the word chinoiserie is hardly less perilous. The decorations on these objects are composed of a gallimaufry of eastern and European motifs which it would be more prudent to term exotic. In the late seventeenth century very few Europeans were capable of drawing nice distinctions between the products of China, Japan, Siam, and India—or indeed between any non-European styles. As we have seen, the exotic tapestries woven at Soho for Elihu Yale were decorated with more Mogul than Chinese motifs. And Robert Robinson, who may have been responsible for their design, happily combined Chinese and Peruvian elements in his paintings—China and Peru being more closely connected in the seventeenth-century conspectus of the world than in Dr Johnson's survey of mankind. Nor was this confusion confined to styles of decoration. The very geography of the Far East was still hazy. To subdivide the exotic ornaments which appear on late seventeenth-century objects into Indienneries, Japonaiseries and Chinoiseries would therefore introduce a note of geographical pedantry wholly foreign to the spirit of the age. Only in the eighteenth century did motifs derived from China and Japan become distinguishable from those taken from other Eastern lands. But these late seventeenth-century exotic decorations are so clearly the forerunners of the purer chinoiseries of the eighteenth century that they may, for convenience, be called by the same name.

To the late seventeenth-century eye the Orient seems to have appeared both infinitely remote and infinitely bizarre—like the Chinese garden in *The Fairy Queen* where 'the Architecture, the Trees, the Plants, the Fruit, the Birds, the Beasts [were] quite different from what we have in this part of the World'. And the products of these strange lands, though prized by men of fashion, were forced to undergo certain modifications to fit them for the European home. Porcelain vases were either mounted in gilt metal or arranged *en masse* in a very un-Chinese fashion; lacquer cabinets were placed on great gilded stands bulging with putti and swags of fruit.

Although a *frisson* at the outlandishness of oriental art was not disagreeable to the late seventeenth-century man of taste, he seems to have admired eastern objects more for their exotic richness than their fantasy. He was attracted principally by the refulgent surface of lacquer—'varnish more glossy and reflecting than polisht marble'—, by the fine clear colours and handsome shapes of Chinese porcelain vases and by the myriad glowing hues of oriental embroideries. These qualities were therefore accentuated in chinoiserie decorations. The fantasy of oriental designs was toned down to suit the taste of the seventeenth-century patron as, at a later period, it was to be exaggerated and made more bizarre. Chinoiseries of the baroque era stress the magnificence and prodigality of the imagined Orient—they abound in opulently robed princes, jungles of burgeoning fruit-trees, herds of strange fauna—while those of the eighteenth century reveal its grace and whimsical charm.

Occasionally in late seventeenth-century chinoiseries, in the gilded details of a lacquer cabinet, the azure decorations on a Delft or Nevers plate, the figures on a Soho tapestry, it is possible to savour a foretaste of rococo chinoiserie. Nowhere is this stronger than in the engraved decorations of Jean Bérain. Indeed, Watteau and Huet adapted elements from his prints. Yet Bérain himself remains essentially and obstinately baroque; the last great decorative artist of the *Grand Siècle*. Only when his mandarins threw off their decorum to break into a tripping dance, only when his monkeys deserted their scroll seats to scamper over wall and ceiling, did the rococo chinoiserie style come into being.

CHAPTER IV

Rococo Chinoiserie

I MONKEYS AND MANDARINS IN THE FRANCE OF LOUIS XV

> Temps fortuné, marqué par la licence,
> Où la Folie, agitant son grelot,
> D'un pied léger parcourt toute la France:
> Où nul mortel ne daigne être dévot,
> Où l'on fait tout . . . excepté pénitence.
>
> VOLTAIRE: *La Pucelle*

Louis XIV's death in 1715 brought to a close a great period in the history of French arts and manners. The old and lonely king had outlived the gilded splendours of his creation and at his death, according to the acid Duc de Saint-Simon: 'le peuple, ruiné, accablé, désespéré, rendit grâces à Dieu, avec un éclat scandaleux, d'une délivrance dont les plus ardens désirs ne doutaient pas'. Almost at once, in the less staid and stilted atmosphere of the Régence court, a gay flirtatious society emerged from a pious and ceremonious one. Reaction against the official Louis XIV style, which had already begun to make itself felt in the first years of the century, quickly transformed literature, music, and the visual arts. Pomp and majesty gave way to charm and elegance and a sense of delicate voluptuousness was diffused over all artistic creations. Whereas the painters of the old regime had slipped only too easily from the sonorous prose of the *Éloge* into the empty rhetoric of the lapidary's inscription, those of the new reign glided smoothly from the scintillating conversation of the *salon* to the sweet nothings of the boudoir. As the Goncourts remarked: 'Plays, books, pictures, statues, houses, everything is subject to the taste for ornamentation and coquetry, to the graces of a delightful decadence. Prettiness, in the best sense of the term, is the symbol and the seduction of France at this airy moment of history. It is the essence, the formula of her genius, the quality of her moral tone and the pattern of her manners.'

To this sophisticated, insouciant and highly cultivated society, chinoiserie naturally made a strong appeal. Connoisseurs were charmed by the limpid porcelain colours of the Chinese palette, amused by the spectacle of quaint little men and monkeys attired in richly embroidered silk robes, and intrigued by the exotic voluptuousness of the Orient—for to the eighteenth-century imagination the harems of China appeared no less titillating than those of Turkey. But, above all, the outlandish waywardness of eastern designs was admired in a period which had laughingly escaped from the tutelary severity of the classical orders. In this frivolous world it is hardly surprising to find Watteau turning from his sad-eyed clowns of the Commedia dell' Arte to the hierophants of an imaginary eastern religion, Boucher endowing the amorous concubines of China with the plump, pink sensuality of his Parisian coquettes, or Voltaire preaching the *Analects* of Confucius and penning classical tragedies in a room lined with Chinese wallpaper.

It has sometimes been suggested that imports from the Far East were responsible for the rise of the rococo style itself; but this is to misunderstand both the eighteenth-century attitude to the Orient and the nature of rococo. As the late Fiske Kimball was at pains to point out, the rococo was an autonomous style dependent on and yet the antithesis of the late baroque; and he traced its first appearance to a chimney-piece designed by Pierre Le Pautre in 1699. Significantly enough, Le Pautre was never, so far as is known, tempted by chinoiserie. Indeed most of the chinoiserie decorations produced between 1700 and 1730 are closer in style to those of the seventeenth century than to those of the 1750s (Pl. 33). The charming, elegant, light-hearted rococo style did, however, lend itself perfectly to exotic treatment. At this period, to quote a contemporary critic, 'tous les genres étaient bons, hors le genre ennuyeux', and there was certainly nothing 'ennuyeux' about chinoiserie. For the first time, therefore, artists of the calibre of a Watteau or a Boucher turned to Cathay for inspiration.

The earliest examples of rococo chinoiserie appear to have been produced by Antoine Watteau. He drew a pair of grotesque decorations, *L'Empereur chinois* and *Divinité chinoise* which were later engraved (Pl. 35) and in about 1719 he painted a series of *Figures chinoises et tartares* for the *cabinet du roi* in the Château de la Muette, destroyed in the middle of the century but known from prints (Fig. 4). He also painted a group of Chinese dancers frolicking on the board of a harpsichord which must have been perfectly suited for the performance of such a deliciously tinkly little piece as Couperin's *Les Chinois*. Small and slight though it is, this painting helps the imagination to colour the engravings of the La Muette decorations with the glowing reds, golden yellows, and acid purples of Watteau's palette. And we may picture the exquisitely painted silks and satins with which he clad the figures, even if it is hardly possible to recapture the sense of mystery and melancholy which were ever the distinguishing qualities of his work. The *Divinité chinoise* print depicts, amid Bérainesque grotesque work, a clearing in a wood with a pagod seated upon a dais which is approached by oriental worshippers. One of the La Muette engravings shows a woman holding a parasol in one hand and what appears to be a feather-duster in the other,

Fig. 4   Idole de la Déesse KI MAO SAO, engraving by Aubert after the painting by Antoine Watteau of *c.* 1719

seated cross-legged on a swirling rococo scroll formed out of the gnarled root of a tree while, on either side, two devout mandarins—one bald with pendant moustaches, the other wearing a sugar-loaf cap—kneel in silent adoration. The inscription reveals that this strange scene represents *Idole de la Déesse* KI MAO SAO *dans le Royaume de Mang au pays de Laos*, another shows *La Déesse* THVO-CHVU *dans l'île d'Haïnan*. As the deities have their names correctly inscribed it has been assumed that Watteau must have based his decorations on similarly inscribed

Chinese paintings, of which a fair number is known to have been in France at this date (forty-nine volumes of Chinese paintings had been presented to Louis XIV by a Jesuit in 1697). This may be so, but if Watteau's models could be identified they would only serve to show with what freedom he had transformed them. For nothing more wittily Gallic and elegantly rococo than these engravings can be imagined. It is interesting to note that the *Ki Mao Sao* scene was translated into porcelain by the 'Muses Modeller' of the Bow porcelain factory in about 1750, but this lumpy group (Pl. 65) is at least as far removed from Watteau as the painting at La Muette must have been from any Chinese prototype. A more successful adaptation, or parody, of the same scene was painted by Christophe Huet in the *grande singerie* at Chantilly where he transformed the seated idol into a Parisian coquette and replaced her worshippers by monkeys in identical postures.

Watteau's chinoiseries had a more profound influence than is suggested by the Bow group and Huet's painting. It is no exaggeration to say that they set the pattern and the tone for rococo chinoiserie decorations not only in France but throughout Europe. The various elements which appeared in them—solemn priests and pagods, obsequious courtiers and devout worshippers, parasol canopies suspended in mid-air, mandarin-headed terms, and temples open to the sky—soon became the essential ingredients of chinoiserie. A comparison between Watteau's *Ki Mao Sao* and the crude engraving of a 'pagod worship in ye Indies' in Stalker and Parker's manual of japanning (Fig. 3), reveals the fundamental difference between the seventeenth- and eighteenth-century attitudes to the Orient. In Watteau's print the mystic rites of the East appear no less fantastic but they have ceased to be grotesque.

The spirit of fantasy in Watteau's chinoiseries was further developed by Christophe Huet in the *grande singerie* which he painted in the Château de Chantilly in 1735 (Pl. 37). The main figures in this room are Chinamen but their attendants are monkeys, amiable and perky little creatures who caper over the walls and ceiling. Monkeys aping the labours and pleasures of man—*babuineries*—had, of course, been familiar denizens of European art since their first appearance in the margins of medieval manuscripts. But these Gothic beasts were only very remote ancestors of the Chantilly breed. *Singes* of the eighteenth-century species seem to be descended from the engraved works of Jean Bérain who first hit on the happy idea of replacing classical fauns with monkeys in his engraved decorations. Then, in 1709, Claude Audran painted an 'arbour with monkeys seated at table' for the Château de Marly and the *singerie* genre was born. Watteau, who had worked under Audran at Marly later painted *Les Singes Peintres* for the Regent as a pendant to Breughel's *La Musique des chats*.

Bérain's, Audran's and Watteau's monkeys are thoroughbred Parisians, as is clear from the cut of their coats, but in the third decade of the century these fashion-conscious creatures donned flowing robes and assumed the airs of the mandarinate. How monkeys first became entangled in chinoiserie is a problem that has vexed several writers. They occasionally appear on Chinese porcelain, and some examples of this type may have been included among the large seventeenth-century importations. Alternatively, *singeries* may derive from the monkeys who assisted Vishnu against the demons, a scene that was depicted on at least one Indian palampore imported into Europe, though none of these monkeys would have been attired as human beings, which is the essential mark of the *singerie*. Whatever the origin of the cult, monkeys came to be associated in the European mind with China before the end of the seventeenth century. As Lord Rochester remarked to his pet ape:

> Kiss me, thou curious miniature of man,
> How odd thou art, how pretty, how japan.

In the *grande singerie* Christophe Huet mixed mandarins and monkeys so freely that it is often difficult to tell whether an individual figure represents a simian Chinaman or a sapient ape. The decorations consist of a series of large grotesque panels framed in elaborate gilt rococo mouldings and painted in gay colours against a white background. Each panel has an individual significance; in one the central figure is a sportsman flanked by monkey gamekeepers and all the grotesque decorations refer to the chase; in another a Chinese apothecary stands at his dispensary assisted by a pair of monkeys and surrounded by the weapons of his craft (Pl. 37). More monkeys appear on the panels of the doors, playing zithers, shooting at dragon-flies, or languidly reclining in hammocks; they also scamper around the stucco scrolls on the ceiling. Huet seems to have taken the general design of his arabesques from Oppenord or Gillot, but individual features and, what is more important, the atmosphere of delicate fantasy clearly derive from Watteau. Partly on account of this influence, the room at Chantilly is one of the most attractive surviving examples of French rococo decoration and the undoubted masterpiece of *singerie*.

Huet painted monkeys on other occasions and he also painted chinoiseries, but never again did he combine the genres with such playful grace as at Chantilly. There are monkeys in a room he decorated in the hôtel de Rohan in Paris, between 1749 and 1752, but they have retreated to the upper parts of the walls leaving the central panels of the *boiseries* free for paintings of *fêtes galantes*. And several groups of his monkey drawings were published under the general title: *Singeries, ou différentes actions de la vie humaine représentées par des singes*.

The best of Huet's chinoiserie decorations were executed for Mme de Pompadour at the Château des Champs shortly after 1747. Here, the *salon chinois* is decorated with a large number of vignettes of Chinamen engaged in country pastimes and exotic birds fluttering through *rocaille* scrolls. Similar scenes, painted on a much larger scale, adorn the walls of the boudoir. In both rooms, however, the paintings were applied to simple *boiseries* of an earlier period which seem to have cramped Huet's style. Delightfully whimsical though the individual scenes may be, the total effect lacks that exuberant sense of fantasy to which he had given full rein at Chantilly. And whereas the *grande singerie* had been the happy result of Watteau's influence, the scenes at Champs reveal the impact of a younger artist—François Boucher, whose *tentures chinoises* had recently been woven at Beauvais.

The originality of Boucher's chinoiserie tapestries can best be appreciated by comparing them with earlier hangings in the same style. The *tentures des Indes* woven at the Gobelins in about 1690 and the Soho chinoiserie tapestries of about 1700, presented a characteristically seventeenth-century vision of the fabulously luxuriant Orient. A distinct change of attitude was marked by a set of *tentures chinoises* woven at Beauvais in the late 1720s. One of these, *The Reception by the Prince*, represents an eastern potentate, probably the Grand Mogul, holding a levee (Pl. 38). He sits beneath a trellis-work canopy, half Moorish, half Gothic, which strangely anticipates the design of a Victorian conservatory, with a somewhat disgruntled elephant peering out from behind his throne; ambassadors kow-tow obsequiously while a princess in a slave-drawn chariot looks on. This hanging was so popular that it was repeated ten times. Other scenes in the same series show the elegant ladies of the court sipping their *café au lait* at an out-door breakfast, the prince conversing with a philosopher who stands on the lowest step of his throne, and peasants harvesting pineapples. In design and detail these hangings are fully rococo, reflecting the light-hearted attitude to the Orient of the early eighteenth century, but it is the pomp and circumstance of the East which they celebrate.

Boucher's tapestries, which were woven at Beauvais shortly after 1742, reveal the charms of an oriental pastoral life rather than the splendours of a court. Even the hanging devoted to the *Emperor's Audience* is conceived as a *fête champêtre* with its rustic and bewildered potentate hemmed in by a motley crowd of concubines, courtiers, attendants and ambassadors of various colours. Other scenes in the same series depict a Chinese fair thronged with merchants, mountebanks and elegant spectators, a bizarre marriage ceremony, a royal breakfast (Pl. 42), a fishing party indulging the pleasures of a simple life on the banks of an artificial lake, and court ladies playing with their parakeets and children in palm-shaded gardens. Boucher is said to have based his cartoons on drawings sent from China by the Jesuit father Attiret, but he could have derived only a few details of costumes and other accessories from this source. The mood of the tapestries is entirely that of European chinoiserie and one may wonder what Emperor Ch'ien Lung thought of the set which he received as a gift from Louis XV. No doubt he found them delightfully outlandish and un-Chinese, but he evidently appreciated something of their Gallic charm, for one panel was still hanging in the Imperial Palace at Peking when it was sacked in 1860. Another set was used, more appropriately, to decorate Mme de Pompadour's apartment at Versailles.

The Beauvais *tentures chinoises* enjoyed wide popularity and were imitated by many other factories. A similar set, for which Boucher probably provided the preliminary sketches, was woven at the Royal Aubusson Factory. But Boucher's essays in chinoiserie were by no means confined to tapestry cartoons. He also painted easel pictures (Pl. 36 and 40) and overdoors, made designs for embroidered fire-screens, painted fans, provided a trade card for Gersaint's shop *A la Pagode* (Pl. 34), made drawings which were engraved as the *Livre des Chinois* and designed the *décor* for Noverre's ballet, *Les Fêtes chinoises*, all in his strongly individual chinoiserie style. For Boucher, the East was neither mysterious nor stately but gay and voluptuous. The gentle caressing air of Cythera is diffused over his paintings and drawings in which every mandarin is a *petit maître* and every Chinese lady a coquette; even his philosophers wear gowns of the smartest cut and walk with a mincing gait. But it would be a mistake to suppose that Boucher was content to dress Parisian figures in oriental silks and satins in the same way that he clothed them in *chic* tatters for pastoral scenes or undressed them for appearance on Mount Olympus. His Chinamen are oriental in both face and figure. These lovers dallying in a bamboo arbour, these courtiers sauntering beside the canal, these elegant young mothers with their pigtailed children tripping at their heels, are true inhabitants of Cathay momentarily succumbing to the fashionable dictates of Paris. They are the descendants of the Chinamen whom Watteau had drawn a generation earlier, though no longer so remote and superior. For after emerging from Watteau's mysterious temple in the woods they acquired the vitality, solidity and graceful sensuality with which Boucher endowed every figure he painted.

As the favoured *protégé* of Mme de Pompadour and, after her death, Chief Painter to the court of Louis XV, Boucher exerted a strong, indeed an all but crushing, influence on French arts. His gods and goddesses, *amorini*, nereids and tritons, shepherds and shepherdesses, mandarins and their concubines, were copied by minor painters throughout France. (In the chinoiserie field his most notable follower was Jean-Baptiste Le Prince who also derived some inspiration from Pillement.) Numerous Parisian hotels and country *châteaux* were decorated with chinoiserie over-doors and painted panels which mimic his seductive style. And by means of engravings his influence was diffused throughout Europe. Not only paintings and drawings, but statuettes in terracotta, bronze and porcelain produced in France, Germany, and England were based on Boucher's designs and reflect his enticing vision of the voluptuous Orient.

Several other artists, most of them dependent on Watteau and Boucher, provided chinoiserie designs for the engravers. Besides publishing prints after Watteau's grotesques, Gabriel Huquier produced some original chinoiserie engravings; Mondon le Fils occasionally abandoned his usual amorous subjects to provide the engraver Aveline with exotic scenes, the most amusing of which represents a monstrous ho-ho bird worshipped by two tremulous Chinamen. A. Peyrotte invented some swirling rococo scroll decorations adorned with flowers and dragons, and also a delightful scene of Chinese musicians performing a sonata for the guitar and *cor anglais*. But of all the artists who drew chinoiseries for the engravers the most outstanding is undoubtedly Jean-Baptiste Pillement, a versatile painter and an exquisite draughtsman.

Whereas Boucher had solidified Watteau's conception of chinoiserie, Pillement, who clearly derived inspiration from the same source, made it more flimsy and more fantastic than ever. The spindly latticed pavilions beneath which his engaging little Chinamen dance, tumble, swing, or sit and fish, appear to have been spun by some exotic, yet innocuous, eastern spider; the flowers with which they are so delicately surrounded look like the minuscule blossoms of lichens and mosses magnified to a thousand times their natural size, and the figures themselves are so buoyant and vivacious that they can hardly keep one pointed toe on the ground. Pillement also designed a number of prints of flowers which, to judge from the number engraved, were especially popular. One set is entitled *Les Fleurs persanes*, but there is no reason why they should be associated with Persia for their natural habitat is plainly Cathay. Some blossoms are in the shape of conical thatched roofs, eminently suitable to cover a rustic pagoda or a hermitage in a chinoiserie garden.

Pillement prints were published in London as well as Paris and they influenced chinoiserie designs in all parts of Europe. Described by the artist as being 'à l'usage des dessinateurs et des peintres', they were applied to objects of every type. They were copied in marquetry by Parisian and German *ébénistes*, and applied to painted chairs, sofas and tables; they were modified and printed on *toiles de Jouy* and wallpapers. They appeared on French gold and Battersea enamel snuff-boxes, on porcelain vases made at Worcester and pottery tiles transfer-printed at Liverpool. Flowers of the species *Pillementiae* are to be found flourishing on walls painted at Drottningholm in Sweden and Vicenza in Italy (Pl. 79). And even today his little Chinamen are sometimes to be encountered dancing on ash-trays and other decorative accessories.

Besides making drawings for prints, Pillement appears to have painted cartoons for Aubusson tapestries, one of which depicts a pair of precariously perched Chinese balancers. For many years he provided designs for the Lyons silk weavers and painters—among these there is a particularly attractive panel of a Chinese astronomer peering myopically through his telescope (Pl. II). He also worked as decorative painter to Stanislas Augustus Poniatowski, King of Poland, for whom he painted a chinoiserie room in the Royal Palace at Warsaw between 1765 and 1767. Later he went to Portugal where, amongst other works, he decorated a pavilion at S. Pedro for the Marques de Marialva, vividly described by William Beckford who saw it in 1787: 'It represents a bower of fantastic trees mingling their branches, and discovering between them peeps of a summer sky. From the mouth of a dragon depends a magnificent lustre with fifty branches hung with festoons of brilliant cut-glass that twinkle like strings of diamonds.' In this congenial setting Beckford and the Marques 'loitered till it was pitch dark'. The pavilion, its painted decorations and its monstrous chandelier vanished long ago.

Recently an example of decorative painting which Pillement executed in Portugal has come to light in an American private collection (Pl. 45). This consists of a series of blue panels with rococo cartouches framing chinoiserie scenes and bunches of gargantuan flowers painted in cream, dull gold, and light red. If, as seems likely, these panels were painted at about the same date as the pavilion at S. Pedro, they must belong to the 1780s by which time the rococo style had been outmoded in Paris and other fashionable centres.

Watteau, Huet, Boucher, and Pillement are the great names in the history of French rococo chinoiserie, for they not only produced many of the finest works in this genre but they provided the patterns for a legion of less original artists and craftsmen. Whole rooms and garden pavilions and every type of household object from writing-tables to fire-dogs, from incense burners to *bourdalous*, were occasionally decorated in the Chinese taste. And although nearly all the larger manifestations of Louis XV chinoiserie such as garden kiosks and complete schemes of interior decoration, have fallen prey to the ravages of time or taste, most of the furniture and bibelots have been preserved by discerning collectors. Deriving from the golden age of French decorative arts, these objects are among the most exquisite of their type ever produced in Europe.

Chinoiserie rooms enjoyed great popularity throughout the reign of Louis XV, and even the classically minded Blondel, who generally disapproved of the oriental cult, conceded that decorations of Chinese and Indian plants and figures might be appropriate for a room 'où l'on passe pour prendre le café'. The vogue for lacquer panelling seems to have survived only until the 1730s —an outstanding example from the hôtel d'Évreux has been preserved (Pl. 33)—when it gave way to the new fashion for painted decorations of the Watteau or Huet type. Sometimes these paintings were set within stucco or carved wood cartouches, as in a room from the hôtel de la Riboissier, now in the Musée Carnavalet in Paris, which appears to have been decorated by a slightly heavy-handed imitator of Pillement. Rooms were occasionally painted by amateurs, and at Versailles, for instance, the Queen, Marie Leczinska, whiled away some hours of her uneventful life by decorating a *cabinet chinois* with chinoiserie garden scenes, though she called in Oudry to perform the more exacting task of depicting Jesuit missionaries preaching to the Chinese. Such

PLATE II   Painted silk panel in the style of J. B. Pillement

rooms remained fashionable even in the 1770's when Rosalie Constant described the chinoiserie delights of Paris. The apartment of the Duc d'Orléans, she said, included a salon 'fait à la chinoise' while the Duchesse de Chartres had a dining-room 'boisée en jaune avec de petits tableaux chinois enchaussés. Le tout très singulier et élégant.'

In less extravagantly decorated *cabinets chinois*, the paintings were confined to the over-doors and over-mantles; or alternatively, and still less expensively, rooms might be hung with *toiles de Jouy* or wallpaper. The *toiles* were often printed with little scenes of fragile buildings or Chinamen in a style imitative of, if not directly derived from, Pillement engravings. Very few such rooms have survived, even in France, and the best example is probably that in the Villa Bianchi-Bandinelli at Geggiano near Siena, where a bedroom is completely hung with Pillementesque *toile* in rusty brown, bought in Paris in about 1790. Chinoiserie wallpapers were painted with large flowering trees and birds and occasionally with little scenes such as *le mariage aux lanternes*. It is perhaps significant that most of the wallpapers simulated small painted decorations or *toile* hangings rather than the wallpapers imported into Europe from the East.

The most elaborate examples of chinoiserie interior decoration were to be found in those charming though sadly perishable buildings with which so many French parks were diversified—pavilions, pagodas, kiosks, and so on. Here exotic tastes were allowed to run wild in a profusion of lattice work, statuary, carved panels, paintings, silk hangings, and trifles of furniture. Of the very few survivors, the most notable is the *maison chinoise* built for François Racine de Monville in that paradise of follies, the Désert de Retz, which was laid out in the 1770s. This elegant little building is of three storeys, each with a curving roof, and is decorated on the exterior with simulated bamboo columns and panels of intricate lattice work. The Chinese effect was heightened by chimneys cunningly made to look like smoking incense burners, and by statues of China-men holding lanterns and umbrellas standing guard at the four corners. Inside, the five rooms were decorated with chinoiserie paintings and silk hangings whose effect can be judged from contemporary prints and water-colours (Pl. 108). Such a delightful folly could hardly be expected to appeal to arbiters of Empire classicism, and in 1808 Alexandre Laborde derisively pointed to it as a prime example of the bad taste which had reigned before the Revolution. 'L'architecture chinoise', he remarked, as if this little folly were a representative example of Ming building, 'ne donne l'idée, ni de l'élégance, ni de la solidité.

Une sorte de légèreté et de papillotage est la seule chose qui la distingue un peu.' Years of contempt and neglect have reduced the *maison chinoise* to ruin, and such buildings, alas, acquire no air of pleasing decay but merely of sad dilapidation.

Of the many vanished pavilions built in late eighteenth-century France, one of the most elaborate must have been that in the park at Chantilly, built in about 1770, decorated on the exterior with statues of Chinese musicians and liberally sprinkled with pseudo-Chinese characters (Pl. 109). Inside the large quatre-foil shaped room was fitted up in the most elegant chinoiserie taste, with paintings of Chinese festivals on the walls and girandoles in the form of chinoiserie term figures. The ceiling was painted to resemble the open sky all alive with fluttering birds in whose midst there hovered an eagle holding in its beak the cord of the enamelled lustre chandelier. The building was so arranged that musicians could be secreted in the cupola whence the sweet sound of airs and gavottes might float down on the company assembled below.

The furniture with which these pavilions and other Chinese rooms were provided seems usually to have been veneered with lacquer panels of either French or oriental origin. But whether the lacquer was eastern or European it was often treated in a somewhat cavalier manner; keyholes were punched in the faces of gilded figures and the tendrils of ormolu mounts were allowed to ramble rankly over the designs. One of the most expert *ébénistes* to make frequent use of lacquer was Bernard II van Risen Burgh (for long known only by his initials B. V. R. B.) who employed coromandel on the furniture he made at the beginning of his career, but later showed a marked preference for the finest and simplest Japanese panels which he treated with rather more respect than most of his contemporaries. On a little console in the Cailleux collection, for example, a panel of Japanese lacquer is set like an exquisite jewel in the ormolu cartouche (Pl. 41). But even he, on one occasion at least (a commode in the English Royal collection) had panels of Japanese lacquer overlaid with French japan to adapt them to the design of the mounts. In many other instances lacquer panels were used as if they were no more than pieces of a very rare wood which might add the last touch of opulence to an article of luxurious furniture. A famous chest of drawers in the Wallace Collection provides a prime example of this attitude. Here some particularly fine panels of Japanese lacquer, augmented by panels of French japan in the same style, are largely obscured from view by a trellis of gilt bronze.

French chinoiserie lacquer seems to have been used principally in conjunction with oriental lacquer on the finest pieces of Louis XV furniture. When used on its own, the designs were somewhat bolder than those which appear on Chinese or Japanese panels and, of course, they are better disposed to fit in with the swirling curves of the ormolu mounts (Pl. 43). But even at this period, when the chinoiserie cult was at its height, the French still seem to have valued lacquer for its *matière* rather than its exotic decorations. It is significant that the Martins who invented the beautiful varnish named after them, seldom if ever applied themselves to decorations in the chinoiserie style. Chinoiserie designs on furniture were sometimes worked out in marquetry (though this practice was not as common in France as in Germany and England); and Sèvres porcelain plaques decorated with Chinese scenes were also, very occasionally, applied to cabinets. A chinoiserie flavour might alternatively be given to furniture by applying ormolu mounts incorporating pagods or dragons, like those on a commode attributed to C. Cressent in the Wallace Collection. But in all these pieces the exotic element is limited to the surface decoration. The French seldom permitted their taste for chinoiserie to influence form and construction and they produced very little furniture comparable with 'Chinese Chippendale' (with the exception of a few chairs and consoles intended for garden buildings in the Chinese taste).

The various ornaments—the bibelots—of the rococo apartment expressed a taste for exoticism in a more whole-hearted fashion. Chinoiserie clocks (Pl. 46 and 50) were particularly popular; they were usually adorned with bronze figures of pagods or Chinamen and sometimes provided with bogus Chinese characters instead of the usual Roman numerals on the dial. Frequently they were made in conjunction with bronze statuettes to form a three-piece *garniture de cheminée*. Similar figures appeared cockling on the rococo scrolls of gilt-bronze fire-dogs. Terracotta figures of the type that French eighteenth-century sculptors modelled with such dextrous facility, were occasionally fashioned as Chinese men, women and children, instead of the usual classical divinities (Pl. 48). Gold snuff-boxes, patch-boxes, vinaigrettes and *étuis* were as often enamelled with gallant as with chinoiserie scenes (Pl. 44). And, of course, porcelain statuettes of Chinamen and porcelain vases painted with Chinese scenes or gay *fleurs des Indes* abounded. Amongst all these strange French *objets de vertu*, a few genuine oriental products might be found, but they were seldom admitted to the boudoir or *salon* before they were suitably dressed. Porcelain vases, especially those of the plain green celadon type, were enriched with swirling tendrils of ormolu which often converted them into ewers. Chinese figures of men, animals and birds were set in gardens of gaily painted Vincennes roses, carnations, jonquils and columbines; lacquer trifles were embellished with gold or silver gilt mounts. At this period, it seems, the unadorned Chinese object was thought insufficiently *chic*—or insufficiently bizarre—to satisfy the French ideal of chinoiserie.

Throughout the long reign of Louis XV, Chinese balls and masquerades continued to beguile the court, while plays set in China were no less popular with the Parisian theatre-goer. Save that the *décor* was in the lighter rococo chinoiserie style, most of these entertainments appear to have differed but little from those of the previous period. Many of the plays and harlequinades have survived only in name and we know nothing of such a piece as *Arlequin pagode et médecin*, performed by Nestier's troupe in 1723 save that the backcloth was said to represent the outside of the Imperial Palace at Peking. A more elaborate spectacle was provided by Jean-Georges Noverre's ballet: *Les Fêtes chinoises* to which the Parisian *monde* flocked in July 1754. Contemporary descriptions reveal that it had sets by Boucher and costumes by Boquet (Pl. 47); as many as eight rows of bedragonned mandarins and attendants were to be seen dancing at a time; pagods in palanquins carried by teams of black and white slaves traversed the stage and Chinese vases magically sprang up to conceal the dancers. *Les Chinois*, a one-act comedy in verse 'meslée d'ariettes. Parodie del Cinese, Par M. Naigeon', which has survived in print, must have relied for its effect principally on the exotic *décor*. The scene was set in a Chinese apartment shut off from the garden by a trellis screen before which Agésie, her heavy father Xiao (a mandarin of the first class) and her lover Tam Tam enact a strikingly simple love story.

A more serious note was struck by Voltaire's *Orphelin de la Chine* first produced in 1755. This was the most notable of the many dramas derived from a genuine Chinese play of which a translation had appeared in Du Halde's great encyclopaedia of oriental lore. The original is a somewhat complicated and gory tale of revenge, but Voltaire gave his work a philosophical tone, styling it 'a dramatization of the morals of Confucius'. He tailored the plot to fit his conception of a classical drama and used it as an answer to Rousseau. In fact, the *Orphelin* owes as much to Aristotle as it does to Confucius but it was given a fashionable chinoiserie setting which made it one of the most popular of eighteenth-century comedies. Probably to stress the country of origin the actors were clothed in full Chinese costumes instead of the mildly exotic garments which had hitherto been worn in plays and operas with oriental settings. A contemporary, Collé, was particularly impressed by this new development and remarked: 'Ils ont observé le costume dans leurs habillements; les femmes étaient en habit chinois et sans paniers, sans manchettes et les bras nus. . . . Les hommes, suivant les rôles, étaient vêtus en Tartares ou en Chinois; cela était bien.'

Other chinoiserie plays of the period, like *Le Chinois poli en France*, were concerned with the plight of the Chinaman who returns to his native land after travels in Europe. Written in a similar vein to the many *Lettres chinoises* which appeared at about the same time, they satirized French fashions and institutions from an outsider's point of view. But such works tell us more about France than the French vision of the Orient and are of little interest to the student of chinoiserie. They may, however, prompt the modern reader to inquire what was the reaction of real Chinamen who visited France at this period. What can they have thought of the *rocaille* chinoiserie paintings and objects which graced every elegant apartment? What, one may wonder, did the two young Chinamen, Ko and Yang, make of Turgot's *Réflexions sur la formation et la distribution des richesses* which was pressed into their hands before they went back to Peking? This work was partly based on the chinoiserie physiocratic theories of Quesnay who had painted a very strange rose-tinted picture of the Celestial Empire to support his economic doctrine.

Behind all the bright elegancies of French rococo chinoiserie there is a serious philosophical strain. We need not assume, indeed it would be foolish to suggest, that Huet, Boucher, and Pillement were influenced by or even conscious of the beliefs and writings of Sinophil savants. Nevertheless, it is hard to escape the conclusion that part at least of the success enjoyed by chinoiseries in France at this period was the result of Voltaire's picture of China as the deist philosopher's empire, and Quesnay's view of the Son of Heaven's benevolent despotism. Voltaire's studies at Cirey and Ferney were embellished with Chinese and chinoiserie decorations. And it is significant that the great patroness of chinoiserise artists, Mme de Pompadour, numbered Quesnay among her intimate friends and, on his suggestion, persuaded Louis XV to follow the Emperor of China's example in guiding the plough at the spring tilling.

2 PORCELAIN

What ecstasies her bosom fire!
How her eyes languish with desire!
How blest, how happy should I be,
Were that fond glance bestowed on me!
New doubts and fears within me war:
What rival's near? A *China* Jar.
   China's the passion of her soul;
A cup, a plate, a dish, a bowl
Can kindle wishes in her breast,
Inflame her joy, or break her rest.

JOHN GAY, 1725

After the failure of the Medici experiment in 1587, few serious attempts were made to produce porcelain in Europe for a hundred years. Optimistic Dutch and English potters took out patents to produce porcelain 'after the fashion of the Indies', but nothing is known of what efforts they made towards this end. In France, Louis Poterat obtained a monopoly for the making of porcelain at Saint-Sever near Rouen in 1673 and produced a small quantity of soft-paste wares during the last quarter of the century. A jug in the Metropolitan Museum at New York, decorated with Persian-style floral motifs and long-tailed Chinese birds in blue underglaze, is a characteristic example of the somewhat undistinguished products of his factory.

Greater success attended the efforts of Mme Chicanneau who controlled a factory at Saint-Cloud from 1679 to 1722. She began to produce soft-paste porcelain shortly before the end of the century and when Martin Lister, the eminent zoologist and virtuoso, visited her factory in 1698 he remarked: 'I was marvellously well pleased, for I confess I could not distinguish betwixt the Pots made there, and the finest *China Ware* I ever saw. It will, I know, be easily granted me that the *Paintings* may be better designed and finisht, because our Men are far better Masters in that Art, than the *Chineses*; but the *Glazing* came not in the least behind theirs, not for whiteness, nor the smoothness of running without bubles; again, the *inward Substance* and Matter of the Pots was, to me, the very same, hard and firm as Marble, and the self same grain, *on this side vitrification*. Farther, the *Transparency* of the Pots the very same.' Lister's views were apparently shared by the young Duchesse de Bourgogne, an ardent collector of orientalia, who made an official visit to the factory two years later. Unfortunately, no ceramics made at Saint-Cloud before 1700 are now known, but those produced shortly afterwards are of good quality despite a slightly yellowish hue in the white body. The factory may well have begun to make the white teapots decorated in relief with sprigs of flowering prunus and the *cachepots*, gaily enamelled with groups of Chinamen, which are its most characteristic products, as early as 1700. But most authorities assign these attractive objects to the years between 1715 and 1730, by which time the Meissen factory was busy turning out true hard-paste porcelain wares.

The story of how the secret of oriental porcelain was discovered at Dresden in the early eighteenth century is as fantastic as any fairy-tale by Grimm. According to an old tradition, Augustus the Strong, Elector of Saxony and King of Poland, was so fanatical a devotee of oriental porcelain that he was prepared to ruin his kingdom to improve his collection. He is said to have spent more than one hundred thousand thalers during the first year of his reign and was rumoured to have swapped a whole regiment of Saxon dragoons for forty-eight of the King of Prussia's porcelain vases. (The 'dragoon vases' in the Green Vaults collection at Dresden.) Special taxes had to be raised to pay for new acquisitions to the elector's collection which grew at an even more alarming rate than his tribe of bastards (three hundred and fifty children are recorded).

It is hardly surprising that his ministers referred to China as the 'bleeding bowl of Saxony' and trembled at the news of each East-Indiaman's arrival in a European port. One of his courtiers who was an amateur alchemist, E. W. von Tschirnhausen, saw that there were only two ways out of this intolerable situation: to make gold out of base metals in order to finance the elector's taste or to produce porcelain in Saxony to satisfy it. Fortunately he plumped for the second alternative. He seems to have guessed that one of the secrets of oriental porcelain lay in the very high temperature at which the clay was fired, and in about 1694 he began a series of experiments in which he persevered, though without success, for more than a decade. Then, by good chance, another alchemist appeared upon the scene, Johann Friedrich Böttger.

Böttger was engaged in the usual search for the Philosopher's Stone and had attracted the encouragement of Friedrich I of Prussia who, like most German sovereigns, was in need of money. Unable to satisfy the king's demands, Böttger thought it prudent to leave Prussia and found a new employer in Augustus the Strong who somewhat ominously sent a military escort to meet him at the frontier and accompany him to Dresden. Given all the facilities for which he asked, Böttger was set to work to make gold from base metals and threatened with various punishments should he fail. After a short time he attempted to escape but was apprehended and put under the supervision of von Tschirnhausen. The two alchemists were now commanded to settle down to the production of gold as speedily as possible. Needless to say, they were unable to comply with the electoral order, and Böttger was clapped into prison.

When Böttger was released from gaol his attention was directed to the still unsolved problem of hard-paste porcelain. This he felt to be an undignified task for an alchemist and above the door of his laboratory inscribed the insolent legend:

> Gott unser Schöpfer hat gemacht
> aus einem Goldmacher einen Töpfer

—God our creator has turned a gold-maker into a potter. His endeavours in this new field were, however, successful, and he fabricated a red stoneware of a porcellaneous nature, much like that which came from Yi Hsing. This pottery hardly answered the elector's expectations, but in 1708, the year of Tschirnhausen's death, Böttger contrived to produce the first piece of unglazed white hard-paste porcelain. The clay he used acted unpredictably in the firing, but the elector was sufficiently pleased with the results to establish the Royal Saxon Porcelain Manufactory at Meissen, twelve miles outside Dresden, in 1710. Next year, a new, much finer clay was discovered and enabled true porcelain of fine quality to be made for the first time in Europe.

Rather surprisingly the patterns of the earliest wares produced at Meissen were derived indiscriminately from European silver and oriental porcelain. A 'pilgrim bottle' in Böttger's red stoneware, for instance, is modelled on a silver prototype with acanthus leaf handles and painted decorations imitative of embossed gadrooning round the base, but the centre is painted with an oriental landscape clearly derived from a panel of Japanese lacquer (Pl. 52). A white teapot of about 1720 is, as might be expected, derived from a Chinese model and ornamented with sprays of prunus blossom in relief—though it has a twisty handle which would never have won a seal of approval in a Chinese pottery. The factory also made a number of porcelain statuettes many of which seem to have been copied from small European bronzes or ivory carvings, but the most famous and influential were of pagods—or pagoda figures as they are often called—squatting, round-bellied, open-mouthed orientals made in imitation, or rather travesty, of Chinese images of Pu-Tai, the god of happiness

(Pl. 53). Comparison of a Meissen pagod with a Chinese joss clearly reveals the light-hearted attitude to the Orient adopted by the eighteenth-century modeller. These grotesque statuettes quickly became the presiding deities of the chinoiserie cult and nearly every porcelain factory in Europe produced imitations of them at some time in the eighteenth century.

Although the secret of porcelain was guarded with the care that might nowadays be applied to a discovery in atomic physics, it soon leaked out. Before 1719 two employees, Christoph Konrad Hunger and Samuel Stölzel, crept away from Meissen and went to Vienna where they helped C. Du Paquier to establish a porcelain factory. In 1720 Hunger moved on to Venice where he provided the essential information which enabled Giuseppe and Francesco Vezzi to begin making porcelain. He tried unsuccessfully to open a factory under the patronage of the King of Denmark in 1737, and in 1743 he was attempting to produce porcelain at St Petersburg, though without much success for want of sufficiently fine clay. From these first factories the art of making hard-paste porcelain gradually spread throughout Europe.

By a curious chance, Stölzel's desertion from Meissen had a happy outcome, for when the renegade returned in 1720 he brought with him Johann Gregor Höroldt who was put in charge of the painting shop and proceeded to make designs for the most delightful chinoiserie decorations. An accomplished enameller and engraver, Höroldt developed a personal vision of Cathay which is reflected in bright colours or gold on many a Meissen vase and teacup. His designs incorporate spidery figures of Chinamen and buildings which are either excessively high or very long and low, according to the shape of the vessel on which they are painted (Pl. 56). Another group of decorations on Meissen vessels produced in the 1720s and 1730s has been ascribed to A. F. von Löwenfinck; they derive from the sparsely spaced designs of the Japanese Kakiemon type but are marked by a strongly European sense of fantasy and frivolity (Pl. 55). Chinese figure subjects were also applied in plain gold to white teapots and cups—which are thus given the appearance of being mounted in filigree—by the *Hausmaler* Seuter of Augsburg and by other outside workmen. But the majority of useful wares made at Meissen were painted with the so-called *indianische Blumen*, gaudy flowers which might well baffle a botanist for they were derived from the *famille rose* and *famille verte* wares which began to arrive from China in the early years of the eighteenth century. (Chrysanthemums and paeonies on which Chinese painters had based their designs were, of course, unknown in Europe at this date.) These flowers were used at Meissen until about 1740 when they gave way to naturalistic *deutsche Blumen*, but they remained popular elsewhere in Europe throughout the eighteenth and well into the nineteenth century.

During the first two decades of its history the Meissen factory produced a few chinoiserie figures besides the pagods to which I have referred. They included a group, modelled by Georg Fritzsche, of a timid mandarin tempting a monstrous bird with a clove which he holds in his outstretched hand. But the great period of the Meissen statuette began only in 1731 when Johann Joachim Kändler was appointed *Modellmeister*. This remarkably prolific artist invented the vast crowd of *Commedia dell' Arte* actors, street vendors, huntsmen, shepherds, animals, monkey musicians, birds, and allegories of seasons and elements which were copied or adapted by nearly every other porcelain factory and invaded fashionable boudoirs and dining-rooms throughout Europe. Some of Kändler's models even reached the far distant Orient where they were imitated by Chinese potters. Of the thousand or more figures with which he has been credited, several were designed to appeal to exotic tastes, notably the large birds and beasts made for the elector's Japanese palace. Perhaps his most extravagant creation was a tea-set in which a pair of Chinese lovers locked in an embrace serve as the sugar caster while the teapot is disguised as a Chinese woman riding a cockerel—side-saddle of course. Kändler's influence is apparent in the work of several other modellers employed at Meissen, notably J. F. Eberlein, who invented a pair of chinoiserie incense burners in 1735, and F. E. Meyer who modelled the figures of two tall oriental musicians, said to be natives of the Malabar coast.

The most important of the many other German porcelain factories which produced chinoiserie figures was that founded at Nymphenburg, near Munich, in 1753. Here the *Modellmeister* from 1754 until 1763 was Franz Anton Bustelli who may well be regarded as the greatest of all European porcelain modellers. Born in the Ticino, the Swiss canton which provided Italy with so many of her best eighteenth-century sculptors, Bustelli combined an Italian feeling for sculptural form with a perfect understanding of the potentialities of porcelain. Despite their tiny scale, his figures have a delicate elegance, vitality and wit which places them among the masterpieces of rococo art. Many represent European figures—actors and amorous couples—but several of the best are chinoiseries. They include a pagod perched on a high altar with a lamp burning before him (Pl. 59), a posturing priest, a devout woman making her sacrifice, children dancing and playing, attenuated musicians holding mandolines or glockenspiels, and a group of a pedagogue with a pupil who clutches his head as he tries to construe an abstruse passage, no doubt from Confucius. These little figures, precisely modelled in the most beautiful hard-paste porcelain ever produced in Europe, catch the effervescent spirit of rococo chinoiserie more successfully than any works other than Boucher's paintings and Pillement's prints.

No other German factory boasted a modeller as accomplished as Kändler or Bustelli, but several produced delightful chinoiserie figures and groups. An unidentified artist at Frankenthal modelled one of the most endearingly absurd of chinoiserie follies, a table-centre consisting of a number of Chinese men, women and children strolling round a square tea-house with a boy and his pet dragon sheltering beneath a parasol on its roof (Pl. 60). This fantasy has sometimes been attributed to the factory's best modeller, J. F. Lück, who has also been credited with a group of Chinamen carousing in the shade of a giant pineapple tree. At Höchst-am-Main a pair of large groups representing the Emperor (Pl. 61) and Empress of China was made in the 1760s by the anonymous *Chinesenmeister* who specialized in such works and modelled figures of Chinese musicians, wizards and children. At about the same time the Ludwigsburg factory, which had been founded by the preposterous Carl Eugen von Württemberg as 'a necessary attribute to the glory and dignity of a prince', was specializing in the production of chinoiserie statuettes of mandarins and their servants, ladies reclining in latticed arbours, and musicians; they were probably made from models by Wilhelm Beyer who later became court sculptor at Vienna. The largest object made by this factory has unfortunately perished—a group of two Chinamen which stood on the roof of a summer house in the grounds of Solitude, near Stuttgart.

During the first four decades of its history, the Meissen factory exerted a strong influence on porcelain painters and modellers not only in other parts of Germany but also in Scandinavia, Italy, and England. France was somewhat less susceptible to German influence, for the factories at Saint-Cloud, Chantilly, Mennecy, and Vincennes had early developed their distinctive styles and methods of production and took few artistic and no technical ideas from Meissen. (The Vincennes and Mennecy factories made a few copies from Kändler's figures.) But after 1756, when Frederick the Great occupied Dresden and took over the Meissen factory, the quality of its products rapidly declined and Sèvres began to emerge as the unquestioned leader of fashion in porcelain: a position it was to occupy for the rest of the century.

Before the beginning of the eighteenth century, the Saint-Cloud factory had begun to produce soft-paste porcelain and this was soon developed into a medium of such exquisite quality that the French were understandably reluctant to abandon it for hard-paste. Indeed, when Paul Anton Hannong began to make hard-paste porcelain at Strasbourg in the early 1750s he met with so little commercial success that he transferred his factory to Frankenthal. The *pâte tendre* used by the French factories was composed of a somewhat strange variety of ingredients including clay, chalk, sand, gypsum, soda, and sometimes soft soap, and was apt to behave capriciously in the firing. But the best pieces have a refinement of form and texture which has for long endeared them to collectors of ceramics.

Chinoiseries predominate in the decoration of the French porcelain produced in the first half of the eighteenth century. The Saint-Cloud factory specialized in the production of *blanc de Chine* wares deriving from Chinese Te-hua porcelain and decorated with sprigs of flowering prunus in relief. It also made *cachepots*, little figures of Chinamen, and such curious trifles as cane handles formed as fantastic Tartar heads, decorated either in underglaze blue or with bright enamel colours reminiscent of the Japanese Kakiemon style (Pl. 58). A factory founded at Chantilly in about 1725, under the patronage of the Prince de Condé who was an avid collector of Japanese porcelain, aimed to imitate the delicately painted vessels in the Kakiemon and Imari styles made at Arita expressly for the European market. But although the vases, cups, and plates made at Chantilly derived many elements from Japanese export ceramics and the colours used in their decorations correspond closely with those on Arita wares, the French nationality of the willowy geishas and stout mandarins painted on them can hardly be mistaken. This factory also produced incense-burners made in a more pronouncedly French chinoiserie style, reclining priests or acolytes holding vases shaped like goldfish bowls and figures of gay oriental sages (Pl. 57). Chantilly figures were occasionally set in ormolu, one of the most charming examples of this treatment being a watch-stand in the form of a latticed arbour entwined with porcelain flowers which swirl round the statuette of a mandarin. In this exquisite piece of frivolity the Japanese influence is limited to the Kakiemon pattern embroidery on the mandarin's robe. Similar wares to those made at Saint-Cloud and Chantilly were confected by the Mennecy factory after 1735 (Pl. 49).

The greatest of all French porcelain factories was, of course, that founded at Vincennes in 1738, granted an absolute monopoly as the *Manufacture Royale de Porcelaine* in 1753 and transferred to Sèvres three years later. In its early years the factory produced table-wares in the Kakiemon style and in the late 1740s it made an outstandingly fine *biscuit* (that is to say unglazed) group of two Chinamen carrying a basket, derived from a print after Boucher. But although it enjoyed the patronage and was under the personal surveillance of that ardent sinophil, the Marquise de Pompadour, and occasionally produced such extravaganzas as the elephant vases, which were on one occasion at least painted with Chinese scenes (Pl. 62), it never specialized in the production of chinoiserie decorations or figures. Mme de Pompadour herself seems to have been less interested in chinoiserie porcelain than in giving a chinoiserie appearance to oriental vases and figures by setting them in elaborate ormolu mounts embellished with the fragile porcelain flowers for which the factory was famous. In 1769 the factory, now well established at Sèvres, began to abandon soft-paste for *pâte dure* and to adopt a severer style in which chinoiserie decorations played a still less prominent part. It is perhaps significant that the gradual rise of Sèvres coincided with the decline in the fashion for chinoiserie porcelain throughout Europe.

The English porcelain industry was a late-starter, and not until the end of the century did it free itself from foreign domination. The earliest soft-paste specimens appear to have been made at Chelsea and are dated 1745, but a factory was founded at Bow in 1744 and was producing soft-paste wares by 1750; other factories were founded soon afterwards at Derby, Worcester, Longton Hall, and Lowestoft. All these factories limited themselves to various types of soft-paste, composed basically of clay, ground glass and bone ash, an ingredient used in no other country. At Plymouth, however, William Cockworthy began to make hard-paste wares in 1768. To satisfy the oriental cult which was so widespread in eighteenth-century England, all these factories made chinoiserie table-wares, vases and ornaments, but the designs of their products were nearly always derived from German or French factories or from engravings after French artists.

White Te-Hua style wares were made by both the Chelsea and Bow factories during their early years, though at Bow the raised decorations were touched with colour which gave them an attractive if curiously un-Chinese appearance. Kakiemon and Imari designs from Japan and *famille rose* patterns from China were also adapted by the English factories. And in England, as in no other European country, the vogue for blue-and-white decorations persisted throughout the century; our sinophils appear to have had a penchant for what Charles Lamb was later to style 'those little lawless, azure-tinctured grotesques that, under the notion of men and women, float about, uncircumscribed by any element, in that world before perspective—a china teacup'. The Worcester factory specialized in such decorations and was so whimsically orientalized—or so naïvely disingenuous—as to use for its trade-mark pseudo-Chinese characters, either a garbled version of the Ming reign mark or a strange rendering of the ideogram for jade. In most instances the marks are as far removed from Chinese originals as the wares on which they are inscribed.

Several English factories produced chinoiserie statuettes which include a very elegant group of a woman helping a child to play diabolo and a group of Chinese musicians (Pl. 64) both made at Chelsea, a conversation piece between a man and a woman made at Derby and a pair of busts of orientals from Bow, all dating from the early 1750s. Like the majority of statuettes produced by English factories, these figures derive from Meissen prototypes and although devout patriots may rank them higher than their originals, they add nothing to our knowledge of the eighteenth-century concept of Cathay. In earthenware, however, the humble artisans of Staffordshire produced such endearingly naïve figures as that of a boy riding a water-buffalo (Pl. 85) which seems to express a peculiarly English rustic dream of the fabulous Orient, though it is in fact closer to Chinese originals than the sophisticated Meissen and Nymphenburg figures. Staffordshire potters also made chinoiserie teapots and tea-poys (Pl. 84) which introduced a whiff of Eastern exoticism into the lowliest of English homes.

On the Continent the decorators of pottery somewhat tardily followed the lead of the porcelain factories, reproducing such exotic designs as *fleurs des Indes* long after they had passed the height of fashion. And the painters of the faience factory at Marseilles, under the rule of *la veuve* Perron, depicted many delightful chinoiserie scenes on their beautifully designed rococo tureens, sauce-boats and plates (Pl. 63). Of the relatively few chinoiserie bibelots produced by continental pottery factories perhaps the most notable is a table-centre made at Marieberg in Sweden: a rococo folly with a little Chinaman climbing a spiral staircase which leads to a flower vase.

3 ROCOCO CHINOISERIE IN GERMANY AND SCANDINAVIA

The French artistic domination of Germany, which had begun to make itself felt in the late seventeenth century, continued to increase throughout the rococo period. French was the language spoken at most princely and electoral courts and Parisian fashions in books, plays, clothes, and interior decoration prevailed in polite society. Nevertheless, it is possible to exaggerate the depth to which this Gallicism penetrated. German princelings might build exquisite chinoiserie pavilions in their parks, but the parties they gave in them tended to degenerate into beery rough-and-tumbles (Fig. 5). Indeed most of them picked up only the thinnest of thin veneers of French sophistication, and although they employed skilled French artists and craftsmen to decorate and furnish their palaces, they frequently called for work which would have caused the raising of *mondain* eyebrows in Paris. A comparison between two pieces of lacquer furniture, a console table in the Cailleux collection and a writing-desk in the *Residenz* in Munich (Pl. 39 and 41) nicely points the contrast between French taste and frenchified-German taste in the 1750s. Both pieces are probably the work of Bernard II van Risen Burgh and both reveal the same high standards of craftsmanship, but whereas the former has a well-bred air of reticence and *bienséance*, the latter is almost vulgar in its exuberance. This lack of restraint was not always a disadvantage, however, and some chinoiseries produced in Germany during the eighteenth century are among the most delightfully fantastic in all Europe.

The so-called Japanese Palace, erected at Dresden for Augustus the Strong between 1715 and 1717, was one of the bulkiest, earliest and best known examples of German eighteenth-century chinoiserie. Intended principally to house the elector's collection of eastern porcelain and to display the products of the recently founded Meissen factory, the building owed its fame to its contents rather than to its architecture. However, a vaguely oriental appearance was given to the exterior by a vast wide-eaved concave roof of a Chinese pattern, and the courtyard was decorated with mandarin caryatids. Inside, a long gallery was set apart for the oriental ceramics, while other rooms were adorned with exotic birds some four feet high, modelled by Kändler, and nearly all the chimney-pieces were decked with *garnitures* of three or five stately *famille rose* type vases painted with engaging chinoiserie scenes by Höroldt and his assistants. Much of the furniture was of lacquer, with tables and chairs of scarlet and gold, heavy ormolu-mounted bureaux, some of which opened to reveal chinoiserie decorations in sky-blue and silver, and *guéridons* which incorporated the heads of mandarins or the figures of monkeys in their contorted supports. Not content with this lavish display of porcelain and lacquer, Augustus the Strong planned an exotic pleasure house at Pillnitz, where every room was to be panelled and roofed with porcelain. Unfortunately, this fragile dream was never realized, but his large *indianisches Lustschloss* at Pillnitz is covered by wide spreading Chinese roofs sheltering a painted frieze on which little Chinese figures frisk and caper (Pl. 68).

While Augustus the Strong was building porcelain castles in the air, other German rulers were commissioning more earth-bound chinoiserie fantasies. Clemens August, Prince Bishop of Cologne, who was so enthusiastic a devotee— —one might almost say high priest—of the oriental cult that he carried out his infrequent diocesan visitations seated mandarin-like on a palanquin, created some of the most attractive chinoiserie follies of his period. He was the son of Max Emanuel of Bavaria who had built the Pagodenburg in the park at Nymphenburg (China-mania seems to have run in families in Germany at this period and the history of chinoiserie might almost be treated as a branch of genealogy.) Soon after his appointment to the see of Cologne, Clemens August rebuilt the magnificent *Schloss* at Brühl where one room, the *indianisches Lackkabinett*, was entirely lined with panels of cream japan on which bunches of flowers and chinoiserie scenes were picked out in bright reds and blues. Slightly later the Prince Bishop employed the young François de Cuvilliés to design another so-called *indianisches Kabinett* for his exquisite little hunting-lodge, Falkenlust, where panels of black japan, gaily painted with chinoiserie scenes, were set on white walls amidst gilded dragons and eddying scrolls of rococo woodwork. Clemens August's next chinoiserie venture was to build a complete *chinesisches Haus*, which was finished before 1750, in another part of his park at Brühl. It consisted of a two-storey central block linked to a pair of smaller pavilions, all capped by bell-hung pagoda roofs, with a double staircase leading up to the main door. Beneath the staircase stood the mandarin fountain which is now in the hall of Schloss Brühl (Pl. 67), a lonely survivor from this elegant folly which is otherwise known only from contemporary prints and drawings.

In about 1734, while work at Brühl was still in progress, Cuvilliés was called back to Munich by his original patron, the Elector Karl Albrecht of Bavaria, Clemens August's elder brother. Here the architect began work on the Amalienburg in the park at Nymphenburg which was to prove his most famous building and, perhaps, the greatest masterpiece of the rococo style. In this exquisite pavilion chinoiserie plays a small but not insignificant part. Two of the smaller rooms, the *Hundekammer* with its dog kennels and gun cupboards, and the *Retirade*, which conceals the electoral *chaise percée*, are painted with chinoiseries in blue on a white ground by Pascalin Moretti. A similar blue-and-white ceiling is in the ornamental kitchen where the walls are lined with colourful Delft tiles, some representing birds and porcelain vases.

The taste for chinoiserie which had been introduced into Prussia by the first king, Friedrich I, the patron of Dagly, was inherited by his grandson, Frederick the Great who became an ardent sinophil and corresponded with Voltaire on a number of Chinese questions. But although he maintained a characteristically level-headed attitude towards the Orient in his letters, and teased Voltaire about his excessive admiration for the organization of the Celestial Empire, this did not prevent him from letting his fancy run riot when he built a chinoiserie tea-house at Potsdam. The fantastic building was designed by the king himself with the technical advice of Johann Gottfried Büring, and erected between 1754 and 1757 (Pl. 73). It is built on a trefoil plan with a conical pagoda roof supported on columns of simulated palm trees and guarded by sandstone statues of Chinamen. Inside, the dome is painted with Chinese figures and porcelain vases. More bizarre than any chinoiserie building previously—or indeed subsequently —erected in Germany, the tea-house provoked the scorn of many contemporary critics, one of whom, amid guffaws of heavy Prussian sarcasm, remarked:

> We know, at any rate, that the Chinese, though they put pagods and images of their gods inside their temples, did not put them on their roofs. Still less do they place effigies of themselves drinking tea or smoking pipes of tobacco in company in front of their houses, and whether they planted palm-trees at regular intervals, in order later on, when they were sufficiently grown, to build roofs on their green stems and to erect dwelling houses under them, is extremely doubtful. Here, however, the architect must be excused, since he had not a free hand, but had to follow a design drawn by the king; and generally speaking, the house would not have been sufficiently characteristic and distinct, had not these palm-trees and effigies of Chinese amusing themselves introduced an obviously Chinese element, seeing that neither real palm-trees nor real Chinese were to be had.

At Sans-Souci, Frederick ordered J. A. Martin, whom he had lured from Paris, to paint decorations of exotic birds and flowers in *vernis martin*, and at Monbijou he had a large number of rooms fitted up *à la chinoise*—they were lined with rose-red and yellow hangings on which chinoiserie scenes were painted, with black-and-green lacquer and with carved *boiseries*, but all were swept away during the Empire period. In the *Stadtschloss* at Potsdam, however, there was until the war an elaborate *Musikzimmer* where Frederick may have played his plaintive flute sonatas in the agreeable company of carved mandarins and pagods. Other rooms in his several palaces were hung with Berlin tapestries woven on cartoons by Charles Vigne and depicting Boucheresque chinoiserie garden scenes. He also infected his sister Amelia, Margravine of Bayreuth, with a taste for chinoiserie by giving her a set of coromandel lacquer panels. These were used to decorate a room in her summer palace, Schloss Eremitage, where they were surmounted by a gilded ceiling inset with Chinese scenes picked out in delicate pinks and blues.

The last great chinoiserie folly created in Germany was also one of the strangest: a complete Chinese village called Moulang built for the Landgrave of Cassel beside the Wilhelmshöhe lake in 1781. It consisted of a scattering of little buildings around a stream which was crossed by an arched and fretted Chinese bridge. The principal house, for the tenant farmer, was of two storeys, but the others were bungalows; there was also a chinoiserie barn, a couple of cow houses and a long low building called a 'sallong' which contained two dining-rooms and a ballroom. In such delightful surroundings Europeans could lead the lives of porcelain figures, fishing in the lake, gardening and sipping tea by day and dancing through the night. It is perhaps appropriate that the best surviving record of this village is on a faience plate.

The vogue for chinoiserie furniture persisted in Germany throughout the rococo period. Most of it was lacquered and much seems to have been imported from France, England, and Holland though Germany possessed some excellent japanners. Among their more extraordinary creations is a clock case and stand made at Augsburg in about 1725 (Pl. 72). The design of the case is classical with four Corinthian columns at the corners, but it is crowned by a double-headed dragon and all the wood-work, columns included, is decorated with chinoiserie devices in bright colours on a white ground. A final touch of exoticism is added by the carved figure of a little Chinaman in a flowered robe and palm leaf hat who squats cross-legged on the stretcher. Other examples

Fig. 5   The Chinese Feast, held at Schloss Favorite, Baden-Baden in 1729

of German japanned furniture were less bizarre; such as a harpsichord case made at Hamburg in 1732 (Kunstindustri Museet, Oslo), decorated with a view of a willow-fringed island, which might be mistaken for French or English work. Furniture of a more fantastic type was produced by Johann Michael Hoppenhaupt who worked for Frederick the Great at Berlin. He published a series of designs, strongly reminiscent of Thomas Chippendale, which included console tables with little pagods, mandarins, and hoho birds perching on the crests of their rococo scrolls.

Chinoiserie designs were also popular for the decoration of inlaid furniture, notably that made by David Roentgen of Neuwied in the second half of the century. Roentgen was undoubtedly the greatest of German cabinet-makers and had few equals even in France where he worked for the latter part of his career and was appointed official *Ébéniste-mécanicien du Roi et de la Reine*— Louis XVI and Marie-Antoinette. But even before he left Germany he based the designs for his furniture on French models and derived many of his chinoiserie decorations from prints after Boucher and Pillement. Occasionally he appears to have used original chinoiserie designs, as on a clock case in the Museum of Kunsthandverk at Stockholm (Pl. 66), but these also have a strongly frenchified air. His works were in great demand in Germany and in France where, in the 1780s, he was regarded as 'le plus célèbre ébéniste de l'Europe'. Naturally he attracted many imitators, some of whom produced fine chinoiserie designs in marquetry (Pl. 71) though none rivalled his accomplishment in this intractable medium. Roentgen long outlived the taste for chinoiserie furniture and his last works were decorated with classical motifs in the Empire style.

From France and Germany the fashion for chinoiserie seems to have spread to Austria, Poland, Russia, and Scandinavia. Complete chinoiserie rooms enjoyed a certain popularity in Austria and several were created in the Palace of Schönbrunn. But the most elaborate example of Austrian chinoiserie is the room made for Count Dubsky's palace at Brünn in the 1730s and now in the Austrian Museum of Decorative Arts at Vienna. Apparently designed to emulate Augustus the Strong's projected Japanese palace, this room is encrusted with panels of chinoiserie porcelain and furnished with porcelain wall-sconces, chandeliers and chimney-piece. Later, probably in the 1760s, Dominik Merlini designed a vast marquee-like chinoiserie orangerie for Lazienski in Poland, but this does not seem to have been built.

In Russia the earliest chinoserie room appears to have been that created for Catherine I in Monplaisir at Peterhof—a relatively simple affair, lined with lacquer, and stacked with porcelain, similar in style to the *Porzellankammer* in the Charlottenburg Palace, Berlin. Catherine II was rather more enterprising and commissioned an Italian architect, A. Rinaldi, to build a Chinese pavilion at Oranienbaum near St Petersburg and, between 1762 and 1768, a much larger Chinese palace richly decorated with lacquer and painted ceilings. One of the ceilings, by the Barozzi brothers of Bologna, represents *Les Noces chinoises* and seems to reflect the tsarina's China-mania as well as her more notorious, and still more sultry, tastes. She also commissioned the Scottish architect, Charles Cameron, to build in the grounds of Tsarskoe-Selo a complete Chinese village based on Sir William Chambers's book of Chinese architecture. (The Oranienbaum pavilion vanished long ago, but the Chinese palace near Oranienbaum is said to survive and most of the buildings in the Chinese village are still intact.)

In Sweden the most outstanding example of chinoiserie is the Chinese House at Drottningholm, built by King Adolf Friedrich for his queen, Louisa Ulrique, a sister of Frederick the Great. The king himself is said to have produced the original design for the pavilion which was first built of wood (1753) and then rebuilt in stone between 1763 and 1769. It consists of a large central block with low wings stretching forward to form a courtyard and is capped by wide-spreading concave roofs. The exterior is painted grey with red panels and embellished with yellow stucco dragons. Delicately painted festoons of flowers, rococo scrolls and chinoiserie scenes derived from prints after Boucher and Pillement, decorate the various rooms (Pl. 74). In 1781 Adolf Friedrich's son, Gustav III, planned to complete the chinoiserie delights of Drottningholm by building a pagoda for which four different artists provided designs. But unfortunately the king took some seven years in selecting his pagoda and by that time the taste for chinoiserie had become *démodé* and the project was abandoned.

4 THE MANDARIN ITALIANIZZATO

When the Earl of Cork and Orrery first arrived in Italy, in 1754, he noted of the Palazzo Reale at Turin that 'amidst all these exquisite decorations not one effeminate toy, not one *Chinese* dragon, nor Indian monster is to be seen, I mention this because many of our finest houses in England are disgraced by the fantastic figures with which they are crowded'. But the noble earl was mistaken, for that great baroque architect Filippo Juvarra had included a lacquer panelled Chinese room in the private apartments of this very palace. Like many later writers, Lord Cork rashly assumed that mandarins, pagods and dragons could not flourish in the classical air of Italy. In fact, the chinoiserie cult was as popular in Italy as elsewhere in Europe during the eighteenth century. Furniture decorated *alla cinese* had been produced at Venice since the late seventeenth century, several villas and palaces boasted Chinese rooms in fresco, stucco, or lacquer, and in 1757 one of the most exquisite and elaborate of all chinoiserie confections, the *salottino di porcellana* was created in the royal palace at Portici where it elbowed the first finds from Herculaneum.

Italians naturally took full advantage of the annual carnival to indulge their fancy for rich oriental costumes, and in the weeks preceding Lent many a bedragonned domino was to be found strutting through the Venetian *ridotti*, sauntering along the Arno in Florence, or stalking around the *piazze* of Rome. Chinoiserie also played a prominent part in the elaborately contrived spectacles for which Italy was so famous. When Augustus the Strong visited Venice in 1716, for example, he was greeted by a junk bristling with parasols, carrying an exotic cargo of Chinese singers, dancers and musicians, and propelled down the Grand Canal by coolie gondoliers (Pl. 76). At Turin *tableaux vivants* of such subjects as the triumph of the Pagod and the Emperor of China were drawn through the straight streets of the city in carnival processions. The *pensionnaires* of the Académie de France in Rome donned oriental attire for the carnival parade along the Corso (Pl. 75). And chinoiserie set pieces were frequently used for firework displays, notably those given in Rome on the *Festa della Cinea*.

But the paragon of all chinoiserie festivals was that held at Colorno in 1769 to celebrate the marriage of Don Ferdinando, Duke of Parma, with the Archduchess Maria Amalia, daughter of Maria Theresa. A handsome elephant folio, printed by Bodoni and illustrated with engravings after the French architect and master of ceremonies Ennemont Pettitot, was published to commemorate the occasion and presents a very full account of the various junketings. After having experienced the thrills of a Gothic tournament and indulged the pastoral delights of an Arcadian *fête champêtre*, the wedding guests were diverted with the spectacle of a Chinese fair. Round a *piazza*, specially built for the evening's entertainment, were ranged a number of shops lit by flickering Chinese lanterns, well stocked with oriental rarities and served by young men and women in Chinese garb. On benches in front of each counter squatted children dressed as pagods, some burning perfume in casolettes or puffing at long clay pipes, others tinkling bells and clanging triangles. The centre of the piazza was given up to a brightly clad crew of charlatans, puppet masters, acrobats, musicians, and men with dancing monkeys and bears. When the courtiers had inspected this lively scene, caravans began to arrive from Tartary, Japan, Java and even China itself, with porters staggering under vast bundles of merchandise labelled in outlandish characters. 'The musicians of each caravan placed themselves on arrival in the corners of the *piazza* and discoursed singular music', the contemporary descriptions records. 'All at once, the puppets acted and danced, the players on musical glasses performed their tunes, and the children jumped over their casolettes or walked on tight ropes while at the same time sounding their bells above their heads.' It must have seemed as if a whole volume of prints by Pillement had come suddenly to life.

In the Italian theatre the vogue for chinoiserie plays and operas was no less strong than in France or England, and many a plump castrato piped his coloratura arias dressed in bizarre garments which were thought to look Chinese. A conical hat, a garishly coloured cloak and a pair of shoes turned up at the toes were deemed sufficient to distinguish a Chinaman on the early eighteenth-century stage, but by the 1750s, when the chinoiserie cult was at its height, complete oriental costumes began to appear. Pietro Chiari claimed to have initiated the new fashion in Venice with *La schiava cinese* (first produced during the carnival of 1752) and such was the success of this complicated comedy of mistaken identity that he at once wrote a sequel, *Le sorelle cinese*, which was performed in the following year. Both plays reveal a delightfully distorted view of the Orient and its flowery customs. In the former, for instance, the very solemn ceremony of tea-drinking is performed to the music of *una grava sinfonia*—the Mandarin drinks a libation to his ancestors, then seven slaves hand seven cups to the participants who drink and wipe their mouths in unison, like automata. It is hardly surprising that one of the characters delivers an eulogy in praise of Marco Polo, the author's evident source for much of his 'local colour'.

In 1753, Venetian audiences were also able to see an adaptation of a genuine Chinese play: Metastasio's operatic version of the *Little Orphan of the House of Chao*, entitled *L' eroe cinese*. Although Metastasio had derived his plot from the same source as that of Voltaire's *Orphelin*, he turned it into a characteristically Italian double love-story embellished with neatly turned 'Arcadian' lyrics. In sharp contrast, Carlo Gozzi presented a somewhat savage picture of the East in his famous play, *Turandot*, which was first performed in Venice in 1761. Here the curtain rose on no flowery garden but on a gate into Peking gruesomely decorated with heads impaled on spears. Punctuated by the clash of cymbals, the rolling of drums and occasional shrieks from women in underground caverns, the play recounted the old Persian fairy-story of ice-cold Princess Turandot and the three enigmas which, on pain of death, her suitors must answer. But despite its picture of medieval Tartar barbarity, *Turandot* is pervaded by that peculiar air of poetic fantasy which distinguished all Gozzi's work. For that reason, perhaps, it is the only eighteenth-century chinoiserie play to survive on the modern stage. Schiller made a characteristically romantic adaptation of it in 1801, and in the early twentieth century first Busoni, then Puccini, composed their still popular operatic versions.

It is probably no coincidence that the most notable Italian chinoiserie plays and operas were first performed in Venice, for the Serene Republic, which had been open to eastern influences since the time of Marco Polo, took more enthusiastically to the oriental cult than any other state in the peninsula.

Japanned furniture was produced here in the late seventeenth century and the inquisitive Maximilian Misson, who visited the city in 1688, remarked that 'the lack of Venice is usually much esteem'd and you may have some of all prices'. Unfortunately no examples are known to survive from this period, and relatively few from the first two decades of the eighteenth century. The earliest pieces, spinets and bureaux, are decorated with gold chinoiseries on a black ground much in the style of those produced in England or Holland. Later in the century rich colours were used with greater daring and the decorations took on a lighter and more obviously Venetian style. Among the most attractive specimens, dating from the 1750s, is a complete suite of furniture now in the Ca' Rezzonico at Venice (Pl. 78), consoles, chairs, looking-glasses, and commodes of bottle-green japan exuberantly painted with Chinese festival scenes in gilt. Venetian *lacca* was always of coarser quality than that produced in northern Europe and its charm resides principally in its spirited decorations. A pair of doors in the Ca' Rezzonico, for example, is painted with such assured elegance and witty fantasy that it was for long ascribed to G. B. Tiepolo or his son (Pl. 77).

Lacca decorated with chinoiseries was applied to all types of furniture and bibelots made at Venice—vast *armadi*, coffee-trays, fans, bellows, and the backs of brushes. So great indeed was the vogue for lacquer in this district that an inexpensive means of imitating it was devised—by pasting cut-out prints on-to painted furniture, and varnishing the whole surface. The Remondini firm of Bassano published a large number of little engravings suitable for this

Fig. 6   Two cut-outs for the decoration of *lacca contraffatta*, engraving by Remondini of Bassano, *c.* 1765

purpose (Fig. 6). The furniture to which *lacca* or *lacca contraffatta* was applied usually conformed to the normal Venetian patterns—if the absurd pot-bellying commodes and attenuated settees then popular in Venice can be called normal. But occasionally the fronts of tables were broken by a little carved and japanned chinoiserie pavilion. And some anonymous Venetian craftsman created a cradle so richly fantastic that it is fit only for the heir-apparent of Cathay—apparently based on the nest of the ho-ho bird, it is suspended in the fork of a gnarled tree on one branch of which sits a stork gazing benignly at the little occupant while a diminutive Chinese parasol dangles from the other to shade his head.

In the mid-eighteenth century the vogue for chinoiserie was extended to the stucco and fresco decorations of whole rooms in Venetian villas. The best of the stuccoes are probably those in the Villa La Barbariga at Stra where several rooms are adorned with exotic flowers and birds which hover over the frontier between European rococo and chinoiserie, while another is elegantly enriched with specifically Chinese motifs—little figures in pagoda hats sitting beneath exotic canopies and mandarins wandering idly amongst spindly trees. Of the fresco decorations the only complete series to survive is that painted by Giovanni Domenico Tiepolo in the Foresteria of the Villa Valmarana at Vicenza in about 1757. The four walls of this room are frescoed with large Chinese scenes which include a market with a group of merchants displaying their wares, and a religious ceremony—a woman offering a basket of tangerines (*mandarini*, presumably) to the gilded statue of a moon goddess, watched by a tall priest who stands, censer in hand, beneath a stone pine (Pl. 79). This room reveals an essentially Venetian vision of the East, far removed from the voluptuous Orient of Boucher or the whimsical Cathay of Pillement (even though Tiepolo seems to have borrowed from the latter's weird botanical illustrations). Here priests and mandarins, and even *contadini*, wear robes of the richest silks or velvets and hats made from the tail feathers of gigantic humming-birds. In the background there are tall pagodas which, at first sight, might be mistaken for Venetian *campanili*, and each scene is suffused by the peculiar sparkling light of the lagoon. If the figures were to speak they would surely lisp the soft Venetian dialect, like Pantalone the Emperor of China's secretary in Gozzi's *Turandot*.

Whereas Venetian artists developed a strongly individual conception of chinoiserie, those in Piedmont were influenced by France. The earliest known example of Piedmontese chinoiserie is a grotesque ceiling painted by Filippo Minei at the Villa della Regina outside Turin in the 1720s. But in this ceiling, as in Bérain's arabesques, chinoiserie monkeys, mandarins and parasols are mere substitutes for the more usual Roman fauns, *ignudi* and fans. In the following decade, however, a magnificent lacquer room was created to the design of Filippo Juvarra in the Palazzo Reale, Turin. It is decorated with sixty pieces of oriental—probably Chinese—lacquer bought in Rome on Juvarra's advice in 1732, and augmented by a number of similar panels japanned at Turin by Pietro Massa. The panels are painted with birds, flowers and Chinese scenes in red, blue and gold on a black ground and set within elegant rococo scrolls on a vermilion wall. For its air of sumptuous princely splendour this room has few equals anywhere in Europe, but the Chinese and chinoiserie motifs are so overshadowed that they contribute comparatively little to its effect. A similar room, destroyed during the war, was in the Villa della Regina and another, much lighter in appearance, lined with panels of red-and-gold japan on celadon green walls, was in the Villa Vacchetti at Gerbido near Turin (now in the Rockhill Nelson Gallery of Art, Kansas City). The vogue for chinoiserie rooms seems to have continued in Piedmont until the 1770s, when a wing of the royal palace at Govone (now the Municipio) was decorated with genuine Chinese wallpapers, helped out by paintings of chinoiserie scenes, teapots and bogus Chinese characters on the dados and panels over the doors and windows.

But for the most elaborate example of Italian chinoiserie decoration we must go south to Naples where a complete porcelain room was created in the royal villa at Portici between 1757 and 1759, and later moved to Capodimonte. This is entirely lined with some three thousand interlocking pieces of porcelain made at the Capodimonte factory. Most of the pieces are of a pure glistening white, but the interstices are covered by festoons of flowers, bunches of ribbons, and trophies of musical instruments while between the windows and above the doors rococo frames enclose groups of Chinamen in high relief (Pl. III). The ceiling is of stucco decorated with fantastic birds and butterflies roosting on rococo scrolls, and chinoiserie scenes similar to those over the doors. From the centre of the ceiling hangs a large porcelain chandelier held in the paw of a monkey. The bright enamel colours of the relief work are dimly reflected in tall grey looking-glasses which give the illusion that this room is but one in a vast pleasure dome with caves not of ice but of porcelain, conjured up by some court magician for the delight of Kublai Khan.

So successful was the Portici porcelain room that when, in the year of its completion, Carlo III succeeded to the Spanish throne, he moved the principal artists of the Capodimonte factory from Naples to Buen Retiro near Madrid, and set them to work on a duplicate for the palace at Aranjuez. Though slightly larger, the Aranjuez room reproduced several decorative motifs of that at Portici—and was lit by a chandelier which must have come from the Capodimonte mould. But the large scenes differ so markedly from those at Capodimonte that it seems hardly possible that they are by the same artist. The Capodimonte figures are slightly awkward in their postures and grouping while those at Aranjuez hold themselves with a sophisticated elegance and reveal a far greater ability of design (Pl. 80). The Aranjuez groups are, indeed, close in style to the frescoes painted by Giovanni Domenico Tiepolo in the Villa Valmarana, Vicenza (*c.* 1757) not only in general composition but also in many details—notably in the stance of several figures and in the richly embroidered robes they wear. Since Giovanni Domenico Tiepolo was in Madrid in 1761 and helped his father to paint the ceiling of the throne room in the royal palace between 1762 and 1764, it seems probable that he had a hand in designing the porcelain reliefs for the Aranjuez room which was created during these years. The room certainly ranks high among chinoiserie decorations in Europe and is much the most accomplished in Spain where, indeed, there are few other examples apart from an octagonal kiosk in the park at Aranjuez and a stucco ceiling by Mattia Gasperini in the royal palace, Madrid. (Spanish textile weavers and the potters of the Alcora factory occasionally made use of chinoiserie motifs, and the rococo plasterwork in the sacristy dome of Santo Domingo, Orihuela, includes a few elements of a faintly oriental flavour.)

The outstandingly high quality of these two porcelain rooms might tempt one to suppose that Naples was an important centre of the oriental cult: but in fact there are few other indications of it in southern Italy. Indeed, the Capodimonte factory does not appear to have produced many chinoiserie figures or even to have used chinoiserie patterns for the decoration of its table wares as extensively as other factories in Italy. In 1775, however, one Nicola Fiore, of whom little is otherwise known, provided a design for a room with chinoiserie painted decorations in the recently completed Palazzo Reale at Caserta (Pl. 81). Unfortunately this very attractive scheme does not survive and it may be doubted whether it was ever carried out. The creation of the two porcelain rooms and the commission of a design for the room at Caserta must be attributed to the Bourbons rather than to any general fashion for chinoiserie in the Kingdom of the Two Sicilies—the wife of Carlo III was a granddaughter of Augustus the Strong of Saxony and it is perhaps significant that the most elaborate specimen of late eighteenth-century Italian chinoiserie, the Villa La Favorita outside Palermo, was built for Carlo III's son, Ferdinando IV.

CHAPTER V

English Rococo Chinoiserie

I THE SINOPHILS AND SATIRISTS OF ENGLAND

> Of late, 'tis true, quite sick of Rome and Greece
> We fetch our models from the wise Chinese;
> European artists are too cool and chaste,
> For Mand'rin is the only man of taste. . . .
> On ev'ry shelf a Joss divinely stares,
> Nymphs laid on chintzes sprawl upon our chairs;
> While o'er our cabinets Confucius nods,
> Midst porcelain elephants and China gods.
> JAMES CAWTHORN: Of Taste, 1756

While continental artists were forsaking the orotundities and grandeurs of the Baroque for the charms and elegancies of the Rococo, England entered her Augustan age of pomp and periwigs—the reigns of Anne and George I. But if the spirit of the times was predominantly classical and found its most notable expressions in Pope's *Essay on Man*, Addison's *Cato*, and the products of Lord Burlington's just and noble rules, the period had a lighter side too, and here chinoiserie played a small but persistent part. Chinese legends were put to moralizing use in *The Spectator*; plays and harlequinades on oriental themes attracted large audiences to the theatre; and many a square unsmiling Palladian exterior sheltered a 'Chinee room' with a few frivolous pieces of chinoiserie japanned furniture. As might be expected, however, chinoiserie was not among the most fashionable styles of interior decoration during the years when Lord Burlington and his 'proper priest', William Kent, ruled the polite world. Only in George II's reign did it return to favour, rising to its peak of fashion in the 1750s.

It has often been supposed that the new epidemic of China-mania, which attacked England in the 1740s and 1750s, was blown across the Channel from France but, as we shall see, this is only partly true. French and German porcelain figures were, of course, copied by English factories; some of the japanned furniture made in England, notably the *bombé* commodes, were derived from French models, and chinoiserie prints after Boucher, Huquier, and Pillement were published in London and used by English craftsmen. Otherwise, however, English rococo chinoiserie was an independent growth. The silver produced in London and embossed with chinoiserie motifs, the furniture made in the 'Chinese Chippendale' style and such a room as that at Claydon House have no parallels on the Continent. Moreover, England's most important contribution to the vision of Cathay, the so-called Anglo-Chinese garden, which later spread throughout Europe, was as English as the oaks and beeches with which it was planted.

During the first half of the eighteenth century a few plays and harlequinades helped to sharpen the Londoner's impression of Cathay. Since the production of Settle's *Fairy Queen* in 1692, no Chinamen seem to have strutted the boards of a London play-house until 1716 when Aaron Hill's *The Fatal Vision* was successfully produced at Lincoln's Inn Fields. In his preface, the author blandly declared that 'our distance from, and dark ideas of, the Chinese Nation, and her borders, tempted me to fix my scene in so remote a location. The fable is fictitious and the characters are all imaginary.' This remark, based on a somewhat dubious assumption, was, of course, no more than an excuse for a wildly improbable story about court intrigues worked out against an exotic backcloth. The elaborate absurdity of the plot can be appreciated from the final recognition scene in which the favourite Eunuch reveals herself as the Empress of China and the *jeune premier*, who has headed a revolt against the regime, is discovered to be the long lost son of the Imperial pair. It is hardly surprising that *The Fatal Vision* was said to have owed its success principally to its exotic new sets and costumes.

In 1720 a harlequinade of French extraction, *Arlequin docteur chinois* appeared in London and introduced a new form of entertainment which held the affection of the public for several decades—*Proteus, or Harlequin in China* being produced at Drury Lane as late as 1755. Noverre's ballet, *Les Fêtes chinoises*, on the other hand, which had scored so great a success in Paris and the French provinces, proved a fiasco when Garrick brought it to London in 1755 as *The Chinese Festival*. Noverre himself was engaged at an extravagant fee, new costumes and *décor* were designed by Boquet, the *corps de ballet* was carefully selected and no expenses spared to make the entertainment the most splendid of the season. Its failure was due to anti-French rather than anti-

Chinese sentiments and, despite the king's presence (carefully engineered by Garrick who had wind of the troubles), the first night was interrupted by cries of 'No French dancers!' The subsequent four performances fared still worse and the last ended with the ballerinas fleeing from the stage before a fusilade of rotten apples.

Garrick lost heavily on *The Chinese Festival* which appears to have been the last spectacular chinoiserie entertainment put on the London stage in the eighteenth century (save for Harlequin's final appearance in Cathay: *The Mandarin, or Harlequin Widower* of 1789). After some years of badgering, however, Garrick was persuaded to produce in 1759 Arthur Murphy's *The Orphan of China*, a version of *The Little Orphan of the House of Chao*. This play, which Voltaire had adapted for France and Metastasio for Italy, had not previously appeared on the London stage though it had been done into English some years earlier by William Hatchett who used it as the cover for a violent attack on Sir Robert Walpole. Meanwhile, the original play, as it appeared in Du Halde's repository, had found a staunch admirer in Richard Hurd (later Bishop of Worcester) who compared it not unfavourably with the *Electra* of Sophocles. Murphy's blank verse adaptation was closer to the original than Voltaire's *Orphelin*, though it was given greater intensity of incident and a more dramatic close. Splendidly produced (probably with the sets originally designed for the ill-fated *Chinese Festival*), it enjoyed a popular success and was occasionally revived in subsequent years.

Literary expressions of chinoiserie were by no means confined to the theatre in mid-eighteenth-century England. One of the most curious is the anonymous *Œconomy of Human Life* which was first published in 1750 and frequently re-printed during the next half-century. This remarkably platitudinous treatise composed in stilted metaphoric language by one of Richard Dodsley's grub-street hacks, if not by the publisher himself, seems to have owed its success largely to the preposterous story that the original had been written in 'Thibetan' by 'An ancient Bramin', translated first into Chinese and then from Chinese into English. Concerned with the 'Duties of Man' and the 'Passions of Men and Women', it abounded in sentiments to which every bosom might return an echo and endowed the distant Chinese with the morals and manners of an Anglican deist.

A different note was struck by Thomas Percy who made a serious attempt to study Chinese literature. He discovered and translated (from the French) a long episodic Chinese novel, *Hau Kiou Choaan*. But this genuine Chinese performance aroused scant interest, and even his friend William Shenstone felt bound to tell the author that 'the novel, tho' in some parts not void of Merit, must certainly draw its chief support from its value as a *Curiosity*; or perhaps an agreeable means of conveying to the generality all they *wish* or *want* to know of the Chinese manners and constitution.' Lavishly supplied with factual footnotes, Percy's book presented a none-too-rosy picture of China redeemed only by a sentimental hero and heroine who so closely resemble the characters in a Richardson novel that one is tempted to accuse the translator of tampering with his text. Percy also combed Du Halde's weighty folios for specimens of Chinese to translate into English, the most notable being the long suffering *Little Orphan of the House of Chao* to which he restored as much of the original directness and simplicity as had survived in the first French version. Having completed these works, Percy prudently turned his scholarly attention from the exotic East to the Gothic North (as did also Richard Hurd) and began to collect *The Reliques of Ancient English Poetry*.

The year 1761, in which Percy's *Hau Kiou Choaan* was published, saw the appearance of a still stranger, yet more widely noticed, performance: Turberville Needham's *De Inscriptione quadam Aegiptiaca Taurini Inventa* which, according to *The Annual Register*, triumphed 'in having overturned the high antiquity of the Chinese by proving that they received hieroglyphics from the Egyptians.' This was the penultimate prolusion on the relative antiquity of the Chinese and Egyptian languages, a question which had perplexed the ingenious since the seventeenth century and had precipitated a large number of books and pamphlets. The problem arose out of a search for the original language spoken before the tower of Babel was so unfortunately raised on the plains of Shinar. Without any means of understanding its script, scholars solemnly debated whether this language was, or was not, Chinese. Sir Thomas Browne applied his mind to the question, though with no more success than he had with the Sirens' song; John Webb, the architect and antiquary, published a modest *Historical Essay Endeavouring a Probability That the Language of the Empire of China Is the Primitive Language*; and although the absurd notion was roundly dismissed by Robert Hook, speaking for the newly founded Royal Society, it still found support among several learned writers during the first half of the eighteenth century. In the course of the long debate Egypt had been frequently mentioned and in 1759 Joseph de Guignes, the curator of the French royal collection of oriental manuscripts, produced the startling theory that the Chinese descended from a colony of ancient Egyptians. His suggestion was promptly answered by M. A. Deshauterayes but found some measure of support among the savants. The interest aroused in England by the controversy may be judged from the space given it in such publications as *The Gentleman's Magazine* and *The Annual Register*. The latter organ hopefully announced in 1762 that Needham had said the last word on the subject, but this was premature. Three years later the Royal Society unmasked his treatise as a deliberate imposture and to this pronouncement no answer came. Scholars were now applying their ingenuity to such new problems as the relative merits of Greek and modern wall paintings and the authenticity of Macpherson's *Ossian*.

Devotees of the Chinese cult had been faced with an increasingly strong opposition ever since the early years of the eighteenth century, but not until the 1760s did Gothic Revivalists and Neo-classicists begin to crowd them out of house and library. One of the first and most loquacious of their opponents was Daniel Defoe who seldom let pass an opportunity for damning Chinese arts, manners and religion, and who even consulted the French sinophobes for points to add to his attack. Others, more moderately, confined their criticisms either to the arts or to the politics of the Celestial Empire. Throughout the century, Lord Shaftesbury's classicist case was stated and restated by other writers and men of taste. In the battle of styles which developed and which so strangely anticipated the still fiercer and grander conflict between Goths and Romans of the mid-nineteenth century, morals and aesthetics were often confused. John Baptist Jackson, the brilliant engraver of *chiaroscuro* prints, mercilessly lambasted 'those who chuse the *Chinese* manner' and remarked that they 'ought to admire, in pursuance of that same Taste, the crooked, disproportioned and ugly, in Preference to the strait, regular and beautiful'. Chinese paintings seemed to him so depraved that he found it impossible

> that any Mind, truly form'd, can without Distaste be capable of letting such objects in upon it through the Eye; where the internal senses are well proportioned and just, these monstrous objects of the external must be displeasing and offensive; in that Breast where the Softer Sensations of Humanity are in any particular Degree, a Love of Beauty generally accompanies them, and the approbation of natural Objects is the Proof of these Sensations in an Individual; as the contrary taste is of the ill Formation or Perversion of that mind which approves of preternatural Appearances. There is a close analogy between the

Love of Beauty in external objects, and a mind truly disposed to feeling all the softer and most amiable Sensations.

The shrill note of grinding axes rings clear through this high-minded vituperation and it may be thought that Jackson had been provoked by the public's obstinate preference for Chinese wallpapers to his own hangings decorated with large relief prints of antique statues.

Satire was a better weapon than argument to attack the Chinese rage, and there were satirists in plenty to shoot their barbs at so obvious a target. In the 1750s when the vogue for chinoiserie was at its height, the satirical barrage reached its fiercest and nearly every periodical echoed with jeers at mandarins and pagods. Batista Angeloni, alias John Shebbeare, declared that in one room of every fashionable house 'all the pagods and distorted animals of the east are piled up, and called the beautiful decorations of a chimney-piece; on the sides of the room lions made of porcelain, grinning and mishapen, are placed on brackets of the Chinese taste, in arbours of flowers made in the same ware. . . .' And he averred that 'so excessive is the love of Chinese architecture become, that at present the foxhunters would be sorry to break a leg in pursuing their sport over a gate that was not made in the Eastern fashion of little bits of wood standing in all directions'. An anonymous writer in *The World* suggested that as the French War interfered with the grand tour, young noblemen should be dispatched to Peking to complete their education. Another writer, in *The Connoisseur* of 1755, predicted that 'the Chinese taste, which has already taken possession of our gardens, our buildings and our furniture, will also find a way into our churches; and how elegant must a monument appear, which is erected in the Chinese taste, and embellished with dragons, bells, pagods and mandarins?'

The satirists overstated their case, but amidst their facetiae one may occasionally find a description of a chinoiserie room or garden which rings true. It is, for instance, pleasing to suppose that many a 'very pretty fellow' in mid-eighteenth-century London possessed a dressing-room like that described by 'Mr Town' in *The Connoisseur*: 'a neat little chamber, hung round with Indian paper, and adorned with several little images of pagods and bramins, and vessels of Chelsea china, on which were set various coloured sprigs of artificial flowers. . . . A looking-glass, inclosed in a whimsical frame of Chinese paling, stood upon a japan table, over which was spread a coverlid of the finest chints. I could but observe a number of boxes of different sizes, which were all of them japan, and lay regularly disposed on the table.' An even more highly coloured account of a chinoiserie interior appears in *The Citizen of the World* where Oliver Goldsmith's imaginary Chinaman, Lien Chi Altangi, visits a fancier of Chinese arts.

When the footman informed her grace that I was the gentleman from China, she instantly lifted herself from the couch, while her eyes sparkled with unusual vivacity. 'Bless me! can this be the gentleman that was born so far from home? what an unusual share of *somethingness* in his whole appearance! Lord, how I am charmed with the outlandish cut of his face! how bewitching the exotic breadth of his forehead! I would give the world to see him in his own country dress. Pray turn about, Sir, and let me see you behind. There! there's a travell'd air for you. You that attend there, bring up a plate of beef cut into small pieces; I have a violent passion to see him eat. Pray, Sir, have you got your chop-sticks about you? It will be so pretty to see the meat carried to the mouth with a jerk. Pray speak a little Chinese: I have learned some of the language myself. Lord! have you nothing pretty from China about you; something one does not know what to do with? I have got twenty things from China that are of no use in the world. Look at those jars, they are of the right pea-green; these are the furniture.' 'Dear Madam,' said I, 'these, though they may appear fine to your eyes, are but paltry to a Chinese; but, as they are useful utensils, it is proper that they should have a place in every apartment.' 'Useful! Sir,' replied the lady; 'sure you mistake, they are of no use in the world.'—'What! are they not filled with an infusion of tea as in China?' replied I.—'Quite empty and useless, upon my honour, Sir.' 'Then they are the most clumsy and cumbrous furniture in the world, as nothing is truly elegant but what unites use with beauty.' 'I protest,' says the lady, 'I shall begin to suspect thee of being an actual barbarian. I suppose you hold my two beautiful pagods in contempt.' 'What!' cried I, 'has Fohi spread his gross superstitions here also? Pagods of all kinds are my aversion.' 'A Chinese, a traveller, and want taste! it surprises me. Pray, Sir, examine the beauties of that Chinese temple which you see at the end of the garden. Is there anything in China more beautiful?' 'Where I stand, I see nothing, madam, at the end of the garden, that may not as well be called an Egyptian pyramid as a Chinese temple; for that little building in view is as like one as t'other.' 'What! Sir, is not that a Chinese temple? You must surely be mistaken. Mr Freeze, who designed it, calls it one, and nobody disputes his pretensions to taste.' . . . She took me through several rooms all furnished, as she told me, in the Chinese manner; sprawling dragons, squatting pagods, and clumsy mandarines, were stuck on every shelf: in turning round, one must have used caution not to demolish part of the precarious furniture.

Lien Chi Altangi was a severe critic of English sinophils. 'I am disgusted, O Fum Hoam, even to sickness disgusted. Is it possible to bear the presumption of these islanders, when they presume to instruct me in the ceremonies of China! They lay it down as a maxim, that every person that comes from thence must express himself in metaphor; swear by Allah, rail against wine, and behave and talk and write like a Turk or Persian.' But an ingenious and genuine Chinaman, Tan Chit-qua, who arrived in England shortly afterwards and enjoyed a *succès d'estime* as a modeller of portrait busts, was well content to profit from the foibles of the Westerner. Cunningly he addressed a letter to some ladies of Oxford, couched in the following terms: 'Some time he makee voyage to Oxford, Christ Church will then open his gates to make Chit-qua welcome he no more tinkee go to Canton again; there he find much bisn. as he so well savee art of modelling Heads, thing much wanted among Mandarinmen of that place. Once more tankee fine present. Adios.' No doubt the mandarinmen and their wives were delighted to give 'bisn.' to so engaging an applicant. But even Chit-qua did not fully answer the expectations of China fanciers and Sir William Chambers felt it necessary to transmogrify him into a chinoiserie character (see p. 158).

2 THE MANAGARETH

When Mrs Lybbe Powys visited Bubb Dodington's house, Eastbury, in 1760 she noted that 'the *Managareth* or Chinese bedroom and dressing-room in the attic story is excessively droll and pretty, furnish'd exactly as in China, the bed of an uncommon size, seven feet wide by six long.' This room, one of the many Chinese bedrooms created in mid-eighteenth-century England, vanished long ago, but happily there are a few others that survive together with a sufficiently large number of chinoiserie furnishings to embarrass the student with their riches. Indeed, the number of surviving objects and satirical references to the Chinese taste, combine to show that chinoiserie reached a height of popularity in England in the 1750s which it attained at no other time and in no other country. Despite the jeers of critics, chinoiseries were applied to every type of household furniture and to every kind of ornament from wine-glasses (Pl. 95) to book-bindings (Pl. 97). In the park, fields were fenced with criss-cross Chinese palings, brooks were spanned by delicately arched Chinese bridges, and a wild profusion of exotic little temples sprang up among the oaks and beeches. Flowered and bedragonned mandarin robes were often assumed on festal occasions and Canaletto depicted a group of figures thus attired in one of his English views. Nevertheless, Lady Frances Ludlow caused some stir when she was carried to the 1753 birthday levee in a sedan chair shaped like 'an *Indian house* with horned corners'. Mrs Delany was delighted by this novel extravagance though she regretted that the old-fashioned tassels had not been replaced by silver bells—'the harmony of the bells' would be delightful, she pointed out.

As we have already seen, the chinoiseries of the 1750s were no sudden growth. Chinese rooms exotically lined with painted panels, lacquer, tapestries, painted cloth hangings or wallpaper, were to be found in late seventeenth-century England. Somewhat surprisingly, however, most of these methods of interior decoration went out of fashion in the eighteenth century. Lacquer panelling was very little used—though a lacquer room was created for the German-born Queen Charlotte in Buckingham House in 1762/3—and painted rooms in the Chinese taste seem to have been very rare. Antonio Joli incorporated some views of Chinese architecture, derived from Fischer von Erlach's book, in the series of panels he painted for the hall of Heidegger's house at Richmond—though the room as a whole can hardly be regarded as an example of chinoiserie—and François Clermont enlivened a few ceilings with monkeys of a vaguely oriental appearance. Chinoiserie tapestries were more popular and the Soho factory continued to produce hangings, in the style of those made for Elihu Yale, throughout the first quarter of the century. This factory may also have produced a remarkable set of panels (now in a German collection), representing a coven of wizards at work, coursing the air on dragons, swinging vast bird-cages which entrap little Chinamen, studying the heavens through telescopes and trading in bizarre talismans. The majority of 'Chinese rooms' were, however, hung either with printed linen or with wallpaper. Of the former type none survives intact outside the pages of contemporary diaries, though we may judge of their appearance from fragments of the materials used (Pl. 100). Fortunately many rooms have retained their eighteenth-century Chinese or chinoiserie wallpapers.

The first wallpapers imported from the East were regarded merely as a cheap substitute for calico or chintz whose importation was later banned by act of Parliament. By the early eighteenth century papers of far higher quality were brought to England, and as they were also far more costly they were deemed suitable even for the most grandiose apartment. Indeed, Lady Mary Wortley Montagu, who thought of buying some pieces to decorate her Italian villa, abandoned the idea on discovering that damask would be less expensive.

Although usually called Indian—a term then applied indiscriminately to imports from the Far East—there can be little doubt that such papers were, in fact, Chinese. In 1750 Horace Walpole referred to a drawing-room in the 'Chinese . . . style that I fancied and have been executing at Mr Rigby's in Essex; it has large and fine Indian landscapes, with a black fret round them, and round the whole entablature of the room, and all the ground or hanging is of pink paper.' (The papers imported from China were, of course, designed to satisfy the European market and were much more elaborate than those painted for Chinese houses.)

The most popular type of oriental wallpaper imported into England at this period shows on each piece a tall tree with exotic birds roosting in its branches and, perhaps, a zigzag fence, a small house and a group of Chinamen in the foreground; landscapes of mountainous prospects liberally diversified with buildings and rustics were also in demand. English paper-stainers imitated the former type so expertly that their hangings, notably a set formerly in a house at Wotton-under-Edge (Pl. 83), should be classed as pseudo-Chinese rather than chinoiserie.

Specimens of this kind of paper were also exported to North America where they appear to have enjoyed some success. In 1738 Thomas Hancock of Boston wrote to a stationer in London enclosing a pattern of a paper he had recently seen and ordered enough to line two rooms.

> 'The pattern is all that is left of a Room Lately Come over here, and it takes much in the Town', he remarked, 'Therefore desire you by all means to get mine well Done and as Cheap as Possible, and if they can make it more beautiful by adding more Birds flying here and there, with some Landskips at the Bottom, Should like it well. . . . About three or four years ago, my friend Francis Wilks, Esq., had a hanging Done in the Same manner but much handsomer, Sent over here by Mr. Sam Waldon of this place, made by one Dunbar of Aldermanbury. . . . In the other parts of these Hangings are Great Variety of Different Sorts of Birds, Peacocks, Macoys, Squirril, Monkys, Fruit and Flowers, &c.'

It is characteristic of the age that 'More birds flying here and there' should be demanded. The relative simplicity of Chinese designs rarely satisfied the chinoiserie fancier and English paper-stainers therefore manufactured wallpapers crowded with oriental motifs, producing an effect strikingly different from those printed in China. In the Victoria and Albert Museum there are several examples: a chocolate-and-cream flock paper of the 1720s decorated with somewhat crudely rendered eastern buildings, exotic trees, birds, and oriental figures; and a panel of a Chinaman mounted on a camel surrounded by gigantic flowering plants, which is still rococo in style though it dates from about 1770.

The rooms in which India papers or English chinoiserie papers were hung, usually a bedroom or dressing-room, were often graced with other fittings in the Chinese taste. In 1746 Mrs Delany had her dressing-room 'hung with the finest Indian paper of flowers and *all sorts of birds* . . . the ceilings are all orna-mented in the Indian taste, the frames of the glass and all the furnishings of the room are well suited; the bedchamber is also hung with Indian paper on a gold ground, and the bed is *Indian work* of silks and gold on white satin'. She may later have learned a wrinkle from her patient correspondent and friend, Mrs Vesey who, she tells us, 'had a whim to have Indian figures and flowers cut out and oiled, to be transparent, and pasted in her dressing-room window in imitation of painting on glass, and it has a very good effect'. Not to be out-done by these lesser blues, Mrs Montagu boasted a dressing-room 'like the Temple of an Indian god . . . the very curtains are Chinese pictures on gauze, and the chairs, the Indian fan-sticks with cushions of Japan satin painted'.

Many another room was adorned with furnishings well suited to the exotic background of India papers. Pier glasses placed between the windows were set within rank growths of rococo tendrils which provided convenient perches for ho-ho birds. Compositions of dragons and luxuriant foliage replaced the classi-cal pediments on door cases. Chimney-pieces were composed of rococo scrolls lapping round the fireplace and frothing up to the central crest which supported a little pagoda-roofed building or a group of chinoiserie figures. Many of the rooms which contained these delightful furnishings have, alas, been dismantled, but the most elaborate and fantastic of all survives intact, in Claydon House, Buckinghamshire.

The various rooms of Claydon House present a strange but by no means unappealing contrast between classical restraint and rococo eccentricity, be-tween Palladianism and chinoiserie. In the entrance hall a battle of styles is in progress: from a classically correct cornice, medallion portraits frown down on niches vibrant with shell-shaped curves, while exotic birds preen themselves on top of Ionic pilasters. Upstairs, in the Chinese room, rococo wins a resounding victory, though one of its last for this extraordinary fantasy was created in the late 1760s when taste was veering away from such frivolities. The room is the work of a Mr Lightfoot, carpenter, building contractor and architect of whom Sir Thomas Robinson remarked that he had 'no small spice of madness in his composition'. Above each door there is a pagoda motif fenced with fretted palings and supported by term figures of mandarins whose necks emerge from eddying scrolls. Similar inscrutable oriental faces peer out from amid the flowers and dripping icicles of the chimney-piece. But the doors and chimney-pieces seem relatively restrained beside the fantastic and exuberant tea-alcove built out from one wall. Liberally hung with bells, bursting with flowers, encrusted with shells and scrolls, and painted on its few plain surfaces with a delicate pattern of lattice work, this astonishing extravaganza has a curiously sub-marine appearance, as if it were a coral temple built far beneath the sunless sea for some Cathaian Neptune (Pl. 87).

The Chinese room at Claydon is the most elaborate surviving example of English rococo chinoiserie, yet it can hardly be compared with the continental manifestations of the cult—such elegancies as the porcelain room at Capodimonte or Giandomenico Tiepolo's frescoed room at Vicenza (Pl. III and 79). Lacking any sense of general design, it appears to have been conceived as a series of independent elements squeezed uncomfortably into too small a rectangular box. Moreover, the execution, especially of the carved figures, is somewhat gauche. Yet, as we shall see from their furniture, English craftsmen were capable of fine work and carved some of the most elegant chinoiserie fantasies of the rococo period. But to trace the development of English chinoiserie furniture we must return to the early years of the century.

In late seventeenth-century England, lacquer furniture had enjoyed a wide popularity which lasted into the reign of George I. Most of the japan produced in the first quarter of the century differed little in style from that of the previous two decades and a barometer in the Science Museum, South Kensington, for instance, might well be dated in the 1680s were it not for an inscription recording that it was made in 1719. At this period japan was especially popular for the decoration of long-case clocks which enjoyed fame throughout Europe. Tables, chairs, and cupboards in the Queen Anne and early Georgian styles were often painted with chinoiseries on a japanned ground. Red-and-black japanned card-tables with claw-and-ball or cabriole legs seem also to have been popular. Most fashionable of all were the cabinets and bureaux which now took the place of the seventeenth-century mounted lacquer chests. But although these splendid pieces of furniture were liberally sprinkled with bizarre figures, flowers and animals, their shapes showed no concessions to an exotic taste and the desks were sometimes crowned with pedimented tops of which the most

PLATE III   The porcelain room at Capodimonte, 1757-1759

exacting neo-Palladian might have approved. The japanning itself is often of such high quality that connoisseurs have had difficulty in determining whether it is English or oriental 'export' lacquer.

The best japanning was, of course, produced by cabinet-makers, but amateurs were still hard at work, mixing their varnishes according to Stalker and Parker's receipts and applying them to a variety of suitable and unsuitable objects. 'Lady Sun. is very busy about japanning', wrote Mrs Delany in 1729, and later that year recorded that 'everybody is mad about japan work; I hope to be a dab at it.' For the benefit of such enthusiasts more books on the craft were published, such as *The Method of Learning to draw in perspective. . . . Likewise a new and Curious method of Japanning . . . so as to imitate China and to make black or gilt Japan-ware as Beautiful and Light as any brought from the East Indies,* which appeared in 1732 with a dedication to Lady Walpole, the Prime Minister's wife. Lady Walpole was herself a japanner and a specimen of her handiwork was preserved by her son at Strawberry Hill. A later manual, *The Ladies' Amusement, or the whole art of Japanning made easy,* published in about 1760 advised its readers of the 'liberties [that] may be taken' with Chinese or Indian designs, 'for in these is often seen a Butterfly supporting an Elephant, or things equally absurd.'

Lacquer seems to have slipped out of fashion in the later 1730s to return shortly before 1750 in a somewhat different form. Elegant Louis XV commodes with gently curving *bombé* fronts had meantime crossed the Channel and the high rococo style began to affect our cabinet-makers. Furniture in the French *goût* was often veneered with oriental lacquer, English japan or a combination of the two materials (Pl. 93). On these pieces, as on all previous examples of lacquer furniture, the oriental motifs were confined to the surface decoration. But such half-measures were insufficiently exotic to meet the demands of English chinoiserie fanciers for whose benefit furniture in the so-called 'Chinese Chippendale' style was now invented—square and angular in outline with, perhaps, a pagoda roof or two and certainly some fretwork after the fashion of the fences to be discerned on Chinese screens and wallpapers. This furniture was not copied from Chinese prototypes. Nor was it in all probability the invention of Thomas Chippendale though he included several prints of such furniture in his *Gentleman and Cabinet-Maker's Director* of 1754, by when this style had already become popular.

In 1749, whilst staying at Tunbridge Wells, Mrs Montagu—the Queen of the Blues—fell to musing, as was her wont, on the ephemeral nature of pleasures and fashions. Describing how quickly the delights of the spa may pall she told one of her correspondents: 'Thus has it happened in furniture; sick of Grecian elegance and symmetry, or Gothic grandeur and magnificence, we must all seek the barbarous gaudy *goût* of the Chinese'. But even queens are subject to changes in taste and she did not fail to add, 'You will wonder I should condemn the taste I have complied with, but in trifles I shall always conform to fashion'. Next year she had so far conformed to fashion as to boast an 'Indian' dressing-room, 'lined with painted paper of Pekin and furnished with the choicest moveables of China', as Mme du Boccage noted. And in 1752 she had a larger room fitted up in the Chinese taste by Mr, probably William, Linnell, whose charges she found excessive. 'Mr Linnell brought me his bill the morning I left town', she told her mentor Gilbert West, 'and I think I will send you a copy of it as a proper warning to Mrs West. . . . Adieu Brocade, Embroidery, and lace, and even the cheaper vanities of lutestring and blonde'. Two pieces of this expensive furniture can be identified with a japanned cabinet and writing-table now at Came House, Dorset. Both are of very high quality; the former has a pair of doors with lattice grilles in front, the latter has lattice reliefs on the doors and similar decorations on the legs and stretcher (Pl. 89). No similar examples of chinoiserie furniture are known, but the style of these two pieces is not far removed from designs published in Chippendale's *Director* two years after they were made.

The fretted work used on Mrs Montagu's furniture was thought to be deliciously Chinese. It had already appeared on garden fences and pavilions—as early as 1702 to judge from a drawing of that year in the Bodleian library—and was soon to spread throughout the country and find its way onto bookcases, cabinets and cupboards, the backs of chairs and the cases of clocks, writing-tables and gaming-tables, beds, library steps, fire grates, and window balconies. These strange palings even forced their way into church and at St Clement's, Old Romney, the altar rails are in this style. Crossing the Atlantic they found favour in the American colonies and were used for chairs and as staircase banisters in several New England homes (in a house at Battersea, Virginia, for example, and Bohemia, Cecil County, Maryland). In England itself they became the hallmark of the 'Chinese Chippendale' style, and as such they have suffered revival in the present century.

Many of the designs in Chippendale's *Director*—especially for standing shelves, fire-screens, chairs, and settees—are enriched with intricate lattice work, and several pieces of furniture which closely correspond with them have survived (Pl. 90, 92 and Fig. 7). But this work, and also the *New Book of Chinese*

Fig. 7 Three chairs in the Chinese taste, from an engraving in Thomas Chippendale: *Gentleman and Cabinet-Maker's Director*, London, 1754

Designs Calculated to Improve the Present Taste by Edwards and Darly, included designs for chinoiserie furniture in a strikingly different style—less angular in outline and more in harmony with the French rococo. They were called 'carvers' pieces', on account of the skill needed to produce them, and include 'sophas' and beds with elaborate canopies guarded by dragons and mandarins, fantastic brackets, girandoles, and looking-glass frames surrounded by sprigs of floral ornament on which birds and pagods perch. A few of these difficult designs were realized, notably those for mirror frames, but whether the surviving examples were made in Chippendale's workshop or merely copied from the *Director* it is seldom possible to say. The furnishings of a famous Chinese bedroom at Badminton House, now in the Victoria and Albert Museum, correspond closely with Chippendale's designs and since they were made in about 1750, before the publication of the *Director*, it seems likely that they were supplied by Thomas Chippendale (Pl. 91). Designs for furniture in a more frenchified *rocaille* style were included in the pattern books published by Thomas Johnson between 1755 and 1758, but these incorporate fewer specifically oriental elements.

Large screens, which seldom figure in the pattern books, maintained their

popularity throughout the first half of the eighteenth century, as is hardly surprising in an age of draughty rooms. Those made of painted or incised Coromandel lacquer were, of course, the most desirable, but they were expensive
luxuries which none but the wealthiest could afford. Cheaper substitutes were
therefore made and frequently decorated in the Chinese taste. Some were
covered with painted paper or fabric similar to wallpaper, others with japanned
leather. Leather screens and painted leather hangings seem to have enjoyed a
wide vogue and were made in London for export as well as the home market.
They were usually decorated with an assortment of oriental motifs derived
from lacquer or wallpaper and crowded together in a slightly uncomfortable
manner. (Similar screens appear to have been made in Holland.)

Among the smaller chinoiserie objects produced in England during the
rococo period, those in silver are by far the most interesting since they appear
to have been peculiar to this country. They also reveal a high level of technical
accomplishment. Whether vast stores of French chinoiserie silver were melted
down at the time of the Revolution we cannot tell but very little has survived
(the most notable piece is a kettle in the form of a Chinaman, by François-
Thomas Germain in the National Museum, Lisbon), and only a few specimens
of Italian silver in this style are known (except for the filigree ornaments made
at Genoa). Although English silversmiths had engraved their wares with somewhat uncouth chinoiserie motifs in the late seventeenth century, the fashion
had died out before 1700. Chinoiseries of the new rococo variety were first
applied to English silver only in the 1740s. One of the earliest examples is a
pair of tea-caddies made in 1744 by the French-born but English-trained master-
craftsman, Paul de Lamerie. Decorated with bats' wings, mandarin heads which
grin out from the corners and exquisitely wrought scenes of tea cultivation,
these caddies reveal a perfect understanding of the French rococo style (Pl. 86).
Other examples of silver chinoiseries of the 1740s are crude in comparison with
Lamerie's caddies. The great period of English chinoiserie silver began in the
early 1750s and lasted for about two decades. During these years salvers and
epergnes and especially the impedimenta of the tea-table—caddies, sugar bowls,
kettles, and teapots—were frequently enriched with chinoiserie decorations.
Epergnes were covered by pagoda roofs, hung round by little bells and crowned
by pineapples, while pagods straddled the curved brackets which held the baskets
of sweet-meats. Tea-kettles, urns and coffee-pots were embossed with scenes of
chinoiserie life and the knobs on their lids were formed like little squatting

Chinamen (Pl. 98 and 99). The greatest variety of patterns and decorations is displayed on tea-caddies: some are square, others pear-shaped, adorned with strange mixtures of red Indian and Chinese motifs, while many are formed like little temples or pavilions with bells jangling from their horned eaves (Pl. 96). Most of the decorations—Chinese tea-parties, musical gatherings, and picnics—show the influence of French engravings, especially those after Pillement, but the idea of applying them to silver appears to have been a whim of the English.

A cheaper substitute for silver was provided by japanned metal—the so-called Pontypool ware—which was given a fashionable appearance by chinoiserie decorations. The discovery of a substance capable of application under heat to metals was made in about 1660 by Thomas Allgood who founded a factory at Pontypool, Monmouthshire, which was carried on and developed by his son. From here the craft spread to Birmingham and to London. By the mid-eighteenth century, a wide range of Pontypool household wares was being produced, notably trays, tea-caddies, and tea-kettles. Most of the objects produced at Pontypool itself were decorated with Chinese figures and landscapes in gold on a lustrous black background. But at Birmingham a greater range of colours and styles was employed. Here a poor writing-master, John Baskerville, set out to supply 'goods painted and japanned as they had never been painted and japanned before'. Obtaining a patent in 1742 he made japanned tin plates in a 'fine flowing mahogany colour, a black no way inferior to that of the most perfect Indian goods, or an imitation of tortoiseshell' to be applied as a veneer to furniture. He also produced an abundance of smaller articles, trays, candlesticks, and boxes. It is interesting to note that the profits from this business were sufficient to subsidise Baskerville's more famous printing works.

The vogue for chinoiserie objects in the rococo style persisted in England until late in the eighteenth century. But after the 1750s the sinophils were faced with fierce opposition not only from classical purists but also from devotees of the Gothic Revival. An account of the relations between the two cults sheds some light on the eighteenth-century English vision of Cathay. Early in the century chinoiserie was well established in the house while in the garden a new vogue appeared for buildings in the Gothic taste. Then, with the importation of the rococo from France, the two styles became confused. In 1754 a critic in *The World* remarked: 'It has not escaped your notice how much of late we are improved in architecture; not merely by the adoption of what we call Chinese, nor by the restoration of what we call Gothic; but by a happy mixture of both.'

CHAPTER VI

The Anglo-Chinese Garden

I SHARAWADGI

Our farms and seats begin
To match the boasted villas of Pekin;
On every hill a spire-crowned temple swells,
Hung round with serpents, and a fringe of bells;
Junks and balons along our waters sail,
With each a gilded cockboat at its tail.

JAMES CAWTHORN, 1756

Writing to a friend in 1763 about 'our skill in gardening or rather laying out grounds', Thomas Gray remarked: 'It is not forty years since the art was born among us; and it is sure, that there was nothing in Europe like it, and as sure that we then had no information on this head from China.' Gray was here contesting a widely held belief that the origins of the English landscape park, which acquired abroad the name of *le jardin anglo-chinois*, lay in the distant and flowery realm of China. The same belief persists among many sinologues today. The Chinese had, of course, laid out irregularly planned gardens, notably the great landscape park, Yüan-Ming-Yüan, around the Imperial Palace at Peking, long before the European garden had escaped from the walls which surrounded the trim symmetrical beds of the medieval pleasance. But only the very haziest notions of the art of Chinese gardening were current in Europe when the first English landscape parks were created, and no pictorial representation of Yüan Ming Yüan appears to have reached Europe before the 1760s, though its irregular lay-out was known from travellers' descriptions.

English eighteenth-century gardens, with their tumbling cascades, wide lakes, neat clumps of trees and mysterious 'awful' woods owed more to the landscapes of Salvator Rosa and Claude than to the artfully contrived scenes of Yüan Ming Yüan. Only certain buildings—a brightly painted chinoiserie temple or a fretwork bridge spanning a brook whose waters were brushed by the boughs of a weeping willow—called up the vision of Cathay. (Very few of the brilliantly coloured Chinese flowering plants, which are now so familiar—camellias, magnolias, azaleas, rhododendrons, wisteria, anemone japonica, double Chinese roses—had as yet reached Europe.) Why then did so many eighteenth-century writers believe that the English landscape garden originated in China; and how far, if at all, was it an expression of chinoiserie? To answer these questions we must consider very briefly the early history of the landscaped park and retrace our steps from the age of 'Capability' Brown's clumps, hahas and shaven lawns to an earlier and more formal period of straight avenues, knot gardens, canals, and 'trees cut like statues, statues thick as trees'.

Before the topiary chessmen in many an English garden had grown to maturity, before the quincunx had darkened and the espaliers met, a whisper of criticism at this manhandling of nature sped across the parterre and echoed down the pleached alley. It is hardly surprising that a feeling of discontent with the formal garden should have originated in England where poets had for long been celebrating the beauties of nature unshackled and unadorned, where Shakespeare had sketched the gentle wildness of the Forest of Arden and where Milton had described Eden as a landscape park *avant la lettre*:

> Thus was this place,
> A happy rural seat of various view;
> Groves whose Trees wept odorous Gumms and Balme . . .
> Betwixt them Lawns, or level Downs, and Flocks
> Grasing the tender herb, were interpos'd,
> Of palmie hilloc, or the flourie lap
> Of some irriguous Valley spread her store,
> Flours of all hue, and without Thorn the Rose:
> Another side, umbrageous Grots and Caves
> Of coole recess, o'er which the mantling Vine
> Layes forth her purple Grape, and gently creeps
> Luxuriant, mean while murmuring waters fall
> Down the slope hills, disperst, or in the Lake,
> That to the fringed Bank with Myrtle crownd,
> Her crystal mirror holds, unite their streams.

The first audible—albeit somewhat muted—note of dissatisfaction with formal gardens, in the work of a theorist, appeared in Sir William Temple's Essay on *The Gardens of Epicurus* published in 1685. 'Among us', he wrote,

> the beauty of Buildings and Planting is placed chiefly in some Proportions, Symmetries, or Uniformities; our walks and our trees ranged so as they answer one another, and at exact Distances. The Chinese scorn this way of planting

. . . their imagination is employed in contriving Figures where the Beautys shall be great, and strike the eye, without any order of Disposition of parts, that shall be commonly or easily observed. . . . We have hardly any notion of this sort of Beauty. . . . Tho' there may be more Honour if they succeed well, yet there is more dishonour if they fail, and 'tis 20 to 1 they will, whereas in regular figures, 'tis hard to make any great and remarkable faults. . . . The Chinese have a particular word to express [this studied beauty of irregularity]— Sharawadgi.

Sharawadgi—an exotic word, once thought to have been an invention of Temple, derives either from the Chinese *sa-ro-(k)wai-chi*, which signifies graceful disorder, or, from the Japanese *sorawaji* 'not being regular'. Temple presumably picked it up during his residence as ambassador at the Hague where he could have met several far-eastern travellers. From them he may also have obtained some account of Chinese gardening to amplify the tantalizingly brief description of Yüan Ming Yüan in Nieuhoff's *Embassy*: 'If I should relate of all the other Artificial Ornaments, as of Gardens, Wildernesses, Pools, and other particulars which adorn this court, I should far exceed the bounds of what I intend, and perhaps to some of belief.' Whatever notions Temple obtained of Chinese gardens and wildernesses from these sources, he probably enlarged them by peering at lacquer screens and porcelain plates which often depicted Chinamen enjoying the delights of rural life among groves of irregularly planted trees. And in this way the idea of irregular gardens came to be associated with the Chinese in the English mind and Sharawadgi lodged there as a part, though unfortunately never a very important part, of the eighteenth-century vocabulary.

Early in the eighteenth century the irregular theme was taken up by two writers, Lord Shaftesbury and Addison. A fierce sinophobe, Shaftesbury felt no need to justify with Chinese precedents his admiration of wild nature 'where neither Art, nor the Conceit or Caprice of Man has spoil'd [her] genuine order by breaking upon [her] primitive state'. He even enthused—in so far as an Augustan philosopher could enthuse—on 'the verdure of the Field . . . the rude rocks, the mossy caverns . . . and broken Falls of Water', which were soon to form the essential features of the landscape park.

Addison, on the other hand, expressed his dissatisfaction with the formal garden by calling in the Chinese. In an essay of 1712 he declared that

Writers who have given us an account of China, tell us the inhabitants of that country laugh at the plantations of Europeans, which are laid out by the rule of line; because, they say, any one may place trees in equal rows and uniform figures. They choose rather to show a genius in works of this nature, and therefore always conceal the art by which they direct themselves. They have a word, it seems, in their language by which they express the particular beauty of a plantation that strikes the imagination at first sight, without discovering what it is that makes so agreeable an effect.

With greater self-confidence, he then issued into an attack on topiary work, modestly conceding that 'I do not know whether I am singular in my opinion, but, for my part, I would rather look upon a tree in all its luxuriance and diffusion of boughs and branches, than when it is thus cut and trimmed into a mathematical figure'. Addison was never a very original thinker, nor was *The Spectator* ever a forum for *avant-garde* ideas, so there can be little doubt that these remarks were calculated to fall on sympathetic ears. He had clearly read his Temple—indeed, he plagiarizes him—and he may have perused some travel literature, but it is significant that he made use of the Chinese here in much the same flippant way as in the oriental fables which he and Steele wrote to satirize contemporary manners. Already the days of the formal garden were numbered; the Earl of Carlisle had deviated from strict regularity in his plantations at Castle Howard; Pope was soon to apply his lash to the ordered lay-out of Timon's park; and within a decade Kent had 'leaped over the fence, and saw all nature was a garden'.

The first great landscape gardens laid out in England developed naturally from the semi-formal garden which, in its turn, had derived from the mid-seventeenth-century formal garden, and they had nothing Chinese about them. As we have already seen, very little was known about the Chinese garden in the early eighteenth century save that it was planted irregularly, a fact that was stated merely as a precedent for irregular plantations in England. But another precedent was to hand. Robert Castell in his publication on *The Villas of the Ancients*, which appeared under Lord Burlington's aegis in 1728, fathered the landscape garden upon the Romans. In the gardens of Pliny's villa, he declared, 'hills, rocks, cascades, rivulets, woods and buildings, etc. . . . were possibly thrown into such a disorder as to have pleased the eye from several views, like so many beautiful landskips'. To an eighteenth-century eye the topography of Pliny's park, of Horace's Sabine Farm or of Cicero's Tusculanum, were to be discerned in the paintings of Claude Lorrain, Gaspard (rather than Nicolas) Poussin, Francesco Albani, and even Salvator Rosa. Scenes in the English park were therefore intended to conjure up reminiscences not of porcelain plates and lacquer cabinets but of such landscapes as

> Lorrain light touch'd with softening hue
> Or savage Rosa dash'd or learned Poussin drew.

At Bowood, for instance, a cascade was modelled exactly on a painting by Gaspard Poussin. Nevertheless, the belief persisted in many circles that the Chinese practised a similar art of gardening. The Prince de Ligne had no difficulty in reconciling the two origins. 'Horace nous a tracé un jardin anglais', he wrote in his *Coup d'œil sur Belœil*, '*quo pinus ingens . . .* etc. est la meilleure description, la plus douce, la plus riante'. And in the very next sentence he remarked: 'Quand je dis jardin anglais qu'on se souvienne que c'est toujours affaire de convention, car c'est plutôt jardin chinois'.

Believers in the oriental origins of landscape gardening must have received a rude shock from Du Halde's voluminous *General History of China* (translated into English in 1736), which states: 'They cultivate their Kitchen gardens, for the Chinese are far from preferring the Agreeable to the Useful: for they seldom make use of their land for superfluous things, such as making fine gardens, cultivating flowers, or making Alleys, believing it more for the public Good, and what is still nearer, their private Benefit, that every Place should be sown in order to produce useful things'. But eighteenth-century sinophils found little difficulty in ignoring such unpleasant truths—when E. C. Dilly made selections from Du Halde for *The Chinese Traveller* (1775) he omitted this statement and substituted Chambers's more imaginative account of Chinese gardening (see p. 157)—and soon they were able to read Père Attiret's more palatable, wholly enthusiastic, description of the Imperial gardens, Yüan Ming Yüan, which appeared in English in 1749. Attiret stressed the vast scale of this park which enclosed a whole village besides a multitude of houses and pavilions nestling among its valleys and decorating the islands of its several lakes. He also noted that it was irregular, that there were no straight avenues and alleys but twisting walks, and that the very bridges 'generally wind about and serpentine'. This passage provoked Horace Walpole to remark that Chinese gardens

> are as whimsically irregular as European gardens are formally uniform, and unvaried—but with regard to nature, it seems as much avoided as in the squares and oblongs and straight lines of our ancestors. . . . Even their bridges must not be strait—they serpentize as much as the rivulets, and are sometimes so

long as to be furnished with resting-places, and begin and end with triumphal arches. Methinks a strait canal is as rational at least as a meandering bridge.

No illustrations of Yüan Ming Yüan were published in Europe until the 1770s when Georges Louis Le Rouge devoted three *cahiers* of his *Détails de nouveaux jardins à la mode 'jardins anglo-chinois'* to a series of drawings sent from Peking by the Jesuits. As yet, very few Chinese plants had appeared in Europe and readers of Attiret were therefore to be excused if they imagined the woods of the Imperial gardens to be composed of oaks, beeches, and laurels. If they wished to believe that Chinese and English landscape parks were similar in appearance, they could obtain further evidence from other travel writers, including Marco Polo who described the beauties of Kin-Sai, that 'Celestial City' where there were gardens with trees of the largest size growing down to the edge of the lake and including 'shady recesses where men might indulge themselves all day in the company of their women'.

Thus the legend grew of spacious landscape gardens strewn as thickly over the Celestial Empire as over Yorkshire and Wiltshire. Amateurs of gardening would have been astonished to learn that the Imperial park was almost unique in China and that the gardens of the mandarins were, by English standards, no more than suburban plots. They would have been dismayed at the symbolical rather than sentimental importance attached to the various parts of a garden in China. And such lovers of the 'amiable simplicity of unadorned nature' as Pope and Addison would have been horrified at the Chinese practice of torturing trees into the forms of animals—an instance of barbarity no better than topiary.

Not until the nineteenth century, when China's gates were forced, did the truth about her gardens leak out. The description of a mandarin's garden visited by the botanist Robert Fortune in 1843 (few changes in the style of gardening are likely to have been wrought within the space of a century in China) provides a striking contrast with the spacious lawns and lakes of an English landscape park.

Amongst the Mandarins' gardens, in the city of Ning-po, there is one in particular which is generally visited by strangers, and is much admired. . . . This old gentleman has the different parts of his house joined together by rude-looking caverns, and what at first sight appears to be a subterraneous passage, leading from room to room, through which the visitor passes to the garden which lies behind the house. The small courts of which a glimpse is caught in passing through, are fitted up with this rockwork; dwarf trees are planted here and there in various places, and creepers hang down naturally and gracefully until their ends touch the little ponds of water which are always placed in front of the rockwork. These small places being passed, we are again led through passages like those already noticed, when the garden, with its dwarf trees, vases, rockwork, ornamental windows, and beautiful flowering shrubs, is suddenly opened to the view. It must be understood, however, that all which I have now described is very limited in extent, but the most is made of it by windings and glimpses through rockwork, and arches in the walls, as well as by hiding the boundary with a mass of shrubs and trees. Here old Dr. Chang—I believe that was his name—was spending the evening of his days in peaceful retirement.

Old Dr Chang's modest demesne is a far cry indeed from Shugborough or Stowe. English gardeners may have adopted the principles of sharawadgi but the results were remarkably unlike Chinese gardens. However, the theory that the English garden owed its informal plan to Chinese inspiration received some adventitious support from the fact that chinoiserie buildings were sometimes included among its delights. But these garden pagodas, fishing houses, and bridges in the Chinese taste merely formed part of a varied assortment of eye-catchers and were usually outnumbered by classical temples, crumbling Gothic ruins and rude hermitages. And it is interesting to note that in France and Germany they were frequently set in formal gardens—at Potsdam, for example, the *chinesisches Haus* was originally surrounded by a Dutch garden which only gave place to the present *englischer Garten* at the end of the eighteenth century.

Though these chinoiserie buildings were merely incidental to the English park, it should be added that they and their immediate surroundings were sometimes arranged to present, as it were, a chinoiserie vignette in the otherwise very un-Chinese landscape garden. They might be planted at the edge of a lake, for example, or on an island connected with the mainland by a Chinese bridge, so that they could be seen in isolation and the more readily provoke a *frisson* of exotic delight. As gaily bizarre and prettily coloured as fretted wood, *papier maché*, and paint could make them, they would often introduce a note of porcelain brilliance into landscapes which were otherwise intended to recall the rich browns and dark greens of thickly varnished Italian paintings. Towards the end of the century they were sometimes surrounded by the flowering shrubs which had recently been imported from China itself: but even before these plants were available, the Chinese fishing house standing beside a weeping willow on the edge of a small lake, with its florid paintwork reflected in the water, may well have served to summon up a vision of Cathay.

Writing to John Chute in 1753, Horace Walpole remarked that at Wroxton 'there are several paltry Chinese buildings and bridges which have the merit or demerit of being the progenitors of a very numerous race all over the kingdom: at least they were of the very first'. Unfortunately, the historian of English gardening failed to mention when they were built, though we may assume that they date from the mid-1740s when Sanderson Miller designed a Gothic rotunda for the same park.

Apart from a little arbour with a fretted railing of vaguely Chinese design which appears in a drawing of the park at Durdans, dated 1702, the earliest recorded English chinoiserie garden building was the House of Confucius at

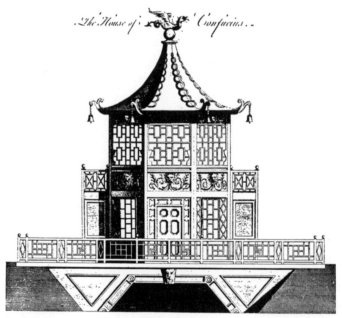

Fig. 8   The House of Confucius at Kew, built *c.* 1745 to the design of J. Goupy

Kew, erected to the design of Joseph Goupy the fan painter in the 1740s. An octagonal structure of two storeys elaborately enriched with lattice work, it stood at the end of a lake. On the ground floor, two closets flanked a larger room, while the upper storey was given up to a saloon which commanded a pleasant prospect over the water and gardens. According to Sir William Chambers, the walls and ceilings were painted with grotesque ornaments and 'little historical subjects relating to Confucius, with several transactions of the Christian missions in China. The sofa and chairs were, I believe, designed by Mr Kent, and the seats and backs were covered by tapestries of the Gobelins.' Chambers included an illustration (Fig. 8) and an account of the pavilion in his book of designs for Kew, presumably to demonstrate the superiority of his own, more 'correct' efforts, in the same style.

Another chinoiserie building dating from the first half of the century has fortunately survived, and has recently been restored, at Shugborough Park, Staffordshire. It was probably erected in about 1747, soon after Commodore Anson, the brother of Thomas Anson who owned the estate, returned from a voyage round the world during which he put in at Canton. Contemporaries said that his Chinese house was 'a true pattern of the architecture of that nation, not a mongrel invention of British carpenters, taken in the country by the skilful pencil of Sir Peircy Brett'. The building originally stood on a lake island, connected with the land by a fretted bridge, but now the waters have receded. A square pavilion with a concave roof and wide-spreading eaves, it was painted on the outside with a fret pattern in pale green against a pink ground; and it may well have been copied from some Chinese building which Anson inspected during his visit to Canton (Pl. 102). But the interior, which has been partly dismantled, was as delightful a specimen of mongrel chinoiserie as ever appeared in England (Pl. 88). The stucco ceiling, now transferred to the main house, is in an elegant rococo style; and an alcove is separated from the main part of the room by a delicate triple ogee-arched screen which might appear Gothic were it not adorned with plaster monkeys holding birds on strings. The whole room was gaily painted in red, pale green, and gold and furnished with Chinese pictures and painted mirrors in delicate pagoda-topped frames (Pl. 94). A particular interest attaches to this house since it was connected with a traveller who helped to destroy the legend that eighteenth-century China was a philosopher's paradise (see p. 27). One of the many eulogists who described the delights of Shugborough in too easy couplets remarked of it:

> Here mayst thou oft regale in Leric Bower,
> Secure from Mandarin's despotic power . . .
> Safe from their servile yoke their arts command
> And Grecian domes erect in Freedom's land.

By 1750 the fashion for chinoiserie buildings was sufficiently widespread to encourage the enterprising William Halfpenny—alias Michael Hoare—to begin publishing a series of *New Designs for Chinese Temples*, and when the fourth part of this work had been issued, in 1752, to produce a further volume of designs of *Chinese and Gothic Architecture properly ornamented*. These neat little books contained a multitude of designs for garden ornaments—palings, bridges, 'A Banqueting House in the Chinese taste' which 'may be executed in a good manner for about £350', a Chinese alcove seat facing four ways at £170, 'a Temple partly in the Chinese taste' and partly in the Gothic, greenhouses in the same style, an obelisk in the Chinese taste and, for the less extravagant, a 'terminary seat in the Chinese taste' which might be 'genteely completed for £45' (Fig. 9). Other draughtsmen, including Edwards and Darly (1754), Edward Oakley and Charles Over (1758) and William Wright (1767) followed Halfpenny's lead in providing designs for chinoiserie buildings. While Paul Decker produced a volume of drawings of *Chinese architecture, Civil and Ornamental, adapted to this Climate* which were so elaborate that one wonders if they were not intended for the use of painters rather than builders and joiners.

Fretwork, bells and dragons played an important part in these delightful, flimsy buildings, none of which has survived. All were elegant and amusing, brightly coloured and delicately enriched, and none, of course, bore much resemblance to a genuine Chinese house. The best description of them comes from a hostile critic, Robert Morris, who remarked that the principles of 'the (improperly called) *Chinese Taste* . . . are a good choice of *Chains* and *Bells* and different colours of Paint. As to the *Serpents*, *Dragons*, and Monkeys &ca. they like the rest of the Beauties may be cut in paper and pasted on anywhere, or in any manner; a few *Laths* nailed across each other, and made Black, Red, Blue, Yellow or any other Colour, or mix'd with any sort of Chequer Work, or impropriety of Ornament, completes the whole.' And he concluded his attack with an amusing advertisement for *A Treatise on Country Five Barr'd Gates. Stiles and Wickets, elegant Pig-styes, beautiful Henhouses and delightful Cow Cribs . . . according to the* TURKISH *and* PERSIAN *manner; a Work never (till now) attempted.*

Before he had become the doyen of the Gothic Revivalists, Horace Walpole permitted himself an occasional chinoiserie folly. In 1750 he told Sir Horace Mann that 'the dispersed buildings—I mean temples, bridges, etc., are generally Gothic or Chinese, and give a whimsical air of novelty that is very pleasing'.

This whimsical air of novelty is certainly the outstanding quality of the designs which appeared in the pattern books and the few buildings that have survived. One of the survivors from this period was in the grounds of Wotton House, Buckinghamshire and has recently been transplanted to Ireland: a square building with a wide-eaved roof and fretted windows in walls which are brightly painted with vases of flowers and chinoiserie scenes (Pl. 103).

A somewhat similar summer house, which used to grace the park at Stowe, was made largely of sail-cloth painted on the outside 'in the Chinese taste' by a Venetian, Francesco Sleter, and hung with India paper inside; the whole place enshrining the figure of a 'Chinese lady asleep'. Bridges were particularly popular, and have survived in greater numbers, possibly because they occasionally served a useful purpose—though the streams they spanned had frequently been created artificially to provide them with a *raison d'être*. A good simple example, dating from the 1740s, has been preserved at Painshill. The longest was probably that built across the Thames from Hampton Court in 1753 and demolished or washed away soon afterwards—though not before Canaletto had made a drawing of it (British Museum).

Of the many chinoiserie follies which have vanished, the most elaborate was probably that built in 1759 on an island in Virgina Water, the lake created by the Duke of Cumberland to provide work for the soldiers who had served under him. Mrs Lybbe Powys was among its many admiring visitors, writing in 1766: 'we went to the Chinese Island, on which is a small house quite in the taste of that nation, the outside of which is white tiles set in red lead, decorated with bells and Chinese ornaments. You approach the building by a Chinese bridge, and in a very hot day, as that was, the whole looked cool and pleasing. The inside consists of two state rooms, a drawing room and bed-chamber, in miniature each but corresponds with the outside appearance.' On the lake itself there floated a Chinese junk, *Mandarine*, which, as Mrs Delany remarked, was 'as rich and gay as carving, gilding, and japanning can make it' (Pl. 104). When entertaining his nephew, George III, on board, the Duke of Cumberland had this junk illuminated and it must have presented an attractive spectacle, shimmering on the water before the red-and-white pavilion and the gently arched bridge.

In the garden, as in the house, the vogue for chinoiserie reached its zenith in the 1750s when few of those who strove to point their prospects, to diversify their surfaces, to entangle their walks and to wind their waters, could resist the temptation to build at least one pagoda-roofed eye-catcher. The indolent visitor viewed the multitude of little buildings with some distaste and Richard Cambridge looked back nostalgically to the 'good time, when the price of a haunch of venison with a country friend was only half-an-hour's walk on a hot terrass; a descent to two square fish-ponds overgrown with frog-spawn; a peep into the hog-sty, or a visit to the pigeon house. How reasonable was this, when compared with the attention now expected from you to the number of temples, pagodas, pyramids, grottos, bridges, hermitages, caves, towers &c.' Among all these delights of the English park the chinoiserie buildings stood out for their brilliance of colouring and exquisite prettiness of ornament, in sharp contrast to the artificially crumbling Gothic or classical ruins which were calculated to summon up tears of a pleasing melancholy sensibility. But into this uninhibited world of chinoiserie frivolity there suddenly stepped the sober figure of William Chambers with a portfolio of designs of Chinese buildings which he claimed to have taken in China. As we shall see, a cat had been set among the ho-ho birds.

In his youth, Chambers had travelled as a supercargo on an East-Indiaman which anchored for a short period off Canton. Having a natural bent towards architecture, he sketched a few of the more interesting temples and pagodas in the district. Some years later, after a more serious training in architecture at Paris and Rome, he set up a practice at London in 1755 and, appreciating the popularity of chinoiserie buildings and furniture, arranged to publish the drawings he had made at Canton. News of this enterprise was abroad in 1756—perhaps a prospectus had been circulated—when Robert Adam's brother, John, remarked of Chambers: 'a book of Chinese affairs he is publishing cannot raise his reputation high among the truly learned in architecture'.

Next year the handsome folio of *Designs of Chinese Buildings, Furniture, Dresses etc.* was published with a dedication to Augusta, Princess Dowager of Wales. In his preface, Chambers cunningly remarked that 'in extensive parks and gardens, where a great variety of scenes is required, or in immense palaces, containing a numerous series of apartments, I do not see the impropriety of finishing some of the inferiour ones in the Chinese Taste'. This broad hint fell on a receptive ear and he soon began building the famous series of Chinese, Moorish, and classical structures for the Princess Dowager of Wales in Kew Gardens.

Chambers's *Designs of Chinese Buildings* must have appeared a little forbidding to his contemporaries, for none of them had that air of whimsical delicacy which was so notable in Halfpenny's work. His designs for furniture were likewise severe and in striking contrast to those in Chippendale's *Director*—not one of them is known to have been executed in England, though they may have exerted some influence on Holland's design for the Chinese drawing-room at Carlton House. Sinophils may well have been disappointed by Chambers's illustrations, and they can have been little better pleased by his text in which he took great pains to show that he was no China-maniac. 'I am far from desiring to be numbered among the exaggerators of Chinese excellence', he sternly wrote; 'I consider them as great, or wise, only in comparison with the nations that surround them; and have no intention to place them in competition either with the antients, or with the moderns of this part of the world. . . .' And he drove his point home by repeated hammer blows, insisting that he found Chinese buildings unsuitable for our climate and looked upon them as mere 'toys in architecture'. The pagoda at Kew, which he completed in 1762, was a very large toy indeed and ironically it has remained the building with which Chambers's name has been most closely connected by the general public. On one occasion only did he afterwards essay the Chinese style, in 1772 when he designed a temple for the Duchess of Queensberry. Two years after the appearance of the *Designs*, Chambers published the first part of his *Treatise on Civil Architecture*, a very solemn disquisition on the beauties of Roman monuments which seems to have been partly intended to excuse his Chinese wild oats.

The buildings at Kew, to which a lavish folio was devoted in 1763, were in a curious gallimaufry of styles, including not only the pagoda, aviary, and bridge in the Chinese taste, but also a Moorish-cum-Gothic mosque and several classical buildings. Of the exotics only the pagoda has survived, shorn of the painted dragons with bells in their mouths which originally peered out from each of its ten storeys, but still towering with delightful incongruity above the copper beeches and wellingtonias of outer London. When built, it was the most scholarly pagoda to be seen in Europe even though it was not modelled on any particular oriental prototype. To chinoiserie fanciers it has always appeared too solemn and to sinologues too inaccurate a copy to win whole-hearted approval. But it quickly became one of the sights of outer London, dear to the general public. Paintings and prints were made of it, and it was also reproduced on chintz (Pl. 101). The other chinoiserie buildings at Kew, the aviary, the bridge and even the open temple which Chambers dignified with the correct Chinese name of 'Ting', were much further from China, much nearer William Half-penny and much more successful. They had all the elegance of bells, pagoda roofs and fretted decorations without the pedantry of the pagoda—or 'Taa', as, with admirable brevity, Chambers called it.

In the history of chinoiserie William Chambers's *Designs of Chinese Buildings* and his folio on the buildings at Kew have very great importance. They mark, first of all, the new attitude to oriental art which was to prevail in the later years of the century and which demanded free but essentially accurate imitations, rather than amusing parodies, of Chinese objects. They inspired garden architects in Scandinavia, Russia, the United States and Germany. Furthermore, the text of the *Designs*, which was widely read on the Continent, gave a new twist to the idea of the Chinese garden. Whereas the theory of sharawadgi had first been propounded in an age of symmetrical plantations and the Imperial gardens at Peking had been cited as a precedent for irregularity, Chambers now used the Chinese as a stalking horse for an attack on 'Capability' Brown's 'natural' lay-outs. For although Chambers had drawn Chinese buildings at Canton he had seen no Chinese gardens and his account of them is largely imaginary.

At first, Chambers restricted himself to a few modest remarks on Chinese gardening. 'Nature is their pattern, and their aim is to imitate her in all her beautiful irregularities', he stated in his *Designs of Chinese Buildings*. Echoing current theories of picturesque beauty he went on to declare that 'the artists distinguish their different species of scenes to which they give the appellations of pleasing, horrid and enchanted'. He had read the travel literature and was able to add that 'they likewise form artificial rocks; and in compositions of this kind the Chinese surpass all other nations'. His only original and imaginative contribution was to suggest that 'as the Chinese are not fond of walking, we seldom meet with avenues or spacious walks as in our English plantations'. This was all mild enough, but it was no more than an overture.

In 1770 Chambers lost to Lancelot Brown the commission for Lord Clive's large mansion, Claremont Park. Two years later he worked off his spleen by publishing *A Dissertation on Oriental Gardening* which was partly an evocation of Cathay and partly a savage attack on Brown. At the beginning he remarked:

> Amongst the Chinese, Gardening is held in much higher esteem, than it is in Europe; they rank a perfect work in that Art with the great productions of the human understanding; and they say that its efficacy in moving the passions,

yields to that of few other arts whatever. Their gardeners are not only Botanists, but also Painters and Philosophers, having a thorough knowledge of the human mind, and of the arts by which its strongest feelings are excited.

In other words, Chinese gardeners are not jumped-up hobbledehoys like Lancelot Brown. 'The scenery of a garden', he proceeded, in direct contradiction to what he had stated in his earlier book, 'should differ as much from common nature as an heroic poem doth from a prose relation', for 'nature is incapable of pleasing without the assistance of art'. Opposing the current belief in the beauty of curves and, in particular, Brown's predilection for serpentine paths, he stated that the Chinese are 'no enemies to straight lines because they are generally speaking productive of grandeur . . . nor have they any aversion to regular geometrical figures, which they say are beautiful in themselves'. The burden of this ill-assorted jumble of ideas is, of course, that the ideal garden was wholly unlike any park laid out by Brown.

But Chambers also gave a few telling glimpses of the exotic ornaments with which his elysium would be diversified. Some of them seem to have been derived from Pillement: structures 'built in large trees, and disposed amongst the branches like nests of birds, being finished on the inside with very beautiful ornaments and pictures composed of feathers'. The 'Halls of the Moon', on the other hand, are as old as Marco Polo; they were large hemispherical rooms to which 'the Chinese princes retire with their favourite women, whenever the heat and the intense light of the summer's day become disagreeable to them; and here they feast and give loose to every sort of voluptuous pleasure'. Chambers also painted a titillating scene of 'beauteous Tartarean damsels, in loose transparent robes that flutter in the scented air . . . giving wines and basketfuls of exotic fruits—mangostans, ananas, fruit of Quangsi—to the visitor who strays into the recesses of the labyrinth'.

This hotchpotch of highly coloured nonsense and acid vituperation met with a mixed reception and elicited from William Mason an *Heroic Epistle* of which Horace Walpole said, 'I laughed till I cried and the oftener I read it the better I liked it.' Chambers had recently been permitted by George III to assume the rank and title of knighthood conferred upon him by the King of Sweden and the epistle therefore began with an invocation to the

Knight of the Polar Star! by fortune plac'd
To shine the Cynosure of British Taste;

Whose orb collects in one refulgent view,
The scattered glories of Chinese Virtu;
And spreads thy lustre in so broad a blaze,
That kings themselves are dazzled while they gaze.

The whole poem is an excellent piece of late Georgian satire; it enjoyed immediate success and went into several editions. It also helped to sell 300 more copies of the *Dissertation* which it attacked.

Sir William Chambers was thus able to reply with a second edition of his work to which he added 'An explanatory discourse' fathered on the portrait sculptor Chit-qua, here designated 'Tan Chet-Qua of Quang-Chew-fu, Gent. FRSS, MRAAP; also MIAAP. TRA, CGHMW, and ATTQ.' All the world, he said,

> knew Chet-Qua, and how he was born at Quang-chew-fu, in the fourth moon of the year twenty-eight; also how he was bred a face-maker, and had three wives, two of whom he caressed very much; the third but seldom for she was a virago, and had large feet. He dressed well, often in thick sattin; wore nine whiskers and four long nails, with silk boots, callico breeches, and every other ornament that mandarins are wont to wear; equalling therein the prime macarones, and scavoir vivres, not only of Quang-chew, but even of Kyang-ning, or Shun-tien-fu. He likewise danced a fandando, after the newest of Macao, played divinely upon the bag-pipe and made excellent remarks.

The discourse which followed merely doubled the strictures on Brown's practice of gardening and Chambers confessed that he had judged it a 'sort of propriety to put into the mouth of a Chinese what further information was wanted relative to his country'. He had written, he said, 'rather as an Artist, to set before you a new style of Gardening; than as a Traveller, to relate what I have really seen'. And later he told a correspondent that he had attributed his system to 'the Chinese whom I thought to be out of range of Critical abuse', an idea as antiquated as most of his reflections in the *Dissertation*. Nevertheless, the book was widely accepted as an accurate account of oriental gardening both in England and on the Continent where it added fire to the controversy about the origin of the landscape park.

The one new and interesting idea in Chambers's book concerned the use of colour in the garden, for he advocated the massing of flowers according to their various hues. But this suggestion was not taken up by any of his contemporaries in England who, though by no means as hostile to flowering plants as is usually supposed, continued to scatter them about their groves without any regard for their colour. Mason, for example, who followed the sprightly *Heroic Epistle* with a long and turgid didactic poem on *The English Garden*, nursed an unfortunate passion for the laurel of which he prophesied with melancholy accuracy: 'swift shall she spread her broad-leaved shade, and float it far and wide.'

The controversy which Chambers's publication precipitated may have helped to sweep the pagoda from the garden. A few theorists, like William Shenstone the owner of that most influential small park, the Leasowes, had always disapproved of 'China's vain alcoves'; Brown seems to have dispensed with Chinese buildings in all the parks he improved and Mason naturally castigated the taste for such delights which his friend Horace Walpole, in an unusually censorious mood, described as 'unmeaning fallaballas of Chinese chequer work'. By the 1770s, therefore, informed taste appears to have been veering away from these frivolities and they never regained the popularity they had enjoyed in the previous two decades. Despite the barrage of critical scorn, however, new Chinese bridges, fishing houses and even a few pagodas were occasionally built in the last years of the eighteenth century and a book of designs for them—the second edition of William Wright's *Grotesques Architecture*—was published as late as 1790.

In the late 1760s a very charming Chinese fishing house, which happily survives (and has recently been restored) was built at Arlesford near Colchester. A square building with a roof shaped like a mandarin's hat and a latticed balcony looking onto the water, it was primarily intended, like the majority of its kind, as a place for picnics and was still being used as such in 1816 when John Constable was commissioned to execute a painting of it (National Gallery of Art, Melbourne). Constable remarked in a letter to his fiancée that the daughter of the owner 'goes [there] occasionally to angle'.

A more grandiose surviving specimen of the genre is the Chinese dairy at Woburn, built in 1787 by Henry Holland. This elegant building, crowned by a small octagonal tower with trellised lights and decorated on the walls with fretted woodwork also stands by a small lake. It is approached through a chinoiserie colonnade which curves round the edge of the water (Pl. 105). The interior is decorated with marble shelves on painted bamboo supports, and niches filled with porcelain dishes ranged on fretwork brackets. An air of freshness and elegant simplicity marks the whole building, and a new note was struck in the surrounding garden which was stocked with some of the Chinese plants recently imported into Europe for the first time.

Only the opulent could indulge in the luxury of Chinese dairies or fishing houses, however; the more modest landowner was forced to content himself with a flimsy covered seat or an erratic fence. Gilbert White of Selborne, so he wrote in his catalogue of intended improvements to the vicarage garden, would

> O'er the gay lawn the flow'ry shrub dispread
> Or with the blending garden mix the mead;
> Bid China's pale, fantastic fence, delight,
> Or with the mimic statue trap the sight.

Yet even the simplest of chinoiserie constructions might help to summon up a vision of Cathay, just as the meanest pile of rubble overgrown with ivy might arouse thoughts of the Gothic Middle Ages. In his miniature park at Amwell, John Scott, the Quaker poet, boasted a modest Chinese temple and here, perhaps, he found the inspiration for his account of Li Po's garden:

> Where Honan's hills Kiansi's vale inclose,
> And Xifa's lake its glassy level shows;
> Li Po's fair island lay—delightful scene!
> With swelling slopes, and groves of every green:
> On azure rocks his rich pavilion plac'd,
> Rear'd its light front with golden columns grac'd;
> High o'er the roof a weeping willow hung,
> And jasmine boughs the lattice twined among;
> In porcelain vases crested amaranth grew,
> And starry aster, crimson, white and blue;
> Lien-Hoa flowers upon the water spread;
> Bright shells and corals varied lustre shed;
> From starry grottoes crystal drops distill'd
> On sounding brass, and air with music fill'd;
> Soft through the bending canes the breezes play'd,
> The rustling leaves continual murmur made;
> Gay shoals of gold-fish glitter'd in the tide,
> And gaudy birds flew sportive at its side.
> The distant prospects well the sight might please,
> With pointed mountains, and romantic trees:
> From craggy cliffs, between the verdant shades,
> The silver rills rush'd down in bright cascades;

O'er terrac'd steeps rich cotton harvests wav'd,
And smooth canals the rice-clad valleys lav'd;
Long rows of cypress parted all the land,
And tall pagodas crown'd the river's strand!
Beneath a bower of sweet Ka-fa, whose bloom
Fill'd the adjacent lawn with rich perfume,
His slaves at distance sat—a beauteous train!—
One wak'd the lute, and one the vocal strain. . . .

It is an enchanting picture and one which beautifully captures the late eighteenth-century vision of oriental gardening.

In the last years of the eighteenth century, exoticism enjoyed a brief but gay Indian summer. 'Capability' Brown had died in 1783; 'Your Dryads must go into black gloves, Madam: their father-in-law, Lady Nature's second husband is dead!' Horace Walpole told the Countess of Upper Ossory. But Lady Nature lost no time in finding a third husband, Humphrey Repton, who proved more indulgent to the whim for Chinese bridges, pavilions, and fences than his predecessor had been. In the guise of Mr Milestone, Peacock represents him looking with horror at the grounds of Headlong Hall, which had 'never been touched by the finger of taste', and asking permission to wave his wand of enchantment over them: 'The rocks shall be blown up, the trees shall be cut down, the wilderness and all its goats shall vanish like mist. Pagodas and Chinese bridges, gravel walks and shrubberies, bowling greens, canals and clumps of larch, shall rise upon its ruins.'

In gardening Repton showed the respect for geographical accuracy characteristic of his age. He it was who suggested that flowers from China should be planted around Holland's Chinese dairy at Woburn. And between 1797 and 1802 he was, he tells us, 'consulted by the owner of Sezincote where he wished to introduce the gardening and architecture of India'. Indeed, he became so enamoured of this novel style that he made bold to declare that England was on the eve of some great change in the arts of gardening and architecture 'in consequence of our lately becoming acquainted with Scenery and Buildings in the interior provinces of India. The beautiful designs published by Daniell, Hodges, and other artists, have produced a new source of beauty and elegance and grace which may justly vie with the best specimens of Grecian or Gothic architecture.' Sezincote is one of the greatest monuments to the taste for picturesque exoticism. But the onion domes, minarets, and multifoil arches of the house and, in the garden, the temple pool, shrine of Sourija and bridge supported on shafts copied from the Elephanta caves are so determined to be Hindu that they fall outside the scope of the present book.

Despite Repton's prophecy about the new vogue for 'Hindoo' architecture and gardening, chinoiserie maintained some popularity throughout the Regency period. The Regent himself admired both styles, which were combined in the pavilion at Brighton, and it was probably on his suggestion that Nash built a pagoda in St James's Park to mark the Peace of 1814. This building united the utility of the Chinese bridge with the charms of the folly, for it was erected on a substructure which spanned the canal and was intended to serve as a permanent means of communication between St James's and Whitehall. Unfortunately it made its *début* as the centre-piece in a firework display when rockets were let off with such gay abandon that the upper storeys caught fire, burst into flames and fell, popping and sizzling, into the water. The bridge and charred stump of the pagoda were allowed to remain for some years; a melancholy monument to a great chinoiserie extravagance. Later, in about 1824, George IV had a Chinese fishing house, with three octagonal spires and dragon-crowned turrets, built on the edge of Virginia Water; this also has perished but a drawing of it by Frederick Crace survives (Pl. 115).

One of the latest and perhaps the most attractive of English pagodas was built some time between 1814 and 1827 in the very elaborate park at Alton Towers, Shropshire (Pl. 106). By a charmingly ingenious device this pagoda, which stands in the middle of a small lake, acts as a fountain, spouting a high jet of water from the top. It consists of three latticed storeys each hung with tongueless bells, but was originally intended to be much taller and to be illuminated by Chinese lanterns lit from a gasometer concealed within. The lowest storey, it is said, was designed as a resting-place for ornamental fowls—mandarin ducks, presumably. One winter night, recently, the fountain was accidentally left on and next morning the pagoda was found sparkling with icicles and looking like the residence of a Cathaian snow queen.

The pagoda garden at Alton is suitably planted with rhododendrons and Lien-Hoa flowers—water-lilies—float upon the lake. It is representative of a new tendency in garden design which was soon to blossom forth in innumerable little gardens within the English park. There were to be Italian gardens, knot-gardens, Japanese gardens, and eventually Alpine gardens, each planted with appropriate trees, shrubs, and flowers. Meanwhile, the *jardin anglais, englischer Garten*, or *giardino inglese*, which had been thought to derive from Chinese precedents, continued to flourish on the Continent.

Fig. 9 Design for a *Terminary Seat in the Chinese Taste*

2 LE JARDIN ANGLO-CHINOIS

Quand je dis jardin anglais, qu'on se souvienne que c'est toujours affaire de convention, car c'est plutôt jardin chinois, et comme peu de gens savent que les Chinois se sont distingués dans ce genre-là, comme bien d'autres, il faut se conformer aux idées reçues. Il est pourtant sûr que c'est à eux que les Anglais doivent leur réputation. Ce sont eux qui ont su mettre à profit ces chutes d'eau, ces abîmes heureux, ces horreurs pleines de charmes, ces cavernes, ces ruines, ces points de vue. . . .

CHARLES JOSEPH LAMORAL DE LIGNE, 1781

'Whatever may have been reported, whether truly or falsely, of the Chinese Gardens', wrote Richard Cambridge in 1756, 'it is certain that we are the first Europeans to have founded their taste.' By this time the English landscape garden with its meandering brooks and walks, irregular plantations and cunning eye-catchers had crossed the channel, first of all to France and then to Scandinavia. During the course of the next forty years it became an essential part of the domain of every continental prince. The full story of how this came about remains to be written; it is as complicated as an artificial wilderness and rambles far beyond the bounds of the present book. In the history of chinoiserie the *jardin anglo-chinois* as it came to be called, is of interest only because it was thought, mistakenly, to have a Chinese origin and because it was frequently adorned with chinoiserie buildings. Our attention will therefore be confined to these two aspects of a much larger subject.

The irregular or English garden sprang from the general revolt against formality and from the new feeling for sensibility which affected all the arts of Europe in the eighteenth century. To highly refined, predominantly urban and, perhaps, over-sophisticated societies, the pleasures of a simple pastoral life, divested of all its hardships and perils, have always seemed especially attractive; but never did they appeal more strongly than to eighteenth-century princes and their courtiers. The English garden provided an appropriate background for such pleasures, presenting, with its unfettered trees and apparently un-planned serpentine walks, an acceptable view of nature, tamed but not sub-dued. It also provided those touching scenes—'ces abîmes heureux, ces horreurs pleines de charmes'—calculated to arouse sentiments of a pleasing melancholy, the 'sad luxury' which, as an English poet remarked, was 'to vulgar minds unknown'. Thus in France, the *jardins anglais* were complementary to the *fêtes champêtres* of Watteau, the pastorals of Boucher and Fragonard and such novels as *La Nouvelle Héloïse* and *Paul et Virginie*. To claim for them a purely English descent would be mere chauvinism. Nevertheless, the essays of Addison, which were translated into French in 1720, and the poems of James Thomson, especially *The Seasons*, which were widely read in France even before they were translated, so perfectly summed up the early eighteenth-century attitude to nature that their influence on the growth of the *jardin anglais* can hardly be denied.

In a very short time the *jardin anglais* became fashionable in France, so much *à la mode*, indeed, that Frenchmen found it difficult to believe so charming a scheme could have been invented by the phlegmatic English. With the sanction of several English theorists, notably Sir William Chambers, they therefore looked to the East for an origin less damaging to their *amour-propre*. Horace Walpole acidly commented in 1771: 'The French have of late years adopted our style in gardens, but, choosing to be fundamentally obliged to more remote rivals, they deny us half the merit or rather the originality of the invention, by ascribing the discovery to the Chinese, and calling our taste in gardening *le goût anglo-chinois*.'

Their belief in this Chinese origin was of course supported by the account of Yüan Ming Yüan sent from Peking to Paris in 1745 by Père Attiret who, recalling the formal gardens of his native land in the early eighteenth century, when he first entered the mission field, naturally emphasized how much Chinese gardeners had striven to imitate nature by planting irregularly. When Georges Louis le Rouge began to publish his great series of quartos on the gardens of Europe in 1776, he therefore entitled the work *Détails de nouveaux jardins à la mode (jardins anglo-chinois)* and blandly remarked in the introduction to the first volume 'tout le monde sait que les jardins anglais ne sont qu'une imitation de ceux de la Chine'. In this work Le Rouge included many plates of English gardens as well as three whole *cahiers* devoted to Yüan Ming Yüan and yet, curiously enough, seems not to have noticed any difference between the broad, smooth sylvan landscapes of the former—inspired by the paintings of Claude—and the jagged, wanton irregularity of the latter with their stunted trees and artificial rocks. But however strongly they believed that the *jardin anglo-chinois* derived from China, the French were careful to copy English precedents rather than the scratchy plates of the Emperor of China's gardens, when they came to lay out their own grounds. And it was to England that French landscape gardeners like Belanger travelled in search of inspiration.

Many of the great formal gardens laid out in France during the late seventeenth and early eighteenth centuries included a *bosquet* or little wilderness, a place to which one might retire when wearied of silent canals, wide avenues and flights of stone steps, when stared out of countenance by too thick a crowd of bronze and marble Olympians. Such was the *bosquet des sources* near the Trianon in the grounds of Versailles itself, where some fifty springs bubbled out of the earth into little streams and where, according to Madame, the Princess Palatine, the trees were so dense that even at midday the sun could not penetrate their boughs.

Madame professed great fondness for natural beauty, remarking in 1719, 'un ruisseau me plaît mieux que de somptueuses cascades; en un mot, tout ce qui est naturel est infiniment plus à mon goût que les œuvres de l'art et de la magnificence'. Her words were echoed nearly two decades later by Voltaire in his *Épître au Prince Royal de Prusse*. But Rousseau was the first French writer to suggest that a whole garden might be laid out on a natural scheme. In *La Nouvelle Héloïse*, published in 1761, he described such a garden with paths and streams winding among plantations where

> vous ne voyez rien d'aligné, ni de nivelé: jamais le cordeau n'entra dans ces lieux, la nature ne plante rien au cordeau; les sinuosités dans leur feinte irrégularité sont ménagées avec art pour prolonger la promenade, cacher les bords de l'île, et en agrandir l'étendue apparente sans faire de détours incommodes et trop fréquents.

When Julie had led her lover through this place he declared that he had been transported into Elysium. It is interesting to note that this garden is owned by an Englishman and that the same book includes an attack on the gardens of the Chinese, 'fais avec tant d'art que l'art n'y paraissoit point, mais d'une manière si dispendieuse et entretenus à si grands frais, que cette idée m'ôtoit tout le plaisir que j'aurois pu goûter à les voir.'

The first English gardens laid out in France seem to have been attached, like the earlier *bosquets*, to formal schemes. Crowded with delights, many of them must have looked nearly as pitiful as that described by Horace Walpole in a letter to John Chute, a prominent member of the Strawberry committee of taste. 'I have literally seen one [garden] that is exactly like a tailor's paper of patterns', he wrote from Paris in 1771.

> There is a Monsieur Boutin, who has tacked a piece of what he calls an English garden to a set of stone terraces, with steps of turf. There are three or four very high hills, almost as high as, and exactly the shape of, a tansy pudding. You squeeze between these a river, that is conducted in obtuse angles in a stone channel, and supplied by a pump; and when walnuts come in I suppose will be navigable. In a corner enclosed by a chalk wall are the samples I mentioned; there is a stripe of grass, another of corn, and a third *en friche*, exactly in the order of beds in a nursery. They have translated Mr Whatley's book, and the lord knows what barbarism is going to be laid at our door. This new *Anglomanie* will literally be *mad English*.'

'There is', he told Lady Ossory, 'something so sociable in being able to shake hands across the river from the tops of the two mountains, that nothing but so aimiable a nation could have imagined it.' This garden, at Clichy in the suburbs of Paris, was probably designed in emulation of Shenstone's famous *ferme ornée*, the Leasowes, of which Thomas Whatley gave a very enthusiastic account in his book. But however much it may have provoked Horace Walpole's scorn, the *Folie Boutin*—as it came to be called—was much admired by French visitors, and the Duc de Croy proudly declared that it 'renferme tous les goûts et pays'.

In France as in England, an oriental air was often given to the garden by planting chinoiserie buildings among its thickets and by spanning its brooks with latticed bridges. These French follies were, if anything, more numerous and often more elaborate than those in English parks, and two of them—at Chantilly and the Désert de Retz—have been described in the account of rococo chinoiserie interior decoration. The *maison chinoise* at the Désert de Retz has, however, an additional importance since it was set in the middle of its own little park approached from the main garden through a pair of gates decorated with hieroglyphics along a path wriggling round clumps of trees and across the many bends of a serpentine stream. Today the stream has dried up and the trees have either fallen to the axe or outgrown their intended size and it is therefore difficult to determine whether the planting of this Chinese garden differed in any way from the surroundings of the several other follies with which the Désert blossomed—the temple of Pan, the ruined church, the pyramid, the hermitage, and the main house which was built in the form of a monstrous fluted column, half shattered and in a carefully contrived state of pleasing decay. The Prince de Ligne, on visiting the Désert de Retz, remarked that 'l'empereur de la Chine avouerait la petite maison chinoise de Monsieur Monville, qui est un modèle en recherches', and he also approved the 'joli ruisseau', but his remarks do not suggest that the garden was more oriental than any other in France.

The Prince de Ligne's park, Belœil (only the formal part of which survives), was one of the largest and most famous in Europe. And the Prince was a prominent amateur of gardening who yielded to none in his belief that the origins of the landscape park lay in China (see the quotation at the head of this section). However, his *Coup d'œil sur Belœil* reveals that the park's only specifically chinoiserie features were a few of its buildings. The joint work of the prince and Joseph Belanger, Belœil was created between 1769 and 1788 to replace a formal lay-out in the style of Le Nôtre. In the first stage of the transformation a little shady garden was created around a brook, charmingly called 'le rieu d'amour'. Later, another part of the park was devoted to a realization of the literary and pictorial pastoral convention, consisting of a *village tartare* of rustic thatched shelters inhabited by picturesquely dressed farm labourers and sleek Swiss cows. The peasants were expected to join in the game of make-believe: herdsmen, their wives and mistresses being required to 'sing and play on their rustic instruments, as clear and cheerful as their voices and, when they are fatigued by the songs of the village, there shall be bag-pipes to rest them, and every kind of horn, and shepherd's pipes, and great flutes like those of the Tyrolese.' The shepherds and shepherdesses were to wear a 'costume worthy of the dignity and simplicity of Nature, of which they are the high priests' (the voice of Rousseau is audible here). And the very animals had to play up to the prince's whims: 'My bulls will have a menacing air', he directed, and the calves were to gambol round a small lake created solely for that purpose.

In sharp contrast to the lively scenes of the *village tartare* there was an English garden where, the prince suggested, 'those with sad thoughts will be able to give themselves up entirely to the little miseries which often afford pleasure, and to which one must yield without a struggle', and where 'those who feel more cheerful can think of reconciliation, hope perhaps, if they like, of change'. Great care was taken in designing this part of the park which was mapped out on a sand tray before planting. It included a ruined temple among the woods and a stream, piped from another part of the estate, which plunged with as much noise as possible into an archway, to reappear very quietly from another close at hand. A number of buildings were also planned, but it is difficult to tell how many of these were erected. There was to be a three-storey Indian Temple built of white painted wood where de Ligne intended to go and eat cream; a Chinese temple was to serve as a dove-cote, and an ice-house was to be concealed beneath a mosque and a clump of lime trees. The prince also gave his attention to the surrounding country and selected an ancient castle for improvement: the exterior was painted in the Italian manner while the interior was transformed into a chinoiserie courtyard lined with marble and blue-and-white tiles. About this strange building there was, he wrote, to be as much oddity, extravagance, even folly as could be contrived.

The Prince de Ligne's penchant for little garden buildings developed into a passion. At Tsarskoe-Selo he remarked that the caprices—they included a Turkish pavilion, a triumphal column in the middle of a lake, several Chinese bridges and kiosks as well as an entire Chinese village—made the garden the most interesting in the world. And his passion was shared by not a few of his contemporaries who scattered their parks with a wild profusion of eye-catchers and pavilions in the classical, Gothic and Chinese tastes: Chinese temples being rather more and Gothic ruins much less popular than in England.

To judge from engravings and printed descriptions most of the chinoiserie buildings were similar to those erected in English parks of the mid-century: octagonal kiosks liberally adorned with monkeys, dragons, exotic birds and flowers, and with bells hanging from the upturned eaves of their roofs (Pl. 113). Chinese tents and merry-go-rounds supported on pagoda-like structures also enjoyed some vogue. But in France, as in England, the relatively inexpensive bridges with brightly painted criss-cross balustrades were the most popular chinoiserie ornaments. They were even incorporated on the strangest of all *jardins anglo-chinois*, that on the roof of Charles Marin de la Haye's hotel in the centre of Paris. Another unusual bridge was in the garden of the Château de Betz near Senlis, laid out between 1780 and 1789. According to a contemporary description, two mandarins with nodding heads, dressed in rich court robes squatted on shell and coral encrusted rocks at one end of this bridge while the other was guarded by a pair of three-headed dragons holding deep booming bells in each of their several mouths.

The names of the artists responsible for these ephemeral erections have seldom been recorded save where they were better known for work in the classical style. Hubert Robert, for example, has been mentioned in connection with the Désert de Retz, but although he occasionally sketched a Chinese scene he is more likely to have been responsible for designing the crumbling classical monuments than the *maison chinoise*. Square and octagonal Chinese summer houses built in the Duc de Penthièvre's garden at Arminvilliers were designed by Jean-Auguste Renard. The only artist who is known to have specialized in such works is the otherwise severely neo-classical Joseph Belanger, the official architect of the *Menus Plaisirs*. At the beginning of his career Belanger visited England where he seems to have been no less taken with the landscape parks than with the pavilions and temples which adorned them. Drawings reveal the elegance of the many chinoiserie kiosks and bridges with which he decorated such notable *jardins anglo-chinois* as Santenay, La Bagatelle, le Jardin de Beaumarchais and his own estate. He lived to survive the revolution and most of his own buildings.

Of all the myriad chinoiserie buildings of late eighteenth-century France only three have survived the combined onslaughts of time and taste: the *maison chinoise* at the Désert de Retz, now sadly tumble-down; a pavilion at Cassan, near L'Isle-Adam, and the stately pagoda which towers above the rolling Touraine countryside at Chanteloup. (In the grounds of the Château de Canon in Normandy there is a very simple latticed pavilion which dates from the early nineteenth century.) The Cassan pavilion is of a type which enjoyed great popularity. Standing on the edge of a lake, it consists of a stout rusticated and Tuscan-columned base supporting an octagonal kiosk with a double pagoda roof and spire. The walls of the kiosk are of lattice work painted red and yellow, and bells dangle from the eaves of the upper roof (Pl. 107). A similar pavilion was in the grounds of Rambouillet; another, which is known from the architect's model, decorated the garden of the hôtel Montmorency-Châtillon, Paris.

The Chanteloup pagoda is a more unusual affair, intended to form the central feature of a *jardin anglo-chinois* which was never laid out. It was designed by Le Camus de Mézières, the architect of the Halle au Blé at Paris, and erected between 1775 and 1778 by the Duc de Choiseul to commemorate the loyalty of some three hundred friends during a period of disfavour at court. The tall seven-storey tower was called a pagoda, but would have startled a priest of Fo, for there is very little that is Chinese about it save for the tapering outline, gently tip-tilted eaves, fretted balconies and a few panels of bizarre abstract carving. Otherwise the detail is severely classical and includes Doric columns and pilasters. It is, indeed, an example of the Louis XVI style without so much as a trace of rococo frivolity (Pl. 111). But it appealed so strongly to Frederick Hervey, Earl of Bristol and Bishop of Derry, that he planned to duplicate it at Ballyscullion on the shores of Lough Beg.

In 1769 the *Avant-Courier* announced, very prematurely, the death of the taste for pagodas. Inspired by Rousseau's back to nature philosophy, many critics arose to denounce the exotic pavilions and artificial ruins which diversified the landscape garden. One of the most prominent, certainly the most voluble, was the Abbé Delille, the author of a long didactic poem on *Les Jardins ou l'art d'embellir les paysages* which begins with the somewhat alarming couplet:

> Le doux printemps revient, et ranime à la fois,
> Les oiseaux, les zéphirs, et les fleurs et ma voix.

The abbé states that he wrote this poem in the 1770s and inflicted many readings of it on his long-suffering friends before it finally reached print in 1782: it subsequently went into twenty editions and was translated into German, Polish, Italian, and English. Although prepared to condone the use of an occasional building in the garden, Delille rigorously declared 'j'en proscris l'abus' and went on to command:

Bannissez des jardins tout cet amas confus
D'édifices divers, prodigués par la mode,
Obélisque, rotonde, et kiosque, et pagode,
Ces bâtimens romains, grecs, arabes, chinois,
Chaos d'Architecture, et sans but, et sans choix,
Dont la profusion stérilement féconde
Enferme en un jardin les quatre parts du monde.

But whatever the purists might say, garden buildings of all types remained popular in France until the deluge descended and classical rotundas, Gothic ruins and Chinese kiosks were swept away on the tide of Liberty, Equality and Fraternity; until the *ferme ornée* was transformed into a work-a-day farm and the Désert became a wilderness indeed.

From the few survivors and the many engravings in Le Rouge's and Krafft's books on landscape gardening, it is possible to obtain no more than a very shadowy idea of the *jardins anglo-chinois* which so delightfully diversified the French countryside in the last decades of the eighteenth century. Only at Cassan may the gay porcelain colours of a *kiosque chinois* still be seen reflected in a silent lake before a densely planted thicket of trees. Fortunately, however, Scandinavia still possesses a number of parks which are rich in lakes, meandering streams, clumps of trees and chinoiserie buildings. Though none of them is as extensive or as thickly planted with follies as Belœil or the Désert de Retz, they give a better impression of how the *jardin anglo-chinois* looked in its heyday —or rather how it was intended to look, for only now, more than a century and a half since they were planted, can they be seen in their majestic maturity.

The earliest of the surviving chinoiserie follies in Scandinavia appears to be a little octagonal pavilion built in 1750 at Stora Nycklviken, outside Stockholm. Here the Chinese elements are very discreet, however, being confined to a bell-shaped roof from which little bells may once have hung. Dating from slightly later and in a more advanced style are two square summer houses, in the park at Linköping and on the shores of Lake Malaren: the former is an attractive, if somewhat modest, little building hung with bells (Pl. 112), the latter has a double pagoda roof, trellissed walls, and a shell decorated interior. At Haga Park (in addition to some Sino-Moresque follies) there is a Chinese temple of the type which Chambers called a 'Ting', looking rather like a Victorian bandstand with eight columns supporting a pagoda roof which curls up at each angle to end in a dragon's head of suspiciously Viking appearance (Pl. 110). Another octagonal temple, based precisely on the 'Ting' in Kew Gardens, was built by an amateur architect Carl Räbergh-Mannerskantz at Värnansäs, near Kalmar, towards the end of the century. Inside, this little building is adorned with Chinese paintings and simulated bamboo furniture.

Even remote and snowy Finland succumbed to the cult of the pagoda, and at Fagervik there is a very elaborate octagonal pavilion with a double roof and dragons leering out from the corners. In Denmark a well-preserved island pavilion and Chinese bridge are to be found in the park of Fredriksborg Castle; and one enterprising Dane even went to the length of importing a genuine Chinese pavilion from China, which still survives in a garden at Klampenborg. But he may well have regretted introducing this cuckoo into the chinoiserie nest.

Chinoiserie pavilions reached Sweden as a part of the *jardin anglo-chinois*. But in Germany they sprung into popularity long before the taste for irregular gardens had manifested itself. As we have already seen, the park at Nymphenburg boasted a Chinese house in the first quarter of the eighteenth century. At Potsdam, the famous *chinesisches Teehaus*—which that arch-connoisseur of follies, the Prince de Ligne, considered 'superbe et bien entendu'—was set in a formal, Dutch style, knot-garden surrounded by metal pagods which gyrated in the wind. Other delights in the same park included a porter's lodge and guard house covered by chinoiserie baldaquins, a so-called dragon cottage and an ornamental seat in the form of a vast umbrella adorned with hanging chains and, on the ferrule, the correct nine rings of the Buddhist 'Taa'. A smaller version of the Potsdam tea-house, with a peaked roof supported on palm trees, was built in the late 1760s in the italianate gardens at Veitshöchheim where it still stands among the mazes, neat geometrical ponds and pleached walks. Designed by Ferdinand Tietz, it delightfully conforms to the mood of his exuberent rococo putti.

Writing *On Modern Gardening* in 1771, Horace Walpole remarked, 'I should think the little princes of Germany, who spare no profusion on their palaces and country houses, most likely to be our imitators; especially as their country and climate bears in many parts resemblance to ours.' At that very moment the first English gardens were being planted in Germany, they took root and flourished in the damp climate, and within a decade had begun to spread throughout the two thousand principalities. The first *englischer Garten* appears to have been that laid out for Duke Francis of Dessau at Wörlitz between 1769 and 1773, and the park of Schloss Rheinsberg also dates from about 1770. But in the very early stages of the new taste C. Hirschfeld published his *Anmerkungen über die Landhäuser und die Gartenkunst* (1773) which included a violent attack on the vogue for little buildings in the park. As a result, a large number of the parks subsequently laid out in Germany were either devoid of follies and delights or only very sparsely diversified with them.

Fortunately, however, several princes were too proud to sacrifice their taste for buildings to the whims of the purist, especially if they already possessed a collection in their formal gardens. At Wilhelmshöhe, the summer palace of the electors of Hess, outside Cassel, the fantastic garden with its water ramp, over which a thirty-feet high copy of the Farnese Hercules presides, was incongruously adapted to suit the new taste. At Schwetzingen, the garden laid out in the manner of Le Nôtre in 1753 and well equipped with buildings in a variety of styles (including the Chinese) was transformed into an English park barely two decades later. A few English gardens, created at this period but now known only from the engravings in the books of Le Rouge and Krafft, were as liberally sprinkled with bridges, pagodas, and kiosks as any in France. The gardens at Oranienbaum, near Dessau, laid out in 1795, still boast a five-storey pagoda, a tea-house on an island and a couple of Chinese bridges. Perhaps the strangest, certainly the richest, was that at Rosswald, near Troppau in Silesia. This large park boasted a Chinese temple, a holy grove, a pagoda, a hermitage, some druid caves, an antique mausoleum to which sacrifices for the dead were ceremoniously brought, and a whole town, including a church, market-place and *Rathaus,* for dwarfs (local children were pressed into service here as dwarfs were expensive and difficult to acquire in quantity). But the most familiar *englischer Garten* in Germany is that at Munich, laid out in the last years of the century. Although it has now been ruined by tarmac walks, it still preserves its groves of trees, an elegant Grecian temple on a hillock and a somewhat stumpy pagoda which was destroyed in the last war but has now been rebuilt on a smaller scale (with three storeys in place of the original five), to serve as a café. Sitting beneath its bell hung roof, surrounded by spruce *Mädchen* carrying cans of beer, and listening to a brass band playing the *Tannhäuser* overture, one may here gain an impression of a robust and distinctly *gemütlich* German Cathay.

By 1770 the taste for the English garden had been established throughout northern Europe, but not for another decade did it cross the Alps. When the

Prince de Ligne visited Italy in the 1770s he was dismayed at what he found and remarked that he had seen no gardens which could give him any pleasure. 'Il n'y a ni la fraîcheur, ni le négligé des Anglais, ni le peigné et la grâce des Français, ni la culture des Hollandais, ni le désordre des Chinois. Les palais des seigneurs italiens sont tout peristiles et escaliers, et leurs jardins, de grands terrains mal tenus, sans goût et sans dessin.' Despite the unsuitable climate and landscape of Italy many English gardens were laid out, notably that at Caserta and the Borghese gardens in Rome. But both these gardens date from the time when chinoiserie follies were going out of fashion and neither displays so much as a Chinese seat.

The pagoda and kiosk had, however, raised their pinnacled heads in eighteenth-century Italy—surviving examples are at Brignano Gera d' Adda (Pl. 114) and the garden of the Bishop's palace at Bressanone—and the theorist of the Italian landscape-gardening movement, Conte Ercole Silva, found it necessary to condemn the use of such follies. One of the last Italian pagodas was raised in the gardens of the Villa Pallavicini at Pegli, near Genoa, in 1837. Perched on a latticed bridge, this building has a more obviously oriental appearance than any of the now familiar Chinese flowering plants which grow around it—for while the plants come from China, the pagoda belongs to the imaginary land of Cathay.

CHAPTER VII

The Last Days of Cathay

I CHINOISERIE AND NEO-CLASSICISM

The serpentine path of the landscape garden has led us from the sparkling rococo world of Voltaire and Boucher to the neo-classical solemnities of Goethe and Jacques-Louis David. Chinoiserie could hardly be expected to flourish, indeed it is surprising to find that it had survived, in this strange new era of Hellenism and the Rights of Man, and soon the flowery Empire of Cathay began to totter. Philosophers no longer justified their deistic beliefs by reference to Confucius; political theorists and economists no longer upheld the Chinese system of government; even the arts of China fell under a cloud. Eyes newly attuned to Doric severities naturally found it difficult to relish the fragile prettiness of a K'ang Hsi vase, and in the *Encyclopédie* Diderot castigated Chinese art, remarking that 'un amas d'ornement confus ne peut avoir de raison apparente; une variété bizarre et sans rapport ni symétrie, comme dans l'Arabesque ou dans le goût chinois, n'annonce aucun dessin.' Perhaps the stark simplicity of a T'ang vase or a Sung bowl might have caused Diderot to change his mind, but no such objects were then to be seen in Europe—nor would they be for more than another century. Oriental porcelain and lacquer imported into Europe in the late eighteenth century was still designed to appeal to rococo taste and could hardly fail to offend the classical purist.

The neo-classical movement which established itself soon after the middle of the century represented more than a revival of interest in the antique; it was primarily a revolt from the frivolities and excesses of the Rococo in favour of the discipline of artistic rules. Rococo artists had indulged in asymmetry and other devices to give their works a sense of glittering movement: they had rarely drawn a straight line when they could use a curved one or shown a figure standing squarely on two feet when it could be represented on tiptoe. Matters were to be ordered differently in the age of neo-classicism. And, it need hardly be said, the new style, calm, restrained, aloof and occasionally a little pedantic, was less well adapted to express the vision of Cathay than the Rococo had been. Yet, despite the better knowledge of the Far East, and despite the pontifications of classicists, the Orient continued to exert much of its exotic appeal. It is significant that Goethe, the presiding genius of the age, should have written a series of chinoiserie poems, *Chinesisch-deutsche Jahres- und Tageszeiten* (1826–7).

Delicate little Chinese pavilions and kiosks continued to be built in the gardens of Europe throughout the last decades of the eighteenth century and the first quarter of the nineteenth. Inside the house, chinoiserie wallpapers, textiles, and furniture remained popular even if they were not quite as fashionable as once they had been. Of course, a large proportion of these objects were in the rococo style. A japanned harpsichord made at Paris in 1786, for example, is decorated with little Chinamen dancing on a puce ground, as lively as any that were painted when the Rococo was the height of fashion (Pl. 119). Were it not for the severe Louis XVI substructure and a dated inscription this piece might well be supposed to date from the 1750s. And at Venice, where the Rococo died hard, neither the outlines nor the decorations of japanned furniture seem to have been much altered until the very last years of the century. In France and England the printers of wallpapers and textile hangings continued to use gay rococo patterns, many of them derived from Pillement prints, making hardly appreciable alterations in the cause of greater simplicity. And Pillement himself lived on in Portugal where he was still painting exotic rococo fantasies in the 'eighties (Pl. 45). Many of the more out of the way porcelain and pottery factories also clung to the rococo style for chinoiserie decorations. *Les Fleurs des Indes* continued to blossom on table-wares and in 1783 the Cozzi factory at Venice was advertising porcelain pagods which, in all probability, were similar to those produced at Meissen some seventy years earlier. Even at the very fashion-conscious Sèvres factory, rococo chinoiseries were sometimes used to decorate vases which otherwise conformed to the new taste for purity and simplicity of outline, the most notable being those on the black-and-gold *écaille noire* wares.

In nearly all parts of Europe, and especially in England, there were, however, some creators of late eighteenth-century chinoiserie who adapted themselves to the new style and presented a vision of Cathay as seen through Grecian spectacles. Having written of baroque chinoiserie and of rococo chinoiserie it would be tempting to describe such works as examples of neo-classical chinoiserie, even though this term might summon up a false impression of high-waisted Chinese nymphs with the coiffure of Mme Récamier, and of naked Carrara marble pagods as lithe as an Apollo or an Antinous. Chinoiseries of this period were sometimes treated with classical restraint: Chinese figures were given a greater sense of nobility and decorum, while decorative motifs were used more sparingly and symmetrically than hitherto. The new style might be called Louis XVI chinoiserie, but that its most notable expressions were created outside France and its popularity lasted long after that unhappy king lost his head to the guillotine.

Neo-classical chinoiseries were not only simpler and less fantastic than those produced by rococo artists; they were also much closer to genuine Chinese objects. An archaeological spirit was abroad which regulated the adaptation of Chinese no less than Gothic and classical styles. This new attitude was already apparent at Kew gardens where Sir William Chambers attempted to imitate a Chinese 'Taa' and 'Ting' with as much care as he applied to the construction of a ruined Roman arch. Though neither of these buildings was a precise copy of a Chinese prototype, both were intended to be scholarly exercises in their style.

Further evidence of the change in the European attitude to the Orient and to oriental art is provided by two sets of Chinese views taken on the spot by William and Thomas Daniell, who made a *Picturesque Voyage to India by Way of China* in 1784, and by William Alexander who travelled to Peking as the official draughtsman in Lord Macartney's hapless embassy of 1793. The water-colour drawings of these artists, and the aquatints etched after them, which were widely diffused, presented for the first time a group of accurate illustrations of the Chinese scene and revealed, of course, a world far different from that presented by Boucher and Pillement. Although these artists appreciated the picturesque qualities of the Chinese landscape, its buildings and the brightly clad figures that thronged around them, they made no attempt to romanticize or sentimentalize them. Their works, lightly coloured and delicately drawn, are suffused by the same clear light of topographical truth as plays over Francis Towne's views of the English lake district. In a striking contrast to these prints are the many little scenes painted at Macao and Canton some thirty years later by George Chinnery whose vision of a quaint nineteenth-century Cathay will be considered in the final chapter of this book.

2 LOUIS XVI CHINOISERIE

In the grounds of the Petit Trianon, Marie-Antoinette had a Chinese merry-go-round, a charming contrivance to which she doubtless resorted when wearied of churning milk and patting butter in her model dairy. One may well imagine her with, perhaps, her husband and children—ladies seated on cushions held up by kneeling Chinamen, the men and boys straddling peacocks—whirling round the central pagoda while labourers, politely concealed from view beneath the earth, turned the wheels, and while other less docile mechanics plotted their ruin beyond the confines of the park. A similar chinoiserie *jeu de bague* diverted the leisure hours of the Duc de Chartres in his *jardin anglo-chinois* at Monceau. In royal circles and, as we shall see, in Paris—where there were *bains chinois*, a *café chinois*, and a *redoute chinoise*—chinoiserie was passing from the drawing-room to the fair ground. No longer did sumptuous Chinese balls and collations occupy the time and excite the jealousies of courtiers, for the royal preference had turned from such dressy functions to the charms of the simple life. Long afternoons were now spent tending the chickens and cows on the royal farm or turning the lathes in the royal locksmith's shop.

The queen could, however, smile on the taste for chinoiserie to which she paid a supreme compliment by including a *cabinet chinois* in her holy of holies, the *Hameau* at Versailles. Most of the chinoiserie porcelain produced at the Sèvres factory was commissioned by her or other members of the royal family. She also made some notable additions to the royal collection of orientalia which was already so vast that it needed a special section in the inventories. Among the choicest objects she owned were a pair of elegant lacquer ewers, hung with fine gold chains and garnished with ormolu dragon heads on the tips of their spouts, now in the Louvre. A more cumbrous, though no less exquisitely worked example of her taste in chinoiserie is provided by the *secrétaire* made for her by the great *ébéniste* Jean-Henri Reisener in the 1780s and now in the Metropolitan Museum, New York. This magnificent if somewhat ponderous piece of furniture is decorated with panels of the finest Japanese lacquer surrounded by rectilinear ormolu frames and discreet garlands and wreaths of flowers which, though they make no concessions to exoticism, harmonize perfectly with the naturalistic plants painted on the lacquer.

The Reisener *secrétaire* is an outstanding example of the type of lacquer-decorated furniture which began to come into fashion in France in the late

1760s. Whereas earlier *ébénistes* had allowed the tendrils of their ormolu mounts to ramble rankly over the inset lacquer panels, those of the new period restrained the ormolu to the borders. The panels of lacquer were framed by the cabinets to which they were applied and were thereby given a greatly increased decorative importance. On a cabinet by P. Garnier in the Louvre, for example, three panels of Japanese lacquer set in narrow ormolu bands form the principal decoration of the front (Pl. 118). The method of mounting oriental porcelain also underwent a change but with dissimilar effect. Ormolu dragons and scrolls were banished and simple classically inspired mounts were substituted for them with the result that the outline of the vessel was retained. But as monochrome vases of an oviform shape were preferred, it is often difficult to appreciate that the porcelain set in mounts of this type owes its origin to the Orient. Even the *écaille noire* wares made at the Sèvres factory in the 1770s were often enclosed in classical mounts in France. Those taken to England, on the other hand, were embellished with dragons only slightly less exuberant than their forebears of twenty years earlier.

Although the *ébénistes* of Louis XVI's reign gave greater prominence to oriental lacquer on their furniture they still seem to have prized it principally as a material of great value which might add the final touch of richness to an opulent piece of furniture whose front would otherwise be decorated with panels of porcelain, *pietre dure* mosaic, or inlays of rare and exotic woods—amboyna from the Moluccas, palisandre from Brazil, satinwood from Ceylon and tulip-wood from Peru. They therefore had no use for lacquer of European make and no French japanner is known to have adapted his style to suit the furniture in the Louis XVI taste. Nor do French craftsmen appear to have produced much simulated bamboo chinoiserie furniture of the type made in England and Germany, other than for such garden pavilions as that of the Folie de St James. For another garden building, the pagoda at Chanteloup, the great *ébéniste* George Jacob made some very unusual chairs with rigid pagoda-shaped backs. But otherwise the only notable example of French neo-classical chinoiserie furniture is provided by a harp, in the Musée des Arts Décoratifs at Paris, painted with oriental motifs chastely arranged as a classical arabesque.

In the design of wallpapers French artists followed English fashions and produced a few hangings suitable to decorate a Louis XVI boudoir. For their finest papers the French had, indeed, been dependent on England and China until after the mid-century. Large non-repetitive patterns similar to the type imitated in the Wotton-under-Edge room (Pl. 83) seem at first to have been popular and were imitated in France with the addition of frenchified chinoiserie figures in the 1760s. But as the pendulum of taste swung towards neo-classicism these soon went out of fashion. In the 1780s the most distinguished French *papiers peints* firm, Réveillon, was specializing in the production of papers which imitated Pompeian paintings. But they also found a market for hangings decorated with staid and distinctly neo-classical groups of Chinamen picnicking or practising falcony. Large panels of wallpaper based on the Chinese non-repetitive type returned to vogue in the Empire period but only as the inspiration for Zuber's and Dufour's famous scenic series which included a set of *Les Vues de la Chine*.

Although relatively few examples of Louis XVI chinoiserie are known to have survived, China appears to have exerted considerable fascination on the Paris of the 1780s. At about this time the proprietors of the Oriental Baths in the Boulevard des Italiens employed S.-N. Lenoir, called *le Romain*, to transform their premises into *bains chinois* (Pl. 117). Prints reveal that this new building was in a curious medley of exotic styles and a contemporary acidly remarked of it that 'L'Architecture qui est turcque, chinoise et persane, est de M. Lenoir, surnommé *le Romain*'. Cuisin celebrated the strange enterprise in a poem:

> Quel pays merveilleux! Sans sortir de Paris,
> Dans le Palais-Royal, vous avez des Chinoises:
> Un orchestre chinois, arrivé de Pékin,
> Exécute, en ronflant, un solo de Martin:
> Mais dans les Bains chinois c'est un autre artifice.
> D'un kiosque élégant tracez vous l'édifice
> Sous des rochers de plâtre en amas rocailleux
> D'une grotte en carton à l'aspect gracieux.
>
> Ainsi le Parisien, tout près de sa maison
> Peut, la canne à la main, aborder à Canton.

The Parisian might visit a Chinese café where he was greeted by a live Chinese porter and served by French waitresses attired in Chinese costume—though whether he could sample *cuisine chinoise* is not recorded. Paris also boasted, in 1781, a *redoute chinoise* in the Foire Saint-Laurent, where Chinese pageants, illuminations, and firework displays were given. Of these three places of entertainment only one survived the Revolution—the *bains chinois*. The cult for exoticism which flourished under the Empire drew inspiration from nearer and more easily attainable parts of the East: Egypt and, at one moment, India on which Napoleon had fixed a covetous eye.

Outside France, examples of neo-classical chinoiserie are rare in continental Europe. In the 1770s the porcelain modellers of Germany changed their style very slightly to give a greater simplicity of decoration and squareness of outline to the chinoiserie groups which they continued to produce. German cabinet-makers at the same time made some pieces of mahogany furniture carved to resemble bamboo. But the Hellenic tyranny over German arts—which began to take effect in the 1760s—created an atmosphere in which it was difficult for exoticism to flourish. Here, as in Spain and Portugal, chinoiserie survived mainly as a part of the rococo style. In Italy, however, a few artists and craftsmen focused their vision of Cathay to bring it into harmony with the rules of neo-classicism.

Of the several known examples of late eighteenth-century Italian chinoiserie none is stranger than a silver candlestick made at Genoa in 1789 (Pl. 120). Its central support is in the form of an octagonal bell-hung temple beneath which there stands the august figure of a Chinese bonze, and the angular arms holding the candles have a vaguely exotic appearance; otherwise the decorations on this piece are classical including two *ignudi* (or semi-*ignudi*) flanking the base and the figure of Pan squatting between the candles. The silversmith responsible for this preposterous object has made an attempt to reconcile classicism with exoticism and although purists—whether sinologists or classicists—may hold up their hands in horror at the result there will be others who can appreciate its wayward fantasy. A more successful synthesis between chinoiserie and classicism was achieved by the decorators of the Villa La Favorita at Palermo and of rooms in the Castello di Rivoli, near Turin, and the Palazzo Braschi in Rome.

La Favorita was built for Ferdinand IV, King of the Two Sicilies, in 1799 when he found it prudent to leave Naples in the hands of the Parthenopean Republic and retire to Palermo. Why he should have decided to build in the Chinese taste is more than a little difficult to determine, though it may be surmised that he wished to retreat from the thundery atmosphere of an unpleasantly realistic Europe into a private world of make-believe. The building seems to have owed its origin to a very elaborate Chinese banquet given for Nelson in May 1799 in a temporary structure run up for the occasion by

Giuseppe Marvuglia. Shortly afterwards the present building was erected to the design of Giuseppe Patricola, the Royal Surveyor and a notable neo-classical architect. It is a square, solid structure of four storeys crowned by a dumpy octagonal pagoda-roofed tower. A minaret enclosing a spiral stairway, which leads to the balcony running round the first floor, juts out from one corner and a semi-circular portico is tacked on to the centre of the garden façade. A profusion of iron railings in the style of Chinese fences enclose the many balconies and the two large loggias on the third floor, while the surface of the building is liberally painted with pseudo-Chinese characters and *trompe-l'œil* architectural details in red on a yellow ground (Pl. 122). An early description records that bells were suspended from various parts of the building. Beside the villa stand the stables, in the form of a vast chinoiserie tent, similarly provided with fretted iron balconies and *trompe-l'œil* decorations. Unfortunately all the paintings on the exterior have faded to a monochrome brown, but they must once have been as brilliant as the rooms inside.

Various styles were employed to decorate the rooms of La Favorita—one is painted to resemble a Roman ruin, another is Moorish, but chinoiserie pre-dominates throughout the house. The *sala da ricevimento* on the main floor is hung with strips of floral Chinese-style wallpaper, framed by bands of painted lattice work, alternating with panels on which pseudo-Chinese and arabic inscriptions are painted. At first sight a discordant note is struck by the ceiling to this room for it appears to be in the Pompeian style. Closer inspection reveals, however, that the motifs are not Roman senators and classical temples but richly dressed mandarins and elaborately fretted pagodas. Of the several other chinoiserie rooms one is painted to resemble a leafy arbour through the boughs of which one may catch glimpses of a Chinese landscape, and the octagon at the top of the house—the *sala del te*—is in the form of a bizarre striped tent hung with genuine Chinese paintings. But perhaps the most effective room is the little *sala da giuoco* where the walls are painted with groups of Chinamen showing off their rich robes under a ceiling in the Pompeian-chinoiserie style. The figures stride and posture with a stiff dignity which marks them as distant subjects of the neo-classical world, and it is hardly surprising to find that the artist who painted them—Giuseppe Velasco—otherwise devoted himself to depicting graceful nymphs and effete heroes similar to those carved by Canova.

The chinoiserie room in the Castello di Rivoli antedates La Favorita by nearly a decade but is painted in a similar vein of restrained exoticism, with diamond-shaped medallions of Chinamen's heads above the windows, narrow half-columns painted with flowers, a frieze on which the Greek key motif has been twisted into a more erratic pattern and a number of Chinese scenes on the ceiling (Pl. 121). Unfortunately the artist responsible for it is not recorded. In the Palazzo Braschi in Rome a Chinese room was decorated in about 1808, probably by Liborio Coccetti, an artist much employed by the Braschi family. It is painted with bamboos, exotic birds, and Pompeian-chinoiserie grotesques similar to those at La Favorita. Two other rooms in the Palazzo Braschi, which were painted at about the same time, are in the Egyptian and 'Etruscan' styles; and it is interesting to note that they have closer affinities than their differences in subject-matter would suggest. The Egyptian style was, of course, very popular in Empire Europe (much more so than chinoiserie), for Egypt now exerted an exotic appeal hardly less strong than that of Cathay and her arts could far more easily be adapted to the canons of neo-classicism.

3   THE PRINCE AND THE PAVILION

> The queerest of all the queer sights I've set sight on;
> Is, the *what d'ye-call't thing*, here, the FOLLY at Brighton.
> The outside—huge teapots, all drill'd round with holes,
> Relieved by extinguishers, sticking on poles:
> The inside—all tea-things, and dragons, and bells,
> The show rooms—*all* show, the sleeping rooms—cells.
> But the *grand* Curiosity's not to be seen—
> The owner himself—an old fat MANDARIN . . .
>   W. HONE: *The Joss and His Folly*, 1820

George IV has usually been given the credit—or the blame—for the revival of chinoiserie in late Georgian England. At Carlton House he commissioned a room which must have been among the most exquisite examples of chinoiserie decoration ever created and in the pavilion at Brighton he left a monument to the Regency vogue for exoticism at its most feverish. Yet neither, in fact, exerted wide influence on the taste of the period. Indeed such were the howls of execration and derision which greeted the Brighton Pavilion—for personal as much as artistic reasons—that it probably had a depressing rather than a stimulating influence on the vogues for indiennerie and chinoiserie.

Chinoiserie had passed the zenith of its popularity by about 1760 in England, but it lingered on fitfully for another half-century and even survived into the opening years of Queen Victoria's reign. Some of its later manifestations in silver, pottery, and textiles were in a *retardataire* rococo style, but the majority conformed to the rules of elegant simplicity laid down by the neo-classicists. For the advent of the neo-classical style in the 1760s by no means banished the Chinese room from the English house. Even Robert Adam, the arch-priest of the new movement, occasionally designed chinoiserie furnishings (drawings by him for lanterns in this style are in the Soane Museum) and he made good use of Chinese wallpaper and japanned furniture at Nostell Priory and the Adelphi; while at his temple of Roman elegance, Osterley, one guest, Lady Proctor, declared in 1772 that she found herself amidst such a 'rich profusion of China and Japan, that I could almost fancy myself at Pekin'. This delightful experience could be enjoyed in one room only, of course, the hostess's dressing-room, though Adam included some exquisite japanned commodes in his strictly neo-classical schemes of decoration elsewhere in the house.

Lady Proctor was not the only writer of the 1770s to enthuse over exotic furniture seen on country-house visits. *A Peep into the Principal Seats and Gardens in and about Twickenham*, written in 1775 by 'a lady of distinction', as the title proudly declares, describes a drawing-room and a bed-chamber in the Chinese style at the Duke of Argyll's house. Here there was also to be seen an as yet unfamiliar import from the East: 'a Chinese instrument called a gong made of copper, almost the shape of a dish which . . . gives a clear, full, and harmonious sound which vibrates a long while and gradually dies away.' Mrs Lybbe Powys, that remorseless and observant county caller, frequently paused in her travels to note an example of chinoiserie decoration. At Kirklington Park, near Bletchingdon, she remarked 'a bed-chamber with hangings, bed and furniture of crimson and yellow velvet is shown as a great curiosity, but I think ugly. The pattern is all pagoda. It was a present of Admiral Lee, my Lord's brother, who had it taken from the loom in China, and the loom broke so that no one else might have the same.' At Fawley Court, she was better pleased with a 'bed-chamber . . . furnish'd with one of the finest red-grounded chintz I ever saw, the panels of the room painted, in each a different Chinese figure larger than life. . . . In the dressing room . . . over the chimney . . . a droll picture of a Chinese pauper.' The chintz was probably English and the papers appear to have been made by the firm of Bromwich and Lee of Ludgate Hill: they were clearly much more to Mrs Lybbe Powys's taste than genuine Chinese hangings—'all pagoda' though they might be.

In 1786 a critic in *The Lounger* remarked that 'a well-educated British gentleman, it may truly be said, is of no country whatever, he unites in himself the characteristics of all foreign nations; he talks and dresses French, he sings Italian; he rivals the Spaniard in indolence and the German in drinking, his house is Grecian, his offices Gothic, and his furniture Chinese.' This comment, which would have passed unnoticed among the many satires on chinoiserie of thirty years earlier, reveals that in 1786 the style still retained enough adherents to stir a writer's scorn. An occasional chinoiserie building was still being erected to adorn an English park; chinoiserie furniture and furnishings were still being made to decorate English homes. Importations from the East—lacquer, wallpaper, silks, and porcelain—continued to flow onto the English market and were as eagerly snapped up as ever. One lady, the Duchess of Dorset, was even so fortunate as to secure that most coveted object in any sinophil's collection—a living Chinese boy. So proud was she of this acquisition that she gave the youth—named Wang-y-Tong—a good classical education at Sevenoaks school and commissioned Sir Joshua Reynolds to paint a portrait of him (now at Knole) dressed in his picturesque costume, clasping a fan in his hand and perched cross-legged on a chinoiserie settee.

Most of the chinoiserie furniture made in England between the mid-1760s and about 1790 is of formal classical outline decorated with japanning or, more rarely, panels of oriental lacquer. Fretwork of the type used in the 1750s remained popular, but gone are the smirking josses squatting on inconvenient corners, the ho-ho birds preening their feathers on the cresting and the pagodas tapering out of seas of rococo waves. Exoticism is confined to the surface: the trees are less luxuriant, the buildings more solid, the figures more decorous and the general style more closely imitative of oriental lacquer. Outstanding among the examples of this type of furniture are Robert Adam's commodes at Nostell Priory and Osterley Park and a similar commode originally at Harewood House and now in the collection of Sir James Horlick (Pl. 127). On these pieces the japanned panels are framed by such favourite neo-classical devices as palmette borders and strings of husk ornament while odd corners are filled with Roman paterae. The Nostell commodes are of a lovely emerald green on which raised figures and landscapes are picked out in gold and silver; but most other examples are painted in flat gold on a black ground. Chinoiserie designs were also applied to painted furniture without any attempt to emulate the appearance of lacquer, as for example in the famous bedroom suite made for David Garrick in about 1770, painted with little landscapes in green on a buff ground (Pl. 126). Some pieces in the same suite are further decorated by strips of simulated bamboo, with the knots painted green, a type of moulding which first began to appear on English furniture at this date and soon became very popular. Usually carved in beech-wood and painted around the knots and buds, these canes were employed both for ornamental borders and the legs of chairs, tables, and cabinets; sometimes they appear on japanned furniture. A magnificent cabinet at Buxted Park (Pl. 125) rests on six tortoises each of which is poised atop a delicately curving and tapering bamboo leg, the whole being covered by a bell-hung pagoda roof. Chinoiserie decorations were also, very occasionally, worked in marquetry.

Smaller chinoiserie objects were also designed in accordance with the laws of the new style. Clocks adorned with proud, upright ormolu mandarins were made by James Cox between 1760 and 1780. (His more extravagant creations in an unbridled rococo style seem to have been intended to delight the eyes of far-eastern potentates.) Pottery and porcelain painters applied chastened chinoiserie landscapes, figures, and posies of flowers to vessels of simple classical outline; silversmiths embossed groups of mandarins onto the new teapots and coffee-pots. One anonymous silver designer of the period hit upon the happy idea of combining the taste for exoticism with the desire for objects of simple rectilinear shape by producing tea-caddies in the form of miniature tea-chests, engraved with the Chinese characters for such words as 'upper', 'spring', and 'direction'—though he no doubt endowed the mysterious symbols with a more romantic meaning (Pl. 133).

Into this world of restrained chinoiserie of the late 1780s there strutted the extravagant figure of George, Prince of Wales (Fig. 10). Born in 1762, the prince had been brought up under the shade of the pagoda in Kew Gardens, a building for which his father bore an inordinate affection which became especially and embarrassingly noticeable whenever his mind was deranged. At these unhappy periods indeed the pagoda had to be bolted against him.

Early initiation into the charms of chinoiserie only whetted the prince's appetite, and it was at his suggestion, perhaps, that his adoring and unfortunate sisters were set to work japanning rooms at Frogmore in red and gold. Not until 1790, however, when the Chinese drawing-room was created in Carlton House, was he able to indulge his taste on the lavish scale he required. Though by no means a novelty in English interior decoration, this room was certainly the paragon of Georgian chinoiserie taste, for it combined a delicate strain of fantasy and a carefully balanced over-all design with brilliant craftsmanship

Fig. 10   Caricature of George IV, after G. Cruikshank

and exquisite materials. Unfortunately the room was dismantled within two decades of its creation, but all the movable furniture has been preserved at Buckingham Palace or at Brighton; and from these pieces and contemporary prints, some impression may still be obtained of its original effect (Pl. 124).

The Carlton House drawing-room was decorated under the supervision of Henry Holland, and despite its obvious surface exoticism, revealed the restraining influence of a classically inspired architect. (Cursory examination of the chimney-piece or even the pier-tables lays bare the Grecian skeleton beneath the chinoiserie dress.) According to the prints and description in Thomas Sheraton's *Cabinet-Maker's and Upholsterers' Drawing Book*, the walls were decorated with Chinese landscapes separated by tall and elegantly simple 'Chinese' pilasters. A vast ottoman upholstered in figured satin with rich trimmings ran across the entire width of one end. In front stood two perfume burners by which, Sheraton explained, 'an agreeable smell may be diffused to every part of the room, preventing that of a contrary nature'—hastening to add that in such an apartment the only disagreeable smell would come from burning too large a number of wax candles. In the centre of one wall stood the marble chimney-piece, a prettily carved confection (now at Buckingham Palace) with Chinese term figures in pagoda-roofed niches and a band of crisp exotic decoration running across the top (Pl. 128). This was balanced on the opposite wall by an appropriately elaborate pier-table (also at Buckingham Palace) with a *rosso antico* top supported by four Chinese terms, painted green, crimson, and gold, and with the figure of a brilliantly dressed mandarin seated on the stretcher. Other pier-tables were slightly simpler, though decorated with dragons pulling back bell- and tassel-hung ormolu curtains. The chairs, upholstered in brilliantly coloured satin, had pagods perching on their backs and serpents twining around their legs. Various bibelots—porcelain vases mounted in ormolu, candlesticks supported by willowy Chinese women—added the final touch of exoticism. Sheraton, somewhat primly and apologetically, remarked that 'the whole effect, though it may appear extravagant to a vulgar eye, is but suitable to the dignity of the proprietor.' And a far greater extravagance was yet to come: the Royal Pavilion at Brighton.

While work was progressing at Carlton House (the Chinese drawing-room dated from the second period of activity there), the prince paid several visits to Brighthelmstone where, in 1787, he commissioned Henry Holland to transform a 'respectable farm-house' into what Daisy Ashford might have called a 'small but costly' marine pavilion. This modest stuccoed villa was soon found inadequate to the prince's needs and further work of enlargement and alteration was begun under the direction of Holland's assistant, P. F. Robinson. In 1802 a long gallery was built to display a recent gift of a set of Chinese wallpapers, and a passage room lit by chinoiserie stained glass windows was also added. At the same time other rooms were given an exotic appearance by the addition of bamboo furniture and numerous Chinese bibelots, while plans were set on foot for a chinoiserie exterior and a Chinese house in the grounds. Much of the finest work on the interior of the pavilion was executed at this period and examples of it have survived both at Brighton and Buckingham Palace.

The furniture designed for the pavilion in about 1802 was in a markedly different style from that produced for Carlton House little more than a decade earlier. The banqueting-room chimney-pieces at Brighton, for example, with their brilliantly enamelled mandarins and fire-breathing dragons make the Carlton House chimney-piece of purple marble and ormolu look almost demure. The movable furniture, on the other hand, the cabinets, tables, and chairs (supplied by Elward, Marsh, and Tatham) was less flamboyant than that made for Carlton House, though no less exotic in intention. Simpler materials were used at Brighton—simulated bamboo and lacquer instead of ebony and ormolu—and the designs were closer in feeling to genuine Chinese furniture of which some specimens were to be found in the pavilion (Pl. 132). While the Chinese drawing-room at Carlton House (and other rooms in the same building) had an air of opulent extravagance emphasized by the richness of the materials used in its decoration, the interior of the Royal Pavilion presented a spectacle of bizarre and gimcrack brilliance. Life-sized statues of Chinamen clad in oriental silk robes greeted the visitor in the corridor. Walls were lined with freshly painted Chinese wallpapers on which exotic flowers unfolded their petals and humming-birds disported themselves against clear turquoise or coral pink skies; gay Chinese silk banners hung from the cornices, and the lightly painted simulated bamboo furniture was loaded with glittering hoards of porcelain, lacquer, and cloisonné enamel. Some visitors, indeed, found the pavilion too garish for their taste and Miss Mary Berry recorded in her diary, in 1811: 'All is Chinese, quite overloaded with china of all sorts and of all possible forms, many beautiful in themselves but so overloaded one upon another, that the effect is more like a china shop baroquement arranged, than the abode of a Prince. All is gaudy without looking gay; and all is overcrowded with ornaments, without being magnificent.' It should be added, that Miss Berry had a headache that day aggravated by a military band playing too loudly in the dining-room.

In about 1803 Henry Holland was succeeded as the prince's architect by William Porden who immediately set about plans for a new pavilion to be built entirely in the chinoiserie style. His drawings show a long two-storey building with a central tower, liberally adorned with dragons and fretted balconies (Pl. 123). Next year he began work on the royal stables, riding school, and coach-house near the pavilion, employing not the Chinese but the Indian style which he had probably acquired while working under Cockerell at Sezincote. Details for these buildings were derived from prints of Agra and Delhi, but when he came to build the vast dome which covers the riding school, Porden modelled his design on the *Halle au blé* at Paris which he richly embroidered with Saracenic ornament. While this work was in progress, an artist who had been more intimately concerned with Sezincote, Humphrey Repton, was ordered on the scene. 'When I was commanded to deliver my opinion concerning the style of architecture best adapted for the pavilion', Repton wrote, 'I could not hesitate in agreeing that neither the Grecian nor the Gothic style could be made to assimilate with what had so much the character of an Eastern building.' He therefore ran through the other available styles: 'The Turkish was objectionable as being a corruption of the Grecian; the Moorish, as a bad model of the Gothic; the Egyptian as too cumbrous for the character of a villa, the Chinese too light and trifling for the outside, however it might be applied to the interior. Thus, if any known style were to be adopted no alternative remained but to combine from the Architecture of Hindustan such forms as might be rendered applicable to the purpose.' No such consideration would have weighed with the creators of exotic buildings half a century earlier; but it is characteristic of the nineteenth century that such stress should have been laid on supposed geographical accuracy.

Repton promptly produced plans to transform the pavilion into a Hindu pleasure dome, and the prince could hardly have been more delighted with them. 'Mr Repton', he exclaimed, 'I consider the whole of this work to be perfect, and will have every part of it carried into immediate execution; not a tittle shall be altered—even you yourself shall not attempt an improvement.'

The attractive scheme was promptly hurried into aquatint and published in 1808, but by this time fresh difficulties had arisen in the princely treasury and the plans had to be shelved. The idea of a Hindu exterior for the pavilion lodged in the prince's mind, however, and when in 1815 he took up the matter again he commissioned his new architect, John Nash, to provide designs for a building in this style (much to Repton's fury). Nash set to work immediately, though it was not until 1821 that the 'presiding genius', now George IV, saw the whole building complete, with its Hindu exterior and chinoiserie interior.

As completed in 1821 the rooms of the Royal Pavilion presented a spectacle of exotic splendour unique in Europe. 'I do not believe', wrote the Princess Lieven, 'that since the days of Heliogabalus, there has been such magnificence and such luxury.' Much of this magnificence is now sadly tarnished and it is only with the aid of Nash's views of 1826 that the modern visitor can recapture the tinsel and lacquer splendour of the pavilion when new. Although it contained much furniture designed for Carlton House and for the 1802 re-decoration of the pavilion itself, the interior of 1821 was marked by an extraordinary difference of emphasis. All had previously been quaint and colourful, almost toy-like: now the atmosphere was more than a little sinister, as if a nest of serpents had suddenly been let loose in the flowery garden of Cathay. Dragons of a hard metallic scaliness abounded, as in no earlier chinoiserie rooms, hanging from the ceilings, and uncoiling their necks across the walls; snakes of peculiar slitheriness twined themselves about the pillars; and even the vast flower-shaped lamps hanging from the ceiling were given a predatory look, reminding one of the man-eating orchid.

Five state rooms on the ground floor are connected at the back by a long corridor lit by a sky-light of chinoiserie painted glass; the walls were originally hung with Chinese pink ground-paper and niches occupied by statues of China-men (Pl. 116). At either end graceful double staircases of cast-iron simulating bamboo led up to the first floor past stained-glass windows representing China-men in fluttering robes. In the banqueting-room the ceiling was painted to resemble the sky partly obscured by a giant plantain from which there hung a great silver dragon clutching in its talons the cords of a vast lustre which incorporates six dragonets holding lotus blossoms of tinted glass in their mouths. There were four smaller hanging lamps in the form of dragons carrying Lien-Hoa flowers—or water lilies—and further light was provided by eighteen-feet high dark blue Spode standards supported on dolphins and crowned with lotus flowers. All these lamps were designed to be lit by gas jets. The walls of the banqueting-room were painted with groups of Chinese figures, much larger than life, said to incorporate portraits of members of the court, including Lady Conyngham. Above them more than a hundred little silvered bells hung from the cornice.

Leading out of the banqueting-room, *en filade*, are the south drawing-room, central saloon, north drawing-room, and the music-room. The two drawing-rooms were comparatively simple—the first with a pink ceiling and white walls on which a Chinese fret pattern was picked out in gold, the second with bright yellow walls, and similar decorations in lilac, which provided a back-ground for a series of Chinese pictures. The central saloon, which owed its oval plan to Holland's building, was more elaborate with a magnificent lotus gasalier, a bell-hung cornice, gilded dragon-headed canopies to the windows and pierglasses, japanned doors, and gilded palm-tree pilasters round which serpents writhed.

Of the music-room at the north end of the pavilion, the enthusiastic topographer Edward Brayley wrote:

> No verbal description, however elaborate, can convey to the mind or the imagination of the reader an appropriate idea of the magnificence of this apartment; and even the creative delineations of the pencil, combined with all the illusions of colour, would scarcely be adequate to such an undertaking. Yet luxuriously resplendent and costly as the adornments are, they are so intimately blended with the refinements of an elegant taste, that everything appears in keeping and in harmony.

Nine water-lily and dragon gasaliers of cut and rose-tinted glass hung from the domed ceiling, the walls were decorated with red-and-gold Chinese landscapes (Pl. IV) set between snake-wreathed pillars and blue panels on which a fretted pattern was picked out in gold. Dragons hovered menacingly over the paintings and supported the curtains. Between the windows stood four remarkably tall pagodas of Yung Chên porcelain. Here it was that George IV, accompanied by a seventy-piece orchestra, would entertain his guests after dinner with such airs as 'Glorious Apollo' and 'Mighty Conqueror' in his strong baritone. The floor was covered with a blue Axminster carpet on which there were more dragons, serpents, and vast flowers. None of the king's private apartments or the upstairs rooms could compete with the state rooms for magnificence, but they did not lack their quota of dragons, mandarins, exotic birds, water-lilies, and lotuses.

Throughout the pavilion, every corner was crowded with a profusion of objects of Chinese virtu—vast Ch'ien Lung vases, exquisitely wrought lacquer boxes, filigree ornaments, fans, screens, enamel bowls, and such curiosities as miniature sampans and junks acquired in China for the royal collection by Dr James Garrett. Among the many chinoiserie objects there were Sèvres *écaille noire* vases in exuberant ormolu mounts, intricate musical clocks guarded by dragons (Pl. 129), dragon fire-dogs and lamps and candlesticks supported by mandarins.

A vast team of artists was employed to decorate the pavilion, most notably John Nash the architect, Frederick Crace (many of whose drawings survive, see Pl. 116), his assistant the painter Lambelet, and Robert Jones who designed much of the furniture. But there can be little doubt that it was to the king himself that the building owed the magnificence and fantasy of its conception. And it is to him, perhaps, that we must attribute the sinister streak in its decorations.

PLATE IV   Painted panel in imitation of lacquer.   The Royal Pavilion, Brighton

Yet it would be a mistake to suppose that the pavilion is a unique phenomenon. Much of the decoration is of the classical Empire variety only slightly disguised by oriental trappings—in the banqueting-room, for example, the ceiling is basically of the popular tent pattern while the trophies of shields and weapons on the walls are unclassical only in their detail. The whole building is, moreover, as much an expression of the age of romanticism as William Beckford's Fonthill Abbey, and is tainted with the same vulgar opulence as that megalomaniac's Gothic phantasmagoria. Even in its present state, stripped of many of its original fittings, the display of wealth seems too extravagantly lavish, the decoration too densely packed and wilfully bizarre. One feels that the creator was straining every nerve to recapture a vision he had glimpsed in childhood.

Courtiers were bound to admire and political opponents to condemn the architecture and furnishings of the Royal Pavilion, and neither the panegyrics of the former nor the often quoted witticisms of the latter—a 'collection of stone pumpkins and pepper boxes' Hazlitt called it—afford much evidence of the impression it made on disinterested contemporaries. Descriptions vary in tone from the enthusiastic pages of Edward Brayley to the savage personal satire of William Hone (quoted at the head of this section). But even in the most effusive accounts one may sometimes detect a subdued note of criticism. It was surely not without a touch of sarcasm that Edward Mogg remarked 'as His Majesty has, in the erection of this terrestrial paradise, placed on British ground the most original, unique and magnificent structure in Europe, it would be a matter of deep regret were it liable to a speedy decay'. For all its picturesque charm the building appeared, and still appears, somewhat gimcrack. Most of those who recorded their impressions of it were critical of the style in which it was built, the garishness of the interior decoration or the extravagance with which money had been lavished on it.

Only one room in England appears to reflect the Brighton chinoiserie style: that decorated for the Dowager Marchioness of Downshire between 1812 and 1814 at Ombersley Park in Worcestershire. Here, in a blue-and-gold colour scheme, the walls are decorated with panels of painted Chinese silk framed by strips of simulated bamboo. The chairs, sofa, and a pier-table are made of beechwood, also carved and painted to resemble bamboo, and are strikingly like those which the firm of Elward, Marsh, and Tatham supplied for the Royal Pavilion in 1802 (Pl. 130). Although Lady Downshire entertained George IV at Ombersley, she is not known to have been a member of the raffish Regency set and the similarity of her room with the earlier rooms at Brighton probably derives only from her having employed the same cabinet-makers.

So it was despite, rather than because of, the Prince's intervention, that the vogue for chinoiserie persisted throughout the last years of the eighteenth and the first decades of the nineteenth centuries. The attitude to the Orient had, meantime, undergone a change which is well illustrated by two plays. James Cobb's *Ramah Droog*, which was performed with universal applause at Covent Garden in 1798, abounds in correct Indian terminology and reveals the new desire for geographical accuracy (its author was a clerk in the East India Company). One stage direction might serve to herald the brief fashion for indiennerie in England:

> Enter the Rajah on an elephant, returning from hunting the tiger, preceded by his hirgarrahs or military messengers and his state palanquin. The Vizier on another elephant. The Princess in a gaurie drawn by buffaloes. The Rajah is attended by his sooth-sayer, his officer of state, and by an ambassador from Tippoo Sultaun in a palanquin; also by Nairs or soldiers from the South of India—Poligars, or inhabitants of the hilly districts, with their hunting dogs—other Indians carrying a dead tiger, and young tigers in a cage—a number of sepoys—musicians on camels and on foot—dancing girls, etc. etc.

Here we are as far from the world of Indo-Cathaian fantasy as in the park at Sezincote.

The other play, or rather comic opera, Andrew Cherry's *The Travellers*, which was produced in 1806, has an Anglo-Chinese theme. The first scene was laid in 'A beautiful garden in the Chinese style—with many bridges, intersecting canals, etc.—the Sun rising slowly in the distance—the curtain is drawn up slowly to a symphony resembling the warbling of birds.' At first this garden may not seem a far cry from Elkanah Settle's *Fairy Queen*, but the story the play unfolds is strikingly different and much of the *décor* was painstakingly accurate —one backcloth was based on a drawing of the Emperor of China's palace and, we are assured, the throne was 'a correct facsimile of that which appertains to the court of Pekin'. The hero of this piece is Prince Zaphimri, heir to the Empire of China, who is sent to England to 'scan those laws which wondering nations silently admire'. On this mission he is accompanied by his Eurasian lover in search of her long-lost father who is, of course, discovered and turns out to be an English admiral. A marriage between East and half-West is promptly arranged, and before the curtain descends the prince strides forward to deliver a paean to the British constitution.

The Last Days of Cathay

China had been put in her place as a 'backward' country, like India, in sore need of British institutions, and the visionary land of Cathay was soon to become as remote historically as geographically. Explaining the success of the Chinese taste, the Rev. Archibald Alison remarked in 1792 that 'however fantastic and uncouth the forms in reality were, they were yet universally admired, because they brought to mind those images of Eastern magnificence and splendour, of which we have heard so much, and which we are always willing to believe because they are distant'.

Some thirty years later, Thomas De Quincey revealed a different attitude to the Orient. 'Southern Asia, in general, is the seat of awful images and associations', he wrote in the *Confessions of an English Opium Eater*. 'The mere antiquity of Asiatic things, of their institutions, histories, modes of faith, etc., is so impressive, that to me the vast age of the race and name overpowers the sense of the Individual. A young Chinese seems to me an antediluvian man renewed.' The magnificence and splendour of the East were reflected in the Brighton Pavilion; so too were some of its 'awful images and associations', which inspired the greatest literary evocation of Cathay, *Kubla Khan*. But in early nineteenth-century eyes the East had also acquired an air of comic absurdity, clearly apparent in Charles Lamb's essays on *The Origin of Roast Pig* and *Old China*.

'I have an almost feminine partiality for old china', Lamb confessed in his garrulous way and proceeded to describe the figures on a china teacup:

> 'Here is a young and courtly Mandarin, handing tea to a lady from a salver, two miles off. See how distance seems to set off respect! And here the same lady, or another—for likeness is identity on teacups—is stepping into a little fairy boat, moored on the hither side of this calm garden river, with a dainty mincing foot, which in a right angle of incidence (as angles go in our world) must inevitably land her in the midst of a flowery mead—a furlong off on the other side of the same strange stream. Farther on—if far and near can be predicted in their world—see horses, trees, pagodas, dancing the hays.'

Many contemporaries must have shared Lamb's partiality; for the English pottery and porcelain factories maintained a steady output of blue-and-white wares decorated with chinoiseries. Of the various designs used, the most popular seems to have been the famous 'Willow pattern' originally engraved by Thomas Minton in about 1780 and subsequently employed by many factories, most notably that of the Spode family (Pl. 134). This pattern, though it incorporated several Chinese motifs, resembled the ideal of an Anglo-Chinese garden rather than any piece of Nanking porcelain. But it soon acquired a romantic story to explain the significance of the pagoda, the houses, the three little figures hurrying over the bridge, and the two birds hovering above them. It was applied to vessels of all shapes and sizes from vast meat dishes to cups and saucers, and even such aberrations of the potter's craft as milk jugs in the form of cows. Eventually it was exported to the East and copied on 'export' porcelain by Chinese painters. The Spode factory produced some variations of the willow pattern, though none achieved equal popularity. They also made some chinoiserie statuettes of a somewhat angular outline.

Wares decorated with brightly coloured polychrome chinoiseries were also produced in great quantity at this period. Japanese Kakiemon or Imari patterns and Chinese *famille rose* chrysanthemums and paeonies which had been so elegantly painted on eighteenth-century porcelain maintained their popularity and were applied to porcelain made at the Worcester, Spode, Derby, and other factories. The designs were, however, coarsened and painted in brighter, sometimes cruder, colours with dark ink blues and flaming cornelian reds predominating. A lavish use of gilt added a further air of sumptuous luxury to these wares. The industrial revolution which was directly or indirectly responsible for the coarseness of design evident in all but the very best early nineteenth-century ceramics, had one beneficial result—the production of large-scale objects.

Perhaps the most interesting of these vast porcelain follies are the chimneypieces and five-feet high vestibule vases, with chinoiserie patterns richly coloured and gilded, made of Mason's patent Ironstone porcelain in the second and third decades of the century (Pl. 135). Such wares have a brio and garish brilliance which reflect the spirit of the decorations in the later Brighton Pavilion. It is perhaps significant that they appear to have been made for the houses of the industrial newly rich rather than the nobility.

Chinoiserie rooms were, however, to be found in houses of all types. In Maria Edgeworth's novel, *The Absentee* (published in 1809), Mr Soho advised his patroness Lady Clonbrony to turn a little room 'temporarily into a Chinese Pagoda, with this *Chinese Pagoda paper*, with the *porcelain border*, and josses, and jars and beakers to match'. In the greater houses such rooms might be hung with Chinese wallpaper, but as these hangings had recently been made prohibitively expensive by a high customs duty, English chinoiserie papers and chintzes were more usual. The chintzes were printed with a wide variety of designs, some derived from Chinese papers, lacquer paintings or porcelain, and some based on the engravings after Pillement and his imitators which had been popular in the eighteenth century (Pl. 137). Others reflected the new desire for exotic richness —heavy designs in strong dark colours with pagoda-roofed buildings and latticed bridges peeping through jungles of flowering plants. But the strangest early nineteenth-century chintzes were designed by Daniel Goddard—the leading artist in this genre—who produced patterns decorated with a mosaic of brightly coloured diamonds, rhomboids, and irregular figures enclosing accurately drawn Chinese characters. And to ensure that the ideograms were correctly printed he cut the blocks himself. Such materials were probably intended to upholster bamboo and lacquer furniture rather than for the lining of walls.

Simulated bamboo furniture held its popularity and a writer of 1826 states that real bamboo was also used, especially for bedroom chairs and tables. This furniture was close in style to genuine oriental pieces, as were many of the designs included in George Smith's *Household Furniture* of 1808. Makers of japanned furniture, on the other hand, did not attempt to copy oriental patterns, but applied their chinoiserie decorations to cabinets, chairs, sofas, and dwarf bookcases of the normal Regency type. Except for those on the doors of cabinets the decorations were very reticent, generally no more than a small group of Chinese figures in an oval or circular frame. Some indication of the continuing fashion for such furniture can be obtained from the London Post Office Directory for 1817 in which seven firms described themselves as japan manufacturers or japan chair makers. Amateur japanners also continued their work and even as late as 1828 Mrs Arbuthnot, the Duke of Wellington's friend, could be found 'making up a japan cabinet I painted last year. . . . The cabinet is really excessively pretty.'

Chinoiserie decorations remained popular with silversmiths during the first decades of the nineteenth century. Generally they were applied to teapots of the austerely classical patterns employed by the Hennells and Batemans; and it must be admitted that romantic views of Chinese gardens, however simplified to accord with the new style, make a somewhat unhappy appearance on such vessels. Frequently chinoiserie, classical, and Gothic motifs were mixed on the same object: knobs in the shape of squatting Chinamen being often applied to otherwise simply decorated wares. A pair of tea-caddies made in 1825 (in the Ionides collection) reveal some knowledge of oriental silver, but no other objects of this type are known.

CHAPTER VIII

China and Japan

I CHINOISERIE SURVIVAL AND REVIVAL

But the curtain which had been drawn around the celestial country for ages has now been rent asunder; and instead of viewing an enchanted fairy-land, we find, after all, that China is just like other countries. Doubtless the Chinese were in that half-civilized state in which they are now, at a very early period, and when the now polished nations of the West were yet rude savages.

ROBERT FORTUNE: *Wanderings in China*, 1847

On the 29th September, 1825, an English portrait and landscape painter, George Chinnery, landed at Macao. He had been living in India for some twenty years and left behind him, at Calcutta, numerous creditors and a termagant wife. (He was said to be heading for Canton where the Chinese authorities would allow no European woman to land.) For the next twenty-seven years, until his death in 1852, Chinnery lived at Macao making occasional expeditions to Canton, and painting innumerable oil and water-colour sketches of common life as well as portraits of such nobilities as the European and Chinese merchants. ('Chinnery himself', said Colonel Newcome, 'could not hit off a better likeness.') Some of these works he sent to England for exhibition at the Royal Academy, and many others must have been taken to Europe and North America by merchants and travellers. They reflected and perhaps helped to diffuse a new picturesque view of southern China—a land in which the barefoot coolie squatting outside his straw hut was more conspicuous than the orgulous mandarin or superstitious priest in all the glory of their silken robes.

Although Chinnery lived on the coast of China for so many years, he remained a member of a foreign colony, unable, and probably unwilling, to mix in native society. The picture he presented of China was therefore very nearly as fanciful as eighteenth-century evocations of Cathay had been. There is, indeed, more than a hint of eighteenth-century chinoiserie in many of his little vignettes of Chinese children playing under vast straw umbrellas (Pl. 139). An attitude of amused condescension informs his works, whether they represent ragged coolies going about their daily tasks or rich Hong merchants, with smiles of senile craftiness on their faces, enthroned amongst gigantic spittoons and piles of bric-à-brac. He showed some interest in Chinese paintings but made only the most perfunctory attempts to learn from them; for to him, as to most of his contemporaries, Chinese art appeared as primitive as the Chinese people themselves, albeit redeemed by a certain quaint picturesqueness.

While Chinnery was quietly painting at Macao in 1839, there broke out the first 'Opium War' which was destined to have a far-reaching and disastrous influence on Chinese civilization. The story of this conflict is not a pretty one from the English (or the Chinese) point of view, but it throws some light on the way in which the flowery vision of Cathay declined into the Far Eastern question. On both sides the war was fought for economic rather than moral reasons; for while the Emperor of China doubtless regretted the demoralizing effect of opium upon his subjects he was more concerned at the drain on the national exchequer. And the British, who made free use of laudanum at home, believed that the export of opium to China provided the basis of the Indian economy. Laws against the opium trade had frequently been promulgated from the Dragon Throne, but the traffic continued with the connivance of government officials, many of whom were partial to the drug.

In 1839, however, a commissioner named Lin was sent to Canton with strict instructions to enforce the laws by whatever means proved necessary. When the British merchants refused to obey his commands, Lin cut off their supply of water and food, obtained most of the opium in their warehouses, liquefied it and poured it into the estuary—composing the while an apologetic address to the Spirit of the Ocean. News of this action incensed the British Government sitting at Westminster: British lives were said to be in danger and Lord Palmerston dispatched sixteen men-of-war and twenty-seven troop-carriers to Canton. The well organized force had little difficulty in routing the Chinese or in marching north towards Nanking and would, no doubt, have advanced on Peking itself had not the emperor prudently decided to temporize by giving way to some of the British claims. By the treaty of Nanking, which was signed in 1842, China paid a heavy indemnity; she ceded the barren island of Hong Kong to the British and for the first time in five hundred years opened four ports (notably Shanghai) to trade and granted foreigners the right to live in them. Foreigners were even allowed to make brief journeys inland from the ports though not, of course, to visit any of the great cities. By a series of further and still less creditable wars, in the course of which Peking was taken and two hundred of the buildings in the Imperial city were sacked (1860), the process of opening China to the West was completed.

The 'unjust and iniquitous war' in defence of an 'infamous and atrocious traffic'—as Gladstone termed the first 'Opium' War—was staunchly opposed by humanitarian thinkers in England. It did not, indeed, throw a very pleasing light on British methods of establishing trade relations. Nor did it enhance the current opinion of China in the eyes of the West. Once more her defences were shown to be pitifully weak, the vast majority of her people backward if not uncivilized, and her administration corrupt and inefficient, while the emperor's proud claims to universal sway were again revealed in all their pompous absurdity. To make matters worse, the Chinese obstinately refused to respond to their conqueror's triumph. The British may have been amused when, in the course of the unequal conflict, the emperor remarked that by cutting off the export of tea and rhubarb he could deprive his enemies of their principal source of pleasure and their only relief from constipation. But they were disappointed by the little interest peasants working beside the Yangtze manifested in the British fleet sailing upstream to Nanking. And when, with proper materialist pride, they pointed to their gleaming steamships they were infuriated to be told by the Chinese: 'Have got plenty, all same inside.'

As a direct and immediate result of the Treaty of Nanking a motley horde of Europeans and British colonials—consular officials, missionaries, engineers, merchants, and freebooters—descended upon the open ports. And the behaviour of many of these settlers must have confirmed the worst Chinese suspicions about the uncivilized state of western nations. There were, however, some worthy and honest men among them, notably Robert Fortune who had been sent out as botanical collector by the Horticultural Society of London. To him we owe several of the Chinese plants now familiar to every European gardener, and it was on his advice and by his collection of seeds that the first tea plantations were established in the Himalayas. He also wrote four travel books which present a vivid account of China in the 1840s and 1850s when it was first opened to the West. Although he was well read in Chinese travel literature, Fortune was none the less dismayed by his first view of the Celestial Empire. Gazing from his steamer at the barren hills which rose above the

Canton estuary he asked himself whether this could be 'the "flowery land" of camellias, azaleas and roses of which I had heard so much in England'. Like many earlier and later travellers he was vexed to find that he had arrived at China and not Cathay.

In the preface to his first book, Fortune declared that he 'was far from having any prejudice against the Chinese people', but although he lived amongst them, on and off, for some fifteen years and acquired enough of their language to pass for a native of a remote province, he appears to have made very few Chinese friends. The dishonesty of the coolies and the duplicity of the mandarins naturally irritated him, and he was no more than amused by the exquisite courtesy of such amiable Chinamen as he encountered. He frequently stayed in their temples, where visitors were always welcome, but his Protestant soul prevented him from having anything but pity for the delusions of their religion. Indeed, the Buddhist ceremonies seemed little better than those of Roman Catholics, and he pondered the conversion of China with scant hope. Only the landscape and the infinite variety of the Chinese flora won his approval and he sent home to England as many seeds and specimens of Chinese plants as he could obtain.

The picture of China as a beautiful landscape populated by a backward semi-civilized race, which Fortune and other mid-nineteenth-century travellers presented, was not an unattractive one. Indeed Fortune's last book, published in 1859, reveals that long familiarity with the country had bred in him a slight decrease in his contempt for its inhabitants. Nevertheless, his account was not designed to stimulate day-dreams about the Celestial Empire. Nor did newspaper reports of the massacre of Christian missionaries enhance the new picture of China which had formed in Western minds. But if China had lost the respect she continued to hold the interest of Europe. Chinese objects were imported in unprecedented quantities and found their way into homes of every type. And a few Europeans continued to create chinoiseries.

The most elaborate example of Victorian chinoiserie is an aviary in the park at Dropmore, Buckinghamshire, probably erected in the early 1850s. Built of iron lattice work painted red and decorated with glazed tiles, it was intended to house a collection of gaudy eastern birds. Near by stands a summer-house, originally decorated inside with floral chinoiserie tiles and split bamboo mouldings and approached, rather surprisingly, through a latticed Doric portico. Part of the surrounding park was transformed into an accurate replica of a Chinese garden, stocked with many of the flowering plants recently imported from the Orient and furnished with Chinese glazed pottery stools.

A still more elaborate garden was laid out at Biddulph in Cheshire in the 1850s, with a joss-house, long latticed bridge and a Chinese verandah among the azaleas and eastern trees. (The same park boasted an Egyptian garden.) In France, at Fleury-sur-Meudon, one Monsieur Pancoucke laid out an extensive park which was diversified by an astonishing variety of buildings—a long *berceau* of chinoiserie lattice work, a replica of William Tell's cottage, a rustic windmill, a thatched house in the Russian style decorated inside with French paintings and eighteenth-century furniture, and a large chinoiserie orangery liberally gilded and decked with Chinese porcelain vases. These were the last of the *jardins anglo-chinois* created in Europe, and in their various parts they revealed that new desire for accuracy which was to mark the nineteenth-century attitude to artistic revivals. A like spirit would, no doubt, have informed the imitation of the Imperial Palace at Peking which Ludwig II of Bavaria intended to add to his collection of gargantuan follies. He ordered the plans and elevations to be drawn on silk.

A somewhat different attitude prevailed in the United States, where some chinoiserie buildings were erected in the nineteenth century. Previously Americans had seldom indulged in the style for entire buildings—the James Reid House in Charleston of 1757 is the only recorded example, though Thomas Jefferson intended to erect a Chinese pavilion in the garden at Monticello—and the first nineteenth-century examples were drawn from European models, such as Chambers's 'tower near Canton' of which a version was raised in the public gardens in Philadelphia in 1827. In the 1840s, however, a new and more pervasive vogue for chinoiserie buildings struck America. The New Haven railway station built in 1848 by Henry Austin incorporated a curious mixture of Chinese, Indian and Italian features (it was destroyed in 1874) and in the same year the great showman P. T. Barnum built 'Iranistan' near Bridgeport—a very bulky house inspired by the Royal Pavilion at Brighton which had deeply impressed the owner when he visited England. Several other oriental villas of a vaguely Indian or Chinese appearance were erected at about the same time and one Mr Valcour Aime adorned his Louisiana garden on the west bank of the Mississippi with a pagoda ornamented with coloured glass and bells.

Some of the smaller chinoiserie objects produced in Europe at this time reflect the nineteenth-century passion for the grotesque—teapots and mustard-pots in the form of grinning Chinamen with their pigtails curving out to serve as handles, and such curiosities as snuff-boxes fashioned like the deformed feet of Chinese women. Others are in a different style, strongly reminiscent of, if not directly copied from, eighteenth-century chinoiserie objects. At the Great Exhibition of 1851, for instance, Messrs John Harrison of Sheffield included among their display of electro-plate 'Tea and coffee services, Chinese and Louis XIV patterns, Kettle and stand, Chinese pattern'. There can be little doubt that this kettle would have been modelled on such a vessel as that made by Whipham and Wright in the early 1760s (Pl. 99).

In the 1830s eighteenth-century art began to return to fashion in both England and France, bringing with it a new vogue for Chinese objects of an eighteenth-century type, and by 1859 L. E. Audot was able to remark: 'Les *Chinoiseries* ont repris faveur dans les dernières années, et les *Magots* et potiches achetés à grand frais ont été réintégrés sur les étagères des petites maîtresses'. These two fashions appealed in many instances to the same collectors—the Goncourts, for example—and were stimulated by similar desires. Although modern China had lost the affection of most Europeans, the elegant world of Cathay, described by Voltaire and depicted by many a porcelain painter, began to exert a new fascination. Théophile Gautier remarked that 'celle que j'aime, à présent, est en Chine'; but the poem he wrote about her clearly reveals that she lived in the Cathay of Boucher and Pillement rather than the Peking of the Emperor Tao-Kuang. It is entitled *Chinoiserie:*

> Ce n'est pas vous, non, madame, que j'aime,
> Ni vous non plus, Juliette, ni vous,
> Ophélia, ni Béatrice, ni même
> Laure la blonde, avec ses grands yeux doux.
>
> Celle que j'aime, à présent, est en Chine;
> Elle demeure avec ses vieux parents,
> Dans une tour de porcelaine fine,
> Au fleuve Jaune, où sont les cormorans.
>
> Elle a des yeux retroussés vers les tempes,
> Un pied petit à tenir dans la main,
> Le teint plus clair que le cuivre des lampes,
> Les ongles longs et rougis de carmin.

China and Japan

Par son treillis elle passe sa tête,
Que l'hirondelle, en volant, vient toucher,
Et chaque soir, aussi bien qu'un poète,
Chante le saule et la fleur du pêcher.

The fashion for collecting French eighteenth-century furniture began in the 1820s and was well established by the middle of the century. By then, too, the imitator had appeared upon the scene and for his benefit historians of the decorative arts produced such pattern books as Guilmard's *La Connaissance des styles* of 1853. The pieces of Louis XIV, Louis XV, and, most popular of all, Louis XVI style furniture made at this period were not, however, intended to deceive their purchasers. *Ébénistes* were instructed to adapt their models freely; indeed, a writer of 1865 remarked that in order to work in the Louis XIV style the craftsman need not 'imiter textuellement une commode de Boulle ou un panneau de Bérain', but should acquire the general principles of the period in order to give his products an 'air de famille' with their ancestors. At the same time the Musée des Arts Décoratifs was founded at Paris, mainly to provide craftsmen with good models especially of the seventeenth and eighteenth centuries. The effect of this revivalist attitude was already marked at the 1878 Exposition Universelle where every example of French furniture shown was imitative of an historical or geographical style, among which eighteenth-century chinoiserie was not lacking. Indeed, nearly every type of Louis XV and Louis XVI lacquer furniture and chinoiserie bibelot seems to have been imitated. Chinoiserie silks *à la Pillement* were also produced, woven in the faded colours which eighteenth-century brocades had by then acquired.

Although English collectors were among the first to appreciate the beauty of French eighteenth-century furniture, they do not seem to have turned their attention to the works of Georgian cabinet-makers until rather later. In the 1860s, however, E. W. Godwin began to collect early eighteenth-century furniture, and in 1872 J. J. Stevenson, hotly followed by Norman Shaw, introduced the 'Queen Anne' style, a synthesis of early eighteenth-century English and seventeenth-century Dutch architectural motifs which secured immediate success. By 1881 it had already become so widespread that Mrs Haweis, an arbiter of interior decoration, complained: 'If people would but let poor Queen Anne rest in her grave! The confusion her ghost has created is ludicrous.' The first building in the new style was the Red House, Bayswater Road, which Stevenson designed for himself and which, Mrs Haweis wrote, 'with its handsome russet façade and niche holding a *Nankeen* vase, has been so continually parodied by cheap builders possessed by the idea that red brick, a blue pot, and a fat sunflower in the window are all that is necessary to be fashionably aesthetic and *Queen Anne*.' This house was lined with Morris wallpapers and filled with sixteenth-, seventeenth-, and eighteenth-century furniture, and there were plenty of Persian tiles and blue-and-white porcelain plates and vases among its ornaments. According to the new doctrine of 'period furnishing' a 'Queen Anne' house must be decorated only with eighteenth-century and earlier objects. Lacquer and japan cabinets and bureaux, and vases of *Delf* or *Nankeen* thus returned to popularity as ingredients of the Queen Anne style. As Max Beerbohm remarked in his essay *1880*: 'men and women hurled their mahogany into the streets and ransacked the curio shops for furniture of Annish days. Dados arose upon every wall, sunflowers and the feathers of peacocks curved in every corner, tea grew quite cold while guests were praising the Willow Pattern of its cup'. But since the demand for 'period' furniture far exceeded the supply, cabinet-makers set to work to make both reproductions, adapted for the modern home, and fakes. Many of their products were decorated with chinoiserie japanning, and they later applied themselves to imitating furniture in the 'Chinese Chippendale' style. This furniture was, of course, intended to summon up a picture of 'Georgian grace' rather than Cathay. Its literary counterpart may be found in the neatly turned poems of Austin Dobson.

The vogue for eighteenth-century furniture which became apparent in Second Empire France and Victorian England was no doubt partly inspired by a new appreciation of craftsmanship. But it also reflected a change of attitude towards the past. Amid the comforts and discomforts of the industrial age, people began to look back wistfully to that remote period before the Revolution when it had been possible, in Talleyrand's phrase, to savour 'la douceur de vivre'. Thus it was in this nostalgic mood that the Empress Eugénie, who seems at times to have thought herself a reincarnation of Marie-Antoinette, furnished her apartments at the Tuileries with genuine and reproduction Louis XVI furniture. Her example was naturally followed by many of her subjects who shared her wish to slip back into the gay, carefree, pre-revolutionary world.

From about 1850 onwards the desire to escape into a romantic past manifested itself throughout Europe more forcefully than ever before. Rich *bourgeois* surrounded themselves with the atmosphere of another, more externally attractive, civilization, though without sacrificing any modern comforts and conveniences. They created a brisk demand for reproduction boiseries, furniture and bibelots among which there was an abundance of Chinese and chinoiserie objects. But in the 1860s the fashion for chinoiserie was largely superseded by a new vogue for japonaiserie, for just at the moment when China was proving herself least worthy of the legend of Cathay, the Empire of the Rising Sun burst on the European horizon. Japonaiserie appealed to many of those who had already succumbed to the cult of the eighteenth century, and it is no coincidence that the Goncourts were devotees, and publicists, of both fashions.

2 JAPONAISERIE

'Mademoiselle, je vous demanderai la recette de la salade que nous avons mangée ce soir ici. Il paraît qu'elle est de votre composition.'
'La salade japonaise?'
'Elle est japonaise?'
'Je l'appelle ainsi.'
'Pourquoi?'
'Pour qu'elle ait un nom: tout est japonais maintenant.'

ALEXANDRE DUMAS fils: Le Francillon, 1887

The rise and decline of japonaiserie forms one of the most surprising interludes in the history of nineteenth-century taste. The vogue began in about 1856; by 1878 it had reached such heights of popularity that a critic complained 'Ce n'est plus une mode, c'est de l'engouement, c'est de la folie'; and within another thirty years it was all but extinct. Brief though the fashion had been, its influence was extraordinarily potent and penetrated all the decorative arts in France and England.

Appearing at a time when many were ready to agree with Baudelaire that 'le beau est toujours bizarre', japonaiserie answered a new demand for exoticism and provided a welcome relief from the classicism of a moribund academic tradition. Its history reflects, as it were in miniature, the longer and more complex story of chinoiserie. In one important respect, however, this new exotic taste differed from the old, for whereas painters and craftsmen of the seventeenth and eighteenth centuries had produced their own highly individual interpretations of Chinese art at the command of their patrons, nineteenth-century painters approached their oriental models, which they discovered for themselves, in a more humble and receptive state of mind. They attempted to understand and master the essential principles on which Japanese art was based. Thus, Japan came to exert a far deeper and more vital influence on the major and minor arts of Europe than China had ever done.

Japan closed her gates against the West much later than China. In the late sixteenth century the work of Christian missionaries in Japan had been conducted with such zeal and attended with such success that the conversion of the entire country seemed to be at hand. One of the several feudal rulers adopted Christianity as the established religion of his domain and in 1582 no fewer than 150,000 converts were recorded. Buddhist priests and the Emperor whose authority was based on the old religious order, viewed this advance with dismay, and they were all the more alarmed when they discovered the exclusive nature of Christianity. The missionaries were asked to leave, proved obdurate and bravely accepted the crowns of martyrdom that were proffered. Intrepid Catholic priests continued to reach Japan disguised among the Portuguese merchants who had, up to now, played the leading part in trade with the West. In 1638, therefore, the Portuguese were expelled from Japan and only the Calvinist Dutch, who had no spiritual designs on the realm, were allowed to remain and keep a trading station on an island off Nagasaki. Having acquired a monopoly of Japanese trade, Holland guarded her privilege jealously and saw to it that no other nation obtained so much as a foothold. When the English East India Company, for example, applied for trading rights in 1673, the Dutch cunningly pointed out that Charles II's queen was a Portuguese princess, and the Japanese promptly returned a categoric refusal.

Throughout the seventeenth and eighteenth centuries, the Dutch kept Europe supplied with Japanese porcelain and lacquer which had usually been made expressly for this market. As we have seen, these wares enjoyed widespread popularity; lacquer panels were extensively used for the decoration of furniture, Imari porcelain was collected and imitated. But they were accepted simply as products of the Orient, for Japan seems generally to have been regarded as a part, and a somewhat dim part, of the Chinese empire. Since no foreigners were allowed to set foot on the main Japanese islands, no travellers could return with tales to create a legend of Japan comparable with that of China, and despite the publication of Kämpfer's *History of Japan* in 1727, it was not until the early nineteenth century that the idea of Japan as an independent nation began to take shape in Europe. The first full account of the country appeared in Golownin's three-volume, *Memoirs of a Captivity in Japan*, which was published in 1819. 'Another of Golownin's volumes on Japan has just come out,' William Beckford wrote with his usual confused enthusiasm:

> Genuine, beautiful Japanese porcelain is hardly ever seen; what is called *Japan* is an inferior variety—heavy, coarse, and much more like faience. The Japanese import much of theirs from China, their own products being horribly dear; they have very few makes of the best quality and it takes a long time to manufacture them. The population of Yeddo [Tokyo] is so immense that it is hard to believe: millions and millions, and more than 180,000 houses. The province where Miaco [Kyotò] and the *Dairi* [Mikado] are is famous for its lovely boys (real *terra papale!*); from there they come to provide the delights of the theatres, inns and brothels! A strange people, a strange country—the only one which still remains to be known.

During the first few decades of the century, the Americans had a few not unamicable encounters with the Japanese. Occasionally an American ship would run aground on the Japanese islands, while Japanese ships were sometimes swept off their course and wrecked among the Aleutians or even on the coasts of Oregon and California; and the sailors of both nations were repatriated without difficulty. In 1845 an American ship returning some Japanese sailors to their native land was able to collect charts of the islands and in the following year the first application was made by the Americans for a trade agreement. The application was curtly refused and, when the next American ship sailed into Nagasaki harbour, her commander was unable to obtain a group of shipwrecked sailors held by the Japanese until he had threatened to bombard the city. This incident revealed the weakness of the Japanese defences and four years later Commodore Perry arrived in Uraga bay with a naval squadron—the famous 'black ships'—bristling with guns and loaded with such benefits of civilization as sewing-machines and miniature railways. The islanders were clearly as terrified by this show of force as they were intrigued by the machines, but they remained reluctant to grant any form of trading agreement. Perry prudently decided to bide his time and, when he returned next year, obtained a treaty which gave Americans permission to use various Japanese harbours and even to go ashore, but not, as yet, to trade.

Similar agreements were signed shortly afterwards with Russia, Holland, and England. Two years later American citizens were allowed to reside in two towns and Nagasaki was opened to foreigners; and in 1858 the long wanted trade agreement was finally signed. A few Japanese *samurai* diehards put up a show of opposition to the infiltration of the western barbarians, but after a lamentable incident in which a British man-of-war bombarded Kagoshima as a reprisal for some amply provoked attacks on British subjects, their influence waned. The last serious outburst of xenophobic feeling was put down by the Japanese Government in 1863. By 1866 Japanese ambassadors in bowler hats and morning coats had made their appearance in most European capitals. The westernization of Japan and the Japanization of Europe had begun. Within a few years Europe was flooded with imports from Japan—lacquer boxes, painted fans, Satsuma porcelain, embroideries, ivories, bronze vases, and, most important of all, wood-block prints.

Writing of the Japanese cult in 1878 Ernest Chesneau commented on the influence of Ukiyo-e and asked who it was who first had the 'bonheur de la main, cette pénétration du regard de découvrir dans les confusions de la Chine morte les clartés du Japon vivant'. Unable to answer his question he told the story of a painter who, some time in 1862, discovered in a curiosity shop certain paintings, coloured prints, and albums of sketches, all with heightened outlines and flat colours, which contrasted sharply with any Chinese works he had ever seen. Whoever this may have been, he was not the first in the field, for in 1856 Jacques Bracquemond discovered a volume of Hokusai prints which was found in a crate of porcelain, obtained it (in exchange for Papillon's rare and valuable book on wood engraving) and is said to have carried it about with him in his pocket until his death. Shortly afterwards, in 1857 or 1858, the young Claude Monet, then but seventeen years old, made his first purchase of Japanese prints at Le Havre. It is clear, therefore, that no one artist can be credited with the discovery of Ukiyo-e. They burst upon the *avant-garde* at the very moment when they were most needed and were to inspire various impressionist and post-impressionist painters in remarkably different ways.

In 1862 Mme Desoye and her husband, who had visited Japan, opened a shop in the rue de Rivoli for the sale of orientalia and caused what a contemporary termed the 'grande explosion japonaise'. Two years later, japonaiserie made its bow in a flurry of rose and silver silk with James McNeil Whistler's *Princesse du Pays de la Porcelaine*, a painting crowded with Japanese detail but owing no more to Japan than Boucher's fantasies had owed to China (Pl. 143). Two years later Zacharie Astruc—an indifferent painter, sculptor, critic, composer, and poet who is best remembered for his loyalty to Manet—published a series of enthusiastic articles on *L'Empire du soleil levant* and, encouraged by their success, wrote a play with a Japanese setting.

A still wider circle of admirers was secured for Japanese arts by the objects sent from Japan to the Exposition Universelle of 1867. Shortly afterwards a group of critics and artists founded *La Société Japonaise du Jinglar* which met at Sèvres for a dinner once a month when chop-sticks were *de rigueur* and the only available drink was saki. A special table service in the Japanese style was designed by Bracquemond and every member received a japonaiserie certificate etched and illuminated by M. L. E. Solon, the porcelain painter. Meanwhile Whistler, who insisted on appearing in a kimono among the frock-coated figures in Fantin's *The Toast* of 1865, now moved from Paris to London where he became known as the 'Japanese artist' and helped to establish the new taste in England.

Japonaiserie was the rage in the Paris of the mid-1860s. Travel books about Japan began to pour from the publishers. Couturiers modified their lines to satisfy the new craze. In fashionable salons the *étagères* groaned beneath the weight of Japanese and japonaiserie objects, and no artist's studio was deemed complete without its Japanese prints and fans and its pile of kimonos. In the theatre a Japanese fantasy by Ernest d'Hervelly drew the city in 1878 and in the same year a Japanese ballet was put on at the *Opéra*: while the Exposition Universelle displayed the first large collection of japonaiserie furniture and ornaments, made chiefly in France, England, and America, as well as a handsome and lavish collection of Japanese art. Commenting on the exhibition, Ernest Chesneau listed the prominent collectors of Japanese art in France: they included Édouard Manet, James Tissot, Fantin Latour, Alfonse Hirsch, Edgar Degas, Claude Monet, Jacques Bracquemond, Jules Jacquemart, M. L. E. Solon of the *Manufacture de Sèvres*, Edmond and Jules de Goncourt (who gradually acquired the vast collection described in *La Maison d'un artiste*), Philippe Burty, Zola, the publisher Charpentier (later a patron of Monet and Renoir), the travellers Duret (who wrote the preface to Monet's 1880 catalogue), Cernuschi, Émile Guimet, and F. Regamey, as well as such industrialists as Barbédienne, Christofle, Bouilhet, and Falize. It is an impressive list and one from which few notable French artists or patrons of the period are absent. (Many of the collections had been begun in the 'sixties when Baudelaire, who died in 1867, was among the chief admirers and purchasers of Japanese art.)

Now that they have been familiar in Europe for a century, it is difficult to appreciate the impact which Japanese prints made on the artistic world of Paris in the 1850s and 1860s. They presented an art which was as vital as it was unfamiliar, opening a window on to a new sense of reality, a new freshness and boldness in the use of colour, and new principles of composition. Chesneau, though he criticized their distortions, remarked of them: 'On ne pouvait se lasser d'admirer l'imprévu des compositions, la science de la forme, la richesse du ton, l'originalité de l'effet pittoresque, en même temps que la simplicité des moyens pour obtenir de tels résultats.' Above all, the use of silhouette, the deliberate flattening of forms and lack of deep perspective in the prints satisfied a new conception of painting which was beginning to emerge in the Impressionist generation. The painters realized that these pictorial devices might be useful in solving their own problems and promptly adopted them or some of them. For, of course, each artist reacted to Japanese prints in a different way and drew different influences from them. Monet was charmed by what he termed their refinement of taste and said that he approved of the suggestions of the Japanese artistic code, evoking a presence by means of a shadow and the whole by means of a fragment. Degas, on the other hand, declared that he had learned from them that 'dessin n'est pas la forme, mais la manière de voir la forme'.

The earliest French painting to show the influence of Japanese prints appears to be Manet's *La Chanteuse des rues* of 1862 (Boston Museum of Fine Arts). Representing a street singer stepping out of a *bistro*, it is rendered with a stark lack of sentiment which appalled contemporary critics. The colouring is flat, without half-tones, and the figure is treated rather in the manner of a cut-out decorated with a pattern of folds and ribbonned hems. In his famous *Olympia* (Louvre) of 1863, Manet seems to have owed a similar debt to Japan in his use of flat planes and in the placing of the figure of the negro. This painting which aroused such a brouhaha in the academic world won the enthusiastic praise of Zacharie Astruc—another devotee of Japanese art—who celebrated it in a fifty-line poem. It was also championed by Zola, and when, in 1867/8, Manet painted the great novelist's portrait he placed a photograph of *Olympia* beside an Utamaro print in the background (Pl. 142). This portrait, with the central figure painted as an arrangement of flattened forms strikingly similar in technique to the Utamaro, provides the clearest indication of Manet's debt to Japan. The presence of the print and the Japanese screen in the picture also serves as a reminder that Zola, like so many of the first patrons and admirers of the Impressionists, was also a collector of Japanese art. George Moore, visiting him in the 1870s, paused on the staircase to observe 'Japanese prints of furious fornications' which, with unusual censoriousness, he deemed 'a rather blatant announcement of naturalism.' The Japanese influence is evident in many of Manet's other works such as the stylized, flatly modelled *Le Fifre* (Louvre). In *La Dame aux éventails* (Louvre) he affords us a glimpse of a fashionable interior where the notorious Nina de Callias, with almost Japanese coiffure, reclines before a group of Japanese fans hung on a wall painted with japonaiseries. And in *Le Chien Tama* he depicted a lap-dog and a doll brought back from Japan by Cernuschi.

Japanese prints exerted a strikingly different influence on Claude Monet who painted his delightful *Panneau décoratif: japonnerie*, better known as *La Japonaise*, in 1876 (Museum of Fine Arts, Boston). This was, he said, 'not a painting of a Japanese but rather of a French girl in a Japanese dress'—a remark more appositely applied to Whistler's *Princesse du Pays de la Porcelaine* (Pl. 143) to which Monet's work owes some debt. For in Monet's painting, the Japanese influence was not confined to the sitter's kimono and the fans on the wall, but determined the attitude of the figure and the whole schematic composition. (Monet seems to have been much addicted to Japanese fans: one appears in an early still-life of about 1863 and Renoir's portrait of Mme Monet shows that the walls of his house were adorned with them.) In his later work the influence of Japan is less tangible though it may be discerned in such a compositional device as the use of cliffs running in a silhouetted zigzag against the sea in his view of the *Douanier's Cottage, Varengeville* (Museum Boymans van Beunigen, Rotterdam). Ernest Chesneau suggested in 1878 that Monet had also learned from Japan 'la sommaire suppression du détail au profit de l'impression d'ensemble'.

The same critic considered that Degas derived from Japanese art 'la fantaisie réaliste de ses groupes, l'effet piquant de ses dispositions de lumières en ses étonnantes scènes de café-concert'. Although he never fabricated japonaiseries comparable with Monet's *La Japonaise*, Degas took close interest in Japanese prints and absorbed much from them, notably their space organization, the effects of violent foreshortening, of cutting figures at unexpected angles and of sharply receding diagonal lines and, not least, the device of placing the principal subject off-centre. His *Bains de mer: petite fille peignée par sa bonne* (Lane Bequest—Tate Gallery and National Gallery, Dublin), for example, might almost be called a Japanese print in French costume; for it combines numerous devices previously found only in Ukiyo-e.

Renoir and Cézanne alone of the great artists of this period seem to have remained almost immune to the Japanese influence, though the former occasionally included such decorative devices as Japanese fans in the backgrounds to his pictures. But the Japanese influence was by no means confined to the *avant-garde*. Zacharie Astruc and the engraver Bracquemond both succumbed to it. The Belgian genre painter Alfred Stevens (not to be confused with his English namesake) exhibited a painting of *La Japonaise* in 1878. Alfonse Legros, James Tissot (a notable collector of orientalia who was himself depicted by Degas seated beneath a Japanese painting in 1868), Diaz de la Peña, Théodore Rousseau, J. F. Millet, and Fantin Latour were among others in whose works contemporaries divined the influence of Japan.

In the field of decorative arts, the Japanese influence seems to have become apparent in France shortly after 1868 under the impact of the Exposition Universelle and was well established a decade later when the second of these exhibitions was held. The most willing student of Second Empire *décor* must, however, admit that its first effects were not of the happiest. Although they sometimes have a certain charm and always a strong period flavour—redolent of cigar smoke and tuberoses—the monstrous lacquer cabinets, over-wrought cloisonné enamel vases, Baccarat glass lamps and porcelain knick-knacks which cluttered the rooms of the Trocadéro in 1878 can hardly be numbered among the most immediately pleasing manifestations of late nineteenth-century taste. Indeed, some contemporaries were alarmed at their appearance. Even L. Falize, who designed japonaiserie cloisonné jewelry, was uncertain whether the influence of Japan was for good or ill, profitable or dangerous, while Ernest Chesneau declared that most of the japonaiseries shown in the exhibition were as pretentious as they were unsatisfactory.

According to Falize, 'le grand prêtre du japonisme' was Émile-Auguste Reiber. 'C'est Reiber qui, chez Deck, a donné la diapason à la céramique, c'est lui qui, chez Christofle, a prêté à l'émail et aux métaux les tons justes pour s'accorder.' Unfortunately these wares have now been so long disregarded by dealers and collectors that they are more difficult to trace than the *objets de vertu* produced in remoter ages. So far as we may judge from contemporary steel engravings, they included goblets, lamps, coffers, jardinières, and clocks, in patinated bronze encrusted with gold and silver, or bright enamel decorated with patterns taken from Japanese lacquer or cloisonné. At first the intention was to imitate objects imported from Japan, but since these models were made specially for the western market the results bear an unmistakable Second Empire impress. Tiffany of New York went so far as to import Japanese craftsmen into America in order to produce *chakoudo* bronze and *mokoumé* gold, silver, and copper wares designed for the American or European home but decorated in an authentic Japanese manner.

In addition to the Japanese imitations, certain objects shown at the Exposition Universelle were in a japonaiserie style evocative but not imitative of Japanese art. A *torchère* in the form of an elaborately robed and coifed geisha standing beside an attenuated tripod table supporting a candelabra (adapted for oil or gas, of course), and a large corner cupboard designed by Reiber, filled a need for a type of furniture not normally made in Japan (Pl. 140 and 141). At the same time, some enterprising industrial artists applied the lessons learned from Japanese artefacts to frankly European furnishings. Félix Bracquemond designed a table service decorated with the flowers of French meadows arranged *à la japonaise*. Textile printers began to abandon their overcrowded patterns for wispier, sparser designs in the style of Japanese silks, though not necessarily incorporating motifs derived from them. And before long the Japanese style merged, imperceptibly, into the first phase of *art nouveau*. Contemporaries were perhaps able to appreciate the Japanese influence on French decorative arts more clearly than we can today. In the early years of the present century Walter Crane remarked of Japan that 'it might almost be said to have taken entire possession of French decorative art, or a large part of it; or rather, it is Japanese translated into French with that ease and chic for which our lively neighbours are remarkable'. But, he continued, 'in modern decoration, the most obvious and superficial qualities of Japanese art have generally been seized upon. . . . On the whole, the discovery of Japanese art on the modern artistic mind may be likened to a sudden and unexpected access of fortune to an impoverished man. It is certain to disorganize him if not to demoralize him.'

In England, the Japanese style first made its appearance in the early 1860s. Whistler had visited London in 1859 and infected the Rossettis with his own newly acquired passion for Japanese prints, painted fans, and textiles. In 1862 the second Great Exhibition presented the first organized display of Japanese art to be seen anywhere in Europe. Shortly afterwards Messrs Farmer and Rogers who had acquired the Japanese objects from the Exhibition opened a shop for the sale of oriental goods in Regent Street, and in 1875 Mr Lazenby

Liberty opened on the other side of the road the still surviving firm which dispensed oriental and oriental style fabrics, furniture, and ornaments. By 1882 W. E. Henley, echoing the words of Chesneau, could complain of the Japanese vogue, 'It is more than a fashion, it is a craze . . . the Japanese dado has become almost a household word and the Japanese fan a household essential'.

Unlike France, England was prepared for the advent of a new style in which freshness of colouring and simplicity of design were the keynotes; the influence of Japan on the decorative arts was therefore happier. The 1851 exhibition had unleashed a storm of criticism at the state of the industrial arts, and its sequel of eleven years later revealed that strides had been made towards a greater purity of design in household furniture. But without some historical style to imitate, designers were at a loss for decorative patterns more appealing than the abstract ornaments, based on the bones and fishes of birds, advocated by Christopher Dresser. The Japanese objects which began to arrive in the 1850s and were shown in force at the 1862 exhibition came as the answer to their prayers. Among those most deeply impressed by the Japanese exhibits was the 'Gothic' architect William Burges who made drawings of the wood-block prints and of the Japanese crests which were soon to form an essential element in every decorator's repertory. Another was E. W. Godwin, who succumbed to the new cult so completely that he promptly redecorated his house in the Japanese style—bare floors sparsely covered with rugs, white walls decorated with Japanese prints—and lest his wife should strike a discordant note, he dressed her in a kimono. Later he built the famous White House for Whistler in Chelsea. In 1867 Whistler himself painted the staircase of W. R. Leyland's house at 49 Prince's Gate, with panels 'imitating aventurine lacquer, decorated with sprigs of pale rose and white flowers in the Japanese taste'. Having performed this task to his patron's satisfaction, he set to work on the dining-room where, he said, the pale rose and silver of his *Princesse du Pays de la Porcelaine*, which Leyland had acquired, were killed by sombre Cordova leather hangings. He therefore transformed the room into a harmony in blue and gold with truculent peacocks strutting round the walls, thus provoking one of the many squabbles which marked his career. But Whistler was now veering away from japonaiserie and after about 1870 Japan ceased to exert any strong influence on his work. The same may be said of other painters in England where the Japanese cult (like the Chinese cult of a century earlier) found expression mainly in the minor arts.

In this realm E. W. Godwin, 'the greatest aesthete of them all', as Max Beerbohm called him, soon emerged as the high priest of movement. Some remarks from his booklet on *Dress* help to point the essential difference between French and English japonaiserie: '. . . to commit beauty—because we cannot help it; to make for the healthy—as a matter of course; to breathe in an atmosphere where the sunbeam throbs with art, and the rain is woven with sanitation, are, perhaps, possible only in the land of Utopia. We might, however, make for that land, and near it . . . by that old Japanesy method of taking delight in all that contributes to beauty and health.' The furniture Godwin designed from 1868 onwards doubtless contributed to health, with its dustproof surfaces free from excrescent decorations, and it is not without a certain beauty. His spindly coffee-tables and cabinets made of lathes of ebonized wood have a simplicity of line and graceful elegance which must have appeared pleasantly fresh, if somewhat stark, to the inhabitants of overcrowded, whatnotted, chenille-hung Victorian parlours. Peter Floud justly remarked that his best works—such as the furniture now in the Bristol Art Gallery and a pair of cabinets in the Victoria and Albert Museum—'show a remarkable capacity for translating into European terms, and into the scale of full-sized furniture, the asymmetrical elegance, the attenuated supports and in particular the subtle three-dimensional interplay of void and solid, which are the main characteristics of Japanese lacquer boxes and cabinets which were then being imported in large quantities.'

Godwin made use of Japanese motifs on plaques and wallpapers for decoration of rooms, and occasionally made use of genuine Japanese objects such as netsuke on his furniture, but his best work is marked by Japanese inspiration rather than explicit japonaiserie. Another designer who employed the Japanese idiom was that prolific artist Christopher Dresser. A pioneer in the quest for functional form, Dresser visited Japan, wrote a book about the country and designed some 'Anglo-Japanese' furniture for the *Art Furnishers' Alliance* which he founded in 1880; but unfortunately few examples have survived. Before long, however, the more commercially-minded designers of the period were answering a popular demand for cruder specimens of japonaiserie than either Godwin or Dresser cared to provide, and the market was flooded with a welter of chairs, cabinets, tables, and whatnots lavishly decorated with imitation bamboo asymmetrical fretwork, and paintings of geishas, birds, butterflies, and flowers. From 1862 onwards the firm of Elkington turned out a stream of cloisonné enamel vases, trays and salvers of a strongly Japanese flavour which even showed a technical advance on similar wares made in Japan. Nor were the potteries slow to follow this lead. By 1862 the Royal Worcester factory was producing a multitude of wares the shapes and decorations of which were derived indiscriminately from Japanese and Chinese objects but were warmly welcomed as japonaiseries. Such objects enjoyed great popularity throughout the 'eighties and into the 'nineties when they began to give place to debased *art nouveau* and revived Hepplewhite patterns.

As drawings and articles in *Punch* reveal, the Japanese cult provoked much robust merriment in Philistine circles.

> Twopence I gave for my sunshade,
> A penny I gave for my fan,
> Threepence I gave for my straw—forrin made—
> I'm a Japan-aesthetic young man

ran a ditty of the 'eighties. And the enterprising Gilbert and Sullivan, who had heartily poked the ribs of the aesthetes with *Patience*, produced in 1885 *The Mikado* which catered abundantly for both parties though it drew a formal protest from the Japanese ambassador. (It also included some harsh remarks about 'the idiot who praises, with enthusiastic tone, all centuries but this and every country but his own'.)

Nevertheless, Japanese fans, porcelain, screens, sword guards, inro (little lacquer medicine boxes) and such little monstrosities as netsukes, were for long destined to adorn the English home. And nearly every English lady might be found tending a miniature Japanese garden with tiny stunted trees, ponds of looking-glass and bridges and temples of porcelain. Not content with such half-measures, that enthusiastic traveller, Miss Ella Christie, laid out a perfect replica of a Japanese garden at Cowden in Scotland; and to ensure that every detail was correct she imported a lonely Japanese gardener who was for many years to be found pining by the Ochils for his lovelier Fujiyama.

Great success was enjoyed by the books of Lafcadio Hearn, who went to live in Japan, married a native wife and eventually became a Japanese subject. He presented a highly idealized and sentimentalized picture of the country. And the vision of Japan as the aesthete's paradise where the life of art and beauty was led amidst groves of abundantly flowering but decently epicene cherry trees, lingered on into the present century, especially among devotees of the Arts and Crafts movement. It is significant that the most famous of modern studio potters, Mr Bernard Leach, served his apprenticeship in Japan under

Ogata Kenzan from whom he learned a skill which had been passed in un-broken succession from master to pupil for some three millennia.

While English aesthetes were remarking the exquisite tints of Japanese fans, men of such a very different stamp as Henri de Toulouse-Lautrec, Vincent Van Gogh, and Paul Gauguin were responding to Japanese art in a more forceful manner. The vogue for japonaiserie had passed its zenith in fashionable Paris by the early 1880s and had begun to slide down the social scale—readers of *A la recherche du temps perdu* will recall that in about 1887 the demi-mondaine Odette de Crécy had furnished her rooms with Japanese silks and fans. But at the same time a revival of artistic interest in Japanese prints became apparent, precipitated no doubt by the Japanese exhibition at the Galerie Georges Petit in 1883 and the *Exposition historique de l'art de la gravure au Japon* at the Galerie Bing three years later. (Another important Japanese exhibition was held at the Galerie Durand-Ruel in 1893.) This new wave of Japanese influence differed in one important way from that of the 1860s and 1870s. Whereas the artists of the Impressionist generation had been interested in Japanese prints mainly for technical reasons and pillaged them for compositional and other devices to help to solve their own artistic problems, the Post-Impressionists were interested in them stylistically. The Japanese influence is therefore more profound, though less obvious, in Post-Impressionist paintings.

Toulouse-Lautrec is a case in point. He is known to have collected Ukiyo-e, and he made sketches of birds either from Japanese prints or drawings. But only in one work, *Le Ballet des 'Lotus'*, is the extent of his debt to Japan made clear. Representing a scene from a ballet performed at the *Nouveau Cirque* in 1892, this painting is dominated by a group of elaborately coifed Japanese heads stuck about with long pins, sharply silhouetted in the foreground. It is as obvious a specimen of japonaiserie as Whistler's *Princesse* or Monet's *La Japonaise*. But the more subtle and profound Japanese influences on the painting, notably the method of composition, the flatness of the figures, the use of silhouette, the abruptly falsified perspective and the linear grace of the figures, are no less strong than in many of his other works—the Jane Avril *Jardin de Paris* poster, for example—where they often go unnoticed.

The Japanese influence on Toulouse-Lautrec is implicit and sometimes rather intangible. But both Van Gogh and Gauguin declared their debts to Japan no less explicitly in their paintings than in their letters. Van Gogh first discovered Japanese prints as a youth in Antwerp. Later, when he went to Paris, he was able to study them more carefully in the shop of the oriental dealer Bing, and in 1887 himself organized an exhibition of Ukiyo-e at the Café Le Tambourin. Although he considered that this exhibition exerted a fatal influence on his friends Émile Bernard and Anquetin, his own enthusiasm for the prints knew no bounds. He even painted free copies of some of them, including Hiroshige's *Ohashi Bridge in the Rain* which is among the most remarkable specimens of japonaiserie (Pl. 144). Japan became an obsession, the symbol of his every desire, and it was partly in the hope of drawing spiritually closer to this land of his dreams that he set off on his momentous journey to Arles in 1888. 'You know there are thousands of reasons why I went south and threw myself into my work there', he told his brother, 'I wanted to see a different light, I thought that to observe nature under a clearer sky would give me a better idea of how the Japanese feel and draw.' He decorated his studio in the Yellow House with *crépons* one of which—a group of women by Sato Torakiyo —appears in the background of his self-portrait with a bandaged ear (Courtauld Institute, London). But Japanese art had a more than decorative importance for him. While at Arles he began to use oriental reed pens in order to follow the technique of Japanese draughtsmen, and he learned from the study of prints the effectiveness of flattened forms, emphatic outlines and areas of simple colour. Of the painting of his bedroom at Arles (V. W. Van Gogh collection, Laren), he wrote: 'the shadows and the shadows thrown are suppressed, the whole is painted flat in large colour areas as in Japanese prints', and the remark might equally well be applied to several other works of this period, including the *L'Arlésienne* (Metropolitan Museum, New York).

Gauguin first showed an interest in Japanese art in his early period when still under the influence of the Impressionists, and in 1884 he made a painting of a Japanese fan. But after the spring of 1888 when he began to work in the style known as *cloisonnisme* or *synthétisme*, Japanese art exerted a more profound influence on him. Émile Bernard, writing in the *Mercure de France* in 1903, claimed that 'l'étude des crépons nous mène (avec Anquetin) vers la simplicité. Nous créons le cloisonnisme—1886'. Gauguin seems, however, to have evolved his new style, in violent reaction to all post-renaissance painting, from a wide variety of other sources as well. He realized, as Mr Douglas Cooper has pointed out, 'that the art which meant most of all to him—the Peruvian idols which had formed part of the decoration of his home, the Romanesque carvings, stained glass and folk-art which he saw in the neighbourhood of Pont-Aven, the Egyptian, Assyrian and far-eastern art which he had seen in the Louvre, the Japanese prints which he had collected—had an emotional force and a vitality, resulting from simplification and directness of approach, which had been lost in European art through the over-refined methods of the Impressionists and their predecessors during the previous four centuries.'

Writing of the *Breton Bathers* which he painted at Pont-Aven in June 1888, Gauguin said that it was not at all like Degas but 'tout à fait japonais par un sauvage du Pérou'. For his somewhat disturbing *Still Life with Three Puppies* (Museum of Modern Art, New York) he appears to have based his piebald dogs on those in a print by Kuniyoshi, while his *La Vague* is clearly influenced by Hokusai's famous print of a wave. Shortly afterwards Gauguin painted *The Vision after the Sermon* (National Gallery of Scotland) which may well be considered the masterpiece of *cloisonnisme*. Émile Bernard wrote of it 'deux lutteurs empruntés à un album japonais furent dévolus à représenter une vision', and the figures of Jacob and the Angel, which appear above the boldly outlined heads of the Breton women, are indeed derived from a pair of wrestlers in a Hokusai print. But the Japanese influence, which is also felt in the tree leaning diagonally across the canvas, has been transmuted, together with the other styles Gauguin studied, and there is no air of japonaiserie about this work. Japan was destined to influence other European artists for many years—one might mention the names of Bonnard, who was called 'le Nabi Japonard', and James Ensor—but their work falls outside the scope of the present book.

It is important to remember that the Japanese influence on nineteenth-century French painters derived not from the great works of Japanese antiquity —which were then and still are too little known in the West——but from popular prints made in the previous hundred years and little valued, if not despised, in their native land. Some notion of the way in which these prints were regarded in Europe may be obtained from Edmond de Goncourt's fantastic statement that Hokusai was the greatest artist of the Far East. Had he but added 'whose works have been exported to Europe', his remark would hardly be disputed, for the prints of Hokusai, Utamaro, and Hiroshige are certainly of a different artistic order from the painted fans and screens, bronzes, ivory carvings, porcelain, and lacquer which otherwise represented the art of Japan in the West at this time. Hence their extraordinary appeal and their power to exert a vital influence on European painters, inspiring a number of works of still higher artistic merit.

And hence the essential contrast which, despite their many similarities, differentiates the history of japonaiserie from that of chinoiserie. Only in the fourteenth century had European artists previously seen wholly indigenous specimens of oriental art, and only then do they appear to have derived any but the most superficial kind of inspiration from them. Moreover, it was only in these two periods that Europeans had the humility to learn from the products of a different civilization.

Nearly all the Chinese and Japanese objects exported to Europe after the fifteenth century (very few filtered in during the previous hundred years) were so carefully designed to satisfy the western collector's conception of oriental art that they reflected the European vision of Cathay. When pre-Ming ceramics, paintings, and sculpture began to reach Europe in the late nineteenth century they were greeted with puzzled surprise. After the end of the century they arrived in greater quantity and began to attract admirers, much to the detriment of the vogue for Japanese art. But not until the Royal Academy exhibition of 1935 was a representative display of such works presented in Europe. And even then Roger Fry remarked that ordinary English art lovers 'may feel happy enough in the presence of trifling bibelots, the "Chinoiseries" of later periods which have become acclimatized in our drawing-rooms, but the great art, above all the religious art, will repel them by its strangeness'.

3 EPILOGUE

> Ching-a-ring-a-ring-ching! Feast of Lanterns!
> What a crop of chop-sticks, hongs and gongs!
> Hundred thousand Chinese crinkum-crankums,
> Hung among the bells and ding-dongs.
> J. R. PLANCHÉ: *The Drama at Home*, 1844

In 1935 Mr Bernard Rackham remarked that 'it is probably no exaggeration to say that, during the present century, knowledge of China and its people and understanding of their philosophy and art have made greater progress in the West than in the whole course of the ages that went before'. Ever since the gates of China were forced in the 1840s, sinologists had been at work revealing the country's artistic heritage, and unfolding the history of a civilization more fascinating and more complex than had hitherto been supposed.

In the 1860s Sir Henry Yule was visiting Chinese towns which no European had seen since Marco Polo, while Dr John Anderson, a naturalist, spent the leisure hours of some twenty years in the Far East acquiring the Chinese drawings which were sold to the British Museum in 1881 and still form the basis of its collection. Slightly later the French sinologues Édouard Chavannes and Henri Maspéro began to apply to the study of early Buddhist sculpture—little valued until then even by the Chinese themselves—archaeological scholarship of a quality previously reserved for Greek and Roman antiquities. Chance diggings connected with the construction of the railway network across northern China had turned up quantities of T'ang and earlier tomb figures and vessels; and archaeologists set to work with pick and shovel to unearth still more. Not until 1909, however, did the first T'ang ceramics reach London where their success was so immediate that by 1912 fakes were already being produced in China. In the next fifty years genuine and fraudulent T'ang horses, camels, and female figures became familiar denizens of the European drawing-room.

Nor was literature forgotten in this quest for the true ancient China. James Legge, a missionary who became in 1875 the first professor of Chinese at Oxford, devoted fifty-five years to translating the Confucian classics into English, supplanting for the first time the Jesuit publications of the seventeenth century. Translations of Chinese verse, either painfully literal or unwarrantably free, began to appear in France and Germany shortly after the middle of the nineteenth century. And in 1918 Mr Arthur Waley published the first of his series of translations which have won the enthusiastic admiration of poetry-lovers and the scholarly commendation of his fellow sinologues. (The influence of these translations on modern English and American poets would make an interesting study.)

Gradually the long history of Chinese civilization was unrolled like some wonderful painted scroll. And as the products of each new and more remote dynasty were brought to light—Sung, T'ang, Sui, Eastern and Western Chin, the period of the three kingdoms (Wu, Shu, and Wei), Han, Ch'in, Chou, and Shang-Yin—to the ever increasing joy of such critics as Roger Fry, the western notion of Chinese art suffered a profound change. No longer was it possible to believe that China had produced one easily recognizable artistic style, characterized by the elegant shape and exquisite colouring of a K'ang Hsi vase, so dear to the lovers of Cathay. Shang-Yin 'Yus' and suchlike were more to the taste of earnest seekers after significant form in the 1930s. The recently discovered wares had an immediate influence on the minor arts in Europe and the noble simplicity of Han, T'ang, and Sung pottery provided industrial designers with a welcome supply of new patterns. Bottles, jugs, bowls, and vases made of pottery and glass during the past twenty-five years frequently owe their design to Chinese vessels dating from the seventh and eighth centuries. Such wares cannot, however, be regarded as specimens of chinoiserie. Indeed, most of those who handle them are probably unaware of their Chinese origins.

Nevertheless, a few examples of chinoiserie have been produced during the last fifty years, albeit they are manifestations of the Georgian revival rather than the cult of Cathay. In 1914, for example, Messrs Jeffrey and Co. were selling a 'Chinese Magpie' paper, based on a Ming dynasty drawing in the British Museum, and a 'Chinese Tree' paper freely copied from a set of Ch'ien Lung hangings in the Victoria and Albert Museum. And such papers are still being produced together with others on which Pillement's figures of China-men, now somewhat tired, dance and jangle their bells. Similar figures may also be found posturing on modern porcelain. Of the gramophone, wireless, and even television sets concealed in supposedly eighteenth-century style japanned cabinets we need say nothing save that they too are intended to harmonize with 'period' furniture.

In the theatre also there has been some vogue for chinoiserie during the present century. In 1915 Busoni wrote an opera on the *Turandot* story with a libretto based closely on Carlo Gozzi's play (see p. 120). Some ten years later Puccini, who had already contributed to the picture of Japan in *Madame Butterfly* (1905), essayed the Turandot theme, and though he left his work incomplete at his death, it has justly achieved greater success. His librettists took considerable liberties with the original, departing from it to include the distasteful scene in which little Liu is tortured and done to death. And the whole opera has a barbaric splendour more strongly reminiscent of Mandeville than Gozzi. But the three court officials, Ping, Pang, and Pong, step straight off an eighteenth-century screen and one of them appears to own a *jardin anglo-chinois*, diversified by a 'laghetto blu, tutto cinto di bambu', at Kiu. Significantly enough, producers have generally chosen to present Puccini's *Turandot* with rococo chinoiserie rather than Chinese costumes and *décor*. Similarly, designers for the ballet have made use of eighteenth-century chinoiserie dresses, notably José Maria Sert and Léon Bakst who derived the costume for a dancer in *The Sleeping Princess* from a print after J.-B. Martin.

Among modern examples of literary chinoiserie the most revealing are probably the slender volumes of whimsical tales, *The Golden Hours of Kai Lung*, *Kai Lung Unrolls his Mat*, and others, written by Ernest Bramah between 1908 and 1940. As Kai Lung himself remarks on one occasion, these stories are 'permeated with the odour of joss-sticks and honourable highmindedness'; but the joss-sticks are those burnt in Louis XV *brûle-parfums* before Meissen pagods, and the highmindedness belongs to eighteenth-century *philosophes*. They derive, by way of Lamb's essay on *The Origin of Roast Pig*, from the elegant eighteenth-century vision of Cathay.

The idea of a contemporary Cathay on the eastern fringes of the world died out in the early nineteenth century and was replaced by a vision of a flowery empire, distant in both space and time, which still survives at the back of the European mind. As I have attempted to show in this book, the vision was based partly on travellers' tales of China, which first filtered through to Europe in the thirteenth century, and partly on Chinese wares, many of them cunningly designed for the European market, which were imported in ever increasing quantities throughout the subsequent centuries. This imaginary picture of Cathay was recorded and preserved for posterity in innumerable chinoiserie buildings, paintings, and *objets d'art*. So that to all but sinologists, politicians, and travellers, the name of China still summons up as many glimpses of chinoiserie as of genuine Chinese scenes. No one now believes in the historical or geographical reality of the exotic world so beautifully evoked by Watteau, Boucher, Pillement, and countless porcelain modellers and japanners in the seventeenth and eighteenth centuries. But the flowery Empire of Cathay survives in the mind—a land of poetry and graciousness, a spacious garden of azaleas, paeonies, and chrysanthemums, where the most serious business in life is to drink tea in a latticed pavilion, beside a silent lake, beneath a weeping willow; to listen to the music of piping and tinkling instruments; and to dance, to dance for ever, among the porcelain pagodas.

Notes

Section 2. The best English edition of Marco Polo's *Description of the World* (as it should properly be called) is that prepared by Sir Henry Yule, revised by Henri Cordier, London, 1903, with an additional volume of notes, 1920. A more readable English text is that translated by R. Latham, Harmondsworth, 1958. The variorum edition by A. C. Moule and P. Pelliot (2 vols., published London, 1938) is as yet incomplete. L. Olschki: *L'Asia di Marco Polo*, Florence, 1957, provides the most up-to-date introduction to Marco Polo's work and dispels several popular fallacies about him, proving, for instance, that he was not a merchant.

Coleridge was reading *Purchas his Pilgrimage*, when he fell asleep; he had also read *Purchas his Pilgrimes*; both books contain accounts of the Khan's summer palace derived from Marco Polo. See J. L. Lowes: *The Road to Xanadu*, London, 1927, pp. 356 ff.

Possibly influenced by Marco Polo, Boccaccio used Cathay as the background for a story of exquisite courtesy—*Decameron*, Day x, Novel 3.

The best English edition of the Blessed Odoric of Pordenone's travels is that translated and edited by Sir Henry Yule, *Cathay and the Way Thither*, London, 1866. 78 manuscripts of Marco Polo and 73 of the Blessed Odoric are recorded in H. Cordier: *Biblioteca Sinica*, Paris, 1904–24; those of 'Mandeville' are innumerable.

For his account of monsters 'Mandeville' drew on Pliny who derived his wilder stories from Megasthenes who appears to have learned them from the Brahmins when he visited India in *c.* 303 B.C. See R. Wittkower, 'Marvels of the East. A Study in the History of Monsters' in *The Warburg Journal*, vol. v, 1942, pp. 159 ff.

The golden vine derives from the spurious 'Letter of Alexander the Great to Aristotle' about the marvels of India, written in the third century by a Greek, see L. Olschki: *Guillaume Boucher*, Baltimore, 1946. In 1630 a Portuguese missionary described a golden creeper, like a melon or marrow plant hung with gold gourds, in the palace at Mrak-u, the capital of Arakan; see M. Collis: *The Land of the Great Image*, London, 1943, p. 155 who states that a similar vine with a stalk of agate, leaves of emeralds, and grapes of garnets was in the Great Mogul's audience hall.

Section 3. For a fuller account of sixteenth-century impressions of China see G. F. Hudson: *Europe and China*, London, 1931. The fullest account in English of Matteo Ricci's career is in A. J. Cronin: *The Wise Man from the West*, London, 1955. For the Chinese view of the Jesuits' activities see Ch'ien Chung-Shu in *Philobiblon*, I (July, 1946), pp. 13–19.

The books to which Evelyn refers are: A. Semedo: *History of the Great and Renowned Monarchy of China*, London, 1655; *Voyages fameux de Sieur Vincent Le Blanc*, Paris, 1658; Mandelso: *Peregrinations from Persia into the West Indies*, translated by John Davies, London, 1662; F. M. Pinto: *His Travels in the Kingdoms of Ethiopia, China, Tartaria*, translated by Henry Cogan, London, 1663. For a fuller list of books on China see A. H. Rowbotham: *Missionary and Mandarin: The Jesuits at the Court of China*, Berkeley and Los Angeles, 1942, pp. 339–61.

Section 4. Lengthy accounts of the impact of Chinese philosophy on Europe may be found in V. Pinot: *La Chine et la formation de l'esprit philosophique en France 1640–1740*, Paris, 1932, and A. Reichwein: *China and Europe: Intellectual and Artistic Contacts in the Eighteenth Century*, New York, 1925; though both these writers seem to overstress the direct influence of Chinese thought.

Section 5. An excellent reconstruction of the Anson incident is given by M. Collis in: *The Great Within*, London, 1941, pp. 219–59, which also includes descriptions of the various seventeenth- and eighteenth-century embassies to Peking. For the Anson incident from the Chinese point of view see A. Waley: *Yuan Mei*, London, 1956, pp. 205–9, with a translation of Yuan Mei's letter about it.

II THE BEGINNINGS OF CHINOISERIE

Section 1. For the best account of early Sino-European commercial relations see M. Rostovtzeff: *The Social and Economic History of the Hellenistic World*, Oxford, 1953, pp. 84 and 864. Trade relations between China and Parthia were firmly established as the result of the two embassies of Chang Ch'ien to Mithridates II, in 128 and 115 B.C. After the beginning of the first century B.C. Chinese ceramics occasionally reached Europe.

The description of Thin, alternatively rendered 'This', appears in *The Periplus of the Erythrean Sea*, of about A.D. 60.

For my account of Roman relations with the Orient I have relied principally on G. F. Hudson: *Europe and China*, London, 1931. A well-balanced account of the Chinese silk trade with the Roman Empire is in W. Willetts: *Chinese Art*, Harmondsworth, 1958, vol. i, pp. 207–19. Mr Willetts considers the question of the silk produced on the island of Cos (to which Aristotle refers) but reaches the conclusion that sericulture was not otherwise practised in the West before the sixth century. Gibbon's account of the introduction of Chinese silk-worm (*Bombyx mori*) eggs is based on Procopius. It seems probable that the persons responsible for introducing the silk-worm eggs were monks of the order of St Basil, in 553 or 554; see F. M. Heichelheim in *Ciba Review*, August 1949, p. 2753.

Section 2. André Grabar: 'Le Succès des arts orientaux à la cour byzantine sous les Macédoniens' in *Münchner Jahrbuch der Bildenden Kunst*, 1951, pp. 32–60, discusses at length the vogue for exoticism in late tenth- and early eleventh-century Byzantium. The inventory of Marco Polo's effects at the time of his death, copied in 1366, is published by A. C. Moule and P. Pelliot, *op. cit.* p. 554.

For the best account of the possible Chinese influence on Simone Martini see G. Paccagnini: *Simone Martini*, Milan, 1957, pp. 22–30. For fuller and more tenden-tious accounts of oriental influence on Italian painters see G. Soulier: *Les Influences orientales dans la peinture toscane*, Paris, 1924 and G. V. Pouzyna: *La Chine, l'Italie et les débuts de la Renaissance*, Paris, 1935. J. Baltrušaitis, *Le Moyen Age fantastique*, Paris, 1955, convincingly suggests that the origin of the devils with bats' wings which began to appear in the mid-thirteenth century is to be found in China and he points out that Tartars were associated with the devils of the Apocalypse (cf. Dante, *Inferno*, xvii, 13-18). Squatting Chinamen or Tartars appear in fifteenth-century illuminations as emblems of gluttony. Mr. Baltrušaitis's other suggestions on the Chinese origins of various features in medieval art are to my mind less convincing. See also *Orient-Occident* (exhibition catalogue), Musée Cernuschi, Paris, 1958.

Notable Chinese textiles of the Yüan period are to be found in the cathedral at Regensburg, the Nikolaikirche at Stralsund, the cathedral at Halberstadt, and the Marienkirche at Danzig: see Otto von Falke: *Kunstgeschichte der Seidenweberei*, Berlin, 1913. Inventories of various churches including St Peter's, Rome, and old St Paul's, London, reveal that many more examples once existed. The practice of using Chinese silks for ecclesiastical vestments seems to have faded out after the end of the fourteenth century and to have been revived only in the eighteenth century. (For an eighteenth-century example see L. Bertolini and M. Bucci: *Mostra d' arte sacra*, Lucca, 1957, no. 105.) Many Lucchese textiles in the oriental style are reproduced by O. von Falke, *op. cit.*, Figs. 388–412.

The porcelain bottle with King Louis of Hungary's arms, now known only from a drawing in the collection Gaignères (Bibliothèque Nationale, Paris, fr. 20070, f. 8), was last recorded when it appeared in the sale of William Beckford's collection at Fonthill Abbey, October 1823. See Y. Hackenbroch in *The Connoisseur*, June 1955, pp. 22–28, who states that the earliest extant example of Chinese porcelain in a Euro-pean silver mount is the mazer cup given to Corpus Christi College, Cambridge, by Archbishop Warham and documented pre-1450.

Chinoiserie

According to W. Heyd: *Histoire du commerce du Levant*, Leipzig, 1885, porcelain was included in the gifts from the Sultan of Egypt to Doge Foscari, 1442, Charles VII of France, 1447, Doge Malipiero, 1461, Caterina Cornaro, 1476, Lorenzo de' Medici, 1487, Doge Barbarigo, 1490, and the Seigneurie of Venice, 1498.

For early collections of porcelain see H. Davillier: *Les Origines de la porcelaine en Europe*, Paris, 1882, pp. 9, 125–7, 130–5.

Loys Guyon on porcelain is quoted by H. Belevitch-Stankevitch: *Le Goût chinois en France au temps de Louis XIV*, Paris, 1910.

The Medici soft-paste wares may not have been the first examples of porcelain produced in Europe: Venetians were making a substance called *porcellana contraffatta* in the fifteenth century, but no samples of it survive and it was possibly an opaque glass.

Section 3. For a fuller account of the trade relations between China and Europe in the sixteenth and seventeenth centuries see G. F. Hudson: *op. cit.* Thomas Platter's remarks on Mr Cope's collection appear in: C. Williams: *Thomas Platter's Travels in England*, London, 1937, pp. 171–3. My account of the Jacobean taste for lacquer is based on J. Irwin in *The Burlington Magazine*, 1953, p. 193.

Section 4. As the words quoted from *L'Ile des Hermaphrodites* were also used to describe a 'pavillon de taffetas de la Chine', owned by Gabrielle d'Estrées in 1599 (see Belevitch-Stankevitch, p. xxxiii) they may refer to genuine Chinese decorations. The reference to Étienne Sager appears in L. Batiffol: *Marie de Médicis and the French Court in the Seventeenth Century*, London, 1908, p. 250.

For Indian elements in Portuguese sixteenth-century architecture, notably the cloister at Batalha, a fountain at Sintra, windows in the Convent of Christ at Thomar and the tower at Belem, see J. Evans: *Pattern*, Oxford, 1931, vol. ii, p. 59. The earliest surviving example of Portuguese pottery with oriental-style decorations is a plate dated 1621 in the Museu Soares dos Reis, Oporto, see G. Martin-Méry: *L'Europe et la découverte du monde* (exhibition catalogue), Bordeaux, 1960, no. 236. Thomas Trevelyon's designs are in the Folger Shakespeare Library, Washington. For Southwark delftware, previously supposed to have been made at Lambeth, see H. Tait in *The Connoisseur*, August, 1960, p. 36 and February, 1961, p. 22. A few figures suffice to indicate the scale on which trade between Europe and China was conducted shortly after the mid-seventeenth century. The journal of the Dutch East India Company at Batavia (quoted by Belevitch-Stankevitch *op. cit.* p. xxxviii) records that on February 9th, 1661, a consignment arrived from Quinam containing 1,100 pieces of Japanese porcelain, 900 pieces of Chinese porcelain, 125 small parasols; on February 11th two more ships brought 5,900 Japanese cups, 1,600 tea-cups, 100 Japanese *pots à bière*, 400 large porcelain vases, 1,062 plates, 500 jugs, 200 parasols besides smaller quantities of many other objects.

Notes

Section 1. For this section I have drawn heavily on H. Belevitch-Stankevitch: *Le Goût chinois en France au temps de Louis XIV*, Paris, 1910, a work of great thoroughness which includes an abundance of literary and inventory references. See also C. Yamanda: *Die Chinamode des Spätbarocks*, Berlin, 1935. For the Trianon de Porcelaine see R. Danis: *La Première Maison royale du Trianon*, Paris, n.d. (*c.* 1926). M. Danis suggested that the arrangement of the five buildings at the Trianon de Porcelaine was based on that of the central court of the Imperial Palace at Peking, and compares them with a print published by Jollain *l'aîné* where the background appears to be derived from a drawing made at Peking. M. Danis's suggestion (repeated by several later writers) that certain panels of Delft tiles in the Château de Rambouillet came originally from the Trianon de Porcelaine has been disproved by Dr. C. H. de Jonge who dates them 1717–23; see *Nederlands Kunsthistorisch Jaarboek*, vol. x, 1959, pp. 125–209.

The terms *façon de la Chine* and *à la chinoise* present a further difficulty, for there are occasions on which they appear to refer to objects of oriental origin while such typically French pieces of furniture as *guéridons* are sometimes described simply as 'chinois' though they were probably made in Europe. As examples of French furniture in the Chinese taste, the following inventory descriptions (from Belevitch-Stankevitch, *op. cit.*) may be quoted: first, a cabinet at Versailles, 'un cabinet, aussi de verny façon de la Chine, enrichy par devant d'un grand ornement d'argent ciselé, d'enfants, crotesques et festons et, au milieu, d'un buste de femme, entourée d'une guirlande de fleurs.' At Choisy in the last decades of the century there were a table and pair of *guéridons* 'dont le dessus est peint en miniature de figures et oiseaux grotesques à la chinoise.' The cabinet might easily escape notice as an example of chinoiserie while the later table and *guéridons* were probably similar to lacquer furniture made in Germany and England.

Colbert remarks that when the king fitted up an apartment for his mother at Versailles in 1663 it was decorated with the two things that pleased her most, 'des ouvrages de filigranes d'or et d'argent de la Chine et des jasmins. Jamais la Chine même n'a tant vu de ces ouvrages ensemble, ni toute l'Italie tant de fleurs.' Anne of Austria may perhaps have acquired a taste for orientalia from Mazarin who possessed a very rich collection of eastern objects before 1658 (see Belevitch-Stankevitch, p. 86); a chest of fine Japanese lacquer probably from his collection, is in the Victoria and Albert Museum (see H. Clifford Smith in *The Burlington Magazine*, October 1916, pp. 299–303).

For a full account of the Siamese episode see M. Collis: *Siamese White*, London, 1936.

Kneller's portrait of Mikelh Xin (or Shen-Fo-Tsing) is reproduced in the illustrated souvenir of the exhibition of *The King's Pictures*, Royal Academy, London, 1946, p. 91.

Les Tentures des Indes are reproduced by H. Göbel: *Die Wandteppiche*, Leipzig, 1928, vol. ii, p. 20, and also the Aubusson panel, vol. ii, p. 277.

The Wallace Collection casket is reproduced by F. J. B. Watson: *The Wallace Collection Catalogues: Furniture*, London, 1956, Pl. 26.

The *Mercure galant* records that on January 25th, 1700, there was a masquerade at Copenhagen in which there appeared 'douze pagodes assises sur de riches carreaux', and the ceiling of the ball-room was in the form of a tent painted 'à la chinoise, avec des figures et ornements grotesques'.

Section 2. A good account of the French domination of eighteenth-century Germany is given by A. Fauchier-Magnan: *The Small German Courts in the Eighteenth Century*, London, 1958. The room at the Neue Residenz at Bamberg was originally called the *holländisches Kabinett* and the japanning was possibly of Dutch workmanship though the name might equally well derive from the similarity of the decorations to lacquer imported by way of Holland from the Far East.

The *Pagodenburg* is illustrated in L. Hager: *Nymphenburg*, Munich, 1955, Pl. 13–15. A little shrine with chinoiserie decorations in gold on a green ground is in the church of Terrugan, between Mafra and Sintra; the paintings are similar to those in the library at Coimbra. I am grateful to Senhor Ayres de Carvalho for drawing my attention to this.

An outstanding example of Japanese lacquer made for a Dutchman is a box in the Victoria and Albert Museum inscribed with the name of Maria van Diemen, wife of the Governor-General of the Dutch East Indies and probably dating from 1636–1645 (see H. Clifford Smith in *The Burlington Magazine*, October 1916, pp. 299–303).

Very few examples of *Bois de Spa*, dating from before the mid-eighteenth century, have been traced but see H. Huth: *Europäische Lackarbeiten*, Darmstadt, 1955 and in *Venezia e l'Europa*, Venice, 1956, p. 374.

The porcelain room in the Charlottenburg Schloss is illustrated by H. Schmitz: *Deutsche Möbel des Barock und Rokoko*, Stuttgart, 1923, p. xxvii.

Section 3. James II's conversation on Confucius with Dr Hyde, the Bodleian librarian, is recorded by Anthony Wood (*The Life and Times of Anthony Wood*, Oxford, 1894, vol. iii, p. 236): 'Then his majesty told Dr Hyde of a book of Confucius translated from the China language by the Jesuits (4 in number) and asked whether it was in the library? To which Dr Hyde answered that it was, and that "it treated of philosophy, but not so as that of European philosophy". Whereupon his majesty asked whether "the Chinese had any divinity?" To which Dr Hyde answered, "Yes, but 'twas idolatry, they being all heathens, but yet they have in their idol temples statues representing the Trinity, and other pictures, which show that ancient Christianity had been amongst them." To which he assented by a nod. After that, his majesty left off asking more questions.'

The Duke of Rutland's vases are illustrated by C. J. Jackson: *An Illustrated History of English Plate*, London, 1911, vol. i, p. 259. The same authority, p. 243, reproduces the Duke of Portland's silver *garniture de cheminée* of 1676, consisting of vases based on the shape of Chinese ginger jars but decorated with characteristic late seventeenth-century English floral motifs.

For my account of japanned furniture I have drawn on R. Edwards and P. Mac-Quoid: *A Dictionary of English Furniture*, London, 1954, *passim*. Captain William Dampier's remark is quoted by R. Fastnedge: *English Furniture Styles*, London, 1955, p. 95

Chinese and Japanese lacquer, that is to say true lacquer, is a varnish made principally from the resin of the *Rhus vernicifera* or Lac tree which grows today only in Annam, south China, Korea, and Japan. The varnish was applied in many layers, each of which was allowed to dry before the next was applied; the surface was then highly polished and decorated in gold leaf. As this resin was unobtainable in Europe and could not be transported from the East, craftsmen resorted to other means to achieve a similar effect and propounded a wide variety of receipts some of which are given by Stalker and Parker in their *Treatise of Japanning and Varnishing*, London, 1688, and by Filippo Bonanni: *Trattato sopra la vernice detta comunamente cinese*, Rome, 1720. Normally the wood was treated with a mixture of whitening and size and then painted with numerous coats of varnish composed of gum-lac, seed-lac, or shell-lac, different preparations of the resin broken off the twigs of a tree on which it is deposited by an insect, the *coccus lacca*: and dissolved in spirits of wine. The decorations were outlined in gold size, built up with a composition made of gum-arabic and sawdust, coloured, polished, and gilt with metal dust. The surface was burnished with a dog's tooth or an agate pebble. Such methods did not produce a substance as hard, waterproof, and glittering as oriental lacquer, but after many experiments European craftsmen made a varnish of great beauty. Voltaire thought they had improved on their models and mentioned the 'cabinets où Martin a surpassé l'art de la Chine'.

The Duke of Marlborough's screen is mentioned by G. M. Trevelyan: *Ramillies*, 1932, p. 62.

For an example of walnut furniture to which japanned decorations have been applied, possibly by an amateur (though the quality of the work is high) see the pair of chairs reproduced by P. MacQuoid: *English Furniture . . . in the Lady Lever Art Gallery*, London, 1928, pl. 52.

The laird of Thunderton's inventory is quoted by M. Plant: *The Domestic Life of Scotland in the Eighteenth Century*, Edinburgh, 1952, p. 40.

For English pottery of the seventeenth century see B. Rackham and H. Read: *English Pottery*, 1924.

James Brydges, later Duke of Chandos, bought his embroidered quilts from Mrs Lee and his damasks from the Indian House in Leadenhall Street, 'the China shop' in the same street and the Golden Anchor in Bedford Street, Covent Garden; see C. H. Collins and M. I. Baker: *James Brydges*, London, 1949, p. 24. An embroidered silk panel with the Duke's arms on it is in the Victoria and Albert Museum, reproduced in R. Fry and others: *Chinese Art*, London, 1935, pl. 47 b.

The taste for 'bizarre silks' in England between 1707 and 1715 has been fully examined by P. Thornton in *The Burlington Magazine*, 1958, p. 265.

The career of the literary impostor 'George Psalmanazar' throws some light on the vogue for orientalia in the opening years of the eighteenth century. A native of the south of France, he was educated by Dominicans but turned mendicant and styled himself a Japanese Christian. This brought him little success, so he represented himself as a pagan Japanese, inventing a language and a religious ritual, and allowed himself to be converted and baptized as an Anglican by William Innes, the chaplain of a Scottish regiment at Sluys. The chaplain was privy to the imposture and recommended Psalmanazar to call himself a Formosan instead of a Japanese. In this guise he arrived in London in 1703 and immediately caused great interest among the learned. Next year he published a wholly fictitious account of Formosa which at first won general credence. In 1708 *The British Apollo* advertised 'fine white Enamell'd work as it is improved according to the right japan way by Geo. Psalmanazar and is now carried on by him and Edward Pattenden to whom alone he has communicated the Secret'. After 1707, when Innes was appointed Chaplain-General to the forces in Portugal as a reward for introducing so spectacular a convert to the Anglican communion, Psalmanazar was deprived of his mentor and found increasing difficulty in maintaining his imposture. But it was not until 1728 that he renounced the fraud and settled down to a career as a writer. The best account of this bizarre chinoiserie figure is to be found in *The Dictionary of National Biography*, vol. xlvi, p. 439.

Section 4. The wares brought back from the East in the *Amphitrite* attained great renown in France and their provenance was recorded; hence the phrase *lacque* (or porcelaine) *d'Amphitrite* which sometimes appears in inventories and contemporary literature. In the cargo were 167 cases of porcelain besides unrecorded quantities of lacquer and textiles—damasks, taffetas, gauzes, crepes and satins.

The English textile troubles are described in greater detail by B. S. Allen: *Tides in English Taste*, Cambridge, Mass., 1937, pp. 221–9.

IV ROCOCO CHINOISERIE

Section 1. The main authority for French eighteenth-century chinoiserie is H. Cordier: *La Chine en France au XVIII⁰ siècle*, Paris, 1910. Numerous objects are reproduced in J. Guérin. *La Chinoiserie en Europe au XVIIIe siècle*, Paris, 1911. For the best account of the French rococo style in architecture and interior decoration see F. Kimball: *Le Style Louis XV*, Paris, 1959.

The quotation from the Goncourts on p. 87 is from E. and J. de Goncourt: *French XVIII Century Painters* (tr. R. Ironside), London, 1948, p. 55.

Several seventeenth-century artists had shown some interest in the exotic clothes of the Orient. Rubens executed five drawings, dated between 1619 and 1627, of Europeans in Chinese (in one instance Korean) dress and appears to have made use of these when he painted an oil sketch of a triumph, now at Bayonne (see C. Stuart-Wortley in *Old Master Drawings*, 1934, vol. ix, p. 35 ff.). Rembrandt owned and copied Mogul miniatures (see O. Benesch, *The Drawings of Rembrandt*, London, 1957, vol. v, pp. 335–42) and some of his own drawings suggest that he may have seen and learned from examples of Chinese or Japanese penmanship; he did not, however, produce anything that could be called chinoiserie. Nor did Kneller who painted a portrait of Père Couplet's protégé Mikelh Xin which he considered his masterpiece; this work may be compared with Reynolds's portrait of Wang-y-Tong of nearly a century later.

A group of drawings of the various orders of Mandarins, from those presented to Louis XIV, was engraved by P. Giffart and published with a text by Père Bouvet as *L'Estat présent de la Chine* in 1697. These engravings seem to reproduce fairly faithfully the spirit of their originals, but comparison of them with the chinoiseries of Bérain and Watteau reveal how little stylistic inspiration the latter derived from this or any other Chinese source.

The first monkeys in a dated work by Bérain appear in an engraving of 1693; a Chinaman appears in a chimney-piece by Bérain published the same year (see F. Kimball, *op. cit.* p. 116).

The rooms painted by Huet in the Château de Champs are illustrated in E. de Ganay: *Châteaux et manoirs de France: Ile-de-France*, Paris, 1938, vol. ii, pl. 30–1. English porcelain copies after Boucher are described by Y. Hackenbroch in *The Connoisseur*, October 1956, pp. 106–10.

Pillementesque flowers appear on a design for a plate, probably prepared by C. Precht for the Marieberg pottery (see G. Munthe: *Konsthantverkaren Christian Precht*, Stockholm, 1957, p. 287). There is a room painted in the style of Pillement in the town hall of Sneek, Frieseland (see S. Sitwell: *The Netherlands*, London, n.d., pl. 86) and another by an anonymous Liégeois artist in the Château de Hex, near Liège (see: *Connaissance*, February, 1960, p. 73).

Beckford's description appears in *The Journal of William Beckford in Portugal and Spain*, ed. B. Alexander, London, 1954, pp. 129–30.

For Marie Leczinska's chinoiserie paintings see P. de Nolhac: *Louis XV et Marie Leczinska*, 1900, pp. 141–2.

The room in the Villa Bianchi Bandinelli is reproduced in *The Connoisseur*,

November 1959, p. 145. A set of chinoiserie *toiles peintes* made at the Fabrique Royale de Marseille in the 1780s is in the Château d'Hauteville, Switzerland, see *Le Château d'Hauteville*, Geneva, 1932.

The Wallace Collection chest of drawers is reproduced by F. J. B. Watson: *op. cit.* pl. 43. A cabinet by Bernard II Van Risen Burgh with porcelain plaques is reproduced in *Connaissance des Arts*, March 1957, p. 59.

The Musée du Louvre possesses a celadon vase with an ormulu mount and another porcelain vase with cover transformed into a *brûle-parfum*, both originally in the collection of Mme de Pompadour.

Section 2. The best stylistic history of European porcelain is F. H. Hoffmann: *Das Porzellan*, Berlin, 1932, though some of his attributions to modellers have been disproved by later authorities. See also W. B. Honey: *European Ceramic Art*, London, 1952 and the brief but useful G. Savage: *Porcelain through the Ages*, London, 1954. For a commentary on M. Lister's account of the Saint-Cloud factory see G. Wills in *The Connoisseur*, March 1958, pp. 74-6. For a biography of Kändler see H. Gröger: *Johann Joachim Kändler*, Dresden, 1956.

The Sèvres figures after Boucher are reproduced in E. Bourgeois: *Le Biscuit de Sèvres au XVIIIᵉ siècle*, Paris, 1909.

Some recently discovered documents on the Bow porcelain factory, together with many illustrations of its products, are in *Bow Porcelain 1744–1776*, catalogue of exhibition at the British Museum, 1959.

Section 3. A painted chinoiserie screen probably made either for the Japanese palace in Dresden or Schloss Pillnitz was included in the exhibition *The China Trade and its Influence*, Metropolitan Museum, New York, 1941.

The lacquer room at Brühl, destroyed in 1944, was described and illustrated in K. Röder and W. Holzhausen: *Das Indianische Lackkabinett des Kurfürsten Clemens August in Schloss Brühl*, Tübingen, 1950.

The contemporary description of the Chinese house at Potsdam is quoted by A. Reichwein: *China and Europe*, 1925, p. 62.

Like Roentgen, the most renowned cabinet-maker of the Louis XVI period, Jean Henri Reisener was, of course, born in Germany, but since he was trained at the Gobelins factory and spent his entire career in France he can hardly be regarded as a German craftsman.

In the palace at Schönbrunn there is one room with panels of oriental lacquer set in elaborate rococo frames; another is decorated with Chinese pictures and plaster relief parasols and swags of flowers.

Merlini's design is illustrated in Władysław Tatarkiewicz: *Dominik Merlini*, Warsaw, 1955, p. 111. There are several other exotic buildings in the park at Drottningholm, but these are in the Turkish rather than the Chinese taste. For the Chinese Palace at Oranienbaum see: *Les Trésors de l'art en Russie*, St Petersburg, 1901, p. 183; the lacquer room in Monplaisir is illustrated *idem*, vol. ii, 1902, pl. 90. For Cameron and Tsarskoe Selo see: G. Loukomski: *Charles Cameron*, London, 1943.

Section 4. A very grand carnival procession *L'entrata del impero della Cina* was held in Turin in February 1749; two of the floats were designed by the court sculptor, Francesco Ladatte (information from MS. notes of Baudi di Vesme, Palazzo Madama, Turin). Caricatures by Marco Ricci of Italian singers in the 'oriental' costumes worn in the early part of the eighteenth century are reproduced in A. Blunt and E. Croft-Murray: *Venetian Drawings . . . at Windsor Castle*, London, 1957, Part II, Figs. 8, 9, and 13.

For Filippo Minei see V. Viale in *Torino*, September 1942, p. 58, and E. Oliviero: *La villa della regina in Torino*, Turin, 1942. The villa was burnt out during the last war. Other Piedmontese artists who produced chinoiseries—though none of their works in this style have yet been identified—are mentioned in L. Rosso: *La pittura e la scultura del '700 a Torino*, 1934, pp. 33–7.

The lacquer room in the Palazzo Reale at Turin is illustrated in *The Connoisseur*, November 1957, p. 144. A room with Chinese paintings and chinoiserie furniture was created in 1747 in the Palazzo Papale, Castelgandolfo. A later lacquer room survives in the Villa Albani, Rome. An unusual example of Italian chinoiserie is provided by two marble pagods attributed to Giovanni Bonazza, see C. Semenzato in *Arte Figurativa*, 1960, No. 4, p. 67.

V ENGLISH ROCOCO CHINOISERIE

Section 1. Fuller accounts of the literary background to English eighteenth-century chinoiserie may be found in B. S. Allen: *Tides in English Taste 1619–1800*, Cambridge, Mass., 1937 and W. W. Appleton: *A Cycle of Cathay*, New York, 1951.

Section 2. Canaletto's painting with figures in Chinese costume was reproduced in *The Burlington Magazine*, February 1938, p. 71. The room with paintings by Joli in Heidegger's house at Richmond was published by E. Croft-Murray in *The Burlington Magazine*, 1941, pp. 105–12 and 155–9. The paintings include views of Basle, the bay of Naples, etc., as well as the Chinese scenes.

The barometer in the Science museum is reproduced in R. Edwards and P. Mac-Quoid, *op. cit.* vol. i, p. 31.

The drawing in the Bodleian library (Gough maps 30) is of a summer-house at Durdans; I am indebted to Mr John Harris for information about it.

Thomas Chippendale was represented as little more than a gatherer of other men's flowers by F. Kimball and E. Donnell: *The Creators of the Chippendale Style*, New York, 1929, who sought to prove that H. Copland was responsible for most of the designs in the *Director*. These conclusions have been scouted by R. Edwards: *Georgian Cabinet-Makers*, London, 1953, and P. Ward-Jackson: *English Furniture Designs of the Eighteenth Century*, London, 1959, and the attribution of the designs to Chippendale has been restored. However, the furniture made for Mrs Montagu by Linnell suggests that the Chinese Chippendale style was formulated and not invented by Chippendale.

Leather screens and hangings are the subject of an article by H. Huth in *The Burlington Magazine*, July 1937, pp. 25–35, where he publishes a hanging at Wilhelmshöhe, signed: *Coventry London*. Doubt may, however, be expressed on whether the screen in the Victoria and Albert Museum which he illustrates is English (as he states), Dutch, or East Indian: the present writer thinks it is probably European.

For the early Gothic Revival and chinoiserie see K. Clark: *The Gothic Revival*, London, 1950, chapter iii. For eighteenth-century chinoiserie buildings in America see C. Lancaster in *Art Bulletin*, xxix, 1947, pp. 183–193, and M. Jourdain: *English Interior Decoration*, London, 1950, Pl. 111, 113.

VI THE ANGLO-CHINESE GARDEN

Section 1. For fuller accounts of English landscape-gardening see C. Hussey: *The Picturesque*, London, 1927; H. F. Clark in the *Journal of the Warburg and Courtauld Institutes*, vol. vi, 1943, pp. 165–89, and *The English Landscape Garden*, London, 1948. The Italian influences are examined by E. Mainwaring: *Italian Landscape in 18th century England*, New York, 1925. O. Siren: *China and the Gardens of Europe*, New York, 1950, also refers to English gardens. He reproduces a photograph of a pile of rockwork at Painshill claiming that this was an artificial rock-work hill made in imitation of a Chinese mount as described by Nieuhoff and others. If it were so it would be unique in Europe, but it appears to be a ruined grotto. For Sharawadgi see *The Architectural Review*, December, 1949, p. 391.

Robert Morris's remarks are quoted from *The Architectural Remembrancer*, London, 1751. The similarity of Chambers's remarks quoted on p. 154 with Blondel's remark quoted on p. 96, may be no coincidence. Chambers worked under J. F. Blondel and later termed him 'mon ancien maître'. For Chambers's relations with 'Capability' Brown see D. Stroud: *Capability Brown*, London, 1950.

The fishing house at Arlesford was published by M. Girouard in *Country Life*, November 6th, 1958, pp. 1040–1.

John Scott's poem, *Li Po* seems to have been first published in his collected works, 1782.

Sezincote House and Park are described and illustrated by C. Hussey: *English Country Houses: Late Georgian*, London, 1958, pp. 66–73.

Section 2. For the landscape garden in Europe see M. L. Gothein: *A History of Garden Art*, London, 1928; O. Siren, *op. cit.*; E. de Ganay: *Les Jardins de France*, Paris, 1949. The best edition of de Ligne: *Coup d'œil sur Belœil* is the variorum text ed. E. de Ganay, Paris, 1922. E. von Erdberg: *Chinese Influences on European Garden Structures*, Cambridge, Mass., 1936, lists many of the most interesting chinoiserie garden buildings in Europe.

Some support is given to the idea that the French *jardin anglais* was thought by contemporaries to have a Chinese appearance by Arthur Young's remarks on the garden of the Petit Trianon which he visited in 1787: 'It contains about 100 acres, disposed in the taste of what we read in the books of Chinese gardening, whence it is supposed the English style was taken. There is more of Sir William Chambers here than of Mr Brown, more effort than nature, and more expense than taste; woods, rocks, lawns, lakes, rivers, islands, cascades, grottos, walks, temples, and even villages. . . . But the glory of *Le Petit Trianon* is the exotic trees and shrubs. The world has been successfully rifled to decorate it. Here are curious and beautiful ones to please the eye of ignorance; and to exercise the memory of science.' (A. Young: *Travels in France*, ed. C. Maxwell, Cambridge, 1950, p. 88.) The architect of the transformation of the garden at Schwetzingen was Friedrich Ludwig von Sckell, who had studied landscape gardening, and particularly 'Capability' Brown in England.

VII   THE LAST DAYS OF CATHAY

Section 2. The best account of late eighteenth-century chinoiserie in France is in H. Cordier, *op. cit.*

For the Sèvres chinoiserie porcelain made for the Royal Family see P. Verlet and S. Grandjean: *Sèvres*, Paris, 1953.

Simulated bamboo chairs formerly in the Folie de St James, were lent from the C. Dior collection to an exhibition at the Musée des Arts Décoratifs, Paris, 1955/6. For an account of the decorations in Palazzo Braschi see C. Pietrangeli: *Palazzo Braschi*, Rome, 1958.

Section 3. It seems possible that some of the many pieces of 'Chinese Chippendale' furniture usually assigned to the 1750s may date from the subsequent two decades.

The Adam brothers had also designed chinoiserie garden ornaments and there are drawings by James Adam, dating from the 1750s, in the collection of Sir John Clerk, Bt.

Sir Joshua Reynolds's portrait of Wang y Tong is reproduced by E. K. Waterhouse: *Reynolds*, London, 1941, pl. 167.

A fine English dressing-table with chinoiserie in marquetry, from the collection of Mrs David Gubbay, was shown in the *English Taste in the Eighteenth Century* exhibition, Royal Academy, London, 1955–6 and reproduced in the illustrated souvenir, pl. 41.

The Brighton Pavilion has been restored to much of its original splendour in recent years, under the guidance of the Director, Mr C. Musgrave. Most of the decorations mentioned in my account of it are still *in situ*—including the vast lamps— and my description is phrased in the past tense only in order to include the objects and decorations which have vanished—the wallpaper in the corridor and central room, the wall-paintings in the banqueting room (the present series dates from the mid-nineteenth century save for one panel), the tall Chinese pagodas in the music-room, and the majority of the smaller objects. Mr C. Musgrave ingeniously suggests (*Royal Pavilion*, London, 1959) that the design of the music-room may owe something to Marco Polo's description of Kublai Khan's pavilion. He also points out that the figures in the music-room paintings (pl. IV), like those in the stained-glass windows on the staircase, are derived from W. Alexander: *The Costume of China*, London, 1805. Fragments from the music-room carpet are in the Royal Collection and reproduced in B. Reade: *Regency Antiques*, London, 1953, pl. 106.

The description of the pavilion by E. Mogg appears in his edition of *Paterson's Roads*, 1831, p. 34.

The pavilion inspired two 'hindoo' buildings in Brighton itself, see C. Musgrave, *op. cit.* p. 153.

The statistics of the japanners working in London in 1817 are derived from B. Reade, *op. cit.*, which provides the best account of Regency furniture.

VIII CHINA AND JAPAN

Section 1. For the best account of George Chinnery and bibliography see: *George Chinnery*, exhibition catalogue, Arts Council, London, 1957.

Robert Fortune's principal works are: *Three Years' Wandering in the Northern Provinces of China*, London, 1847 (2nd ed. amplified); *Journey to the Tea Countries*, London, 1853; *A Residence Among the Chinese*, London, 1857; *Yeddo and Peking*, London, 1863.

The aviary and Chinese garden at Dropmore are reproduced by O. Siren, *op. cit.*, where they are, probably incorrectly, dated 1790; the aviary alone is reproduced and described by G. Nares in *Country Life*, October 18th, 1956, pp. 834–7.

The buildings in M. Panckoucke's garden are illustrated in L. E. Audot: *Traité de la composition et de l'ornement des jardins* (6th ed.), Paris, 1859, Pl. 96–101.

For chinoiserie architecture in America see C. Lancaster in *The Art Bulletin*, vol. xxix, 1947, pp. 183–93.

The comments by Mrs Haweis appear in *Art in Decoration*, London, 1881; and *Beautiful Houses*, London, 1882.

Notes

T. Gautier wrote a Chinese novel and several articles on Chinese themes. In about 1863 he employed a Chinaman, Tin-Tun-Ling, as tutor to his daughter who published a series of free translations of Chinese poems (*Le Livre de jade*, 1867) and later wrote a novel set in Japan. See M. D. Camacho: *Judith Gautier*, Paris, 1939.

Among the direct imitations of Chinese art created in nineteenth-century Europe the bulkiest and most interesting were various exhibition buildings. A Chinese temple of wrought and cast iron was shown at the Philadelphia exhibition of 1876, shipped across the Atlantic and re-erected for the Paris exhibition of 1878, and then bought by the Corporation of Norwich and set up in Chapelfield Gardens where it remained for some forty years. (See *The Architectural Review*, November 1959, p. 231.) A Japanese pagoda built for the Paris exhibition of 1900 was re-erected at Laeken in the suburbs of Brussels where it yet stands.

Section 2. Accounts of the influence of Japanese prints on French painters are given by J. Rewald: *The History of Impressionism*, New York, 1946, and *Post Impressionism from Van Gogh to Gauguin*, New York, 1950; D. Cooper: *Toulouse-Lautrec*, Paris, 1955, in *The Burlington Magazine*, June 1957, p. 204 (Van Gogh) and his exhibition catalogues *Paul Gauguin*, Edinburgh, 1955, *Monet*, Edinburgh, 1957; Y. Thirion in *Gazette des Beaux-Arts*, January 1956, pp. 95 ff. (Gauguin); T. S. Madsen: *The Sources of Art Nouveau*, Oslo, 1956; J. Richardson: *Édouard Manet*, London, 1958. Ernest Chesneau's article 'Le Japon à Paris' is in *Gazette des Beaux-Arts*, September 1878, pp. 385 ff.; and 406 ff.; the article on the decorative arts by L. Falize is in the same issue, pp. 217 ff. For an appreciation of Japanese art characteristic of the '90s see L. Gonse in *Revue des Arts Décoratifs*, xviii, 1898, pp. 97–116. For Bracquemond see L. Bénédite in *Art et Décoration*, xvii, 1905, p. 37 ff. An account of Mme Desoye is given by E. de Goncourt in his journal, March, 13, 1875.

A very early and hitherto unnoticed example of japonaiserie painting is provided by a water-colour of a Japanese girl (Wallace Collection) by D. Papety who died in 1849; it incorporates some surprisingly correct Japanese (and a few Chinese) details but owes nothing to the artistic influence of Japan.

For the Japanese influence on English decorative arts see A. Bøe: *From Gothic Revival to Functional Form*, Oslo and Oxford, 1957; C. Lancaster in *The Art Bulletin*, xxxiv, 1952, pp. 297-310 (with special reference to Art Nouveau); P. Floud in *The Concise Encyclopaedia of Antiques*, ed. L. G. G. Ramsey, London, 1957, pp. 25 ff.; G. B. Hughes in *Country Life*, August 29th, 1957, pp. 382-3 (English cloisonné); J. Lowry in *Country Life*, April 10th, 1958, pp. 752-3. For E. W. Godwin see D. Harbron: *The Conscious Stone*, London, 1949. Godwin published a book of designs for Anglo-Japanese furniture in 1877. Japanese influences are sometimes evident in the work of C. R. M. Mackintosh, see T. Howarth: *Charles Rennie Mackintosh*, London, 1952, p. 135. The first of the Japanese gardens in Europe was laid out for M. H. Krafft at

Jouy-en-Josas, *c.* 1885 (see *La Vie à La Campagne*, April, 1, 1909, p. 198 ff.) but this has vanished. Surviving Japanese gardens include the Jardin Kahn, Boulogne-sur-Seine (*c.* 1900), Tully House, County Kildare (*c.* 1906), The Cheynies, Cottered, Herts., and Kyoto Court, Bognor Regis: they were all designed by Japanese gardeners.

Though Proust's time scheme is a little erratic the description of Odette de Crécy's house may be dated *c.* 1887 from a reference to Dumas's *Le Francillon* a few pages later.

Section 3. The ballet designs by Sert and Bakst are reproduced in C. W. Beaumont: *Ballet Design Past and Present*, London, 1946.

The last large chinoiserie buildings appear to be the cinema *La Pagode*, rue de Babylone, Paris, and the premises of C. T. Loo et Cie, Rue de Courcelles, Paris, erected in 1926. I am grateful to Mlle Loo for this information.

1 Eleventh-century Byzantine ivory casket

2 Fourteenth-century Lucchese silk

3 Detail from *The Feast of the Gods* by Giovanni Bellini and Titian

4 Ming bowl and vase set in English silver-gilt, *c.* 1585

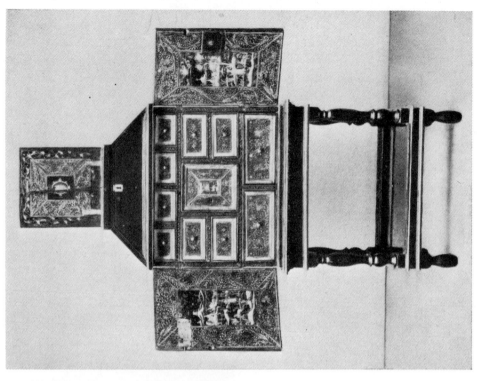

7 English japanned cabinet, c. 1620

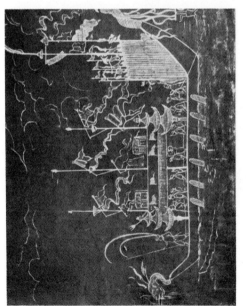

5 Detail of seventeenth century japanned decoration

6 Dutch japanned coffer, c. 1610

9 Four Delft tiles, *c.* 1650

8 Soft-paste porcelain vase made at the Medici factory, *c.* 1575–87

10 Faience ewer made at Nevers, *c.* 1650–80

11 Panel of English crewel work, *c.* 1680

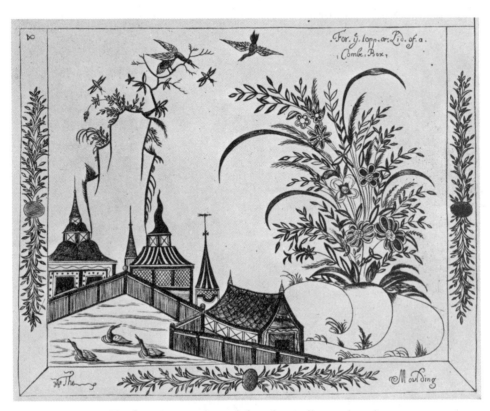

12 Design for a japanned comb box by Stalker and Parker, 1688

13 Tin-glazed earthenware plate made at Rouen, *c.* 1700

14 Delft tulip vase, *c.* 1725   15 French needlepoint panel, *c.* 1710

17 Delft jug, c. 1680–92

16 Mme de Sévigné's writing-desk

19 Dutch japanned doll's house cabinet, c. 1720

18 Design for a masquerade costume by Jean Bérain, c. 1700

20 Japanned tea-tray by Martin Schnell, *c.* 1720

21 Japanned cabinet by Gerard Dagly, *c.* 1710

22 Room in Schloss Ludwigsburg, Württemberg, 1714–22

24 English silver-gilt sconce, 1665

23 Design for a Chinese room by Daniel Marot, c. 1700

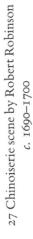

27 Chinoiserie scene by Robert Robinson
c. 1690–1700

25 Silver box, London, c. 1685

26 Silver toilet service, London, 1681–3

28 Panel of Soho tapestry, *c.* 1700

29 Panel of Soho tapestry, *c.* 1720

30 English japanned cabinet, *c*. 1690

31 English japanned cabinet, *c*. 1715   32 Japanned chest of drawers made at Boston, *c*. 1700

33 French *boiserie, c.* 1725–30

34 Trade card after a design by François Boucher

35 *Divinité chinoise*, drawing after Antoine Watteau

36 *Chinese Fishing Party*, by François Boucher, 1742

37 *Singerie*, by Christophe Huet, *c.* 1735

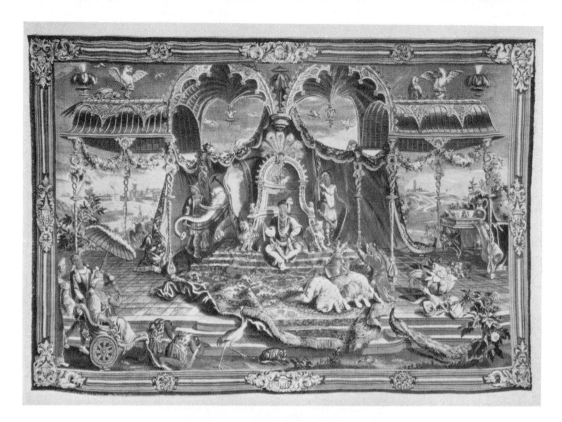

38 *The Audience*, Beauvais tapestry, *c.* 1725–30

39 Writing-desk, probably by Bernard II van Risen Burgh, *c.* 1750

40 *The Chinese Lovers*, by François Boucher, 1742

41 Console table by Bernard II van Risen Burgh, *c.* 1750

42 *The Emperor of China's Feast*, Beauvais tapestry, *c.* 1743

43 French japanned commode by Pierre II Migeon, *c.* 1750

44 A group of gold snuff-boxes and *nécessaires*

45 Panels by Jean Pillement, *c.* 1790

46 French ormolu clock, *c.* 1750   47 Design for ballet dancer's costume by Boquet, *c.* 1755

48 French terracotta statuette, *c.* 1750   49 French ormolu and porcelain clock, *c.* 1735

51 French japanned metal tea-kettle, c. 1740

50 French ormolu clock, c. 1750

53 Meissen porcelain pagod, c. 1720

52 Pilgrim bottle in Böttger's red stoneware, Meissen, c. 1715–20

54 Meissen porcelain *garniture de cheminée*, *c.* 1725–30

55 Meissen porcelain tankard, *c.* 1735   56 Meissen porcelain clock, *c.* 1735

57 Chantilly soft-paste porcelain statuette of a Joss, *c.* 1735

58 Saint-Cloud soft-paste cane-handle *c.* 1740

59 Nymphenburg porcelain pagod by Bustelli, 1756

60 Frankenthal porcelain tea-house, 1755

61 *The Emperor of China*, Höchst porcelain group, *c.* 1760

62 Sèvres porcelain vases, *c.* 1760

63 Marseilles faience tureen, *c.* 1760

64 Chelsea soft-paste porcelain group, *c.* 1755

65 Bow soft-paste porcelain group, *c.* 1750–5

66 Clock case by David Roentgen, *c.* 1770   67 Fountain at Schloss Brühl, *c.* 1750

68 The Indian House at Pillnitz, 1720–32

70 Detail of plate 66

69 Detail of German japanned cabinet door, *c.* 1740

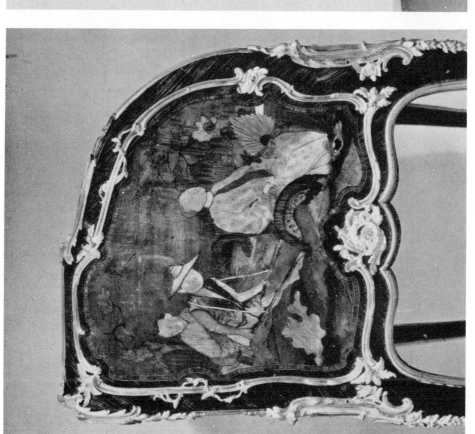

71 Inlaid woodwork on a German bureau, c. 1765

72 German japanned clock and stand, c. 1725

73 The Chinese tea-house at Sans-Souci, Potsdam,
1754–7

74 Exterior and detail of painted decoration inside
the Chinese House at Drottningholm

75 *The Asian Procession*, by Jean Barbault, Rome, 1751

76 Engraving of a regatta barge, Venice, 1716

77 Detail of a Venetian japanned door, *c.* 1750

78 Venetian japanned commode, *c.* 1750

79 Fresco paintings by Giovanni Domenico Tiepolo, c. 1757

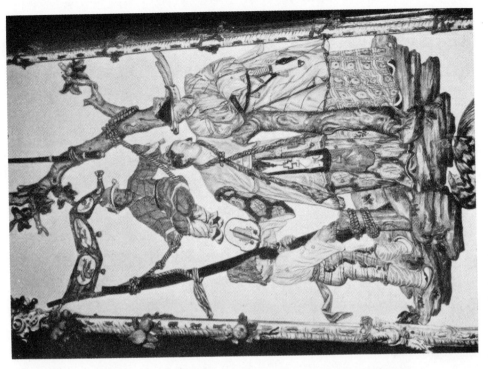

80 Porcelain reliefs by Giuseppe Gricci, 1761–5

Stanza di Compagnia del Palazzo Reale di Caserta - 1775 Nicola Fiore

81 Design for a room at Caserta by Nicola Fiore, 1775

82 Title page by William De La Cour, 1741

83 Panel of English wallpaper, *c.* 1740

84 Staffordshire earthenware tea-poy, *c.* 1750   85 Staffordshire earthenware water-buffalo, *c.* 1750

86 Silver-gilt tea-caddy by Paul de Lamerie, London, 1747

87 (a and b) Details of the Chinese room at Claydon House, 1769

87 (c and d) Details of the hall and Chinese room at Claydon House, 1769

88 Interior of the Chinese summer house
in Shugborough Park, c. 1747

89 English japanned writing-table, 1752

90 English settee, *c.* 1755

91 English japanned bed, probably by Thomas Chippendale, 1750–4

92 English japanned standing shelves, *c.* 1755

93 Commode veneered with oriental lacquer and English japan, *c.* 1765

94 Chinese painted mirror in an English frame, *c.* 1747

95 English wine-glass, *c.* 1780

96 Silver tea-caddy, London, 1763

97 English vellum book-binding by James Bate, c. 1765

98 Silver coffee-pot, London, 1769

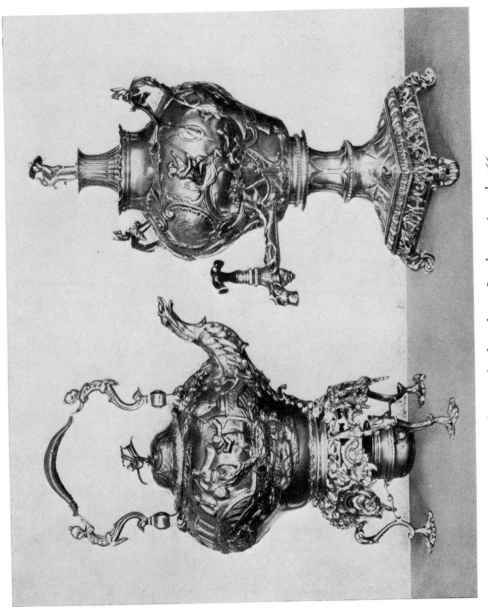

99 Silver tea-kettle and urn, London, 1761 and 1766

100 Panel of English plate-printed cotton, 1765

101 Engraving of the pagoda in Kew Gardens, 1763

102 Summer house in Shugborough Park, *c.* 1747

103 Chinese pavilion at Harnstown House, County Kildare, *c.* 1750

104 Engraving of the Duke of Cumberland's Chinese yacht, 1754

105 The Chinese dairy in Woburn, 1787

106 The pagoda fountain at Alton Towers, *c.* 1824

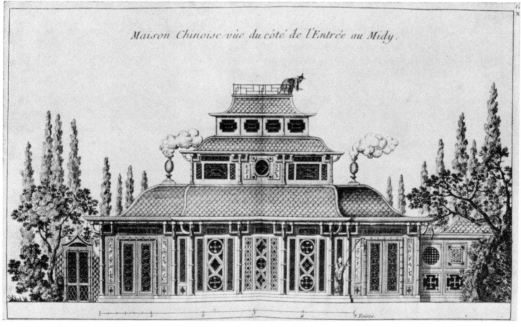

Maison Chinoise vûe du côté de l'Entrée au Midy.

107 Pavilion at Cassan, L'Isle-Adam, *c.* 1778
108 Engraving of the *Maison chinoise* at the Désert de Retz, 1785

109 Water-colour of a kiosk in the park at Chantilly, 1784

110 Pavilion in Haga Park, Sweden, *c.* 1770

111 The pagoda at Chanteloup, 1775–8   112 The Chinese pavilion at Sturefors, Sweden, *c.* 1760

113 The Chinese pavilion at Bonnelles, engraving, *c.* 1776

114 Summer house at Brignano Gera d' Adda, *c.* 1770

115 Water-colour design for a fishing pavilion by Frederick Crace, *c.* 1824

116 Design by Frederick Crace for the Chinese Gallery in the Brighton
Pavilion, 1815–19

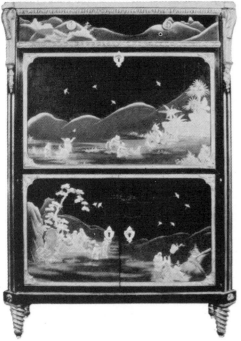

117 Engraving of the Chinese Baths in Paris, *c.* 1800

118 French *secrétaire* decorated with panels of Japanese lacquer, *c.* 1780

119 French japanned harpsichord case, 1786

120 Silver candlestick made at Genoa, 1789

121 A room in the Castello di Rivoli, near Turin, *c.* 1790

122 Exterior and games room in the Palazzina La Favorita, Palermo, 1799

123 Unexecuted design for the Royal Pavilion at Brighton by William Porden, 1803

124 Engraving of the Chinese drawing-room at Carlton House, 1793

125 English japanned cabinet, *c.* 1780–90

126 English japanned wardrobe made for David Garrick, *c.* 1770

127 English japanned commode, *c.* 1765

128 Marble chimney-piece made for Carlton House, 1792

129 English musical clock, *c.* 1820   130 English chair of simulated bamboo, *c.* 1812–14

131 Marble and ormolu chimney-piece made for the Royal Pavilion at Brighton, *c.* 1817

132 Cabinet made for the Royal Pavilion at Brighton, 1802

134 Staffordshire willow pattern plate, 1818

133 Silver tea-caddy, London, 1767

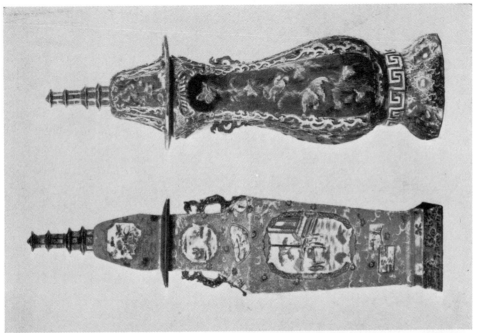

136 Ironstone china vestibule vases made in Staffordshire, c. 1828

135 Ironstone china chimney-piece made in Staffordshire, c. 1829

137 English block-printed cotton, 1806
138 Engraving of the bandstand in Cremorne Gardens, 1857

139 Water-colour by George Chinnery, *c.* 1825–52

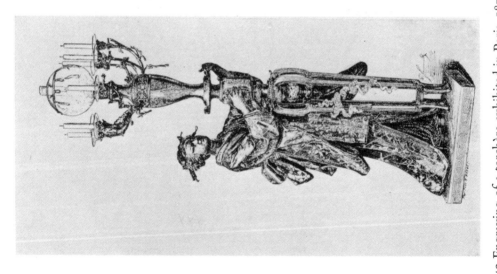

140 Engraving of a torchère exhibited in Paris, 1878   141 Corner cupboard designed by Émile Reiber, 1869

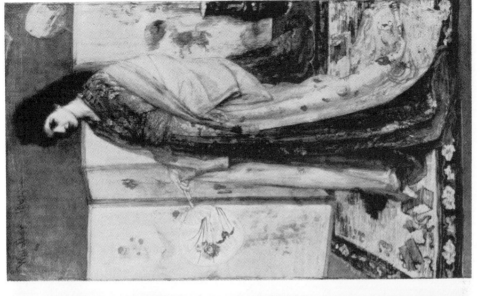

143 *The Princess from the Land of Porcelain*
by James McNeill Whistler, 1864

142 Portrait of Émile Zola by Édouard Manet, 1867–8

144 Copy of a Japanese print by Vincent Van Gogh, 1886–8

Catalogue of Illustrations

Catalogue of Illustrations

The phoenix on the two end panels of this mid-eleventh-century casket has few parallels in Byzantine art (another appears in a mid-tenth-century MS., present whereabouts unknown, see K. Weitzmann: *Die byzantinische Buchmalerei des IX. und X. Jahr.*, Berlin, 1935, pl. xxi). It seems almost certain that this bird was derived from a Chinese silk and is a manifestation of a cult for exoticism which enjoyed some popularity at the Byzantine court in the tenth and eleventh centuries.

Bibl.: D. Talbot Rice (ed.), *Masterpieces of Byzantine Art* (Exhibition catalogue), London, 1958, p. 51 with full bibliography.

2 Fragment from the back of a chasuble; silk; 106 × 70·5 cm. Lucchese, fourteenth century.

The Cleveland Museum of Art, Ohio.

One of the numerous Italian silks decorated with Chinese motifs in the fourteenth century. A few paintings of the period show figures dressed in such textiles, notably a *St Ursula* by the Cologne Master at Prague. The motif of the swooping phoenix is one of the commonest in Chinese textiles and appears as early as the Han dynasty. Here it has been integrated into a Gothic pattern together with Arabic motifs and a lion-dog. Other fourteenth-century textiles are decorated with fire-breathing birds, lions, lotuses, etc.

Bibl.: *Cleveland Museum of Art Bulletin*, March 1929, p. 51; *Ciba Review*, June 1950, p. 2927.

3 *The Feast of the Gods*, By Giovanni Bellini and Titian, detail showing two Ming porcelain bowls. 1514–*c*. 1525.

National Gallery of Art, Washington (Widener Collection).

Several gifts of Chinese porcelain from the sultans of Egypt to the Doges of Venice in the late fifteenth century are recorded, and one of these presumably provided Bellini with his models for the dishes in this picture. The first recorded appearance of Chinese porcelain in European painting is a bowl in Andrea Mantegna's *Adoration of the Magi* of *c.* 1490 (see E. Tietze-Conrat: *Mantegna*, London, 1955, pl. 150). Albrecht Dürer made a drawing of a Chinese porcelain vase (British Museum), possibly on his visit to Venice in 1505 or in the Low Countries in 1520. Chinese porcelain, together with lacquer, was to appear in several late sixteenth- and early seventeenth-century Dutch paintings (cf. Holzhausen, pp. 284–8).

Bibl.: J. Walker: *Bellini and Titian at Ferrara*, London, 1956 (for dating and authorship of the various parts of the panel).

4 Chinese bowl and vase, porcelain of the Wan Li period (1573–1619), set in English silver-gilt, *c.* 1585. Bowl, 21·6 cm. high; vase, 34·6 cm. high. The Metropolitan Museum of Art (Rogers Fund), New York.

The practice of mounting oriental porcelain in Europe in gold or silver began before the end of the fourteenth century and became highly fashionable in the sixteenth century. In the Landesmuseum, Cassel, there is a Yüan cup with a fifteenth-century silver gilt mount (see the catalogue, *Mostra d'Arte Cinese*, Venice, 1954, No. 438). The earliest dated English example, the Lennard Cup (Percival David Foundation) has hall-marks for 1569 (cf. *Connoisseur*, June 1955, pp. 23–7. Doubt has been cast on an earlier example with a mount of 1550 which may have been made for a vase other than that to which it was attached when it recently passed through the London salerooms). Later in the century Lord Burghley owned a small collection of Chinese porcelain from which the two pieces illustrated here probably came; two other pieces he gave to Queen Elizabeth I as handsels in 1587 and 1588. Other notable examples of Chinese porcelain with English silver mounts are in the British Museum and the Victoria and Albert Museum. Continental mounts for porcelain are seldom dated: a rare exception is that of 1608 on a bowl in a private collection in Copenhagen (see G. Boesens and C. A. Bøje: *Old Danish Silver*, no. 313).

Bibl.: A. J. Collins: *Inventory of the Jewels and Plate of Queen Elizabeth I*, London, 1955, pp. 349, 590.

5 A Chinese junk; detail of japanned decoration in Rosenberg Slott, Copenhagen.

A room in the Rosenborg Castle was decorated with panels of green imitation lacquer set in simulated tortoiseshell frames for Christian IV in 1615–16, by Simon Clause, This appears to be the earliest surviving example of japanned decoration in Europe. Mr Th. H. Lusingh Schleureer has, however, noted that some panels are derived from Nieuhoff's book and must therefore date from after 1665.

Bibl.: H. Huth: *Europäische Lackarbeiten*, Darmstadt, n.d., p. 12.

6 Coffer, japanned wood; 22·5 × 25 × 17·5 c.m. Dutch, *c.* 1610.

The Royal Archaeological Society, Rijksmuseum, Amsterdam.

Bibl.: W. Holzhausen: *Lackkunst in Europa*, Brunswick, 1959, p. 54.

7 Cabinet, japanned oak wood, *c.* 130·8 cm. high. English, *c.* 1620.

Victoria and Albert Museum, London.

One of a small group of examples of early seventeenth-century English japanning, this cabinet shows similarities of style with the japanned decoration on a ballot box dated 1619 in the possession of the Saddlers' Company, London.

Bibl.: R. Edwards in *The Burlington Magazine*, 1936, p. 232.

8 Vase, soft-paste porcelain; 27·5 cm. high. Florence, 1575–87.

Musée du Louvre, Paris.

All the surviving products of the Medici factory are decorated in blue on a white ground (save for one in the collection of Baron Maurice de Rothschild, painted with blue, green, and yellow grotesques) with motifs derived principally from the Middle and Far East. It has sometimes been suggested that potters from Isnik were employed at the factory, but a comparison between its products and the pseudo-Isnik wares made at Padua slightly later and possibly decorated by Turkish artists throws doubt on this. The exotic decorations on Medici porcelain could all have been derived from the Chia Ch'ing and Wan Li wares or Persian pottery imported into Italy. It is significant, however, that despite their evident skill in draughtsmanship, the decorators did not copy oriental motifs precisely.

Bibl.: G. Liverani: *Catalogo delle porcellane dei Medici*, Faenza, 1935. A. Lane: *Italian Porcelain*, London, 1954, pp. 1–7.

9 Four tiles, tin-glazed earthenware; each 12·5 cm. high. Delft, *c.* 1650.
Museum 'Het Princessehof', Leeuwarden.
Bibl.: C. H. De Jonge: *Oud-Nederlandsche Majolica en Delftsch Aardewerk*, Amsterdam, 1947, p. 107.

10. Ewer, tin-glazed earthenware; 43·5 cm. high. Nevers, *c.* 1650–80.
The Victoria and Albert Museum, London.
The Nevers factory made vessels of European and Chinese shape decorated with either European or chinoiserie scenes. On this example a baroque ewer has been decorated in blue with a chinoiserie scene; but whereas the landscape and the bored lady are clearly intended to be Chinese, the servant who holds the parasol is attired in European clothes.
Bibl.: A. Lane: *French Faience*, London, 1948, pp. 10-14.

11 Panel of crewel work; 137·5 × 66·7 cm. English, *c.* 1680.
Museum of Fine Arts, Boston.
This panel presents, in reverse, a design which appears on two hangings, one of painted cotton, the other of cotton embroidered with silks, both of which were made in Gujarat, Western India, for the European market in about 1680 and are now in the Victoria and Albert Museum. In an analysis of this design Mr John Irwin has conclusively shown that it derives from an English original sent out to India to be copied. The design on which the Boston crewel-work panel is based therefore derives, in all probability, from a pattern drawn some years earlier.
Bibl.: J. Irwin in *The Burlington Magazine*, April 1955, pp. 106-14.

12 Design for a japanned comb box, engraving from John Stalker and George Parker's *Treatise of Japanning and Varnishing*, London, 1688.

The British Museum, London.

See p. 71.

13 Plate, tin-glazed earthenware decorated in blue and red on a white ground; 55 cm. diameter.

    Rouen, *c.* 1700.

    Musée des Arts Décoratifs, Paris.

    For the fullest account of the Rouen factory see A. Lane, *French Faience*, London, 1948, p. 20. An oval dish of similar design is in the Metropolitan Museum, New York.

14 Tulip vase, tin-glazed earthenware decorated in blue on a white ground; 108 cm. high. Delft, *c.* 1725.

    The Royal Archaeological Society, Rijksmuseum, Amsterdam.

    This type of vessel, which owes its design to the Chinese pagoda, appears to have been produced at Delft before the end of the seventeenth century and to have held its popularity while tulipomania raged in Holland. The majority of examples are decorated with European motifs. Another very fine pair of *c.* 1700 is also in the Rijksmuseum.

    Bibl.: Catalogue of exhibition of Delft, Musée National de Céramique de Sèvres, 1954–5, no. 205.

15 Needlepoint panel, silk; 248 cm. high. French, *c.* 1710.

    Collection of Judge Irwin Untermeyer.

    Although this panel has usually been assigned to the *Régence* period its decorations are in a style which accords better with baroque than rococo chinoiserie and the little scenes are somewhat reminiscent of those which appear on Soho tapestries of *c.* 1699. Other examples of late Louis XIV chinoiserie textiles are the hangings of a bed shown in the exhibition, *Louis XIV: Faste et Décor* (Paris, 1960, no. 1) a set of bed hangings and a pair of curtains formerly in the Untermeyer collection now in the Baltimore Museum of Art and the Metropolitan Museum.

    Bibl.: Y. Hackenbroch: *English and Other Needlework in the Irwin Untermeyer Collection*, London, 1960, p. 60.

16 Bureau, thuya wood lacquered in black with flat decorations in gilt; 100 cm. high; probably made in China, *c.* 1680.

    Musée Carnavalet, Paris.

    The bureau originally belonged to Mme de Sévigné and bears on the fall the arms of Rabutin and Sévigné. As the woodwork is marked with Chinese characters it would appear that the desk was made and decorated in China. The decorations are, however, in a very unusual style and seem to have been intended to satisfy the French taste for restrained exoticism which marked the late seventeenth century: they are much less bizarre than those on cabinets imported into England from the Orient at the same period. (I am grateful to M. Bernard de Montgolfier, Conservateur-Adjoint of the Musée Carnavalet, for information about this desk.)

Photograph by courtesy of M. Bulloz.

17 Jug, tin-glazed earthenware; 26 cm. high. Delft, 1680–92.
Rijksmuseum, Amsterdam.
This piece is marked with the monogram *RIHS* and a moor's head for Rochus Jacobsz. Hoppesteijn.
Bibl.: C. H. de Jonge: *Oud-Nederlandsche Majolica en Delftsch Aardewerk*, Amsterdam, 1947, p. 215.

18 Masquerade costume designed by Jean I. Bérain; engraving French, *c.* 1700.
Bibliothèque Nationale, Paris.
The costume is said to have been designed for the Duc de Bourgogne.
Bibl.: R. A. Weigert: *Jean I. Bérain*, Paris, 1937, vol. ii, p. 189, no. 250.

19 Cabinet made for a doll's house; wood japanned in black with relief decorations in gold; 28 cm. high. Dutch, *c.* 1720.
Rijksmuseum, Amsterdam.
The best japanned furniture produced in seventeenth-century Europe is sometimes said to have been made in Holland, but very few surviving specimens can with certainty be traced to a Dutch origin. This miniature piece reveals, however, the excellence of Dutch japanners on a small scale. For the fullest account of Dutch lacquer see W. Holzhausen: *Lackkunst in Europa*, 1959, pp. 52–62.
Bibl.: Th. H. Lusingh Schleureer: *Catalogus van Meublen en Betimmeringen* (Rijksmuseum), Amsterdam, 1952, no. 358.

20 Tea-tray by Martin Schnell; wood, japanned in red and gold. Dresden, *c.* 1720.
Ehem. Residenzschloss, Dresden.
Martin Schnell (1675–1740), a pupil of Dagly, was the most notable of japanners working in Germany in the early years of the eighteenth century. The tray was destroyed in the last war.
Bibl.: R. von Arps-Aubert in *Zeitschrift des Deutschen Vereins für Kunstwissenschaft*, 1936, pp. 342 *et seq.*

21 Cabinet, wood japanned in white with relief decorations in gilt and blue; 71 cm. high, by Gerard Dagly. Berlin, *c.* 1710.
Herzog Anton-Ulrich Museum, Brunswick.

For an account of Dagly's career see H. Huth in *The Connoisseur*, vol. 95, 1935, pp. 14–18, though one of his attributions has been corrected by W. Holzhausen. *Bibl.*: W. Holzhausen: *Lackkunst in Europa*, Brunswick, 1959, p. 177.

22 Room decorated with japanned panels by Johan Jakob Saenger. Württemberg, 1714–22.
Schloss Ludwigsburg, Württemberg.
Schloss Ludwigsburg is one of several German palaces built to emulate Versailles. This is particularly evident in its plan and baroque decorations; the lacquer room may therefore be in a style similar to the long vanished *petits appartements* at Versailles, many of which were panelled with lacquer or japan. An earlier and less elegant example of a German *Lackkabinett* is in the Neue Residenz at Bamberg; others dating from the first quarter of the eighteenth century are in the Pagodenburg pavilion, Schloss Nymphenburg, and the royal palace at Berlin.
Bibl.: W. Holzhausen: *Lackkunst in Europa*, Brunswick, 1959, pp. 140–52. H. Huth: *Europäische Lackarbeiten*, Darmstadt, n.d., p. 21.

23 Design for a chinese room by Daniel Marot, engraving from D. Marot: . . . *Nouvelles Cheminées . . . c.* 1700.
The Victoria and Albert Museum, London.
Trained in France but forced into exile early in his career, Daniel Marot was one of the artists chiefly responsible for the diffusion of the Louis XIV style in Europe. His classical designs reflect the earlier decorations at Versailles and it seems possible that the design for a lacquer and porcelain cabinet reproduced here derives from the same source. The method of massing oriental porcelain appealed to Mary II in England and is revealed in some of the designs (cf. *Wren Society*, vol. iv, pl. xxxvii), possibly by Marot himself, for the interiors at Hampton Court. The figures shown on the japanned or tapestry panel, however, are close in feeling to Soho tapestries and the paintings of Robert Robinson (pl. 27 and 28).

24 Sconce, silver-gilt; dimensions unrecorded; London, 1665 (maker's mark: W G crowned); formerly in the collection of Col. Norman Colville.
This is the earliest recorded piece of English silver with chinoiserie decorations, though the engraving may have been added some time after the sconce was made.
Bibl.: R. Edwards and P. MacQuoid: *Dictionary of English Furniture*, London, 1954, vol. iii, p. 46.

25 Box, silver; 9·8 cm. wide. London, *c.* 1685. (Maker's mark *P.D.* crowned.)
The Victoria and Albert Museum, London.
A rarity among examples of Charles II chinoiserie silver, this little object is decorated in relief with figures which seem to derive from carved lacquer instead

of the usual engraved decorations (see pl. 24). An inscription on the bottom reveals that the box was 'The Gift of K: Charles 2 to Mrs: Gwin: Her Son Charles Duke of St. Albans Gave this to me Lawrance Answorth 1720 Who had then the Honour to be Head Butler to Him'.

26 Toilet service, silver, consisting of mirror (not illustrated) and six caskets of various sizes (the largest one 25·4 cm. wide), stamped with the maker's mark *R L* (probably Ralph Leeke or Richard Lassels). London, 1681–3.
    Private collection.
    The same maker's mark appears on a larger toilet service decorated with similar engravings, formerly in the collection of the Earl of Harewood and exhibited at Queen Charlotte's Loan Exhibition, Seaford House, 1929, no. 334.

27 Chinoiserie scene, oil on wood; 215 × 89 cm., by Robert Robinson. London, 1690–1700.
    The Victoria and Albert Museum, London.
    One of a set of eleven panels, two of which are painted with coats of arms (Skelton of Northumberland and Nourse of Woodheaton, Oxfordshire) and the rest with exotic scenes in which chinoiserie motifs predominate. Robert Robinson (*fl.* 1674–1706), to whom they have been attributed on stylistic grounds, was responsible for a series of exotic paintings now in Sir John Cass's Schools, Aldgate, London (see E. Tristram in *Walpole Society*, vol. iii, pp. 75 ff.) and is also known to have worked for the stage. A similar collection of Mogul motifs appears in a mid-seventeenth-century painting by Willem Schellinks in the Musée Guimet, Paris (see exhibition catalogue: *Orient-Occident*, Paris, 1958, no. 380).
    Bibl.: E. Croft-Murray in *Country Life Annual*, 1955, pp. 174–9.

28 Panel of tapestry, silk and wool on woollen warp; 274 × 400 cm. Soho (London), *c.* 1700.
    Private collection.
    The earliest set of chinoiserie tapestries produced at the Soho factory was probably that made for Elihu Yale in about 1699, formerly at Glenham House, Norfolk, now at Yale University. The Yale set is signed by John Vanderbank who ran the factory from 1689 to 1727. A set was made for the withdrawing room at Kensington Palace at about the same time as the Yale set. The panel illustrated here is one of a pair recently sold at Christie's and is similar to those in the Yale set, though it has a more elaborate frame. It is possible that Robert Robinson may have designed the Soho chinoiserie tapestries (see no. 27) and based parts of his designs, which freely mix Indian with Chinese motifs, on Mogul miniatures brought back to England by Elihu Yale.

Bibl.: H. Marillier: *English Tapestries of the Eighteenth Century*, London, 1930, pp. 34–5.

29 Panel of tapestry, silk and wool on woollen warp; 236 × 387 cm. Soho (London), *c.* 1720.

Collection of Christabel, Lady Aberconway.

Though similar to the Soho tapestries woven under Vanderbank's direction (see no. 28), this panel, signed by the otherwise unknown *M. Mazarind*, is clearly a little later, the heavy floral frame having been replaced by a more delicate chinoiserie border. Among other examples of these tapestries are the set at The Vyne, Hampshire; Belton Hall, Lincolnshire; the Victoria and Albert Museum and the Barbican Museum, Lewes (four badly damaged panels). Later in the century, probably *c.* 1730, an English factory produced a lighter and more rococo version of the Soho chinoiseries; a unique series is in the collection of H.S.H. Erbergrossherzog Nikolaus Herzog von Oldenburg, at Güldenstein. (See *Catalogue of the Exhibition of the Age of Rococo*, Munich, 1958, no. 903.)

30 Cabinet, wood japanned in black with relief decorations in gold, on a carved and gilded wood stand; 159 cm. high (including stand). London, *c.* 1690.

The Victoria and Albert Museum, London.

This cabinet, of a type very popular in late seventeenth-century England, is one of very few recorded examples which clearly show the influence of the designs published in Stalker and Parker's *Treatise* (see p. 71).

Bibl.: W. Holzhausen: *Lackkunst in Europa*, Brunswick, 1959, p. 66.

31 Cabinet, wood japanned in blue with raised decoration in gold on a carved and gilded wood stand; 231 cm. high. England, *c.* 1715.

William Rockhill Nelson Gallery of Art, Kansas City.

32 Chest of drawers, wood japanned in black with relief decorations in gold; 161·4 cm. high. Boston, *c.* 1700.

The Metropolitan Museum of Art (Joseph Pullitzer Fund), New York.

One of the earliest known examples of American japanning, this piece reveals the influence of English furniture of a decade earlier. Several examples of American japanned furniture survive from the first half of the eighteenth century. In 1748 David Mason, advertising in *The Boston News Letter*, recorded that he did 'all sorts of Japanning, Vernishing, Painting and Gilding' while those who visited his shop might be 'entertained with a great variety of experiments in Elictricity'.

Bibl.: L. Powell in *Apollo*, October 1958, p. 104.

33 *Boiserie*, oak carved, painted cream, and partly gilded with an inset panel of Chinese lacquer. Paris, *c.* 1725–30.

Messrs Jansen, Paris.

This detail is from the panelling of a room originally in the hôtel d'Évreux, 19 place Vendôme, Paris, built for Antoine Crozat in the first decade of the eighteenth century. The interior of this house was largely redecorated in the mid-eighteenth century (see F. Kimball: *Le Style Louis XV*, Paris, 1949, p. 210), but this panelling clearly dates from an earlier period and is close in style to the *grand salon* of about 1730 in the other hôtel d'Évreux which Kimball (p. 155) attributed to Oppenord. It is perhaps significant that Antoine Crozat's brother, the more famous Pierre (Watteau's patron) employed Oppenord in 1730 to decorate his house in the rue de Richelieu. The *boiserie* here reproduced is in a style which hovers on the border of full *rocaille*, but the type of decoration, with panels of Chinese lacquer, belongs to the late Louis XIV or *Régence* period (cf. Huet's much lighter *singerie* of *c.* 1730, Pl. 37).

Bibl.: Catalogue of exhibition: *Chefs-d'œuvre de la curiosité du monde*, Paris, 1954, no. 127.

34 Trade card of the art dealer Gersaint; engraving, after François Boucher. Paris, 1740.

Bibliothèque Nationale, Paris.

35 *Divinité chinoise*, drawing; 26 × 38·1 cm., after Antoine Watteau, probably by Gabriel Huquier, 1729–30.

Cooper Union Museum for the Arts of Decoration, New York.

An undated engraving of this grotesque design was published in Paris, inscribed: *A. Watteau Inv. Huquier Sculp.* The paintings which Watteau executed in the *cabinet du roi* of the Château de la Muette have been variously dated 1709 (Mathey) and 1719 (F. Kimball, *op. cit.* p. 150); since the house was not decorated for the young king's use before 1719 the latter is more acceptable. Watteau's only other essay in chinoiserie is a harpsichord panel now divided into three parts, see J. Mathey: *Antoine Watteau: peintures réapparues*, Paris, 1959, p. 44.

36 *Chinese Fishing Party*, oil on canvas; 38·1 × 52·1 cm.; by François Boucher, 1742.

Museum Boymans Van Beuningen, Rotterdam.

The painting is probably identical with one of the two *paysages chinois* which adorned the drawing-room of Mme de Pompadour in the Château de Bellevue. It is closely connected with the series of Beauvais tapestries for which Boucher provided the designs in 1742 (see Pl. 42).

Bibl.: E. and J. de Goncourt: *Madame de Pompadour*, 1888, p. 95; Hannema: Catalogue of the Van Beuningen Museum, no. 107.

37 *Singerie*, oil on panel with carved and gilt surround, by Christophe Huet, *c.* 1735.
Musée Condé, Chantilly.

The Prince de Condé, for whom these paintings were executed, was a collector of orientalia and is said to have owned Chinese drawings. He was also responsible for founding the Chantilly porcelain factory. The paintings at Chantilly were attributed to J. B. Huet until Christophe Huet's signature on one panel was discovered.

Bibl.: L. Dimier in *Gazette des Beaux-Arts*, 1895, ii, pp. 352 ff., 487 ff.

38 *The Audience*, wool and silk tapestry; 358 × 529 cm. designed by G. L. Vernansal, J. B. de Fontenay, and J. J. Dumons. Beauvais, *c.* 1725–30.
Residenzmuseum, Munich.

From a series of *Tentures chinoises* woven at the Beauvais factory under the direction of N. A. de Mérous and repeated ten times.

Bibl.: H. Göbel: *Die Wandteppiche*, 1923–4, vol. ii, p. 221.

39 Writing-desk, wood, Japanese lacquer, and ormolu; 107 cm. high; probably by Bernard II van Risen Burgh with mounts by Jacques Dubois. Paris, *c.* 1750.
Residenzmuseum, Munich.
See Pl. 41.

Bibl.: Catalogue of the Exhibition: *The Age of Rococo*, Munich, 1958, no. 890.

40 *The Chinese Lovers*, oil on panel; 106 × 145 cm.; by François Boucher, 1742 (signed and dated).
Collection of Mr C. L. David, Copenhagen.

41 Console table, ebony, Japanese lacquer, ormolu, and marble; 90 cm. high; by Bernard II van Risen Burgh.
Cailleux collection, Paris.

Bernard II van Risen Burgh, until recently known only by the initials on the stamp used by his family, B.V.R.B., became a *maître ébéniste* before 1730 and was one of the first to adopt the full rococo style; he died in 1765 or 1766. Other examples of his work, also adorned with panels of Japanese lacquer, are to be found in the English royal collections (see: H. C. Smith: *Buckingham Palace*, London, p. 245).

Bibl.: J.-P. Baroli in *Connaissance des Arts*, March 1957, pp. 56–63.

42 *The Emperor of China's Feast*, wool and silk tapestry; 320 × 370 cm., woven after a design by François Boucher. Beauvais, *c.* 1743.
Collection of the Earl of Rosebery, Dalmeny House.

Boucher's oil sketches for this tapestry and the others in the same series are in the Musée des Beaux-Arts at Besançon (see *Besançon*, catalogue of exhibition at the Musée des Arts Décoratifs, Paris, 1957, pp. 7–8). Two of the preparatory drawings are in the collection of M. Cailleux, Paris, another is in the Cooper Union Museum for the Arts of Decoration, New York. The cartoons for the tapestries were drawn by J. Dumont. One set of tapestries was sent to the Emperor of China and hung in the Summer Palace at Peking until that building was sacked in 1860 (a panel from this set is now in the museum at Cleveland, Ohio).

    Bibl.: H. Göbel: *Die Wandteppiche*, Leipzig, 1928, Teil II, vol. i, p. 226.

43 Commode, wood japanned in red, gilt, and cream on a chocolate brown ground, with ormolu mounts and marble top; 87 cm. high, by Pierre II Migeon. Paris, *c.* 1750.

    Musée des Arts Décoratifs, Paris.

44 Group of seven boxes:

    (a) Snuff-box, gold, varnish and mother of pearl; 3·5 cm. high, by Alexandre Lefèvre, Paris, late eighteenth century. Musée du Louvre, Paris.

    (b) Snuff-box, gold and enamel; 3·7 cm. high. Probably Geneva, mid-eighteenth century. Musée du Louvre, Paris.

    (c) *Nécessaire*, blue glass and gold; 5·6 cm. high. Probably English mid-eighteenth century. Musée du Louvre, Paris.

    (d) *Nécessaire*, gold, red lacquer, and mother of pearl; *c.* 5 cm. high. Paris, 1762–3. Musée du Louvre, Paris.

    (e) Snuff-box, mottled white quartz inlaid with gold and mother of pearl, 6·3 cm. high, by Johann Martin Henrici, Dresden; *c.* 1750; Messrs Charles Woollett and Son.

    (f) Snuff-box, gold with basse-taille blue enamel; 3.8 cm. high; by Noel Hardvilliers, Paris, 1753.

Collection of Mr. Villiers David.

    (g) Snuff-box, gold, and semi-precious stones; 3·8 cm. high; mid-eighteenth-century panels reset by Adrien Vachette, Paris, 1809–19. Musée du Louvre, Paris.

45 Two panels painted in oils; 231 × 200 cm. (upper) and 139 × 59·5 cm. (lower), by Jean Pillement, *c.* 1780–96.

    Private Collection.

    Two of six panels painted in cream grisaille on a pale blue ground, formerly in the collection of Riccardo Espirito Santo, Lisbon. It seems probable that these panels were painted by Pillement during his second visit to Portugal from 1780 to 1796.

    Bibl.: *The Connoisseur*, December 1956, p. 270.

46 Clock, ormolu with Vincennes porcelain flowers; 32·2 cm. high. Paris, *c.* 1750. Howard and Company, London.

47 A Chinese dancer, drawing in pen and wash; by Boquet, *c.* 1755.
    Musée de l'Opéra, Paris.
    Boquet, who is otherwise unknown, designed the costumes for Noverre's *Fêtes chinoises* (see p. 100) and this drawing may be connected with that ballet.

48 Statuette of a Chinese woman; terracotta; 45 cm. high. France, *c.* 1750.
    Formerly in the collection of M. Adrien Fauchier-Magnan.
    One of a pair of figures, the other representing a Chinese fisherman.
    Bibl.: J. Guérin: *La Chinoiserie en Europe au XVIIIe siècle*, Paris, 1911, pl. 78.

49 Clock, ormolu and porcelain; 33 cm. high. France (the porcelain flowers Mennecy), *c.* 1735.
    The Antique Porcelain Company.

50 Clock, ormolu; 65 cm. high, by St-Germain. Paris, *c.* 1750.
    Musée des Arts Décoratifs, Lyon.
    The movement of the clock is by J. B. du Tertre and the ormolu is signed: *St-Germain.* A similar clock with ormolu by the same *ciseleur-fondeur*, from the collection of the Earl of Shrewsbury, was sold at Sotheby's, December, 9, 1960.

51 Tea-kettle, sheet-iron japanned in black and gold; 26·5 cm. high. French or English, *c.* 1740.
    Herbig-Haarhaus Lackmuseum, Cologne.
    A kettle of somewhat similar design appears in Gersaint's trade card (see Pl. 34), but see also the English silver kettle of 1761 (Pl. 99).
    Bibl.: W. Holzhausen: *Lackkunst in Europa*, Brunswick, 1959, p. 293.

52 Pilgrim bottle; Böttger's red stoneware japanned in black and gold; 17 cm. high. Meissen, *c.* 1715–20.
    The Metropolitan Museum, New York.
    (Reproduced by courtesy of the Metropolitan Museum of Art, Gift of R. Thornton Wilson, 1943, in memory of his wife, Florence Ellsworth Wilson.)

53 Pagod, porcelain; 9·5 cm. high. Meissen, *c.* 1720.
    The British Museum (Franks collection), London.
    Originally in the Japanese Palace at Dresden.

54 *Garniture de cheminée*, porcelain, central vase; 66 cm. high. Meissen, *c.* 1725–30.
The Wadsworth Athenaeum, Hartford, Connecticut.

55 Tankard, porcelain and silver gilt; 14·7 cm. high. Meissen, probably decorated
by Adam Friedrich von Löwenfinck, *c.* 1735.
Rijksmuseum, Amsterdam.
The signature L. F. which appears on this piece is generally assigned to
Löwenfinck, though it has also been claimed for Johann Tobias Locke, another
porcelain painter.
Bibl.: Catalogue of the Exhibition: *The Age of Rococo*, Munich, 1958, no. 741.

56 Clock, porcelain; 42·5 cm. high. Meissen, *c.* 1735.
The Cooper Union Museum for the Arts of Decoration, New York.
The modelling is attributed to Johann Gottlieb Kirchner, and the paintings
are in the style of Höroldt (see p. 105).

57 Statuette of a Joss; soft-paste porcelain; 24 cm. high. Chantilly, *c.* 1735.
Musée des Arts Décoratifs, Paris.
The figure is possibly intended to represent the Taoist immortal, Shou Lao.
His robe is painted with the Kakiemon patterns in which the Chantilly factory
specialized.

58 Cane-handle, soft-paste porcelain; 6·5 cm. high. Saint-Cloud, *c.* 1740.
The Metropolitan Museum, New York (Gift of Mrs Morris Hawkes, 1924).

59 Pagod, porcelain; 28 cm. high, by F. A. Bustelli. Nymphenburg, 1756.
Bayerisches Nationalmuseum, Munich.
Bibl.: F. H. Hoffmann: *Geschichte der Porzellanmanufaktur Nymphenburg*, 1921–
1923, vol. iii, p. 423.

60 A Chinese tea-house, porcelain; 50 cm. high; by Paul Hannong. Frankenthal,
1755.
Collection of S.K.H. Berthold Markgraf von Baden, Salem.
This table-centre was listed in the inventory of the factory as 'Chinesenhaus
worauf ein Chinese sitzt mit Parapluie in der Hand'. It is signed with the initials
P. H. for Paul Hannong who moved from Strasbourg to Frankenthal in 1755.
Bibl.: E. Heusser: *Porzellan von Strassburg und Frankenthal*, 1922, p. 284.

61 The Emperor of China, porcelain; 37·5 cm. high. Höchst, *c.* 1760.
Museum für Kunst und Gewerbe, Hamburg.
The modeller of this piece was responsible for many other chinoiserie groups

produced by the Höchst factory and is usually known as the 'Chinesenmeister'.
Bibl.: K. Röder and M. Oppenheim: *Das Höchster Porzellan*, 1950, pl. 52.

62 Pair of vases, porcelain; 31·5 cm. high, modelled by Duplessis and painted by Dodin. Sèvres, *c.* 1760.
The Walters Art Gallery, Baltimore.
Vases of this pattern were occasionally painted with European-style decorations.

63 Tureen, faience; 22·8 cm. high. Marseilles, *c.* 1760.
The Wadsworth Athenaeum, Hartford, Connecticut.

64 The Chinese musicians, soft-paste porcelain; 36·5 cm. high. Chelsea, *c.* 1755.
The collection of Judge Irwin Untermeyer, New York.
Bibl.: Y. Hackenbroch: *Chelsea and other English Porcelain . . . in the Irwin Untermeyer Collection*, Cambridge, Mass., 1957, p. 53.

65 The Goddess Ki Mao Sao, soft-paste porcelain; 17·8 cm. high. Bow, *c.* 1750-5.
Messrs Charles Woollett and Son, London.
The group is based on an engraving after Watteau (see Fig. 4) and is the work of the anonymous artist usually known as the 'Muses Modeller', who appears to have been working at Bow between 1748 and 1752.
Bibl.: Y. Hackenbroch: *Chelsea and other English Porcelain . . . in the Irwin Untermeyer Collection*, Cambridge, Mass., 1957, p. 171.

66 Long-case clock, inlaid wood; 318 cm. high; case by David Roentgen, *c.* 1770.
National Museum, Stockholm.
See Pl. 70 (detail).
Bibl.: *Masterverk I Nationalmuseum: Konsthandverk*, Stockholm, 1954, p. 113.

67 Fountain, painted lead; 145 cm. high. German, *c.* 1730–50.
Schloss Brühl.
The fountain formed part of the exterior decoration of the *chinesisches Haus*, built for the Kurfürst Clemens August in the pheasantry of the Park at Brühl before 1750 and destroyed in 1832. The building may have been designed by François de Cuvilliés.
Bibl.: A. Renard: *Clemens August Kurfürst von Köln*, 1926.

68 The Indian House, Pillnitz, by M. D. Pöppelmann and Zach. Longuelune, 1720–1732.
See p. 112.

Bibl.: E. von Erdberg: *Chinese Influence in European Garden Structures*, Cambridge, Mass., 1936, p. 174.

Photograph by courtesy of the Deutsche Fototek, Dresden.

69 Door of a bureau, wood japanned in blue with relief decorations in gold, silver, and brown; from the workshop of Martin Schnell. Dresden, *c.* 1740.

Museum für Kunsthandwerk, Frankfurt-am-Main.

Bibl.: W. Holzhausen: *Lackkunst in Europa*, Brunswick, 1959, p. 167.

70 Detail of marquetry on long case clock, Pl. 66; by David Roentgen, *c.* 1770.

Nationalmuseum, Stockholm.

David Roentgen frequently made use of chinoiserie designs for the decoration of his furniture, see H. Huth: *Abraham und David Roentgen*, Berlin, 1928.

71 Detail of a cylindrical bureau, various inlaid woods, and ormolu; over-all height, 99 cm. German, *c.* 1765.

Collection of Graf Georg Schönborn-Buchheim, Vienna.

An inlaid coat-of-arms reveals that the bureau was made for Graf Eugen Franz Erwein von Schönborn-Buchheim and his first wife, whose marriage took place in 1751 (the Gräfin died in 1775).

Bibl.: Catalogue of the Exhibition: *The Age of Rococo*, Munich, 1958, no. 861.

72 Clock and stand, japanned wood and gilt bronze; 208 cm. high. Augsburg, *c.* 1725.

Bayerisches Nationalmuseum, Munich.

The dial of the clock is signed by a maker from Friedberg, near Augsburg, and dated 1725.

Bibl.: *Rococo Art from Bavaria* (commemorative exhibition catalogue), London, 1956, no. 56.

73 (a) The Chinese tea-house, by J. G. Büring, 1754–7.

(b) and (c), sandstone figures outside the Chinese tea-house, by J. P. Benkert and Heymuller, 1754–7.

Sans-Souci, Potsdam.

Frederick the Great erected several other chinoiserie buildings at Sans-Souci, notably a four-storey pagoda called the Dragon House.

Bibl.: F. Heppner in *The Architectural Review*, vol. ciii, March 1958, pp. 117–20.

74 (a) The Chinese House, Drottningholm, Sweden, probably by C. F. Adelcrantz, 1763–9. Built by King Adolf Friedrich of Sweden for his consort in 1753, the first Chinese House at Drottningholm was of wood and destroyed in about 1763 to

make way for the present structure. The exterior is painted red and grey with the relief sculpture picked out in gold.

> *Bibl.*: O. Siren: *China and the Gardens of Europe*, New York, 1950, p. 171.

(b) The Green Salon at Drottningholm, the walls painted in green and gold with chinoiserie designs after Boucher and Pillement.

(c) Detail of painted decoration in the Chinese House at Drottningholm, probably by Johan Pasch after J. B. Pillement.

75 The Asian Procession, oil on canvas; 40 cm. high; by Jean Barbault, Rome, 1751 (signed and dated).

> Musée des Beaux-Arts, Besançon.

Detail from *Mascarade des quatre parties du monde*, a project for, or record of, the Académie de France's masquerade procession in the 1751 carnival at Rome. This procession was more than usually magnificent on account of the presence in Rome of the Marquis de Marigny, Directeur Général des Bâtiments de France and brother to Mme de Pompadour. Barbault appears to have executed another painting of this procession (whereabouts unknown).

> *Bibl.*: *Besançon* (catalogue of exhibition at the Musée des Arts Décoratifs), Paris, 1957, no. 2.

76 The Chinese barge, engraving by Andrea Zucchi after Alessandro Mauro, Venice, 1716.

> Museo Correr, Venice.

The barge formed part of the regatta held on 27 May 1716, in honour of Augustus I King of Poland and Elector of Saxony (Augustus the Strong).

> *Bibl.*: G. Lorenzetti: *Le feste e le maschere veneziane* (exhibition catalogue), Venice, 1937, p. 45.

77 Panel from a door, wood japanned in gold and colours; 55 cm. wide, *c.* 1750.

> Ca' Rezzonico, Venice.

Perhaps the finest example of Venetian eighteenth-century japanning, the pair of doors from which this detail is taken were once attributed to G. B. and G. D. Tiepolo. A similar door from the Ca' Rezzonico is in the Art Institute, Chicago. A series of doors probably by the same hand is in the Palazzo Papadopoli, Venice.

> *Bibl.*: G. Lorenzetti: *Lacche veneziane del settecento* (exhibition catalogue), Venice, 1938, no. 320.

78 Commode, wood japanned with relief figures in gold on a green ground; 86 cm. high; Venice, *c.* 1750.

> Ca' Rezzonico, Venice.

The commode forms part of a suite of green japanned furniture originally in the Calbo-Crotta collection.

79 (a) and (b) details of fresco paintings by Giovanni Domenico Tiepolo, *c.* 1757. Villa Valmarana (ai Nani), Vicenza.

One of the series of fresco decorations painted by Giovanni Domenico Tiepolo in the *foresteria* of the Villa Valmarana is signed and dated 1757. In the weird trees at the side of (b) it is possible to discern the influence of Pillement's prints (cf. Pl. 45).

Bibl.: R. Pallucchini: *Gli affreschi di Giambattista e Giandomenico Tiepolo alla villa Valmarana*, Bergamo, 1945.

80 (a) and (b) two details from the porcelain room, figures modelled by Giuseppe Gricci, 1761–5. Palacio Real, Aranjuez.

The porcelain room at Aranjuez was begun soon after the establishment of the Buen Retiro porcelain factory in 1760 and appears to have been completed in 1765. It is slightly larger than the porcelain room originally at Portici (now Museo di Capodimonte, Naples, see Pl. III), but in many ways similar to it: the raw material was probably imported from Naples, the same modellers were employed (one panel is signed by Giuseppe Gricci), many of the decorative motifs in the two rooms are identical. There is, however, a striking difference between the large reliefs of Chinamen in the two rooms. The Aranjuez groups are, in fact, remarkably close in style to the frescoes painted by Giovanni Domenico Tiepolo in the Villa Valmarana, Vicenza (Pl. 79). And since G. D. Tiepolo was working in Madrid from 1761 to 1770 it seems probable that he may have provided designs for the figures at Aranjuez.

Bibl.: A. Lane: *Italian Porcelain*, London, 1954, p. 53. *The Connoisseur*, November, 1960, p. 183.

81 Design for wall decoration, pen-and-ink drawing with water-colour; 62·3 × 54·6 cm., by Nicola Fiore, Naples, 1775. The Cooper Union Museum for the Arts of Decoration. New York.

The inscription reveals that this drawing was executed as a design for the decoration of a room in the Palazzo Reale at Caserta. The interior decoration of this palace was begun in 1773. If these decorations were carried out (which seems unlikely) they have since perished.

82 Title page to William De La Cour's *First Book of Ornament*, 1741, engraving. The Victoria and Albert Museum, London.

This volume contains the earliest set of rococo furniture designs published in England.

Bibl.: P. Ward-Jackson: *English Furniture Designs*, London, 1958, p. 346.

83 Panel of wallpaper, hand drawn and painted; 170 cm. high. English, *c.* 1740.
   The Victoria and Albert Museum, London.
   Detail from complete set of paper hangings taken from a house at Wotton-under-Edge, Gloucestershire, in 1924. A floral border was added in the late eighteenth century to replace the original trellis-work border. Comparison with Chinese papers of the same type reveals how the artist responsible for this piece has drawn motifs from such hangings but rearranged and overcrowded them in a singularly unoriental fashion.
   Bibl.: C. C. Oman: *Catalogue of Wallpapers* (Victoria and Albert Museum), London, 1929, pp. 15, 16, and 76.

84 Tea-poy, salt-glazed earthenware; 9·5 cm. high. Staffordshire, *c.* 1750.
   The Victoria and Albert Museum, London.
   Tea-poys of this type appear to have enjoyed widespread popularity in mid-eighteenth-century England; they were, of course, intended for humbler owners than those who possessed such silver caddies as that illustrated on Pl. 86. This example is decorated with a relief representation of the tea plant, here called the herb *Cia*, derived from an illustration in J. Nieuhoff's *An Embassy . . . to the Grand Tartar Cham Emperour of China* (London, 1669, p. 248).

85 Boy on a water-buffalo, earthenware; 20 cm. high. Staffordshire, *c.* 1750.
   The Victoria and Albert Museum, London.
   Like the tea-poy (no. 84) this statuette was intended for a fairly humble class of patron. Strangely enough, however, it is nearer in feeling to Chinese art (especially hard-stone carvings) than any of the exquisite chinoiserie ornaments produced by continental porcelain factories.

86 Tea-caddy, silver gilt; 13·5 cm. high, by Paul de Lamerie, London, 1747.
   The Worshipful Company of Goldsmiths, London.
   One of a pair of caddies. The repoussé and embossed scenes on the sides are intended to illustrate the cultivation of tea. A similar caddy by the same maker, dated 1744, is in the Metropolitan Museum, New York.
   Bibl.: J. B. Carrington and G. R. Hughes: *The Plate of the Worshipful Company of Goldsmiths*, London, 1926, p. 98.

87 Details of the Chinese room and hall at Claydon House; carved and painted wood; by Lightfoot, *c.* 1769. (a) Carving in alcove, (b) alcove, in the Chinese room, (c) niche in the hall, and (d) chimney-piece.

Claydon House, Buckinghamshire.

The building of Claydon House was begun in 1754 but the mysterious Mr Lightfoot, who was responsible for the fantastic rococo decorations in several rooms, is not known to have been on the scene until 1768, and he was dismissed in 1769. No other documented works by this remarkable craftsman are known.

Bibl.: C. Hussey in *Country Life*, November 7th, 1952, p. 1483; C. Hussey: *English Country Houses: Early Georgian*, London, 1955, p. 249.

Photographs by courtesy of *The Connoisseur*.

88 Alcove in the Chinese Summer house, Shugborough Park; wood carved and painted and stucco, *c.* 1747.

Shugborough Park, Staffordshire.

See p. 151 and Pl. 102.

Bibl.: *Country Life*, 15 April, 1954, p. 1126–8.

89 Writing-table, japanned wood; 96 cm. high; by William Linnell, London, 1752.

Came House, Dorset.

This table was made for Mrs Elizabeth Montagu in 1752, together with several other pieces of furniture in the Chinese taste, see p. 138.

Bibl.: A. Oswald in *Country Life*, April 30th, 1953, pp. 1328–9.

90 Settee, carved mahogany; 152 cm. long, English, *c.* 1755.

Collection of C. D. Rotch, Esq.

Bibl.: *English Taste in the Eighteenth Century* (Catalogue of Exhibition at the Royal Academy), London, 1955–6, no. 240.

91 Bed, wood japanned in red and gilt; 380 cm. high; probably by Thomas Chippendale, 1750–4.

The Victoria and Albert Museum, London.

This bed formed part of the furniture of a bedroom at Badminton House, Gloucestershire, probably supplied to the fourth Duke of Beaufort by Thomas Chippendale and certainly completed by 1754 (see *The Travels through England of Dr Richard Pococke*, Camden Society, Cambridge, 1888–9, vol. ii, p. 31). The Duke of Beaufort was a subscriber to the first edition of Chippendale's *The Gentleman and Cabinet Maker's Director*, London, 1754, which included many chinoiserie designs several of which are in a style close to this bed. The room at Badminton House was hung with Chinese painted paper and the other furniture included chairs, a commode, dressing-table and four china stands all japanned in red and gold.

Bibl.: R. Edwards and P. MacQuoid: *op. cit.*, vol. i, p. 64.

92 Standing Shelves, wood japanned; 200 cm. high. English, *c.* 1755.
Collection of Viscount Scarsdale.
The pagoda roofs to these shelves show similarities with several of the designs for china shelves published in Chippendale's *Director* of 1754.
Bibl.: R. Edwards and P. Macquoid, *op. cit.*, vol. iii, pp. 117–18.

93 Commode, wood, veneered with oriental (probably Chinese) lacquer on the front and japanned on the sides and top; 107 cm. high. English, *c.* 1765.
The Shaftesbury Estates Company.
Bibl.: R. Edwards and P. Macquoid, *op. cit.*, vol. ii, p. 114.

94 Chinese painted mirror in carved wood and gilt English frame; *c.* 1747.
Shugborough Park, Staffordshire.
Made for the Chinese House (see Pls. 88 and 102) in Shugborough Park. The painted glass is of a type made extensively in China for the European market (see M. Jourdain and S. Jenyns: *Chinese Export Art in the Eighteenth Century*, London, 1950) and these pieces may have been brought back from Canton by Admiral Anson, the owner of Shugborough in the 1740s.

95 Wine-glass, cut and engraved glass; 12·7 cm. high. English, *c.* 1780.
Collection of L. G. G. Ramsey, Esq., F.S.A.

96 Tea-caddy, silver; 17·7 cm. high; by Samuel Taylor, London, 1763.
Collection of the Hon. Mrs Ionides.

97 Book-binding; green vellum tooled in gold; 32 × 20 cm. by James Bate, *c.* 1765.
St John's College, Cambridge, reproduced by courtesy of the Master and Fellows.
The binding encloses a MS of the *Khamsa* of Nizami dated 1540, part of the Benares loot captured after the battle of Buscar in 1764; bought by Richard Bate, an East India merchant, who sent it home to his father, the Rev. James Bate, rector of Deptford. The Rev. James Bate had it bound by his other son, James Bate of Cornhill, London, in what he described as 'the tawdry Mahometan taste' and bequeathed it to St John's College.
Bibl.: Browne: *Supplementary Handlist of Mohammedan MSS in Cambridge*, Cambridge, 1922, no. 1434; E. Hawe: *A List of London Book Binders*, London, 1950, H. 8 and p. xxxiv.

98 Coffee-pot, silver; 29·5 cm. high. London (maker's mark C. W.), 1769.
Collection of Hugh Farmar, Esq.

99 Tea-kettle and urn, silver; 43 cm. and 53 cm. high; by Thomas Whipham and Charles Wright, London, 1761 and 1766.

Collection of the Hon. Mrs Ionides.

Compare the tea-kettle with the French japanned metal example on Pl. 51; it is possible that the designs of both derive from the same (probably French) pattern book.

100 Panel of cotton, plate-printed in blue; detail from panel 70 × 95 cm. England, 1765.

The Cooper Union Museum for the Arts of Decorations, New York.

English plate-printed cottons, commonly called *toiles de jouy* after the factory founded at Jouy near Versailles by Obercampf in 1760 (some twenty years after they had first appeared in England!), enjoyed great popularity for the decoration of bedrooms. Many were decorated with chinoiseries similar to those on this example which reveals the influence of Pillement. This piece came from Bromley Hall.

101 The Pagoda in Kew Gardens, engraving, after a drawing by William Marlow, 1763.

The British Museum, London.

The engraving is in William Chambers: *Plans, Elevations, Sections and Perspective Views of the Gardens and Buildings at Kew in Surrey*, London, 1763. Pl. 43.

See p. 155.

102 Chinese house, *c.* 1747.

Shugborough Park, Staffordshire.

A water-colour of *c.* 1780, at Shugborough, shows that the Chinese house was originally surrounded by the lake on three sides and approached by a chinoiserie bridge, but the lake has now receded. The contents of the building (see Pl. 94) were removed to the main house in about 1885. The little building has recently been restored. See p. 151 and Pl. 88.

Bibl.: C. Hussey in *Country Life*, April 15th, 1954, p. 1126.

103 Chinese Pavilion, *c.* 1750.

Harnstown House, County Kildare.

This building was originally erected in the grounds of Wotton House, Buckinghamshire, and moved to Ireland in 1957.

Bibl.: *Country Life*, July 8th, 1949, p. 112.

104 *The Mandarine*, a chinoiserie yacht belonging to the Duke of Cumberland, detail from an engraving by Paul Sandby after a drawing by Thomas Sandby, 1754.

The British Museum, London.

Drawings connected with this print are at Windsor Castle, the British Museum, and the Sir John Soane Museum. The yacht sailed on Virginia water where a chinoiserie building was erected on an island, to the design of T. Sandby. John Adam recorded in his diary in June 1759 'the Chinese building is not finish'd on the inside, but is said to be elegant of its kind'. (Clerk of Penicuik Papers.)

Bibl.: A. P. Oppé: *The Drawings of Paul and Thomas Sandby . . . at Windsor Castle*, Oxford and London, 1947, p. 83.

105 The Chinese dairy at Woburn, designed by Henry Holland and built 1787.
Woburn Park, Bedfordshire.

In 1791 a certain Léon Peliceix was paid for 'treillage work' at Woburn, possibly the balconies to this dairy.

Bibl.: D. Stroud: *Henry Holland*, London, 1950, p. 37.

106 The pagoda at Alton Towers, designed by Robert (?) Abraham, *c.* 1824.
Alton Towers, Staffordshire.

Robert and one H. R. Abraham designed garden buildings and conservatories for Charles, 15th Earl of Shrewsbury at Alton in 1824. According to J. C. Loudon, only the lower part of the pagoda was complete in 1826 when he visited Alton. Loudon obtained, presumably from Abraham, a drawing for the pagoda which he published in his *Encyclopaedia of Gardening*. This shows a six-storey pagoda 88 feet high which was to be approached across a richly ornamented bridge; the ground floor was to be of stone and the upper storeys of cast iron; forty elaborate Chinese lanterns, lit from a gasometer concealed inside the building, were to hang from the horns of the eaves while dragons spouting water were to peer out from the angles of each roof. A column of water some 70 or 80 feet high was to squirt from the spire of the pagoda.

Bibl.: J. C. Loudon: *Encyclopaedia of Gardening*, London, 1850, p. 262; H. Colvin: *A Biographical Dictionary of English Architects*, London, 1954, p. 27.

107 Chinese pavilion at Cassan, about 10 m. high, probably by J. M. Morel, *c.* 1778.
Cassan, L'Isle-Adam.

The *anglo-chinois* garden at Cassan was laid out for the financier Pierre-Jacques Bergeret in the late 1770s by J. M. Morel who probably designed this Chinese pavilion.

Bibl.: O. Siren: *China and the Gardens of Europe*, New York, 1950, p. 134.

108 *Maison chinoise* in the Désert de Retz, engraving, 1785.
The British Museum, London.

From Le Rouge: *Détails des nouveaux jardins (jardins anglo-chinois)*, 1776–87, 13th *cahier*, pl. 12. See pp. 97 and 167.

Bibl.: O. Siren: in *The Architectural Review*, November, 1949, p. 327.

109 *Kiosque chinois* in the park at Chantilly, detail from a water-colour drawing, by Chambé, 1784.

Musée Condé, Chantilly.

This drawing, together with others of the Château and park at Chantilly, were executed in 1784 for the Prince de Condé who gave them to Catherine the Great of Russia. The *kiosque chinois*, built in 1770, to the design of Jean-François Leroy, was decorated with sculpture by Bernard, paintings by Jeanteau and furniture by Toussaint; it was destroyed during the revolution.

Bibl.: H. Cordier: *La Chine en France*, Paris, 1910, p. 70; *Connaissance des Arts*, June 1958, pp. 102–7.

110 Chinese pavilion at Haga Park, by Jean-Louis Desprez, *c.* 1770.

Haga Park, near Stockholm.

See p. 171.

Bibl.: O. Siren: *China and the Gardens of Europe*, New York, 1950, p. 193.

111 The pagoda at Chanteloup, designed by Le Camus, 1775–8.

Chanteloup.

The Duc de Choiseul who lived at Chanteloup in disfavour during the last four years of Louis XV's reign built this tower to commemorate the loyalty of some three hundred friends who cheered his exile from Court and whose names are inscribed on marble tablets inside. Some chinoiserie chairs appear to have been made for the pagoda by G. Jacob. (See catalogue of the Decour sale, Paris, 30th June, 1936, lot 57. I am indebted to Mr Francis Watson for this reference.)

Bibl.: O. Siren: *China and the Gardens of Europe*, New York, 1950, p. 133.

112 Chinese pavilion, at Sturefors, *c.* 1760.

The English Park, Sturefors near Linköping, Sweden.

This little pavilion appears to be the sole survivor from the many hundreds of similarly modest chinoiserie delights which adorned the gardens of Europe in the second half of the eighteenth century.

Bibl.: O. Siren: *China and the Gardens of Europe*, New York, 1950, p. 177.

113 The Chinese pavilion and Philosopher's house at Bonnelles; engraving, *c.* 1776.

The British Museum.

From G. Le Rouge, *op. cit.*, 12th *cahier*, pl. 12. The plan shows a characteristic *jardin anglo-chinois*.

114 Summer house, *c.* 1770.
   Palazzo Citterio (ex Visconti), Brignano Gera d' Adda, Bergamo.

115 Design for a fishing pavilion, water-colour by Frederick Crace, *c.* 1824.
   Cooper Union Museum for the Arts of Decoration, New York.
   The drawing is inscribed *The Fishing Temple, Virginia Water* and belongs to
   a series of drawings by Frederick Crace and his assistants, most of which are
   connected with the Royal Pavilion at Brighton. Contemporary descriptions suggest that the Fishing Pavilion at Virginia Water, built as part of the improvements to Windsor Park begun by George IV in 1824 and sometimes attributed
   to Sir Jeffry Wyatville, was based on this design by Crace. The pavilion was set
   at the edge of a lake, near an aviary and a fountain stocked with gold and silver
   carp. A long gallery, from which the king and his courtiers might fish, extended
   the length of the building on the lake side, and there were three other
   rooms. The whole exterior was brilliantly coloured. E. W. Brayley's *Topographical History of Surrey* records that the building was undergoing repair in
   1850 but it was demolished before the end of the century and replaced by a
   Swiss cottage.
   Bibl.: Letter from C. S. Hathaway in *Country Life*, December 24th, 1959,
   p. 1270.

116 Design for the Chinese Gallery in the Brighton Pavilion, water-colour 33·6
   × 51·3 cm., by Frederick Crace, 1815–19.
   The Cooper Union Museum for the Arts of Decoration, New York.
   This design is similar to the decoration as executed.
   Bibl.: *The Prince Regent's Style* (catalogue of exhibition at the Cooper Union),
   New York, 1953, p. 18 and p. 19, no. 2.

117 The exterior of The Chinese Baths, in the Boulevard des Italiens, engraving,
   Paris, *c.* 1800.
   Musée Carnavalet, Paris.
   See p. 180.

118 *Secrétaire*, ebony and gilt bronze with panels of Japanese lacquer; 147 cm. high,
   by Pierre Garnier, *c.* 1780.
   Musée du Louvre, Paris.
   Compare the treatment of the lacquer on this *secrétaire* with the console table
   and writing-desk of three decades earlier, Pls. 39 and 41.
   Bibl.: C. Dreyfus: *Mobilier du XVIIᵉ et du XVIIIᵉ siècle* (Louvre catalogue),
   Paris, 1922, no. 66.

119 Harpsichord case, japanned wood: 194·5 cm. long (Instrument signed by Pascal Taskin). Paris, 1786.

> The Victoria and Albert Museum, London.
>
> See p. 176.

120 Candlestick, silver; 36 cm. high. Genoa, 1789.

> Collection of Signor Martelli, Genoa.
>
> See p. 181.
>
> *Bibl.*: *Argenti italiani* (exhibition catalogue), Milan, 1959, no. 112.

121 A corner of the Sala Cinese, (now destroyed), *c.* 1790.

> Formerly Castello di Rivoli, Turin.
>
> Six rooms at Rivoli were decorated in a Bérainesque style with chinoiserie motifs by Filippo Minei in the early eighteenth century (see V. Viale in *Torino*, 1942, September, p. 58) but the room illustrated here dates from the end of the century when the Duca d' Aosta, later Vittorio Emmanuele I, redecorated much of the castle. The work of 1790 was carried out under the direction of the architect Carlo Randon (see G. Briolo: *Nuova guida . . . di Torino*, Turin, 1822, p. 183); the name of the decorative painter employed is not recorded. Several Torinese artists are said to have specialized in work 'alla cinese' during the eighteenth century (see p. 123) including Leonardo Marini (1730–97) who painted 'abbondanza ornati e figure alla cinese' (L. Rosso: *La pittura e la scultura del '700 a Torino*, Turin, 1934, p. 36).

122 (a) Exterior and (b) view of games room, in the Palazzina La Favorita, designed by Giuseppe Patricola, 1799.

> Palazzina La Favorita, Palermo.
>
> The building has occasionally been ascribed, incorrectly, to Giuseppe Marvuglia. The paintings in the games room are by Giuseppe Velasco or Velasquez. See p. 182.
>
> *Bibl.*: E. Croft Murray in *Country Life*, 10 October, 1947, pp. 724–5.

123 Design for the Royal Pavilion at Brighton, pen and water-colour; 59 × 109 cm., by William Porden, 1803.

> The Royal Pavilion, Brighton.
>
> See p. 189. This design shows a certain stylistic affinity with the Palazzina La Favorita built a few years earlier, cf. Pl. 122.
>
> *Bibl.*: C. Musgrave: *Royal Pavilion*, London, 1959, p. 32.

124 The Chinese drawing-room at Carlton House, engraving; 18·3 × 27·9 cm., by J. Barlow, 1793.

The Victoria and Albert Museum, London.
From Thomas Sheraton: *The Cabinet Maker's and Upholsterer's Drawing Book*, London, 1791–4. See p. 187.

125 Cabinet, wood japanned with gilt decorations on a black ground; 170 cm. high, English, *c.* 1780–90.
Collection of the Hon. Mrs Ionides.

126 Wardrobe, wood japanned with green decorations on a buff ground; 167 cm. high. London, *c.* 1770.
The Victoria and Albert Museum, London.
Part of the furniture made for David Garrick's bedroom.

127 Commode, japanned in black with flat decorations in gilt; 95 cm. high. England, *c.* 1765.
Collection of Sir James Horlick.
Photograph by courtesy of *The Connoisseur.*

128 Chimney-piece, marble; 112 cm. high, designed by Henry Holland, 1792.
Buckingham Palace, reproduced by gracious permission of H.M. the Queen.
This chimney-piece originally stood in the Chinese drawing-room at Carlton House.
Bibl.: H. C. Smith: *Buckingham Palace*, London, 1931, p. 105.

129 Musical clock, glass, gilt bronze and other metals; 103·5 cm. high. English, *c.* 1820.
Collection of Mr B. E. Hokin.
The clock is said to have been made for the Prince Regent, probably to adorn the pavilion and the dragon on its top is close in style to those incorporated in the central light in the pavilion banqueting room.

130 Chair, wood (beech) carved and painted to simulate bamboo; 66 cm. high, probably by Elward, Marsh, and Tatham, *c.* 1812–14.
Ombersley Court, Worcestershire.
The chair forms part of the furniture of the Chinese room decorated for the Marchioness of Downshire between 1812 and about 1814.
Bibl.: A. Oswald in *Country Life*, January 16th, 1953, pp. 152–5.

131 Chimney-piece, marble and ormolu; 131·7 cm. high, probably designed by Robert Jones, *c.* 1817.
Buckingham Palace, reproduced by gracious permission of H.M. the Queen.

This chimney-piece was originally in the banqueting room of the pavilion at Brighton. It should be compared with the more restrained chimney-piece designed by Holland for Carlton House some years earlier (Pl. 128).

Bibl.: C. Musgrave: *op. cit.* p. 106.

132 Cabinet, wood carved and painted to simulate bamboo cane, ormolu, and marble; 102 cm. high, by Messrs Elward, Marsh, and Tatham, London, 1802.

On loan to the Royal Pavilion, Brighton; reproduced by gracious permission of H.M. the Queen.

One of a pair of imitation bamboo cabinets made for the Pavilion in 1802. See p. 189.

Bibl.: *The Connoisseur*, June 1956, p. 17.

133 Tea-caddy, silver; 9 cm. high, by Augustus Le Sage, London, 1767.

The Ashmolean Museum, Oxford.

At least two other caddies were made in the form of miniature tea-chests, by John Parker and Edward Wakelin, 1769 (Collection of the Hon. Mrs Ionides), and by Louisa Courtauld and George Cowles, 1773 (Victoria and Albert Museum).

134 Plate, earthenware printed in blue with willow pattern; 22·5 cm. diameter. Staffordshire, 1818.

The Victoria and Albert Museum, London.

The inscription: *Thomasine Willey* presumably refers to the owner of the plate.

135 Chimney-piece, ironstone china; 112 cm. high, by Messrs Charles Mason, Staffordshire, *c.* 1829.

Hanley Museum and Art Gallery, Stoke-on-Trent.

The Mason factory seems to have been the only one in England to make ceramic fireplaces.

Bibl.: G. B. Hughes in *Country Life Annual*, 1958, pp. 98–103.

136 Two vestibule vases, ironstone china, vase on left 152 cm. high, made by Messrs Charles Mason, Staffordshire, *c.* 1828.

Hanley Museum and Art Gallery, Stoke-on-Trent.

An advertisement in the *London Morning Herald*, 21 April, 1828, records that a sale of Mason's ironstone china wares would include 'the most noble, splendid and magnificent jars some of which are nearly five feet high.'

Bibl.: G. B. Hughes in *Country Life Annual*, 1958, p. 100.

137 Panel of cotton, block-printed in colours, designed by J. J. Pearman and printed at Bannister Hall, 1806.
> The Cooper Union Museum for the Arts of Decoration, New York.
> *Bibl.*: B. Morris in *The Connoisseur*, June 1958, pp. 36–7.

138 The Chinese bandstand in the Cremorne Gardens, steel engraving; 15 × 23·2 cm., published in *The Illustrated London News*, 1857, p. 515.

139 Chinese Scene, water-colour; 12·8 × 17·9 cm., by George Chinnery, *c.* 1825–52.
> Birmingham Art Gallery, J. Leslie Wright Collection.
> See p. 199.

140 Torchère, engraving, Paris, 1878.
> The British Museum, London.
> The torchère, modelled by Guillemin, was reproduced in the *Gazette des Beaux-Arts*, September, 1878, p. 226.
> See p. 215.

141 Corner cupboard, ebony, palissandre, bamboo, gilt bronze and cloisonné enamel; 195 cm. high, designed by Émile Reiber, 1869.
> Musée des Arts Décoratifs, Paris.
> Made under the direction of Henri Bouilhet in the Atelier Christofle for Napoleon III, and exhibited at the Exposition Universelle, Paris, 1878.
> *Bibl.*: *Gazette des Beaux-Arts*, 1878, vol. xiii, pp. 226–30.

142 Portrait of Émile Zola, oil on canvas; 144 × 113 cm., by Édouard Manet, 1867–8.
> Musée du Louvre, Paris.
> See p. 212.
> *Bibl.*: J. Richardson: *Édouard Manet*, London, 1958, pp. 19 and 122.

143 *Rose and Silver—The Princess from the Land of Porcelain*; oil on canvas; 199·9 × 116·1 cm.; by James McNeill Whistler, 1864 (signed and dated).
> Freer Gallery of Art, Washington.
> The painting was bought by F. R. Leyland in 1867 and installed in the dining-room of his house at 49 Prince's Gate which Whistler decorated to his own satisfaction as the notorious Peacock Room. In 1864 Whistler painted three other japonaiserie subjects: *Le Paravant doré* (Freer Gallery), *The Lange Lijzen of the Six Marks* (John G. Johnson Collection, Philadelphia) in which he depicted porcelain from his own collection, and *Le Balcon* (Freer Gallery), a group of girls in Japanese dress on a balcony overlooking the Thames at Battersea. The influence of Japan is notable also in his later *Nocturnes*.

Bibl.: L. Bénédite in *Gazette des Beaux-Arts*, xxxiv, 1905. p. 142 ff. P. Ferriday in *The Architectural Review*, June 1959, pp. 407–14.

144 Copy of a Japanese print, oil on canvas; 72·2 × 53·5 cm., by Vincent Van Gogh, 1886–8.

Collection of V. W. Van Gogh, Laren.

A copy of *Ohashi Bridge in the Rain*, by Hiroshige. Van Gogh also painted copies of a print of a tree by Hiroshige and a print of an actor by Kei Sai Yeisen.

Bibl.: J. B. de la Faille: *L'Œuvre de Vincent Van Gogh*, Paris, 1928, no. 372.

FIGURES IN THE TEXT

9. Design for a *Terminary Seat in the Chinese Taste*, engraving from W. Halfpenny: *New Designs for Chinese Temples*, London, 1750. The British Museum.   p. 163

10. Caricature of George IV, engraved illustration after G. Cruikshank from an anonymous pamphlet: *The Queen's Matrimonial Ladder* (probably by W. Hone), London, 1820.   p. 187

The print reproduced on page 86 is from J. Stalker and G. Parker: *Treatise of Japanning and Varnishing*, London, 1688; that on page 142 is from Edwards and M. Darly: *New Book of Chinese Designs Calculated to Improve the Present Taste*, London, 1754.

Index

Roman numerals refer to the colour plates; numerals in *italic* type refer to the black-and-white plates; numerals in italics preceded by the letters *fig.* refer to the illustrations reproduced in the text.

Index

Index

Index